ELEVENTH EDITION

A Student's Guide to History

Jules R. Benjamin

Ithaca College

Bedford/St. Martin's

Boston ◆ New York

For Bedford/St. Martin's

Publisher for History: Mary Dougherty
Director of Development for History: Jane Knetzger
Senior Editor: Heidi L. Hood
Developmental Editor: Michelle McSweeney
Production Editor: Lindsay DiGianvittorio
Production Supervisor: Sarah Ulicny
Executive Marketing Manager: Jenna Bookin Barry
Copyeditor: Patricia Herbst
Indexer: Steve Csipke
Cover Design: Sara Gates
Cover Art: T804 Map of the World, from the *Atlas sive cosmographicae . . .*, pub. by Gerard Mercator (1512–1594), Duisburg, 1585. (Bridgeman Art Library)
Composition: NK Graphics, a Black Dot Group Company
Printing and Binding: Haddon Craftsmen, Inc., an RR Donnelley & Sons Company

President and Publisher: Joan E. Feinberg
Editorial Director: Denise B. Wydra
Director of Marketing: Karen R. Soeltz
Director of Editing, Design, and Production: Marcia Cohen
Assistant Director of Editing, Design, and Production: Elise S. Kaiser
Managing Editor: Elizabeth M. Schaaf

Library of Congress Control Number: 2009928932

4   3   2   1
f   e   d

For information, write: Bedford/St. Martin's, 75 Arlington Street, Boston, MA 02116 (617-399-4000)

ISBN-10: 0-312-53502-3
ISBN-13: 978-0-312-53502-5

Acknowledgments

Page 14 image: FY 1404 Takyuddin and other astronomers at the Galata observatory founded in 1557 by Sultan Suleyman, from the Sehinsahname of Murad III, c. 1581 (vellum) by Turkish School Istanbul University Library, Istanbul, Turkey/The Bridgeman Art Library.
Page 28: Charles Ambler, "Popular Films and Colonial Audiences: The Movies in Northern Rhodesia." *American Historical Review,* Vol. 106, No. 1 (February 2001): 81. Published by the University of Chicago Press. © American Historical Association 2001. All rights reserved.
Page 180: From Louisa A. Burnham, *So Great a Light, So Great a Smoke: The Beguin Heretics of Languedoc.* Ithaca: Cornell University Press, 2008. Copyright © 2008 by Cornell University. Used by permission of the publisher, Cornell University Press.

To Elaine, Aaron, Adam, Rose, and Vincent

Preface

I first wrote *A Student's Guide to History* in response to a barrier I noticed between my students and the historical material I was teaching. Although this barrier differed somewhat from one student to the next, the core issue was always the need to learn basic study, research, and writing skills. If my students could not take thoughtful and concise notes, tackle common assignments, write clearly, and understand what an exam question required of them, my efforts to explain the meaning of the past would be thwarted by their inability to respond effectively. Since then, new ways of accessing historical evidence have made it possible for students to work with a wide variety of primary sources. While this vastly enlivens the teaching and learning environment, it raises barriers of its own. To absorb the richness of the new kinds of evidence, students need to master digital searching and visual interpretation, among other skills. This edition complements the basics of study, research, and writing with the skills that students need in today's learning environment.

In each edition, my goal has been twofold: to provide instructors with a resource that they can easily incorporate into history courses at all levels, and to equip students with a reference that they can refer to throughout their undergraduate careers and beyond. I have made an effort to keep the book thorough yet not overwhelming, covering, in a clear, accessible writing style, all the skills students need to succeed. Like earlier editions, the eleventh edition of *A Student's Guide to History* relies on concrete advice, numerous examples, and helpful Guidelines boxes to introduce students to the discipline of history and to cover a broad range of skills, but it has been reorganized into eight new easy-to-reference chapters to emphasize important concepts more clearly.

New Organization

Chapters 1 and 2 introduce the study of history and the basic skills needed in any history course. Chapter 1 discusses why people study history, explains how historians go about their investigations, and introduces students to the differing approaches to history and the various fields of historical research. It also examines how the study of history can prepare students for a variety of careers. Chapter 2 teaches fundamental skills that students need to be successful in history classes: keeping up with reading assignments, taking notes in class, and participating both in class and in online discussions.

Chapters 3, 4, and 5 focus on historical sources and writing. Chapter 3 introduces students to historical evidence and how to work with it. In more than a dozen examples and clear explanations, students are shown how to read and interpret a wide range of sources, including primary texts, scholarly articles, maps, and photographs. Chapter 4 focuses on writing skills, taking students through the steps of building and revising an essay and providing guidance on matters of style and mechanics. Chapter 5 offers guidelines and examples for specific types of writing assignments, including single-source and comparative analyses, sample book reviews, oral presentations, and exams.

Chapters 6 and 7 address the complex tasks of preparing and writing a research paper. Chapter 6 takes students through the research process: choosing and narrowing a topic, formulating a research question, planning a search strategy, and finding and working with sources in print and online. It also warns of the dangers of plagiarism and helps students understand how to avoid it. Chapter 7 covers the writing of research papers, stressing the importance of an effective thesis, explaining how to organize evidence with an outline, and giving practical advice such as how to incorporate quotations and visuals. The complete, annotated sample research paper that concludes Chapter 7 models how to pull together research findings, incorporate visual materials, and document sources.

Chapter 8 is devoted entirely to preparing notes and bibliographies according to *The Chicago Manual of Style*. It includes over one hundred models and displays a wide range of history sources. A quick-reference guide to these documentation models is included in the beginning of Chapter 8 (on p. 175) as well as on the inside back cover.

Appendix A points students toward hundreds of the best print and electronic history resources, highlighting the most helpful indexes, reference sources, document collections, and periodicals. **Appendix B** includes sections on local and family history. The **glossary** includes all of the key terms that appear in boldface throughout this book.

The book's **companion Web site**, A Student's Online Guide to History Reference Sources, at **bedfordstmartins.com/benjamin**, provides an easy-to-navigate, interactive version of the appendixes with direct links to the Web sites listed there.

New to This Edition

In my ongoing efforts to improve and update *A Student's Guide to History,* I have turned to my own students and to students and instructors across the country, asking what changes they would like to see in future editions. The revisions and additions I have made for the eleventh edition reflect the needs of today's history students:

- **Expanded coverage of working with sources.** Chapter 3 now focuses solely on historical evidence, showing students how to examine any type of source, whether primary or secondary, written or nonwritten, print or digital. Chapter 3 also includes three new Guidelines boxes on working with sources and an all-new section on interpreting sound and video recordings. Numerous new examples in this chapter help prepare students for the kinds of source-based assignments that they are most likely to encounter in history courses.
- **More attention to analytical writing.** A new and expanded Chapter 5 contains two new sections, with full-length examples, on writing about primary sources — one on analyzing a single source, another on comparing multiple sources. Chapter 5 also includes a new section on critiquing scholarly articles and a new sample book review. These assignments teach students how to approach historical evidence, frame a compelling thesis, and present supporting evidence.
- **Revised research coverage emphasizing argument.** Chapters 6 and 7 provide more guidance on how to write a paper in support of a thesis. New Guidelines boxes, revised examples, and detailed instruction throughout help students formulate debatable research questions, draft assertive thesis statements, create outlines with supporting evidence, and write persuasive papers.
- **New visual aids for documenting sources.** In Chapter 8, five new Guidelines boxes for citing sources use visuals to illustrate how to find documentation information for books, published letters, print articles, database articles, and Web sites. Information on sample source pages is keyed to accompanying notes and bibliographic entries, showing students how to turn publication information into a citation.
- **Updated guide to research sources.** Appendix A, "Resources for History Research," is an annotated compilation of some of the best research tools — in print and online — currently available to history students. The appendix is divided into broad general categories such as reference type and geographical region, as well as specialized subcategories such as historical eras and specific subject areas. In addition, an online version of the appendixes at the book's companion site (**bedfordstmartins.com/benjamin**) includes links to all of the Web sources.

Acknowledgments

Every edition has benefited from comments and suggestions made by some of the hundreds of instructors who have assigned *A Student's Guide to History* and by some of the hundreds of thousands of students who have read it over the years. I particularly wish to thank the many people who reviewed the tenth edition in preparation for the revision: 89 student reviewers, plus these instructors: Sean Adams, University of Florida; Alan Baumler, Indiana University of Pennsylvania; Deborah Buffton, University of Wisconsin–LaCrosse;

Thomas Burnell Colbert, Marshalltown Community College; Ken Cruikshank, McMaster University; Roger P. Davis, University of Nebraska at Kearney; Richard Hirsh, Virginia Tech; David L. Kenley, Elizabethtown College; David Lewis, California State Polytechnic University at Pomona; Charles W. Sanders Jr., Kansas State University; Michael Shirley, Eastern Illinois University; Linda Simmons, Northern Virginia Community College; Kenneth Wilburn, East Carolina University; James H. Williams, Middle Tennessee State University; and Amanda Wunder, Lehman College, CUNY.

I want to express my great respect for those at Bedford/St. Martin's who have contributed to this edition of *A Student's Guide to History*: Mary V. Dougherty, Jane Knetzger, Heidi L. Hood, Jennifer Jovin, Lindsay DiGian-vittorio, and Patricia Herbst. I also want to thank my collaborator, Sean Adams, associate professor of history at the University of Florida. Sean made many useful additions and revisions, especially in Chapters 3 and 5. He provided a new sample book review, two new source analyses, revisions for the sample research paper, and a host of new documentation models.

Special thanks go to my developmental editor, Michelle McSweeney, who accomplished so much so well. Authors can be possessive creatures, unwilling to part with a word or even a punctuation mark. Michelle took big heaps of words from me yet left me at ease. Most notable of all, she guided me toward authorial decisions that I otherwise might not have made.

As no one lives by e-mail alone, I want to thank my wife, Elaine. Her aid passeth understanding.

Jules R. Benjamin
Ithaca College

Contents

Preface   *v*
A Note to Students   *xvii*

1   The Subject of History   *1*

What History Can Tell You   *1*

How Historians Work   *3*

Approaches to History   *4*

Philosophies of History   *5*

Historiography   *7*

Fields of Historical Research   *8*

How You Can Use History   *11*

2   Succeeding in Your History Class   *12*

Keeping Up with Reading Assignments   *12*

Navigating a Textbook   *12*

Reading a Textbook   *13*

Taking Notes in Class   *15*

From Class Lectures   *15*

Guidelines for Taking Lecture Notes   *16*

From Slides and Films   *20*

Taking Notes in a "Wired" Classroom   *20*

Classroom Participation   *21*

Classroom Discussions   *21*

Guidelines for Speaking in Class   *21*

Group Work   *21*

Guidelines for Peer Reviewing   *22*

Communicating Online   *23*

3 Working with Historical Evidence *25*

Primary Sources *25*

Secondary Sources *28*

When a Secondary Source Becomes a Primary Source *28*

Accessing Sources in Print, in Person, and Online *29*

Reading Written Sources *30*

    Primary Texts *31*

        Guidelines for Working with Written Sources 31

    Scholarly Articles *32*

        Guidelines for Identifying Scholarly Articles 34

    Monographs *35*

    Anthologies *35*

    Historical Novels *35*

"Reading" Nonwritten Sources *36*

    Maps *36*

        Guidelines for Interpreting Nonwritten Sources 36

    Statistical Data *39*

    Illustrations, Photographs, and Other Visual Material *41*

    Sound and Video Recordings *45*

    Artifacts *48*

4 Building a History Essay *51*

Why Clear Writing Is Important *51*

Preparing to Write *51*

    Examining Sources *52*

    Drafting a Thesis Statement *53*

    Creating a Writing Outline *54*

Drafting Your Essay *55*

    A Clear Introduction *55*

    A Cohesive Body *56*

        Sentences: The Building Blocks of Writing *56*

        Cohesive, Connected Paragraphs *58*

    A Meaningful Conclusion *59*

Revising Your Essay *60*

        Guidelines for Revising Your Essay 61

Proofreading Your Essay *60*

The Danger of Plagiarism *61*

5   Preparing Specific Writing Assignments   63

Writing about Primary Sources   *63*

   Single-Source Analysis   *64*

   Comparative Analysis   *67*

Writing about Secondary Sources   *70*

   Book Reviews   *71*

      Guidelines for Writing a Book Review   75

   Article Critiques   *76*

   Comparative Reviews and Critiques   *76*

Writing Short Essays   *77*

Giving Presentations   *78*

   Oral Presentations   *78*

      Guidelines for Giving an Oral Presentation   78

   PowerPoint Presentations   *79*

Taking Exams   *79*

   Objective and Short-Answer Exams   *80*

      Example of a Short-Answer Question   *80*

      Example of an Identification Question   *81*

      Example of a Multiple-Choice Question   *81*

   In-Class Essay Exams   *82*

      Composing Sample Questions   *82*

      Guidelines for Writing In-Class Essay Exams   82

      Taking the Test   *83*

   Take-Home Essay Exams   *83*

      The Dangers of Plagiarism   *87*

6   Researching a History Topic   88

Beginning the Research Process   *88*

      Guidelines for the Research Process   89

   Choosing a Topic   *89*

   Narrowing Your Topic   *90*

   Formulating a Research Question   *90*

      Debatable Questions   *91*

      Narrow Questions   *91*

      Significant Questions   *91*

      Researchable Questions   *92*

   Planning a Research Strategy   *92*

      Budgeting Your Time and Staying Focused   *92*

Keeping an Open Mind *93*

Maintaining a Working Bibliography *94*

Conducting Research *94*

Using the Library's Online Catalog *95*

Searching by Subject or by Keyword *95*

Searching by Author and by Title *98*

Locating Materials by Using Call Numbers *98*

Using Print and Electronic Reference Works *99*

The Problem of *Wikipedia* *99*

Atlases, Dictionaries, and Encyclopedias *100*

Subject Bibliographies *100*

Using Print and Electronic Periodical Databases *101*

Locating Articles in Scholarly Journals *101*

Guidelines for Using Periodical Databases *104*

Locating Articles in Magazines and Newspapers *105*

Searching for Primary Sources *105*

Primary Sources on the Web *105*

Primary Sources in Published Collections *106*

Primary Sources in Museum Archives *106*

Interviews as Primary Sources *107*

Using Internet Search Tools *107*

Searching Efficiently *107*

Previewing Search Results *108*

Evaluating Sources *109*

Evaluating Secondary Sources *109*

Reviewing Secondary Sources for Basic Information *109*

Reading Secondary Sources for Signs of Bias *110*

Guidelines for Evaluating Secondary Sources *111*

Evaluating Primary Sources *111*

Written Primary Sources *111*

Guidelines for Evaluating Written Primary Sources *112*

Nonwritten Primary Sources *113*

Guidelines for Evaluating Nonwritten Primary Sources *113*

Special Problems of Evaluating Web-Based Sources *114*

Evaluating Web Sites *114*

Guidelines for Evaluating Web Sites *114*

Evaluating Material Found on Web Sites *115*

Guidelines for Evaluating Material Found on Web Sites *116*

Interpreting Sources and Taking Notes   *116*

    Reading Your Sources   *117*

    Summarizing and Paraphrasing without Plagiarizing   *118*

        Summarizing Your Sources   *118*

        Paraphrasing Your Sources   *118*

    Quoting without Plagiarizing   *120*

    Organizing Your Notes   *121*

        Taking Notes on Note Cards   *121*

        Taking Notes on a Computer   *121*

        Photocopying, Downloading, or Printing Sources   *123*

Avoiding Plagiarism   *126*

    Plagiarism and Working Online   *126*

    Plagiarism and Group Work   *127*

    Guidelines for Avoiding Plagiarism   *127*

7   Writing a Research Paper   *128*

Asserting Your Thesis   *128*

    Why Your Paper Needs a Thesis   *129*

    What Makes a Thesis Effective   *129*

    Guidelines for Developing an Effective Thesis   *130*

Organizing Your Evidence with a Writing Outline   *131*

Writing the Text   *135*

    The Rough Draft   *135*

    Clear Writing: A Matter of Continuity   *136*

    Quotations: When and How to Use Them   *137*

        When to Quote Sources Directly   *137*

        How to Format Quotations   *138*

    Incorporating Visual Materials into Your Paper   *139*

    Guidelines for Incorporating Visuals   *140*

    When to Use Footnotes and Endnotes   *140*

Revising and Rewriting   *142*

    Guidelines for Revising and Rewriting   *143*

Example of a Research Paper   *143*

    How the Thesis Was Developed   *144*

    The Writing Outline for the Paper   *145*

    Formatting a Research Paper   *146*

    Sample Student Research Paper   *146*

8 Documenting Your Paper: How to Cite Sources in *Chicago* Style *173*

Formatting Footnotes and Endnotes *173*

Organizing a Bibliography *174*

  Directory of Documentation Models for Notes and Bibliography Entries *175*

Documentation Models *176*

  Overview of Notes *176*

  Overview of Bibliography Entries *176*

  Author Variations *177*

  Books *179*

    Guidelines for Citing Books *180*

    Guidelines for Citing Letters in Published Collections *184*

  Periodicals *186*

    Guidelines for Citing Articles in Print Journals *188*

    Guidelines for Citing Articles in Electronic Databases *189*

  Public Documents *191*

  Multimedia Sources *192*

    Guidelines for Citing Information from Web Sites *194*

  Other Published Sources *197*

  Unpublished Sources *198*

Appendix A Resources for History Research *201*

Historical Dictionaries, Encyclopedias, and Atlases *202*

  Historical Dictionaries—World *203*

  Historical Dictionaries—United States *203*

  Historical Encyclopedias—World *204*

  Historical Encyclopedias—Europe *205*

  Historical Encyclopedias—United States *206*

  Historical Atlases—World *206*

  Historical Atlases—United States *207*

Biography Collections *207*

  International Biography Collections *207*

  United States Biography Collections *208*

Newspaper Indexes and Databases *209*

  Newspaper Indexes and Databases—General *209*

  Newspaper Indexes and Databases—United States *210*

Periodical Indexes and Databases   *210*

    Magazine Indexes and Databases   *211*

    Journal Indexes and Databases   *211*

Public Documents   *212*

    Public Documents—Britain and Canada   *212*

    Public Documents—International   *213*

    Public Documents—United States   *213*

Historical Statistics   *215*

    Historical Statistics—General   *215*

    Historical Statistics—National and Regional   *215*

    Historical Statistics—United States   *216*

General Resources in World History   *218*

    Reference Works and Bibliographies   *218*

    Web Sites   *219*

Specialized Resources in World History   *221*

    Ancient History   *221*

    Europe—General   *223*

    Europe—Medieval   *224*

    Europe—Early Modern   *226*

    Europe—Modern   *226*

    Britain—General   *228*

    Britain before 1800   *229*

    Britain since 1800   *231*

    Ireland and Scotland   *232*

    Eastern Europe   *233*

    Russia and the Soviet Union   *233*

    Africa   *234*

    Middle East and North Africa   *235*

    Asia—General   *236*

    South Asia—India, Pakistan, and Sri Lanka   *237*

    China   *237*

    Japan and Korea   *238*

    Australia and New Zealand   *239*

    Latin America and the Caribbean   *239*

    Canada   *241*

General Resources in United States History   *242*

    Reference Works and Bibliographies   *242*

    Web Sites   *243*

Specialized Resources in United States History   *245*

Regional, State, and Local   *245*

Colonial, Revolutionary, and Early National, 1607–1800   *246*

Native American   *248*

Slavery and the Civil War   *248*

African American   *250*

Women's   *252*

Immigrant and Ethnic   *252*

Social and Cultural   *254*

Political   *256*

Foreign Relations, International, and War   *259*

Science, Technology, Environment, and Medicine   *260*

Labor, Business, Economic, and Urban   *261*

Religious   *262*

Appendix B   Historical Sources in Your Own Backyard   *263*

How to Research Your Family History   *264*

Sources for County and Local History   *265*

Sources for Family History and Genealogical Research   *266*

Glossary   *268*
Index   *274*

A Note to Students

I have written this book to introduce you to the enormous world of history that is the heritage of people everywhere. This world is as fascinating as the world of today or as any vision of the future. I hope to convince you that the study of history is not a journey into a dead past but instead offers a way to understand and live in the present. You can use the tools of historical research to succeed not only in history courses but in your future career. And you can use them to answer important questions about your own life and your relationship to the rest of the world. This broader purpose is what makes the study of history so valuable.

Jules R. Benjamin
Ithaca College

(Acknowledgments, continued from p. ii)

Page 184: From *Reading the Man: A Portrait of Robert E. Lee Through His Private Letters* by Elizabeth Brown Pryor, copyright © 2007 by Elizabeth Brown Pryor. Used by permission of Viking Penguin, a division of Penguin Group (USA) Inc.

Page 185: The original document is in the Gilder Lehrman Collection at the Gilder Lehrman Institute for American History under catalog no. GLC1071, Robert E. Lee to John Mackay, June 27, 1838.

Page 188: Copyright © Organization of American Historians. www.oah.org. Reprinted with permission.

Page 189: Laura Edwards, "Status without Rights: African Americans and the Tangled History of Law and Governance in the Nineteenth-Century U.S. South." *American Historical Review,* Vol. 112, No. 2 (April 2007): 365. Published by the University of Chicago Press. © American Historical Association 2007. All rights reserved.

Page 194: Smithsonian Arctic Studies Center, *Sharing Knowledge,* http://alaska.si.edu.

CHAPTER

1

The Subject of History

WHAT HISTORY CAN TELL YOU

The Interstate Highway System connects all of the major cities of the United States. The speed limits are high, and local traffic is carried over or under the Interstates. Traveling at seventy miles per hour, you may not realize that these highways have a history — that construction of the Interstate System began in the 1950s.

The car that carries you down the Interstate and the music that plays on your car's audio system have a history even older than the highway's. Your car has the same basic components — engine, rubber tires, steering wheel, axles — as the boxy touring cars of the 1920s, whose design was based on the design of horse-drawn carriages. The rock or rap music playing on the audio system is a descendant of country music, folk music, and jazz, with roots extending into the distant past. American folk music traces its roots to the British Isles, from which it was brought to the Appalachian Mountains of the eastern United States in the eighteenth and nineteenth centuries. Jazz traces its roots to the music of enslaved Africans brought to the American South and the Caribbean in the seventeenth and eighteenth centuries.

Looking for the signs of history in the world around us is something like the task of the geologist or archaeologist. However, instead of digging into the earth to uncover the past, the historical researcher digs into the visible, everyday elements of society to find the historical roots from which they sprang. The Interstate Highway System, parts of which are still being built today, is in the uppermost layer of history. If a study of the newest super-highways can take us back fifty years, what about the historical roots of older highways or country roads? How far into the past can we travel on them?

Turn off the eight-lane Interstate, past the huge signs over the multistory motels, and onto U.S. Route 51 or 66 — older highways built in the 1940s and 1950s. As you ride along at a slower pace, there are no signs saying "Downtown Freeway 1/2 mile" or "Indiana Turnpike — Exit 26N." Instead, signs say "Lubbock 38 miles" or "Cedar Rapids 14 miles." As you approach Lubbock or Cedar Rapids, you may see small, single-story motels. They may be wooden cottages with fading paint and perhaps a sign that says "Star Motor Court" or "Stark's Tourist Cabins." Instead of fast-food restaurants, you may pass "Betty's Restaurant" or "Little River Diner." The older restaurants, stores, and gas stations that you see provide clues to the history of the road on which you are riding. Places like the Star Motor Court and the Little River Diner probably were built when the road was new. Unless they have been modernized, they are relics of a previous historical period — when Franklin Roosevelt and Harry Truman were president and when cars had rounded hoods, trunks, and fenders. The diner isn't air-conditioned, and the sign over the tourist cabins proudly proclaims that they are "heated." This is the United States of sixty or seventy years ago.

Turn off at State Route 104 where the sign says "Russell Springs 3 miles" or "Hughesville 6 miles." Again the speed limit drops. You are on a road built in the 1920s or earlier (some country roads are a hundred or more years old). Time has claimed many of the buildings that once stood along this road, but a surviving single-pump gas station displays faded advertisements that promote NeHi Orange and Red Man Chewing Tobacco. (Figure 1.1 below shows an image from this era.) If you see a restaurant or motel, it may

FIGURE 1.1   **Highway Travel in the 1920s**
Country stores like this one added gas pumps to serve their new customer — the automobile driver.
SOURCE: *Droster Store, Image No. Whi-31934. Wisconsin Historical Society.*

be boarded up because the people who used to stop in on their way to Russell Springs or Hughesville now travel on major highways or moved to a nearby city. Many old homes, however, are still standing along Route 104. They were built when only farmland straddled the road, and they may date back to a time when horses pulled traffic past the front door. Relics of early technology such as wringer washing machines and iceboxes may stand on the tilting wooden porches, and a close look behind the tall weeds beside the dirt driveway may reveal the remains of a 1926 Ford. As you stop before one of the old farmhouses, the past is all around you. With a little imagination you can reconstruct what life was like here on the day in 1918 when the Great War in Europe ended.

The line linking past to present never breaks. The farmhouse itself has a history, as do the people who once lived in it. The main bedroom upstairs has a fireplace with the date "1878" carved into the stone. On the table near the bed is the family Bible marked with the year the family came to the United States and the dates in the early nineteenth century when the parents of the immigrants who built the house were born.

The story could extend much further into the past, although the evidence would become slimmer and slimmer. From county records you could find out who owned the land before the house was built, perhaps going back to the time when the people who lived on the land were Native Americans. Evidence of Native Americans could be found not only in written records but in **artifacts**[1] (physical objects) such as arrowheads lying under the foundation of the house. In distance, you may have traveled only ten or twenty miles from the Interstate Highway, and the trip may have taken less than an hour. But while looking in the present for signs of the past, you traveled more than a hundred years into history.

If you think about and study the passage of time between the building of the old farmhouse on the country road and construction of the luxury motel by the Interstate, you may come to understand some of the social, political, and economic forces that moved events away from the old wooden porch and sent them speeding down the superhighway. The more you know about this process, the more you will learn about the time when the farmhouse was new and the more you will understand why the Interstate Highway came into being, what you are doing riding on one, and into what kind of future you may be heading.

HOW HISTORIANS WORK

The past is a fascinating place. Almost everyone feels this. We are easily drawn into films, novels, and histories that bring us vivid images from that strange land. Historians in particular wonder about it and, unlike most people, "travel" back into it.

---

[1]Terms in **boldface** are defined in the Glossary at the back of the book.

Some historians record their journey of research into the past in order to convey, as best they can, something of the experience of living in a very different world — for example, the life of a Russian serf in the eighteenth century or the building of Great Zimbabwe in southern Africa. Other historians hope to find a storehouse of useful knowledge, even wisdom. They feel that if we can understand the ways of life of past generations, we will better understand our own lives, perhaps because accounts of earlier accomplishments and failures will provide yardsticks by which we can measure the quality of our lives and the success of our social arrangements. Historians are trained to study the past systematically and to use the knowledge they gain to help explain human nature and the roots of contemporary affairs. Many are moved by the possibility that their study of the past will help solve the problems of the present.

What kinds of answers can history give? What are the ways in which the historian can dig into the complex world of the past? Historians begin their work by asking questions to which they hope historical research can provide answers: What was the effect of the replacement of kerosene lanterns and, later, gas lamps by electric light bulbs? What **evidence** is there that some of the native peoples of South America may have originally come from islands in the Pacific Ocean?

Historians must compose important (but not impossible) questions. They need to know what kinds of evidence exist, how to examine that evidence, and how to determine what about the past it might explain. (For details on how to research a history topic, see Chapter 6.)

APPROACHES TO HISTORY

A historian's choice among important questions is determined by personal values and experience, by academic training, by the nature of the time in which the historian lives, or by some combination of all of these. The ways in which these influences operate are complex, and historians themselves often are unaware of them.

After the historian chooses his or her subject, many questions still remain. For example, does historical evidence dealing with the subject exist? If it does, where can it be found? If someone wanted to study gypsy music from medieval Europe, and that music was never written down or mentioned in historical accounts of the Middle Ages, then historical research would uncover little or nothing about this subject. Even when records exist on a particular subject, the historian may be unaware of them or may be unable to locate them. Why? The records may be in a language unfamiliar to the historian, or they may be in the possession of individuals or governments that deny access to them.

If records do exist and they are accessible, the historian still faces a series of formidable questions: How complete is the evidence? Are there significant gaps in it? How credible or reliable is the evidence? Is it genuine? How accurate are the records, and what **biases** were held by the people who created them? If sources of information are in conflict, which source is correct? Or is it possible that most of the sources are in error? Historians must pick and choose among the sources they uncover, and that is not always easy to do. The historian's own biases also cloud the picture, making impartial judgment extremely difficult.

Philosophies of History

The results of historical investigation depend on the aspect of human nature or society that the historian emphasizes and on the kind of information that he or she obtains. The results of historical investigation also depend on the philosophy of history that the historian subscribes to. A philosophy of history offers an explanation of the most important causes of specific events and of the broadest developments in human affairs. It explains the *forces* of history, what moves them, and in what direction they are headed. At any particular time, the *dominant* philosophy of history is the one that most closely reflects the beliefs and values of that time, and most of the historians writing at that time write from the perspective of that philosophy.

There are several philosophies of history. Perhaps the oldest school of thought is the **cyclical school**. According to this view, events recur periodically — history repeats itself. The essential forces of nature and of human nature are changeless, and patterns of events repeat themselves endlessly. As the saying goes, "There is nothing new under the sun." The Aztecs conceived of history this way, as did the ancient Chinese. This view of history was dominant from ancient times until the rise of Christianity.

In contrast, Old Testament history is an advancing narrative — the story of the relationship between God and the Jewish people. And in societies influenced by the Christian Church — especially in Europe in the Middle Ages — the concept of divine intervention also undermined the cyclical view. The resulting philosophy of history, the **providential school**, held that the course of history is determined by God. Thus, the ebb and flow of historical events represents protracted struggles between forces of good and evil, but the eventual victory of good is inevitable.

The providential school's belief that history is characterized not by ceaseless repetition but by direction and purpose became an element in the thinking of the more secular age beginning with the eighteenth century. In this new age of scientific inquiry and material advancement, there arose the **progressive school**, whose central belief was that human history illustrates neither endless cycles nor divine intervention but continual progress. According to this interpretation, the situation of humanity is constantly improving, and this improvement results not from divine providence but from the efforts of human beings themselves. The power of human reason directs this process. Each generation builds on the learning and improvements of prior generations and, in doing so, reaches a higher stage of civilization. The idea of history as continual progress remains powerful. Currently, many variations of the progressive philosophy share the field of historical investigation.

In the eighteenth and nineteenth centuries, political rule shifted from monarchs to parliaments (legislative bodies similar to the U.S. Congress). Historians of the progressive school interpreted the development of democratic institutions as an important sign of progress. The rise of popular government in Europe, however, was accompanied by social problems such as rapid urban growth, exhausting forms of industrial labor, and the growth of poverty. In the mid-nineteenth century, Karl Marx introduced the idea of materialism and class conflict as a way of understanding this historical development. According to Marx, the industrial revolution was producing very wealthy capitalists (owners of industrial enterprises) on the one hand, and masses of desperate workers on the other. Marx predicted that conflict between these two groups would determine the direction of modern history.

As a result of the problems of industrialization, the progressive school examined the history of "progress" for clues to their solution. The further development of democratic societies in the twentieth century (despite the parallel rise of fascism) gave rise to a variety of progressive perspectives. An important one, influenced by Marx's ideas and by the progressive emphasis on democracy, began to study history "from the bottom up." These progressives saw history as producing freedom for more and more groups in society, and scholars influenced by these ideas began to look at the histories of subordinate groups. Historians of the United States began to examine evidence of the roles played by Native Americans, African Americans, Hispanic Americans, women, and, most recently, gays and lesbians.

One of the newest philosophies of history is **postmodernism**, which has not replaced the progressive view but has raised significant questions about the inherent nature of human progress. Postmodernism has influenced many academic disciplines. In history, it raises the fascinating question of whether the past can truly be understood from the perspective of the present. Evidence from the past, say the postmodernists, takes on new meanings because the present is so different from the past that past and present cannot directly communicate with one another. According to postmodernists, when historians search the records of the past, the understanding of the past that they bring back is heavily influenced by the methods they use or the questions they ask. They do not "find" history or discover how things really were; rather, they "create" history in the process of looking for it.

Another aspect of postmodernism concerns language. In the postmodernist's view, written (and even nonwritten) documents hide, rather than reveal, their true meanings. Their words must be "deconstructed" — decoded — to reveal not what the authors intended to say but what their words disclose about the authors themselves and the influence on them of the worldview of their times. Few historians wholly subscribe to the postmodernist view, but it has affected and weakened the idea of historical objectivity — the idea that, with time and effort, the historian can avoid bias and uncover the "truth" about history.

Unlike postmodernists, most historians consider themselves capable of discovering and understanding the past. There is, however, disagreement over the best method for doing so. Two ideas dominate the debate: **positivism** and **historicism**. Positivism utilizes the scientific method: positivists believe that history contains a true record of the past. If the historical record is examined objectively, they reason, then the historical "truth" can be uncovered. The historicist position, in contrast, holds that although complete objectivity is desirable, it is not possible. Most scholars are historicists, believing that some degree of bias always influences historical research. Historicism maintains that the facts of history require interpretation, and historians who undertake this interpretation employ not only reason but intuition as well. Unfortunately, a scientific experiment cannot be conducted on the facts of history to prove the correctness of a particular interpretation.

Historiography

A different approach to the study of history examines earlier writings by historians themselves. This area of study, known as **historiography**, examines changes in the methods, interpretations, and conclusions of earlier generations of historians. Often, earlier studies of historical topics reached conclusions that historians today find surprising. For example, between 1920 and 1939, most of the major histories of World War I placed principal blame for the war on Germany. The prevailing view was that Germany's aggression against its neighbors caused the war. At the end of the war, the Treaty of Versailles required Germany to disarm, to accept blame, and to pay reparations to the countries it fought against for the great damage the war had caused, even though Germany too had suffered greatly. Despite this general agreement on the cause of World War I, the experience of World War II, lasting from 1939 to 1945, led many scholars to rethink the origins of World War I. Historians began to ask how the Nazi movement in Germany, which directed unprecedented brutality against civilians both before and during World War II, had been able to rise to power through elections. Why were so many Germans willing to follow Hitler?

Before coming to power, the Nazi Party repeatedly charged that Germany had to avenge itself for the war guilt placed on the German nation by the Treaty of Versailles. Slowly, historians of World War I realized that the idea that Germany alone was responsible for that conflict had helped the Nazi Party to exploit the patriotism of the German people. Historians looked more closely at the world of 1914 and concluded that there were *many* reasons for the erupting of World War I. Germany was no longer considered to be the sole culprit. Economic and strategic competition among the major powers (Germany, England, France, Russia, and the United States) was seen as an important factor. Intensified nationalism in all these nations — not just in Germany — had increased tensions. Also, it was realized that a series of interlocking alliances among the great powers — which turned a minor conflict in the Balkans into an all-European war — was another source of the explosion.

The simplistic verdict of German guilt gave way to a complex explanation of the aims and security concerns of many nations. In this case, an attempt to understand Germany's role in World War II led to a new understanding of the German role in World War I. This kind of reinterpretation is not uncommon in history.

Historians' views of Reconstruction, the period in U.S. history after the Civil War when the defeated South was under the military and political control of the victorious North, also changed. During Reconstruction, for the first time in U.S. history, black people, many of them former slaves, were allowed to be elected to and hold political office. Prior to the 1930s, almost all the books written on this subject (whether by northern or southern historians) concluded that southern politics was corrupted and made ineffective during the Reconstruction period by selfish northerners and ignorant black southerners. Since the 1950s, however, scholars have reached very different conclusions. Most now believe that southern blacks' participation in state and local government was a healthy development and that the standard of politics in the South was generally equal to that of other regions of the nation at that time.

One reason for this new interpretation was the later historians' more effective use of basic sources describing the work of the Reconstruction governments of the southern states. Also, historians compared southern Reconstruction politics with politics in northern and western states of the period (an example of comparative history). And after looking back over the older literature and placing it in the **historical context** of race relations existing at that particular time, most scholars now conclude that an understanding of racist attitudes toward African Americans does much to explain the negative conclusions of earlier historians. Historiography lets historians use the tools of historical research to study themselves and, in the process, come to new conclusions about old questions. This process ensures that the judgments of historians do not fossilize. The reexamination or reinterpretation of earlier research, often called **revisionism**, is constantly evolving and may result from a variety of factors. In some cases, younger scholars examining new topics, or older scholars using new perspectives, may provide new ways of understanding past events. These reinterpretations can be seen in the previous examples: the changing views of Reconstruction and the new perspectives regarding Germany's role in World War II.

Another source for revisionists is the discovery of new evidence. For centuries, there was little hard evidence to support the claim that Thomas Jefferson had several children by one of his slaves. Current DNA testing makes it possible to support this claim, and historical studies of Jefferson now reflect this new evidence.

Fields of Historical Research

When historians investigate the questions that interest them most, they are influenced in their approach by their own values and experiences, their academic training, and their beliefs about which aspects of human nature, hu-

man institutions, and the human environment are most important in understanding those questions. As a result, historians might examine their chosen
topic from a wide range of perspectives. These differing perspectives or views
can be grouped into dozens of major fields (and even more subfields), each
of which has a particular focus or concern. For example, when examining
the decline of the Ottoman Empire in the late nineteenth century, one historian might choose to focus primarily on political matters, and another might
pay more attention to economics. Although the fields of historical study are
numerous and varied, they have all evolved over time, nearly all of them influence others, and many of them overlap.

Some fields are more traditional than others. Political approaches to historical questions have been employed by historians for many years, and have
given rise to such fields as military history, diplomatic history, and history of
empire. Political historians are generally concerned with major changes in a
country's government or political landscape — changes that reset its internal structure or reshape its place in the world. To answer a question regarding
the Ottoman Empire's decline, a military historian might look at the growing
superiority in weapons and training of British, French, and German troops
compared to those in the army of the sultan (the highest authority in the
empire). A historian of empire might compare the ailing system of taxation
under the last of the sultans to the more successful systems of the early Ottoman rulers. A diplomatic historian might examine the Ottoman Empire's
changing relationship with neighboring powers to explain its demise.

Other long-established approaches to historical questions include views
that focus on religious, intellectual, and economic matters. To continue the
example of the decline of the Ottoman Empire, a religious historian might
compare the roles of Islam and Christianity in the process, whereas an intellectual historian might examine the work of important Muslim scholars (Ulama)
in the decades leading up to the empire's demise. By contrast, a historian spe-
cially trained in the field of economic history might focus on the great increase of indebtedness of the empire to European investors and banks and
how this situation arose.

Some economic historians have taken up the field of quantitative history.
They use as their primary sources numerical data — election returns, price
levels, population figures, and others — that they trace over time. Quantitative data are uniform, allowing study of amounts and rates of change. Different kinds of change can be correlated — such as political party affiliation
with price levels — in an attempt to describe the conditions under which certain changes occur.

Over time, relatively new historical fields have arisen to probe neglected
areas of study such as social and cultural issues. Social historians often focus
their research on the development of human communities and their interaction with the larger society, incorporating two of the most rapidly expanding
areas in recent decades: women's history and gender studies. Because women
have been mostly absent from traditional history texts until recent decades,
women's history scholars attempt to fill in the gaps, showing the impact that

women have had on all aspects of history. If we return to the example of the decline of the Ottoman Empire, a researcher of women's history might explore the growing use of transparent veils by women in late-nineteenth-century Istanbul. Historians of gender study look at the ways in which ideas of masculinity and femininity have influenced history; they might compare the coffee house (male) and the bath house (female) as places of gendered socialization.

In addition, historians of the family and private life have taken up the examination of the structural and emotional development of small, intimate groups and the interaction of these groups with powerful social forces such as wars, depressions, class and ethnic conflict, and technological change. A historian in this field might examine the reasons for the segregation of space by gender in the homes of the wealthy.

Another fairly recent area of historical study is cultural history — a field in which historians focus on group attitudes and behaviors and how these change over time. If we look again at the Ottoman Empire example, a cultural historian might want to know the significance of the loosening of the clothing laws at the middle of the nineteenth century or of the new forms of public leisure activity, especially among the growing middle class. Numerous subsets of cultural history — the history of classical music, the history of media, the history of sport — focus on one particular aspect of popular or high culture.

History can be applied to a host of other academic disciplines, resulting in very specific genres. A historian of science, for example, might seek to understand why Islamic medicine, so advanced in earlier centuries, was outpaced by European advances in the nineteenth century. An ethnic historian might study the many non-Islamic peoples of the Ottoman Empire and the status they held in Islamic society.

As fields of historical study slowly but constantly emerge and evolve, they are influenced by many external factors, including current events. For example, just as pollution and global warming have emerged as important issues in our current world, environmental historians have begun to examine the interaction between previous human communities and their habitat. Globalization has influenced the growth of "world" history, which, among other topics, studies large-scale migrations of peoples and the mutual impact arising from the contact of civilizations.

In addition, changes in one historical field, or the emergence of a new field, can influence another. For example, as social history has become more influential, it has led other historians to incorporate a social aspect to their studies. A military historian might expand his or her research of weapons and tactics of the sultan's army to include an examination of the groups in society from which soldiers were recruited.

Historians also welcome ideas and methods of analyzing evidence that arise in other related but nonhistorical fields. Some examples include the influence of psychology on family history, the influence of sociology on demography, and the influence of anthropology on ethnohistory. For example, theology might influence a historian of religion to examine the arguments for a return to Islamic law (Sharia) despite the rising secularization of the late Ottoman Empire.

HOW YOU CAN USE HISTORY

Through the study of history, we make other people's experiences our own. In this way, we touch other times and places and add to our lifetime's knowledge the knowledge gained by others. In more practical terms, there are any number of careers in which the tools of the historian are directly employed. You yourself could teach history at the secondary or college level. You could work in the archives of a library, museum, historical site, or large corporation with a record-keeping department. Labor unions have staffs of historians who research the history of important unions.

The field of public history is a very large one, and you could be hired to the research staff of the U.S. government's National Archives and Records Administration, the Library of Congress, or any of the Cabinet departments or U.S. intelligence agencies. There are even more opportunities at the state, county, and local levels. For example, you could work for a local or county historical society. You might do archaeological research at the site of an ancient Indian village or a Civil War battlefield, or you might organize the nineteenth-century records of a great natural disaster or of a major exhibition of farm or industrial machinery. You could be hired to construct a family history from the photographs, diaries, and letters of one of the founding families of a town. Every step back in time calls on the skills of a historian.

The study of history also is excellent preparation for a wide variety of nonhistorical professions. Students often employ the research and writing skills acquired in their study and interpretation of history when they work toward advanced degrees and then practice in the fields of law, journalism, medicine, and many areas of business. The tasks of a course in history — formulating a research topic, laying out a clear research path, locating a wide range of **primary sources** and **secondary sources**, analyzing and organizing those sources, and effectively presenting a well-supported and clearly written **argument** — are all elements of sharpening, managing, and expressing your thoughts. Not only will these skills support you in any career you may choose to follow, but they will enrich your life.

CHAPTER

2

Succeeding in Your History Class

KEEPING UP WITH READING ASSIGNMENTS

The most common assignment in a history class is reading: many courses have one or more required textbooks, which are often supplemented by **primary sources** and **secondary sources**. (For details on reading primary and secondary sources, see Chapter 3.) Your syllabus will clearly list the due dates of readings for the entire semester, yet many students put off reading until right before an exam. Keeping up with reading assignments, however, will give you the background knowledge you need to understand the lectures and to succeed in the class. Since many instructors make classroom discussion a significant portion of the grade, it is especially important that you keep current with the assigned readings.

Another common mistake students make is to skip required readings altogether, assuming that the instructor's lectures will provide all the necessary information. But in most courses, the lectures are designed to embellish the background material provided in the readings, and instructors assume that students have completed assigned readings in preparation for class. A lecture on the economic aspects of the American Revolution may be confusing if you have not read the textbook discussion of the mercantilist theories behind many of the colonists' grievances.

Navigating a Textbook

A textbook is a complicated work, and you will need to take a close look at yours before you do the more serious work of reading it. In some textbooks you will find an introduction for students. Its purpose is to familiarize you with the organization of and various features within the book. Read this introduction at the beginning of the semester in order to lay the groundwork for the reading assignments ahead.

Most textbooks have a "brief" table of contents, which lists only chapter titles, as well as a complete table of contents, which includes subheadings and additional features such as chapter summaries, review questions, lists of terms, sources for research, and other aids. The index, of course, provides even more detail than the table of contents does, and it should be used when you are searching for a very specific term or topic. In addition to the tables of contents and index, at the beginning or end of a textbook you are likely to find components such as timelines, lists of maps, appendixes of historical documents, and glossaries, all of which can be useful study and reference guides.

Because textbook chapters typically contain an abundance of information, they usually are designed to help students absorb the content most effectively. For example, most textbook chapters open with an introduction or preview and an image that represents the time period being covered. Within each chapter, headings identify the major topics, and visuals with captions illustrate important concepts. In addition, chapters usually contain tables, timelines, and maps to help contextualize the material being presented. Unfamiliar terms are usually defined on the spot or in a glossary at the back of the book. Some chapters have sidebars presenting detailed information on particular sources of interest, such as political decrees or historical figures. Textbook chapters typically end with a summary or review, a list of study questions, and a bibliography for further reading.

As you read through each chapter, pay attention to all these features and use them to your advantage. Although they may not be explicitly mentioned in your reading assignment, these features are meant to enhance the main text of the chapter and are therefore worth your time and attention.

Reading a Textbook

Before you begin to read, preview the assigned chapter or section to get a sense of its organization. Read any introductory material and scan the headings throughout the chapter. Browse the visuals and their captions to take note of some of the more important aspects of the material contained in the chapter. (Because space is limited, textbook authors typically include visuals only for the concepts that they feel are most important.) Also look at the chapter summary to get a general idea of the territory you will be traveling through.

After previewing the chapter, read through it thoughtfully and actively. (See Figure 2.1 on p. 14 for an example of an annotated textbook page.) Underline or highlight the most prominent factual information. Also underline important generalizations, interpretations, and conclusions. Make marginal notes wherever you wish to remind yourself of something important or to raise a question that you might bring up in class. In addition, look for passages that in the formation of the modern global system after 1500. These new crops and the development of the intensified agricultural techniques that often accompanied them contributed to increased food production, population growth, urbanization, and industrial development characteristic of the Muslim Middle East in early Abbasid times.

Technology too diffused widely within the Islamic world. Ancient Persian techniques for obtaining water by drilling into the sides of hills now spread across North Africa as far west as Morocco. Muslim technicians made improvements on rockets, first developed in China, by developing one that carried a small warhead and another used to attack ships.[30] Papermaking techniques entered the Abbasid Empire from China in the eighth century, with paper mills soon operating in Persia, Iraq, and Egypt. This revolutionary technology, which everywhere served to strengthen bureaucratic governments, spread from the Middle East into India and Europe over the following centuries.

Ideas likewise circulated across the Islamic world. The religion itself drew heavily and quite openly on Jewish and Christian precedents. Persia also contributed much in the way of bureaucratic practice, court ritual, and poetry, with Persian becoming the primary literary language of elite circles. Scientific, medical, and philosophical texts, especially from ancient Greece, the Hellenistic world, and India, were systematically translated into Arabic, for several centuries providing an enormous boost to Islamic scholarship and science. In 830, the Abbasid caliph al-Mamun, himself a poet and scholar with a passion for foreign learning, established the House of Wisdom in Baghdad as an academic center for this research and translation. Stimulated by Greek texts, a school of Islamic thinkers, known as Mutazalites ("those who stand apart"), argued that reason, rather than revelation, was the "surest way to truth."[31] In the long run, however, the philosophers' emphasis on logic, rationality, and the laws of nature was subject to increasing criticism by those who held that only the Quran, the sayings of the Prophet, or mystical experience represented a genuine path to God.

But the realm of Islam was much more than a museum of ancient achievements from the civilizations that it encompassed. Those traditions mixed and blended to generate a distinctive Islamic civilization with many new contributions to the world of learning.[32] (See the Snapshot.) Using Indian numerical notation, for example, Arab scholars developed algebra as a novel mathematical discipline. They also undertook much original work in astronomy and optics. They built upon earlier Greek and Indian practice to create a remarkable tradition in medicine and pharmacology. Arab physicians

A Muslim Astronomical Observatory
Drawing initially on Greek, Indian, and Persian astronomy, the Islamic world after 1000 developed its own distinctive tradition of astronomical observation and prediction, reflected in this Turkish observatory constructed in 1557. Muslim astronomy subsequently exercised considerable influence in both China and Europe. (University Library, Istanbul, Turkey/The Bridgeman Art Library)

Islamic world disseminated:

1. Technology
– drilling for water
– rockets
– papermaking

2. Ideas
– religion
– politics
– science
– literature

Why did this happen?

Islamic world's contributions:
– algebra
– astronomy and optics
– medicine and pharmacology

FIGURE 2.1   Textbook Page with Student Annotations

This sample page shows how a student might actively read a textbook. Keywords, phrases, and sentences are underlined and circled to highlight the textbook author's interpretations and conclusions. In addition, the student writes notes in the margin, summarizing main points and raising questions to be pursued later.

SOURCE: *Robert W. Strayer,* Ways of the World: A Brief Global History *(Boston: Bedford/St. Martin's, 2009), 326.*

surprise you or with which you disagree, and write your reaction or summary of these passages in the margin. (For more advice on reading, see Chapter 3, pp. 30–36.)

If you read your textbook carefully and actively throughout the semester, you will have ready-made study materials when it comes time to prepare for a test: you will be able to reread the underlined material and your comments and obtain a quick review of a chapter's content. Before the exam, however, you may want to reread the textbook itself. (See Chapter 5, pp. 79–87, for detailed advice on taking exams.)

TAKING NOTES IN CLASS

The time you spend in class is vital to your learning. True, you can learn on your own outside of class, but the interaction with your instructor and other students is most intense during class time. Learning to record that interaction in your notes is an important skill.

From Class Lectures

The first rule of note taking is simple: pay attention. Learn to concentrate on what is being said. Read assigned texts before going to class so you won't end up taking notes on the material in the book. If everything the instructor says is new to you, you will spend so much time writing that you may not be able to grasp the subject of the lecture. If you have obtained some basic information from outside readings, however, you will be able to concentrate on noting points in the lecture that are new or different.

An instructor is most likely to prepare exam questions from the material that he or she considers most important. It is therefore essential in preparing notes to determine which points in the lecture are given most prominent attention. Some instructors are very open about their preferences and clearly emphasize certain points, often writing them on the board or displaying them on overhead projectors or slides. Never fail to note something that the instructor indicates is important. Other instructors are less explicit about their biases and values, and you will have to try to figure them out. Listen closely, and make note of interpretations and generalizations that seem to be stressed, especially when they differ from the approach in the textbook. You should not feel obliged to parrot your instructor's interpretations in an exam, but ignorance of them could work against you.

Write your notes legibly, and begin with the date and subject of the lecture. The notes should reflect a general outline of the material covered, with emphasis on major interpretations and important facts not covered in the textbook. It is often best to write on every other line or to leave a large margin on at least one side of the page. This will allow you to add material later and to underline your notes and write additional comments without cluttering the page. Don't worry about taking down every word that comes out of your instructor's mouth; instead, try to summarize major points and put detailed information such as dates, statistics, and particular names into your outline format. If you simply have a list of facts without any organization, the notes will not make sense to you when you review them for an exam.

If possible, reread your notes later in the day on which they were written. If your handwriting is poor or your notes are disorganized, it is best to rewrite them. Check the spelling and definitions of any unfamiliar words, and be sure that your notes are coherent. Remember, your notes are an important source of information in your studies.

To illustrate some of the essentials of good note taking, compare Figures 2.2 and 2.3, which show portions of two sets of class notes taken from the same lecture. Figure 2.2 (p. 17) illustrates many of the common errors of note takers; Figure 2.3 (p. 18) is a well-written set of notes. A third example, Figure 2.4 (p. 19), shows a rewriting of the good notes. The subject of the lecture was early European contact with Africa.

What is it about the poor notes (Figure 2.2) that makes them inferior? First, they are not well organized. They do not even record the title of the lecture, the course number, or the date — omissions that could be problematic if the notes get out of order. They are little more than a series of sentences about gold, trade, spices, Portugal, and slaves. The sentences are not in any particular order and do not say much of anything important. Even the factual information does not cover the major points of the lecture. By paying too much attention to trivial points about sea monsters, China, Jerusalem, Bartholomew Diaz, and Columbus, the note taker missed or did not have time to record the principal subject of the lecture: the relationship be-

---

Guidelines for Taking Lecture Notes

- Prepare for a lecture by reading all related course materials ahead of time.
- Write the course information, lecture subject, and date at the top of each page of notes.
- Be selective. Don't try to write down everything a lecturer says.
- Be sure to write down anything that the instructor (a) puts on the board or presents in an overhead; (b) says is important; or (c) emphasizes as he or she speaks.
- Leave room in your notes to add material later if necessary.
- Reread your notes later in the day on which they were written.
- Underline especially important points.
- Look up the meaning of any unfamiliar words.
- Rewrite any parts of your notes that are poorly organized.
- If something important in your notes is unclear to you, ask your instructor about it.

tween European-Asian trade and the religious struggle between Islam and Christianity. The note taker also missed another major point: the connection between the enslavement of Africans and the need for plantation labor in the New World. Without those two points, this student cannot write a good exam essay on this subject.

The good notes (Figure 2.3), in contrast, follow the organization of the lecture and touch on the major points made in class. The notes make sense and can serve as the basis for reviewing the content of the lecture when the note taker studies for exams. These notes have a wide margin for extra comments and the marking of important passages. Notice the sections marked "important." The instructor emphasized these points in class, and by specifically identifying them, the student will be sure to master them.

The rewritten version (Figure 2.4), which eliminates unimportant or repetitious phrases and smoothes the language into connected sentences, is even better as a study guide. Taking notes during a lecture is difficult, and even a good set of notes can be greatly improved by being rewritten, so these notes were rewritten within a day of the lecture, while the material was still fresh in the student's mind. Notice how much clearer everything becomes.

The greatest value of rewriting notes, however, is that re-creating the lecture material in essay form helps it to become part of the note taker's own

---

Colonization of Africa — People were afraid to sail out. Afraid of sea monsters. But they liked the stories about gold in Africa. The Portuguese King Henry sailed south to find the gold mines and built a fort at Elmina.

England and France want to trade with Africa. They begin trading. Competing with Portugal. These countries got into wars. They wanted to control Africa.

China had spices. They traded with Cairo and Venice. The Asians wanted gold, but the Islams stopped all trade. They fought wars about religion for hundreds of years. Fought over Jerusalem. The Pope called for a crusade. This was in the Middle Ages.

Spices came from Asia. In Europe they were valuable because the kings used them to become rich. They also ate them. The Portuguese wanted to explore Africa and make a way to India. Their boats couldn't get around until Bartholomew Diaz discovered the Cape of Good Hope in 1487.

Most of all, the Portuguese wanted slaves. They shipped them back from Africa. Columbus took them after he discovered America (1492). The Pope made a line in the Atlantic Ocean so the Catholics wouldn't fight. The colonies needed slaves. They sent 15 million from 1502 to the 19th century. Slaves did the hard work. They got free later after the Civil War.

FIGURE 2.2   Example of Poor Note Taking

Early European Contact with Africa   *History 200*
Why Did Europeans Come to Africa?   *10/23/08*

1. *Desire for gold*
   - *Medieval legends about gold in Africa.*
   - *Prince Henry (Portuguese nobleman) sent men down coast of Africa to find source of gold. (Also to gain direct access to gold trade controlled by Muslims.)*
   - *Portuguese built forts along the coast. Their ships carried gold and ivory back to Portugal (16th century).*
   - *Then the other European states came (England, Holland, France, Spain) to set up their own trading posts.*
   - *Competed with each other for African trade. (Will talk about rivalry next week.)*

2. *Wanted to trade with Asia and weaken the Muslims (The Muslims had created a large empire based on the religion of Islam.)*
   - *Religious conflict between Christianity and Islam. Fought a religious war in the 11th–12th centuries — the Crusades.*
   - *The Muslims had expanded their empire when Europe was weak. In 15th century they controlled North Africa and they dominated trade in the Mediterranean. They controlled the spices coming from Asia, which were in great demand in Europe. In Europe they were used to preserve meat. So valuable, sometimes used as money.*
   - *Portugal and Spain were ruled by Catholic monarchs. Very religious. The Catholic monarchs wanted to force the Muslims out of Europe. (They still held part of Spain.) Wanted to convert them to Christianity.*
   - ***Important***   *The Muslims controlled North Africa and Mediterranean trade. If the Portuguese and Spanish could sail to the Indian Ocean directly, they could get goods from China and the Muslims couldn't stop them. The way to Asia was the sea route around Africa.*

3. *The Europeans wanted slaves*
   - *When the Portuguese explored West Africa (15th century), they sent back the first slaves (around 1440).*
   - *The Spanish conquered the New World (Mexico, Peru, etc.). (Columbus had made several trips for Queen Isabella I of Spain.)*
   - *In America (the name for the New World), they needed slaves. Most slaves were sent to America.*
   - *Native Americans died from diseases of white men. They were also killed in the wars. There was nobody to work the mines (gold and silver).*
   - ***Important***   *Sugar plantations of the Caribbean (and Brazil) needed labor. Cotton and rice plantations in the south of U.S. also. It was hard work and nobody wanted to do it.*
   - *15 million slaves were brought to work the plantations starting in 1502 until mid-19th century.*

FIGURE 2.3   **Example of Good Note Taking**

Early European Contact with Africa   History 200
What Drew Europeans to Africa?   10/23/08

1. GOLD

There were medieval legends that there was a lot of gold in West Africa. Access to the gold was controlled by non-Christian powers (Muslims—believers in Islamic religion). Tales of gold lured the Portuguese (led by Prince Henry) to explore the coast of West Africa in the late 15th century. By the 16th century, the Portuguese had built several trading posts and forts along the West African coast and were bringing back gold, ivory, and pepper.

By the 17th century, English, Dutch, French, and Spanish ships challenged the Portuguese trading monopoly and set up their own trading posts. This was the start of European rivalry over Africa's wealth.

2. DESIRE TO WEAKEN THE POWER OF THE ISLAMIC EMPIRE (MUSLIMS) AND EXPAND TRADE WITH ASIA

Conflict between Christianity and Islam was an old religious conflict (the Crusades as an example in 11th and 12th centuries). The Muslims controlled North Africa and the Mediterranean. They also controlled the spice trade from Asia. Spices were important in Europe because they were the only known way to preserve meat.

The Catholic states of Portugal and Spain wanted to fight with the Muslims. They wanted to drive them out of Spain and challenge the large Muslim empire in Africa, the Middle East, and Asia. They hoped to convert them to Christianity. _The Muslims were strong in North Africa, but if European powers could discover a way around Africa into the Indian Ocean, they could outflank the Muslims and obtain direct access to the trade with India and Asia._

3. SLAVES

Portuguese trading posts in Africa had sent a small number of slaves to Europe starting in the late 15th century. With the discovery and conquest of America at the turn of the 16th century, a new and larger slave trade began to European colonies in the New World (America).

The Native Americans died (they were killed in war and by European diseases in great numbers). There was a shortage of labor. In the 17th and 18th centuries, large sugar plantations were set up in the Caribbean and Brazil and rice and cotton plantations in the southern United States. _The need for laborers to do the hard agricultural work led to the importing of millions of slaves from Africa._ Approximately 15 million Africans were sent to America as slaves between 1502 and the mid-19th century. This slave trade made Africa valuable to the European powers.

FIGURE 2.4   Example of Rewritten Good Notes

thinking. The mental effort that goes into revising lecture notes serves to impress the material and its meaning upon the mind. This makes it much easier to review the material at exam time.

From Slides and Films

Some instructors use visual aids or show video clips in class. Note taking in these instances presents special problems. If a lecture is accompanied by slides, you will need to include in your notes information about what the slides illustrated (for example, the Pyramid of Cheops, the novels of Willa Cather, the assassination of John F. Kennedy, the dances of Martha Graham) and anything of importance your instructor said about the slides.

Taking notes on films or videos also presents the unusual problem of dim lighting. The greatest problem, however, may be the film itself. In our culture, films are a medium of entertainment rather than education. Your natural response may be to sit back and relax your mind, but you will need to fight this response and learn to probe a film as you would a reading or a lecture. If a film is essentially factual (*Walled Cities of the Middle Ages*), note the major facts and interpretations as you would when reading a secondary source or listening to a lecture. If a film is dramatic rather than documentary (*Hotel Rwanda, Citizen Kane*, or *Schindler's List*), examine the emotional message and artistic content as well as any historical facts it describes (or claims to describe). Ask yourself, What is the movie director trying to say, and what dramatic and technical devices does he or she use to say it? Your notes should record important narration and dialogue that illustrate the theme of the film. Finally, you will need to take note of cinematic elements (camera angles, sets, lighting, gestures and movements, facial expressions) because the impact of a dramatic film is essentially visual. For more on working with video recordings, see Chapter 3, pages 45–48.

Taking Notes in a "Wired" Classroom

A newer form of class presentation is the multimedia lecture, which usually combines traditional lecturing and questions with digital media. The use of nonprint material requires a looser form of note taking, one that will help you to recall a mixed-media presentation.

The key to note taking here is to follow carefully the ways in which the use of new media complements the instructor's lecture. In general, the purpose of incorporating new media is to present you with a richer and more dramatic exposure to a wide variety of historical sources. This material helps to get across the main points that the instructor is covering. Ask yourself, How do the photographs, or timelines, or audio recordings complement the subject of the lecture? Be sure to take notes not only on the media themselves but also on their relation to the subject under discussion. Perhaps your instructor will use media to reinforce a fact — how something looked or sounded. Most likely he or she will also explain the "meaning" of an image or recording:

the way it represents nineteenth-century European romanticism, or the popular culture of a large city in the twentieth century, or the connection between rice paddies and villages in twelfth-century China. Don't fill your notes with long descriptions of images or sounds. Instead, focus on the aspects of the topic that the new media bring to life.

CLASSROOM PARTICIPATION

In most history classes, you will be expected to actively participate in your own learning. This section discusses some ways of doing so.

Classroom Discussions

Many instructors encourage class participation. Some base a portion of the final grade on it. Come to class prepared to answer (and to ask) questions. Follow the discussion as it develops. If you are called on, contribute what you know. Remember that sometimes the instructor is asking for your informed opinion and that you won't be judged on whether your comment is "correct" or not. If some part of an instructor's presentation or a classmate's comments is unclear to you, don't hesitate to ask a question. If class ends and something remains unclear, raise your question with your instructor after class or during your instructor's office hours.

Group Work

Your instructor may ask you to be part of a small group and carry out an assignment working with members of that group. Conducting research and preparing a group paper or presentation can be tricky but also rewarding. The key to success is to clarify who in the group is to do what part of the assignment

---

Guidelines for Speaking in Class

- Be familiar with the subject under discussion.
- If you are unclear about something the instructor or another student has said, compose and ask your question.
- If you disagree with something said, make your point clearly and constructively.
- Be respectful of others; always treat your classmates as you would expect to be treated.
- If you don't have a chance to raise a question in class, ask your instructor after class.

and to be sure that each member is prepared when the time comes. This will become especially important if the instructor assigns a group grade, rather than individual grades for the project.

Another kind of group work takes place outside the classroom. Known as **peer reviewing** or peer editing, this type of work requires you to evaluate the work of a classmate. For example, you may be asked to read and comment on a student's rough draft of an assignment. Your peer review may take the form of an informal one-on-one review in which you go through the paper with the author point by point. Some instructors may ask you to write your evaluation or mark up a draft with comments; others may want your review in the form of a class presentation. No matter what the format is, remember to provide *constructive* criticism that will help your classmates develop their papers. Be sure to point out a paper's strengths in addition to any weaknesses.

If you are asked to peer-edit the work of a classmate, remember also to pay particular attention to the **thesis** of the paper. Ask yourself whether the thesis is stated clearly and whether there is sufficient **evidence** to support it. In addition, you should consider whether the information has been presented in an organized manner, such that your classmate's conclusions are justified. Unless specifically told to do so, don't focus on minor issues, such as misspellings and other typos, especially when reviewing a **rough draft**.

Learning to work collaboratively will be of use when you leave school and enter a working environment in which these kinds of personal and digital interactions are common. Moreover, the ability to accept constructive criticism and use it to improve a piece of work is a skill that will help you no matter what career you choose after your history course. The sooner you get used to sharing drafts via e-mail or posting your comments on a peer project online,

---

Guidelines for Peer Reviewing

- Don't be overly critical. Your goal is to assist your classmate in seeing the strengths and weaknesses in her or his draft. Your ability to do this comes from your outsider status: you have not been submerged in the research and are able to take a fresh look at the essay.
- Pay special attention to the thesis of the essay. Is it stated in clear terms?
- Does the body of the paper provide important evidence to support the thesis?
- Are the points made in support of the thesis well organized, and are they clear to you as a reader?
- Are the paper's conclusions justified by its arguments and documentation?
- Whether your comments to your classmate are written or oral, be supportive. Give the writer the kind of help you hope to get from your own peer reviewer.

the more comfortable you'll feel receiving this kind of feedback. In the end, this give-and-take is an important building block for critical thinking, good writing habits, and a host of other skills necessary for graduate and professional work.

COMMUNICATING ONLINE

Some professors and students use online resources to enhance or expand their academic experience. Some instructors, for example, post the course syllabus and assignments online, perhaps in a secure environment such as Blackboard or WebCT. Other instructors may incorporate a slide show from a museum's Web site into their lecture, or provide a set of links to primary sources for you to discuss in a class chat room. Whenever you find yourself researching or communicating in an online environment, it is important to be aware of your instructor's expectations as well as the general rules of behavior (or "netiquette") of the medium.

Using tools such as e-mail and listservs, and working in online environments such as chat rooms, message forums, and blogs, you can virtually communicate with peers as well as experts on topics that interest you. Listservs are a way of managing e-mail lists of people interested in a particular topic. Instead of allowing one-to-one or one-to-many communication — as with e-mail — listservs send out everyone's messages to everyone else on the list. Listservs are especially valuable in settings that emphasize group-oriented work. Chat rooms allow users to have real-time discussions with others who are in a specific "room"; online message boards or forums are similar, but discussions are posted and archived for later viewing. Chat rooms provide users with immediate communication, but unlike e-mail or listservs they do not provide users with any tangible record of the dialogue. Some professors maintain blogs (Web logs) for posting additional information or thoughts about the course, and they may expect you to post comments there as well.

Professors generally set up these interactive environments so that students can raise issues, pose questions, or simply discuss a particular topic. Be sure that you know what the general content and tone of the particular environment is before you jump in with your commentary.

If your class uses a listserv, message board, or blog, you might submit the following post:

I understand Prof. Capra's discussion of the factors that led to an anticommunist belief/paranoia in the U.S. during the late 1940s and early 1950s. However, I'm confused about which groups expressed these fears. From the readings it appears that only the Republicans did; however, Prof. Capra's lecture leads me to believe that both Republicans and Democrats did. Can anyone help me with this point?

By posting this message, you are assessing what you know and what you don't know and trying to deepen your understanding. Your message may stimulate another student's thinking. A classmate might offer the following reply:

> I think that is exactly Prof. Capra's intention. As I understand it, both Republicans and Democrats expressed these fears; however, they employed different means to achieve the same ends. Because the Democrats' activities were less dramatic, the Republicans charged them with being "soft" on communism.

Responding gives the student an opportunity to think about the material, understand the connections, and see how the material works.

Despite the advantages of online environments, there are dangers as well. Most of this kind of communication is unmediated or unedited, especially if it takes place in a forum outside your class Web site. This means that anyone can say anything at any time. Perhaps someone with whom you are communicating tells you that the Holocaust was a Hollywood creation. Although it is important to be open to new theories, it is equally important to read electronic communication with a skeptical eye. If someone says something with which you are unfamiliar, it is perfectly acceptable to ask for references where you could find more information on that topic. The best advice is to know the individuals with whom you communicate, read messages critically, and don't be afraid to challenge someone if you have reason to believe that he or she is wrong.

Web communication can also help with advanced course work. If you decide to tackle an obscure topic, you can use the Web to find and contact scholars who have done research in that area. If possible, contact several scholars so that you have more than one interpretation of the topic. The scholars and archivists with whom you would communicate are busy individuals. When contacting them, introduce yourself, describe your research, and outline your reason for writing to them. Be sure that you are knowledgeable about your topic, that your contact can actually help you, and that you ask specific questions. (For information about conducting research on the Web, see Chapter 6.)

The cooperative learning fostered through online communication is of great value. Remember: historians do not work in a vacuum; historical research relies on access to the discoveries, interpretations, and analyses of others. Virtual means of communicating, much like seminar-type classes, are fueled by cooperative learning. By exchanging information, you are increasing and solidifying your knowledge, pointing out errors, and sharing important findings. This experience will give you insight into an important principle of the humanistic disciplines: your best work will result from dialogue with other researchers.

CHAPTER

3

Working with
Historical Evidence

As you will learn in Chapter 6, historians usually begin the research process with a pointed question that provides a focus for their study. A historian might ask, for example, "Why did China deemphasize naval exploration and trade by the Middle Ages?" or "What led the Populist Party in the United States to fuse with the Democratic Party in 1896?" Once a historian has settled on a **research question**, he or she will begin looking for **evidence** that can lead to an answer. The evidence available to historians falls into two general categories: primary sources and secondary sources.

PRIMARY SOURCES

The raw materials that historians use as they reconstruct the past are known as **primary sources**. These are the firsthand remnants of an event that come directly from a historical actor (for example, a person, a corporation, a government agency, or a religious institution). *Written* primary sources include personal documents, such as letters and diaries, and published works, such as memoirs and newspaper articles. Official statements such as royal decrees, church edicts, advertisements, and political party platforms are considered primary sources, as are official records and statistics such as marriage, birth, and death statistics, census data, property deeds, contracts, and transcripts of legal proceedings. Eyewitnesses have also left us with *nonwritten* primary sources such as maps, illustrations, and, in more recent generations, photographs, audiotapes, and videos. **Artifacts** are yet another type of nonwritten primary source. These are things made and used by people in the past: houses, public buildings, tools, clothing, and much more. Figures 3.1 and 3.2, as well as Figures 3.4 through 3.16, are examples of primary sources.

$_____ KNOW ALL MEN BY THESE PRESENTS, That we are held and
firmly bound unto *Colin Clarke*
in the just and full sum of *twelve Dollars & fifty cents ($12.50.)*
to be paid to the said *Colin Clarke, his agents,_____* executors,
administrators, or assigns, on or before the *first day of april next* A. D. 1848.
*In the like sum to be paid on the first of July 1848. In
the like sum to be paid on the first of October 1848. and
in the like sum to be paid on, or before the first day
of January in the year Eighteen hundred and forty
nine (1849)_____*
being for the hire of *a negro man slave named, Anthony, to be
employed as a farm hand, or gardner, for the year Eighteen
hundred forty eight (1848)*
Said negro — to be furnished with the customary summer clothing, and to be returned to the said
Colin Clarke_____ or to *his* agent*s*
in Richmond, on the *twenty fifth* day of *December next,* with
a good winter suit. *a hat and a blanket—*

For the true and faithful performance of which we do hereby bind ourselves, our heirs, executors and administrators, jointly and severally, firmly by these presents,

As witness our hands and seals this *6th* day of *January*
A. D. one thousand, eighteen hundred and *forty Eight (1848)*

Robt Baird [SEAL.]
P W Harwood [SEAL.]
[SEAL.]

N. B.—Should the above named negro   require medical aid in the course of the year, notice must be given to the
said *Colin Clarke _____* or to *his* agent*s* in Richmond,
if practicable, if not, Doctor*s R. of M. Cabell_____* and no other Physician must be employed.

FIGURE 3.1   Example of Primary Evidence (1848)

If you were pursuing the research question "How common was the practice of
hiring out slaves in antebellum Virginia?" you might find this 1848 contract to be
an informative primary source. Consider the blend of printed and handwritten
text on this page. What does the preprinted nature of the form tell us about the
practice of slave hiring? What is implied by the schedule of payments and the other
conditions of the transaction? Can we learn anything about the "negro man slave
named Anthony" from this document?

SOURCE: *Image of a slave contract between Colin Clarke and Robert Baird, dated January 6, 1848, in the
Robert Baird Papers located in the Rare Book, Manuscript, and Special Collections Library, Duke University.*

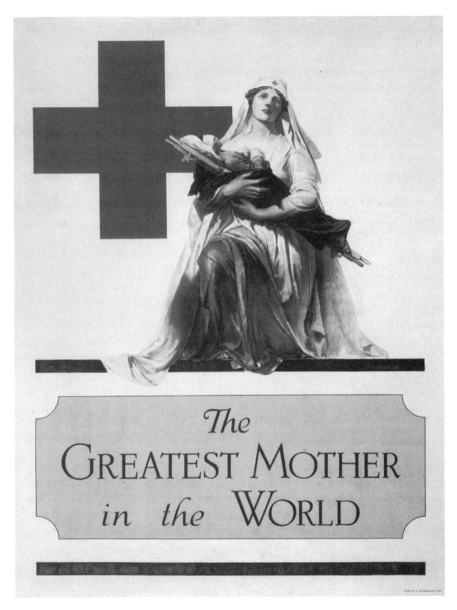

FIGURE 3.2   Example of Primary Evidence (1918)

This World War I–era poster depicts a Red Cross nurse holding a wounded U.S. soldier on a stretcher. What message do you think the artist is trying to promote here? What audience do you think the poster is aimed at? Do you think a similar image would be effective in the United States today?

SOURCE: *Library of Congress Prints and Photographs Division.*

During the 1940s and 1950s, no visitor to the copper mining cities of colonial Northern Rhodesia (Zambia) in central Africa could escape the visible marks of the impact of American films.[1] In the vast company compounds that housed the African miners and their families on the Copper belt, groups of African boys, "dressed in home-made paper 'chaps' and cowboy hats, and carrying crudely carved wooden pistols," were a ubiquitous presence running through the streets and alleys in endless games of cowboys and Indians. Others appeared "more sinister, . . . with a black mask over their eyes and a wooden dagger in the belt." As they engaged in their mock battles, they could be heard shouting, "Jeke, Jeke," a local corruption of "Jack," the universal term among urban moviegoers in the British central African colonies for the heroes of cowboy films.[2] In the same streets, young men affected styles of dress that plainly showed the influence of westerns and gangster films — ten-gallon hats, kerchiefs, and so forth.[3]

[1]The British colony of Northern Rhodesia became Zambia at independence in 1964. During the 1950s, Northern Rhodesia was linked with Southern Rhodesia (Zimbabwe) and Nyasaland (Malawi) in a Central African Federation dominated by white settler interests.

[2]H. Franklin, "The Central African Screen," *Colonial Cinema* 8 (December 1950): 85. "Jack" was supposedly a tribute to the actor Jack Holt. Also see "The Cinema in Northern Rhodesia," *Colonial Cinema* 2 (June 1944): 22.

[3]R. J. Allanson to Director, Department of Information, Lusaka, January 27, 1956, National Archives of Zambia (hereafter NAZ), Sec. 5/16, I, no. 88.

FIGURE 3.3 Example of Secondary Evidence (2001)
This example is the opening paragraph of a scholarly article by Charles Ambler entitled "Popular Films and Colonial Audiences: The Movies in Northern Rhodesia," which appeared in the *American Historical Review* in 2001. Notice that note 3 refers to a primary source that Ambler used as evidence.

SECONDARY SOURCES

Secondary sources are the findings of writers who were not participants in a historical episode but have investigated primary evidence of it, as historians do when they conduct their research. When historians publish the results of their research, they create secondary sources, which are read by other scholars and by students. Most history books and articles are secondary sources, and their **notes** and **bibliography** identify the primary sources that the historians examined. If your own work is based on primary sources, your research paper will become a secondary source for others to read. For an example of a secondary source, see Figure 3.3 above.

WHEN A SECONDARY SOURCE BECOMES A PRIMARY SOURCE

It is important to understand the basic differences between primary and secondary sources, for in certain situations a secondary source becomes a primary one. Here are two examples:

1. A contemporary historian is writing a book that discusses the views of early-twentieth-century historians on the reasons for the decline of the Roman Empire. The works from the early twentieth century that the historian uses as his sources would generally be considered secondary works because they were written more than fifteen hundred years after the end of the Roman Empire. However, for the contemporary historian's study, they are primary sources because they provide *direct* evidence of what early-twentieth-century historians thought about the decline of the Roman Empire.

2. In 1990 a U.S. senator writes an article about the background of the men in his state who signed the Declaration of Independence. The senator's article is a secondary source because it is based on primary sources from the time of the American Revolution rather than on his direct experience. However, if a later historian writes a biography of the senator that includes an analysis of the senator's views about the period of the Revolution, then the senator's article becomes a primary document because it represents *direct* evidence about the senator's views.

ACCESSING SOURCES IN PRINT, IN PERSON, AND ONLINE

Historians can access sources in a variety of ways, as explained in detail in Chapter 6. Primary and secondary documents can be found in books, **scholarly journals**, Web sites, **databases**, and museum exhibits, among other places. These repositories of information may in turn be accessed in one or more ways: in print, in person, or online. You might, for example, view John Singer Sargent's painting *Gassed* in a printed collection, in a museum, or on a Web site. The quality of the image may vary somewhat, and your own viewing experience may change depending on the environment in which you view it — a small computer screen versus the real-life painting, which is twenty feet long — but the artwork itself, which Sargent painted as he witnessed soldiers during World War I, remains a primary source no matter how you access it. There might also be subtle tweaks to the source — the image might be cropped or have captions added by an editor — but reputable repositories will leave the core of the primary source unchanged.

As another example, a book might be out of print and difficult to track down physically, but it may be available in digital format on a Web site such as Project Gutenberg. The important point to keep in mind is that a primary source book, such as *The Autobiography of Malcolm X,* is still a book and still a primary source whether it is accessed online or in print. An artifact, such as the ones shown on page 49, is still an artifact and still a primary source whether you encounter it in person or in a text such as this.

Secondary sources also maintain their status as secondary regardless of the way they are accessed. A scholarly journal article might be available both in print and in an electronic database such as *JSTOR*. But whether you read the print version or the electronic version, you are still reading a journal article (not a Web site), and it is still a secondary source.

NOTE: Thorough historians constantly interrogate their evidence whether it comes from a traditional archive, a printed collection, a database, a Web site, or elsewhere. For a full discussion of finding and evaluating all types of sources, see Chapter 6.

READING WRITTEN SOURCES

Reading history can be a satisfying experience, but to enjoy the landscape you must first know where you are: you must have a general sense of the subject and of the manner in which it is being presented. If you begin reading before you get your bearings, you may become lost in a forest of unfamiliar facts and interpretations. Before you begin reading any written document, look it over carefully. If you are reading a book, look at the preface or **introduction**. This should tell you something about the author and his or her purpose in writing the work. For articles, read through the brief **abstract** (article summary), if there is one, to get a sense of the central **argument**. Also scan the table of contents of a book to get a sense of the way in which the author organized the subject. Next, skim the text itself, reading headings and glancing at illustrations and graphed material. If you have the time, preread the opening and concluding chapters of a book (or the opening and concluding paragraphs of an article) rapidly before reading the full work. For further advice on reading written sources, see the guidelines on page 31.

After scouting the ground, you will be ready to read. By this time, you should be familiar with the source's **topic** (what aspects of history the source covers), the background of the author (politician, journalist, historian, eyewitness, novelist, etc.), when the document was written (a hundred-year-old letter, the most recent book on a subject, etc.), how it is organized (chronologically, topically, etc.), and, most important of all, its **thesis** and **conclusions**. The thesis is the principal point that an author wishes to make on a subject: that the geography of Spain was a significant factor in that nation's failure to industrialize in the eighteenth and nineteenth centuries; that disagreement on moral issues between J. Robert Oppenheimer and Edward Teller delayed development of the hydrogen bomb. Most authors set out their thesis in a preface or introduction. If you understand the principal point the author is trying to make, then the organization and conclusions of the work will become clear to you. The author will be organizing evidence and drawing conclusions to support the thesis. The ability to recognize and describe a weak thesis or unsupportive evidence is part of learning history too. (For a discussion of thesis and argument, see Chapter 4, pp. 53–54, and Chapter 7, pp. 128–31.)

NOTE: Primary sources, even written ones, may or may not have a thesis. A political memoir, for example, might center around an argument intended to justify a particular policy or ideology. But a raw primary source, such as a birth certificate or a list of committee assignments, will not contain a thesis. When you are assessing sources, the presence of a thesis statement is not as significant for primary sources as it is for secondary sources, which almost always should have a clear thesis statement or argument.

Primary Texts

One of your most important concerns when reading a primary source is determining its reliability. Primary sources can be fraudulent, inaccurate, or **biased.** Eyewitness accounts may have been deliberately distorted in order to

Guidelines for Working with Written Sources

- Find a place with very few distractions, and allot enough time to complete the reading assignment in one sitting.
- Consider the main purpose of your reading in order to place it in context. How does it relate to the other readings for your course or for your research? How might it apply to or enhance your class assignments or lectures?
- Before reading a book or long article all the way through, preread it by looking over the table of contents and scan it for headings or visual matter. Skim the text to get a quick sense of what it covers.
- Look for a paragraph or two that provides information about the author. Is he or she a scholar in the field? Does he or she appear to have any particular motivation or bias in writing the piece?
- For primary texts, read through any headnotes or captions that provide background information on the source, keeping in mind that such material constitutes *secondary* source matter.
- As you read through the source, constantly interrogate it. Why does the author say that? What sources is he or she citing to support that point? Why is he or she spending so much time on a particular point?
- Read actively, taking notes on any points that strike you as particularly strange, persuasive, surprising, illuminating, or otherwise significant. If you are working from your own printout or copy of the book, mark it up and write in the margins; otherwise, take notes in a notebook or on your computer.
- For details on evaluating written primary and secondary sources, consult pages 109–16 in Chapter 6.
- For advice on writing about readings, see Chapter 5.

avert blame or to bestow praise on a particular individual or group. Without intending to misinform, even on-the-scene judgments can be incorrect. Sometimes, the closer you are to an event, the more emotionally involved you are, and this involvement distorts your understanding of it. We can all recall events in which we completely misunderstood the feelings, actions, and words of another person. Historians have to weigh evidence carefully to see whether those who participated in an event understood it well enough to describe it accurately. Official statements present another problem — the issue of propaganda or concealment. A government, group, or institution may make statements that it wishes others to believe but that are not true. What a group says may not be what it does. This is especially true in politics.

The *inherent* bias of a source also presents difficulties. People's unspoken attitudes toward the world influence the way they interpret events. For example, you and your parents may have different attitudes toward music, sex, religion, or politics. These differences can cause you to disagree with them about the value of a rock concert, a Sunday sermon, or the president. (See also "Evaluating Sources" in Chapter 6, pp. 109–16.)

To check the reliability of evidence, historians use the tests of consistency and corroboration: Does the evidence contradict itself, and does it disagree with evidence from other sources? Historical research always involves checking one source against another. For example, Figure 3.4 (p. 33) presents two primary documents that report the fighting at Lexington and Concord, Massachusetts, in 1775 — battles that began the Revolutionary War. In what important ways do the two accounts differ? How do you think the conflicting goals of the colonists and the English soldiers biased each report of the battle? What phrases could you pull out of each document to highlight the bias? Notice that the American version talks of "some inhabitants of the colony" who while "travelling peaceably" were "seized and greatly abused" by the English soldiers. The English officer, in contrast, says that the Americans were "drawn up in military order, with arms" and that his troops were "without any intention of injuring them." You should be able to find other important differences in the two reports of the fighting. Also, as you read the documents, consider what additional sources would help you decide which report is more accurate. The two accounts agree on some facts but disagree on the responsibility for the fighting. Eyewitness accounts from other English soldiers and from American colonials who were there will help in determining which description is more accurate. It might turn out, for example, that parts of *each* account are correct and other parts are distorted in some way. Sometimes there is no *one* true source for the history of an event. Still, the more primary sources you read, the closer you will come to knowing the event in all its details and meanings.

Scholarly Articles

One of the most important ways that historians present new scholarship in their field is through the publication of **scholarly articles**. These secondary sources are essays of about thirty to fifty pages that are found in academic

AMERICAN ACCOUNT OF THE BATTLE OF LEXINGTON:

Account by the Provincial Congress at Watertown, Massachusetts,
April 26, 1775

By the clearest depositions relative to this transaction, it will appear that on the night preceding the nineteenth of April instant, a body of the king's troops, under the command of colonel Smith, were secretly landed at Cambridge, with an apparent design to take or destroy the military and other stores, provided for the defence of this colony, and deposited at Concord — that some inhabitants of the colony, on the night aforesaid, whilst travelling peaceably on the road, between Boston and Concord, were seized and greatly abused by armed men, who appeared to be officers of general Gage's army; that the town of Lexington, by these means, was alarmed, and a company of the inhabitants mustered on the occasion — that the regular troops on their way to Concord, marched into the said town of Lexington, and the said company, on their approach, began to disperse — that, notwithstanding this, the regulars rushed on with great violence and first began hostilities, by firing on said Lexington company, whereby they killed eight, and wounded several others — that the regulars continued their fire, until those of said company, who were neither killed nor wounded, had made their escape — that colonel Smith, with the detachment then marched to Concord, where a number of provincials were again fired on by the troops, two of them killed and several wounded, before the provincials fired on them, and provincials were again fired on by the troops, produced an engagement that lasted through the day, in which many of the provincials and more of the regular troops were killed and wounded. . . .

By order,
Joseph Warren, President.

ENGLISH ACCOUNT OF THE BATTLE OF LEXINGTON:

Report of Lieutenant-Colonel Smith to Governor Gage, April 22, 1775

I think it proper to observe, that when I had got some miles on the march from Boston, I detached six light infantry companies to march with all expedition to seize the two bridges on different roads beyond Concord. On these companies' arrival at Lexington, I understand, from the report of Major Pitcairn, who was with them, and from many officers, that they found on a green close to the road a body of the country people drawn up in military order, with arms and accoutrements, and, as appeared after, loaded; and that they had posted some men in a dwelling and Meeting-house. Our troops advanced towards them, without any intention of injuring them, further than to inquire the reason of their being thus assembled, and, if not satisfactory, to have secured their arms; but they in confusion went off, principally to the left, only one of them fired before he went off, and three or four more jumped over a wall and fired from behind it among the soldiers; on which the troops returned it, and killed several of them. They likewise fired on the soldiers from the Meeting and dwelling-houses. . . . While at Concord we saw vast numbers assembling in many parts; at one of the bridges they marched down, with a very considerable body, on the light infantry posted there. On their coming pretty near, one of our men fired on them, which they returned; on which an action ensued, and some few were killed and wounded. . . . On our leaving Concord to return to Boston, they began to fire on us from behind the walls, ditches, trees, &c., which, as we marched, increased to a very great degree, and continued without intermission of five minutes altogether, for, I believe, upwards of eighteen miles. . . .

I have the honor, &c.,
F. Smith, Lieutenant-Colonel 10th Foot.

FIGURE 3.4 **Two Conflicting Primary Documents**

(scholarly) journals. (For tips on how to identify scholarly articles, see the guidelines below.) Academic journals, such as the *American Historical Review*, differ from popular magazines, such as *Time*, because their articles are based on original research into primary sources. In addition, articles in most academic journals are **refereed** or **peer-reviewed**, which means that other experts in the field assess the essay's quality before it is published in the journal. An excerpt from a scholarly article appears in Figure 3.3 on page 28.

If provided, an abstract at the beginning of a scholarly article will tell you the gist of the essay, but you'll need to read the entire essay in order to get the nuances of the article and in order to evaluate it properly. Every article should have a clear thesis or central argument stated either explicitly or implicitly at the beginning. If there is an abstract, it is likely to summarize the thesis of the article.

To read an article most effectively, identify the thesis right away and consider whether the evidence that the author used supports it. (For more details on evaluating scholarly articles, see Chapter 6, pp. 109–11.) Once you've read through the article, you should consider its wider place in the literature. In other words, you'll want to know not only what an author is saying but why he or she is saying it. Is this a case study meant to explore a theory developed elsewhere? Is the author challenging another historian's interpretation of a

---

Guidelines for Identifying Scholarly Articles

- Look at the publisher of the article. Does the piece appear in a journal or in an anthology published by a university press or nonprofit institution (such as the Organization of American Historians)?
- Examine the author's credentials. Authors of scholarly articles typically hold an academic position.
- Read the complete title of the article. Scholarly article titles usually include a lengthy description of the article's content.
- Review the editorial apparatus surrounding the article. Is there an abstract at the beginning? Are there footnotes or endnotes that cite both primary and secondary sources? Is there a bibliography or a works-cited section? Your article need not have all of these elements, but if it has none of them, it lacks the methodological rigor demanded of scholarly research.
- Consider the article's physical appearance. Most scholarly articles consist of text alone and rely on few or no fancy typefaces and graphics. If the article contains images, charts, or tables, they should have citations explaining their origin. Articles published in scholarly journals will also have fewer advertisements around them than those in popular magazines.
- If you still have doubts about whether an article is scholarly, check with a reference librarian or ask your professor for help.

subject? Does the article revise a commonly accepted historical viewpoint? Take notes on the article before, during, and after you read it to help you digest its main points and analyze its underlying philosophy.

NOTE: Historians commonly reserve broad philosophical questions for their footnotes or endnotes. In order to assess the larger purpose of the article, be sure to pay attention to the source's citations — footnotes, endnotes, and bibliography. (For more detail on historical philosophies, see Chapter 1.)

Monographs

One of the most common secondary sources of historical work is a **monograph** — a book-length study of one specialized topic. When you are reading a monograph, pay special attention to the point of view, for your instructor may expect you to learn not only about the topic but also about the argument and evidence presented in the work. You will need to determine the author's assumptions and values, and to understand his or her thesis and conclusions. Read this kind of work not only to absorb the facts but also to analyze, question, and criticize. If you own the book, you can do your questioning and criticizing in the margins. If the book is not yours, or if you wish to have an organized set of notes about it, summarize the contents and the author's thesis in a notebook or computer file. You can then review your notes or annotations before the exam. (For more on taking notes, see Chapter 6, pp. 116–25.)

Anthologies

Another kind of work in history is an anthology — a book of readings on a particular subject, usually primary documents (such as letters or memoirs) or excerpted sections from larger secondary works. All of the general suggestions concerning the reading of historical sources apply here as well, but this type of assignment often calls for a particular kind of reading. Each selection usually discusses a different aspect or interpretation of the subject, and some pieces are likely to be in serious disagreement. Instructors expect students to be able to assess the arguments of the various authors and on occasion to take a position in the debate. Therefore, you should read this particular kind of book with an eye to analyzing the arguments of the different authors or to comparing their different approaches to the subject. A good way to do this is to summarize briefly the argument or approach of each selection.

Historical Novels

A historical novel is a work of fiction based on actual occurrences and real people. Historical fiction is often more dramatic and more personal than an article or monograph and describes the presumed feelings of individuals caught up in important historical events. Reading a historical novel gives you a feel for the times in which it is set and for the historical material it contains. A novelist who knows a historical period or event well can bring it to life in ways that scholarly works cannot, but be cautious not to treat a fictional text as historical truth.

"READING" NONWRITTEN SOURCES

Depending on the assignment, you may need to interpret maps, videos, sound recordings, artwork, photographs, statistical data, and other nonwritten sources. To use these kinds of resources effectively, you will need to learn how to understand their historical significance. The guidelines below provide general advice for interpreting nonwritten sources; the sections that follow provide details on how to examine specific types of nonwritten documents.

Maps

Important aspects of the historical record can be displayed in maps. The landscape is one of history's fundamental settings. The rise and fall of empires, the course of wars, the growth of cities, the development of trade routes, and much more can be traced on maps of large areas. Figure 3.5 (p. 37) indicates the years in which parts of Africa came under European colonial

---

Guidelines for Interpreting Nonwritten Sources

- If a source is accompanied by written background information, such as a caption or a headnote, read it to gain a fuller understanding of the source.
- Consider where, when, and by whom the source was created. As with written sources, understanding the historical context in which a nonwritten document was made can help you to make sense of it.
- Consider the original purpose of the source. Was it designed to inform, persuade, or entertain (or some combination of these)? Was it utilitarian in nature?
- Determine why the source still exists. Why has it been preserved or included in a collection for present-day audiences? The act of making a source available may imply a particular agenda or point of view.
- If you are dealing with a restoration or reproduction of an item, such as a reconstructed temple or a print of a cave drawing, find out if any alterations in color, size, or scope have been made.
- Make certain you know whether any audiovisual materials you are using (including photographs and sound and video recordings) have been edited from their original format.

rule. This map tells you which European countries controlled which parts of Africa and when this control was established. Analyzing the map, you can see that Britain and France had the largest colonial empires in Africa and that most of Africa was still free of colonial rule before the 1880s. Figure 3.6 (p. 38) indicates the dates on which the nations of Africa became independent. By comparing this map with Figure 3.5, you can determine which countries changed their names upon achieving independence. Comparing the dates on the two maps, you can figure out how long colonial rule lasted in different countries. Notice also that the first wave of independence came in the

FIGURE 3.5   **The March of Colonialism in Africa**

1960s and that the dates of Namibian and Eritrean independence are only two decades ago.

Small area maps can show the layout of villages, the outcome of battles, or the location of mines, canals, and railroads. To read a map, you must understand the *key*, which translates the symbols used on the map. A line on a map may identify a road, a river, or a gas pipeline. The key tells you which it is. The *scale* of a map tells you the actual size of the area the map represents. Maps are an important aid in understanding history because they display the physical relationships between places. Never ignore maps in a textbook or

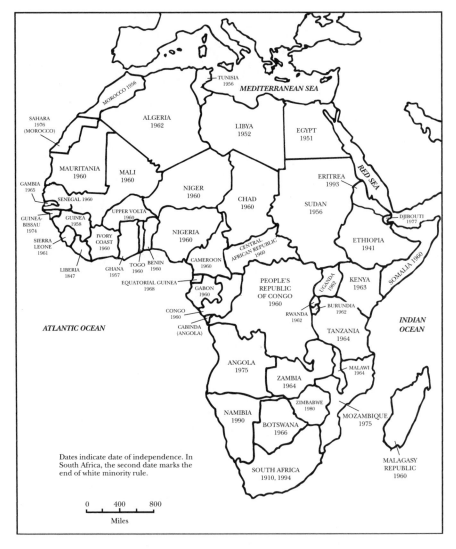

FIGURE 3.6   The March of African Independence

other reading. It is also wise to put a good map of the area you are studying near your desk so that you can see the location of places mentioned in lectures and readings.

Old maps are primary documents. The way that old maps describe the territories they cover can give you clues as to what was going on in the mind of the mapmaker — an eyewitness to that era — when the map was created. A good example of the mapmaker's perspective can usually be found in the artwork around the border.

Statistical Data

In addition to maps, history resources often include statistical data arranged in charts, graphs, or tables. These data describe the amounts of something (such as warships, marriages, schools, bridges, or deaths from smallpox) at a specific time in the past, and usually they compare these amounts (such as the number of marriages in relation to the number of schools) or trace changes in amounts over time (such as the number of warships in 1820, 1830, and 1840).

Figure 3.7 below shows a tabular arrangement of statistical data with an explanation of how to read them. The table organizes population statistics from different regions and across two and a half centuries. Reading across the rows allows you to trace the changes in population of a particular region at fifty-year intervals. You can note the change for each region and the rate of change. For example, the population of Africa barely increased in the fifty years between 1750 and 1800, but it more than tripled in the fifty years between 1950 and 1999. Reading down the columns, you can compare the populations of each region during the same period. In 1750, the population of Latin America and the Caribbean was eight times greater than the population of Northern America. In 1950, the two populations were nearly the same, and by 1999, the Latin American population had begun to outpace the Northern American population once again.

More complex comparisons can be made from Figure 3.7 by combining the differences between regions (reading down) and their rates of growth over time (reading across). For example, you can discover that whereas the

Major area	1750	1800	1850	1900	1950	1999
Africa	106	107	111	133	221	767
Asia	502	635	809	947	1,402	3,634
Europe	163	203	276	408	547	729
Latin America and the Caribbean	16	24	38	74	167	511
Northern America	2	7	26	82	172	307
Oceania	2	2	2	6	13	30

FIGURE 3.7   Estimated World Population, 1750–1999
Numbers represent millions of persons.
SOURCE: *Population Division, Department of Economic and Social Affairs, United Nations Secretariat.*

population of Asia grew more than that of any other region in absolute terms, its *rate* of growth from 1850 to 1999 (809 million to 3,634 million, or about 450 percent) was much less than that of Africa (111 million to 767 million, or around 700 percent) in the same time period.

Even the cold statistics of a table can provide images of the great drama of history. The negligible increase in African population between 1750 and 1850 may tell us something of the impact of the slave trade, and the large increase in the U.S. population between 1850 and 1900 tells us something about the history of European emigration.

The information in the table can be presented differently in order to highlight different aspects of the data. In Figure 3.8 below, the numbers for each region are represented as percentages of the total world population. By changing the numbers from absolute amounts to percentages, this table facilitates the comparing of populations and population growth.

Another way of presenting data is in the form of a graph. Notice that Figure 3.9 (p. 41) makes more obvious the differences between numbers and thus makes comparisons easier. However, ease of comparison is traded for loss of precision; the graph gives less specific numbers (along the vertical axis) than the table. A graph also often requires more space than a table to convey the same information. If Figure 3.9 included all six geographic regions listed in the table in Figure 3.8, it would be very large.

The more detailed the data and their arrangement are, the greater is the amount of historical information that can be displayed and the more intricate the comparisons that can be made. Figure 3.10 (p. 42) presents a table that lists the percentage of the total vote and the number of deputies elected to the German parliament (the Reichstag) by each of the major political parties in each election from 1919 to 1933. (Notice that in a parliamentary system, elections do not come at regular intervals.)

This table allows you to follow the changing fortunes of each political party. A wealth of information on German political history is contained in these figures. Between the lines one can also find pieces of the social and economic history of Germany. For example, the strength of the Communist

Major area	1750	1800	1850	1900	1950	1999
Africa	13.4	10.9	8.8	8.1	8.8	12.8
Asia	63.5	64.9	64.1	57.4	55.6	60.8
Europe	20.6	20.8	21.9	24.7	21.7	12.2
Latin America and the Caribbean	2.0	2.5	3.0	4.5	6.6	8.5
Northern America	0.3	0.7	2.1	5.0	6.8	5.1
Oceania	0.3	0.2	0.2	0.4	0.5	0.5

FIGURE 3.8   Estimated World Population, 1750–1999

Numbers represent percentages of the total world population.

SOURCE: *Population Division, Department of Economic and Social Affairs, United Nations Secretariat.*

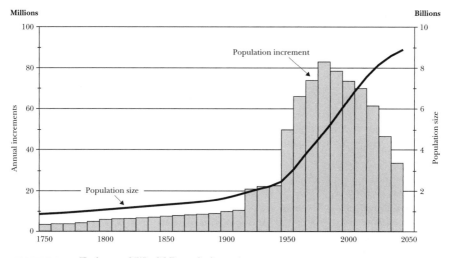

FIGURE 3.9   Estimated World Population, 1750–2050
SOURCE: *Population Division, Department of Economic and Social Affairs, United Nations Secretariat.*

and Social Democratic (Socialist) parties attests to the deep dissatisfaction of many German workers with the state of the economy during the period known as the Weimar Republic. Even more striking is the tremendous growth of the National Socialist (Nazi) Party after 1930. This development brought Adolf Hitler to power in 1933, and the results of that event would eventually reverberate around the world. As you can see, a table is more than just numbers.

Illustrations, Photographs, and Other Visual Material

Visual material also can present historical information. Gathering information from old paintings, drawings, and photographs, however, can be surprisingly difficult. First, you need to recognize the actual information that they present — what Columbus's ships looked like, how Hiroshima appeared after the explosion of the atomic bomb, and so on. Then you need to interpret them. Interpreting requires an effort to understand what the artist or photographer is "saying" in the work. When an artist draws something and when a photographer takes a picture, he or she is not simply recording a visual image but is sending a message to everyone who looks at the work. In this way, artists and photographers are like writers whose written work needs to be interpreted.

Another important aspect of a visual source is its artistic style. This refers not only to how a visual looks but also to where it fits in the history of art or photography. Is it a painting in the style of the Italian Renaissance (fifteenth century) or abstract expressionism (twentieth century)?

Party	1919	1920	1924	1928	1930	1932	1933
Communist							
# of deputies	0	4	45	54	77	89	81
% of total votes		2.1	9.0	10.6	13.1	14.3	12.3
Social Democratic							
# of deputies	165	102	131	153	143	133	120
% of total votes	37.9	21.7	26.0	29.8	24.5	21.6	18.3
Democratic							
# of deputies	75	39	32	25	20	4	5
% of total votes	18.5	8.3	6.3	4.9	3.8	1.0	0.9
Centrum							
# of deputies	91	64	69	62	68	75	74
% of total votes	19.7	13.6	13.6	12.1	11.8	12.5	11.2
Bavarian People's							
# of deputies	0	21	19	16	19	22	18
% of total votes		4.4	3.7	3.1	3.0	3.2	2.7
German People's							
# of deputies	19	65	51	45	30	7	2
% of total votes	4.4	13.9	10.1	8.7	4.5	1.2	1.1
National People's							
# of deputies	44	71	103	73	41	37	52
% of total votes	10.3	15.1	20.5	14.2	7.0	5.9	8.0
National Socialist							
# of deputies	0	0	14	12	107	230	288
% of total votes			3.0	2.6	18.3	37.3	43.9

FIGURE 3.10   Reich Elections, 1919–1933
Under the electoral system provided for in the Weimar Constitution, each party received approximately one representative for every sixty thousand popular votes cast for its candidates. Various small parties, not listed here, were underrepresented in the Reichstag.
SOURCE: *Adapted from E. Kolb,* The Weimar Republic, *2nd ed. (New York: Routledge, 2005), 224–25.*

Figures 3.11 (p. 43) and 3.12 (p. 44) present two illustrations of the Spanish conquest of Mexico. See whether you can detect what they are saying.

Figure 3.11 is by a European artist and shows Hernán Cortés, who conquered Mexico for Spain, being offered young Indian women by a coastal tribe. The Indians seem happy to greet the Spaniards. Figure 3.12 was drawn by an Aztec Indian and shows Cortés's soldiers (having fought their way from the coast to the Aztec capital) massacring Indians in their main temple. Not all drawings have such obvious (and opposite) messages: the Spanish as friends of the Indians and the Spanish as murderers of the Indians. The interpretation of some visual material requires knowledge about the subject matter, the artist, the style, and the context in which the work appeared. Like written descriptions of past events, art does not simply "speak for itself."

Now look at Figure 3.13 (p. 45), a photograph of a clash in 1968 between Chicago police and demonstrators opposing the war in Vietnam. Like the illustrations in Figures 3.11 and 3.12, it too contains information. Even a casual glance shows confusion and violence. Examining it closely, you can see the kinds of weapons used by the police and the facial expressions of some of the demonstrators. The more difficult part, again, is interpreting the photograph. Is this a scene of provocation by lawless demonstrators or an attack by the police? A careful look at the picture may help you answer this question. In any case, you need more evidence. Although an unaltered photograph does show something that actually happened, another photograph — even one of the same event — might show something very different. In most cases, the person taking the photograph has made an effort to say something, and you need to take this motive into account, as well.

Not all pictures have controversial interpretations. Figure 3.14 (p. 46) is a photograph of a city street in Ithaca, New York, in the 1890s. There is a wealth of information here about nineteenth-century town life. Notice that at this early date the town already had electric trolleys. Notice also that the horses are pulling not wagons or carriages ("buggies," as they were called) but sleighs ("cutters"). This simple fact opens up a window to farm life in winter. When roads were covered with snow and ice, the flat, smooth wheels of wagons could not navigate, but the sharp runners of the cutter dug into the ice and gave the sleigh stability.

FIGURE 3.11   **Indian Offerings to Cortés**
SOURCE: *Courtesy of the Bancroft Library, University of California, Berkeley.*

FIGURE 3.12   Massacre of the Aztec Indians

SOURCE: *From* The Broken Spears, *by Miguel Leon-Portilla. Copyright © 1962, 1990 by Miguel Leon-Portilla. Expanded and Updated Edition © 2007 by Miguel Leon-Portilla. Reprinted by permission of Beacon Press, Boston.*

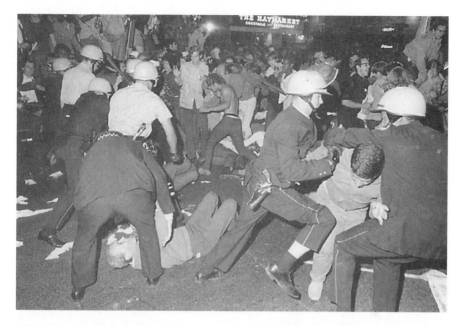

FIGURE 3.13   Antiwar Demonstration at the 1968 Democratic National Convention in Chicago
SOURCE: *Copyright © Bettmann/Corbis.*

Sound and Video Recordings

Electronically or digitally recorded sounds and pictures now make up a large category of nonwritten primary sources. These nonwritten records of past events allow history to come alive before the researcher's eyes. They provide an immediacy and sense of the past that is palpable in ways that written sources can rarely convey. Audiovisual sources, however, require special attention when being interpreted for historical research. Sound and video recordings typically do not have authors in the usual sense of the word, and their purpose can range from artistic to journalistic to persuasive.

Like photographs, sound and video recordings need to be interpreted, particularly in terms of what they choose to place before your eyes or ears and how they do so. Although they might not have traditional authors, sound and video recordings have been created and perhaps edited by one or more individuals, usually to suit a particular political, commercial, personal, or artistic purpose. Being aware of the message behind the image or sound is critical to assessing that source's credibility. For example, sound clips might intentionally be taken out of context or edited together in such a way as to misconstrue a person's meaning. Make sure you are aware of the entire speech or interview before judging one or two sentences.

FIGURE 3.14   Town Life in Ithaca, New York, during the 1890s
SOURCE: *Courtesy of The History Center in Tompkins County, Ithaca, New York, General Photo Collection.*

As with other types of sources, it's also important to know the historical setting of audiovisual materials so that you don't take an **ahistorical view** of them. If, for example, you were watching footage of athletic events from the 1964 Olympiad in Tokyo, it would be helpful to know that these were the first Olympic Games to be held in an Asian nation. Knowing that historical context would allow you to analyze the reaction of some of the crowd, the symbols you can see in the background, or the commentary provided by the television crew in ways that go far beyond the competition on screen.

Historians need to be very careful to distinguish between aesthetic analysis and historical analysis when examining sound or video recordings. Take, for example, the short educational film entitled "Duck and Cover," which was created in 1951 by the Federal Civil Defense Administration (see Figure 3.15, p. 47). The film blends animation and live action in order to train young American students how to seek refuge in case of a nuclear attack. The main character, Bert the Turtle, demonstrates this technique by slipping into his shell when confronted with a lit firecracker. When a nuclear explosion occurs, the film's narrator explains, children should immediately "duck and cover" under their school desks or in the nearest ditch. If we view this source from an aesthetic standpoint, it now comes across as quaint and silly at best, and at worst as a morbid set of instructions that would provide little protection in case of a nuclear attack. But if we leave artistic merit aside and consider the historical context of the Cold War, "Duck and Cover" reveals much about the mentality of the American public in 1951. To a populace unfamiliar with the threat of direct attack or the devastation of an atomic bomb, the film would have seemed necessary and, in many cases, reassuring. Historians thus must take a serious approach to a source within its appropriate context, even when the content now appears silly or antiquated.

For a researcher, it is also important to note that establishing the authorship of modern video (and audio) productions is very problematic. Music videos, TV episodes, product and political commercials, among others, are produced by large production crews and often are assembled (mixed, dubbed, reworked, etc.) from various pieces of different kinds of media. Moreover, digitized versions of sound and video sources are easily shared, altered, or deleted. As a

FIGURE 3.15   Short Film from 1951
A screenshot from the Federal Civil Defense Administration's 1951 film "Duck and Cover." As silly as it looks to our eyes, what might this video tell us about everyday life in the 1950s?

result, it is almost impossible to distinguish "copy" from "original." Only a very clear trail of evidence can indicate if the "original" was altered. To understand complex, modern media, you need to know their "media context" — a vital aspect of their historical context. When analyzing digital media, be sure to keep the following questions in mind:

- What is the *form* of the source: videotape, audiotape, CD, digital TV, digital video, Web page, digitized print document, something else?
- What was the *technical process* by which the source was originally produced? (You need to know this in order to understand the way in which the source was created and thereby the ways in which it might be altered.)
- What is the *form, genre,* or *style* of the artistic aspects of the source? (This information places the source in the history of its form of art.)
- What is the social and cultural context?

Artifacts

An artifact is a physical object from the past: a radio from the 1920s; a rifle from the U.S. Civil War; the ruins of a fourteenth-century church in Paris; a 10,000-year-old arrowhead. Whether you examine an artifact in a museum, in an attic, or in a field, keep in mind that sometimes even the simplest artifact can be interpreted to reveal surprising and sophisticated historical information.

Suppose you are hiking in the American Southwest and you notice a couple of stones that look out of the ordinary. The smaller of the two has a rectangular shape that doesn't seem natural, and the larger one is flat and has an indentation that has clearly been carved into it by human hands. As you look around the surrounding brush, you find shards of pottery and other evidence that suggests this arid area was once inhabited by people. As you place the two stones together, you see that they fit perfectly, and when you grind them, some powdery material shakes loose from them. You've found a *mano* and a *metate* — two common tools used by American Indians to grind corn (see Figure 3.16, p. 49). Once the corn is ground into a fine meal, it can be stored or made into food.

In order to place your artifacts into a wider context, consider the landscape around them. This area is arid today, but you see a few shallow ditches that seem to be arranged in a particular pattern. The crumbled stones in front of a dried-up water basin might have been a dam that once fed those ditches. Could this have been an irrigation system? The pottery shards are also important to consider. The thickness and coarse nature of their construction suggest that they were once heavy-duty containers, distinct from the more fragile decorative or ceremonial vessels that you've seen in museums. A more detailed scientific analysis of your artifacts might uncover the remnants of ground corn that was indigenous to the area and that date back over one thousand years. Once you've put the mano and metate into their historical context, you can surmise that this area had a more cultivated landscape than it does now, and that your found artifacts might have been part of a now-defunct agricultural system.

Although field discoveries such as this will be rare in your undergraduate work, consider the benefits of exploring historical artifacts in their original setting. If you had found an image of these artifacts on the Web or in a book on Native American culture, you wouldn't have had the experience of running your fingers over the mano and metate, and you wouldn't have gained the sense of how slow and difficult this work would have been and how coarse the resulting corn meal might have felt. You also would have missed exploring the objects' immediate environment, and some of their meaning would have been lost. Fieldwork can add new dimensions to any research project.

However an artifact is initially examined, it is usually helpful to conduct additional research and consider the artifact's wider implications. The immediate suggestion might be that corn was an important part of Native American diets in the Southwest. But more research might reveal that the mano and metate were important tools in women's labor, that grinding increases

FIGURE 3.16   Mano and Metate
Pictured here are a mano (the smaller grinding stone) and metate (the flat grinding surface) from the southwestern United States. In a museum, these artifacts might be displayed along with a bowl of dried corn and some ground cornmeal. Would you know what the tools were for without such context? How might a museum-style presentation alter your perception of the artifacts?

SOURCE: *Photograph courtesy of the Arizona State Museum, the University of Arizona, photographer, Jackie Kinman.*

the nutritional yield of corn meal, and that cooking processed corn meal requires less time and therefore less fuel than cooking whole kernels. This information tells us a great deal about the everyday life of the ancient residents of this land, but we can take that information a step further and glean even wider insights from the found artifacts. Many of the factors influenced by the mano and metate — a gendered division of labor, increased nutritional yields, less demand for wood fuel — allowed the population of American Indian societies like the Anasazi to expand across the arid environments of the American Southwest, which in turn resulted in the construction of sophisticated cities like Mesa Verde, in modern-day Colorado. As it turns out, the mano and metate that you found are an important link between everyday life and the grand scope of human development. Not all artifacts have such wide-reaching implications, but you never know until you explore them fully. After all, you thought you had just found some unusually shaped rocks!

CHAPTER

4

Building a History Essay

WHY CLEAR WRITING IS IMPORTANT

Writing is a task of great significance. It is far more important than simply completing a college assignment. Your writing skills tell the reader a lot about your ability to read critically and think clearly. A few years after graduating, you may no longer remember the meaning of Confucianism or when the Egyptian pharaohs of the eighteenth dynasty reigned, but if you sharpened your writing skills in history assignments, you acquired an asset that will last a lifetime.

Clear writing accomplishes two important goals. First, it demonstrates that your thinking about a subject is logical. You cannot write clearly about something that you do not understand clearly. Second, it enables you to convey to your readers in a convincing way exactly what you want them to understand. Clear writing is persuasive.

PREPARING TO WRITE

When you are given a writing assignment in a history course, you are being asked to gain command over a series of documents — **primary** or **secondary**, print or visual. You are also being asked to turn your understanding of that material into an essay — one that responds directly to a question or **topic** and demonstrates your understanding of the topic or documents.

When confronted with a writing assignment, keep the following questions in mind:

51

- What is the nature of the assignment?
- What kind of writing is required?
- What kind of sources are required (and allowed)?
- What is the best way of organizing these sources?

What are you being asked to do? The question that is asked (or the topic that is assigned) helps determine the kind of writing best suited to the answer. The question "Who invented the light bulb?" can be answered more directly and concretely than can the question "Why was electricity spoken of in spiritual as well as technical terms in the late nineteenth century?" The second question requires more background knowledge and more interpretation of **evidence**. An essay in response to the second question will need to be more complex and more carefully organized than a response to the first one. It will need to approach the answer in stages, and the conclusions will need to be more speculative.

The nature of the question will also help determine the kind of evidence needed to answer it. What sources are you expected to use? Are they identified for you, or do you need to find them? Even before you begin to think about writing, be sure that you have a clear idea of the kind of evidence you will need and that such evidence is available to you.

Once you understand the question and the kind of answer and sources expected of you, consider the kind of information you will need to take from those sources. As you gather that information, think about which part of it answers which part of the question. Begin to consider the organization of your essay.

Examining Sources

In many cases, the topic of your writing assignment will be given to you, and you may even be directed to a set of particular sources for examining. For example, your assignment might be "Based on the travel reports of Marco Polo and Ibn Battuta and on the article 'Crossing Asia: Messengers and Messages,' support or challenge the view that Christians and Muslims had distinct views of Asia in the thirteenth and fourteenth centuries." In other cases, assignments may be very broad, and you will be responsible for narrowing a topic down to one manageable aspect. (Refer to p. 90 in Chapter 6 for advice on narrowing a topic.)

In either event, once you have a specific topic to write about, you will need to do some exploring. Read about your topic, using the sources assigned or, if necessary, the sources you find on your own. (See Chapter 6, pp. 94–109, for advice on tracking down sources.) As you examine your sources, consider important points such as when the source was created, who its author or creator was, and why it was written or made. As discussed throughout Chapter 3, critical thinking about the meaning of a source will lead you to your own conclusions about historical questions.

Drafting a Thesis Statement

After reading through and examining your sources, you will be ready to draft a **working thesis**. A working thesis is tentative; it helps you to organize your ideas and plan your paper. Once finalized, your **thesis** will be the *central point* of your essay; your goal as a writer is to convince your readers that your thesis is correct. Like a lawyer before a jury, you present the evidence that your research has uncovered, and you argue that this evidence demonstrates the correctness of your thesis.

NOTE: Most, but not all, assignments will require a thesis statement. Some assignments, such as summaries, should remain neutral. See Chapter 5 for details on various types of writing assignments.

A thesis statement is not a restatement of your topic or a summary of your research; it is a specific claim that you will pursue in the essay and that the evidence that you present will support. Don't be concerned about the exact wording of your thesis statement while you are just beginning your research. You may need to refine the statement as you learn more about your subject and even as you draft your paper. (For more details on drafting and revising a thesis, see Chapter 7, pp. 128–31.)

Consider the following writing assignment: "Write an essay explaining why navigators in the time of Columbus were afraid to voyage beyond the sight of land." A paper based on such an assignment could be organized around one of several thesis statements. One essay might argue that navigators were afraid of being eaten by sea monsters. (Belief in sea monsters did exist in that era.) Another essay might argue that navigators in the fifteenth century were afraid of sailing off the edge of the (flat) earth. An examination of the relevant evidence would lead you in the direction of a particular thesis. For example, if you were impressed by the evidence about navigational instruments, your essay might begin like this:

> In the fifteenth century, very few navigators believed that the earth was flat, although some did fear sea monsters. The greatest concern was that the Atlantic Ocean was huge and the lack of accuracy of navigational instruments could leave a ship hopelessly lost until it was hit by a fatal storm or ran out of supplies. It was, therefore, not irrational fear but rather lack of technical knowledge that kept ships' courses in sight of land. This essay will examine the problems of ship-building and navigation that stood in the way of transoceanic voyages in the fifteenth century, arguing that the inadequacy of ship design and lack of precise navigational instruments lay behind the more realistic fears of fifteenth-century navigators.

Here, for comparison, is an example of an opening paragraph that would *not* serve as a thesis statement:

> Some sailors in the fifteenth century were frightened of sea monsters, but nobody thought the earth was flat. They were afraid of going out in the ocean because nobody had ever done it before. They could become lost if their navigation equipment failed. This essay says that sailors were afraid to voyage out of sight of land because they were afraid of becoming lost. It also says they were afraid of storms. The basic problem was that they didn't have the equipment they needed to sail across the ocean safely.

This paragraph is far too general (and vague) to serve as a thesis statement. It mentions several concerns of fifteenth-century navigators without separating them clearly one from the other. It does not explain to the reader which concern will serve as the thesis. In fact, it does not state *any* formal thesis.

Creating a Writing Outline

Once you have arrived at a thesis for your paper, you need to think about the structure of your essay. Just as a thesis statement helps you to stay focused on the main purpose of your paper, a writing outline will help you organize your thoughts and present your evidence. As you work on the outline, keep in mind the length of your essay. Also think about the kinds of evidence you expect to use and the places in your essay where you will need specific kinds of evidence. Because you still have research to do, don't be concerned if your outline needs to be revised as you go along. It is normal to adjust an outline as you gather information and refine your thesis.

A sample outline, based on the writing assignment given on page 52, is shown below. Notice that the student includes a rough sketch of the thesis statement, the four main areas to cover (one with subheadings), and the conclusion. (For more on outlining, see Chapter 7, pp. 131–35.)

EXAMPLE OF AN OUTLINE FOR A HISTORY ESSAY

Thesis: Christians and Muslims had distinct views of Asia in the 13th and 14th centuries.

Points to Cover: 1. Variety of travelers

                  1a. European, African, eastern Mediterranean (evidence from "Crossing Asia")

                  1b. Religious; merchant; soldier (evidence from "Crossing Asia")

2. Views of Marco Polo (evidence from primary source)

3. Views of Ibn Battuta (evidence from primary source)

4. Comparison of views

Conclusion: Summary of evidence in support of thesis

NOTE: If, in your research, you come across information that could support a thesis very different from your own, you should address such evidence, which is known as **counterevidence**, in your outline and, eventually, in your paper. Your knowledge of opposing viewpoints, and your ability to disagree with them, indicates that your research has been thorough. No history paper can ever expect to "prove" its thesis correct. What historians claim when they defend a thesis is that the evidence presented strongly supports the thesis. It is up to other scholars, in their own research, to support, challenge, or go beyond a particular thesis.

DRAFTING YOUR ESSAY

Having examined sources, drafted a thesis, and sketched a writing outline, you have created the basic framework for your essay. Your next step is to flesh out the text into a **rough draft**. In this early stage of writing, don't worry too much about grammar or style. Get your most important ideas and the evidence that supports them down on the page. Find a place for any valuable new ideas and evidence that were not part of your original outline. If necessary, consider shortening or dropping any section that now seems less important.

Regardless of the kind of essay you are writing, the essay should open with an **introduction** that includes a clear statement of your thesis. Then, in an organized manner, the body of your essay should present the evidence supporting your thesis. Most essays should end with a **conclusion** that restates the thesis and summarizes how it is supported by the evidence.

NOTE: Writing is a nonlinear process. You do not have to create the introduction first. Many writers draft the body of the paper first and then write the introduction and conclusion. In addition, you probably will need to revise parts of the essay as you go. Refer to "Revising Your Essay," on pages 60–61 of this chapter, for details.

A Clear Introduction

Your first paragraph describes your topic for the reader. It also contains your thesis statement and a brief preview of the kinds of evidence you will be using. Some other ways of looking at the topic may be mentioned as well. In a long essay, you may need two paragraphs or more to accomplish these goals.

Here is the first paragraph of an essay on the topic "the origins of slavery in seventeenth-century Virginia":

> The English settlers in the part of North America that became the United States did not arrive with the intention of creating a system of slavery. Yet, within several decades, each of the British colonies had imported African slaves. Historians have debated the reasons for this development for many years. Some emphasize the racist views of the English toward the Africans, which were quite strong well before British settlement of North America. They point out that Europeans ("whites") were never enslaved in the colonies nor were Native Americans, with a few exceptions. Other historians emphasize the growing need for labor in the colonies. With the development of tobacco agriculture in Virginia, landowners could not find enough European fieldworkers. The thesis of this paper, which is based on the diaries of seventeenth-century Virginia plantation owners, is that these landowners made a decision to solve their manpower problem by using the labor of African slaves, which they could purchase from Caribbean colonies already organized around slave labor. This paper will also argue that, without the belief that slaves were an absolute necessity for the success of the new plantations, the slave labor system might never have been established in what became the United States.

The above introductory paragraph is excellent preparation for the reader. It provides background information and briefly describes the historical debate between the "racial" and the "labor" arguments about slavery in North America. It ends with a statement of the thesis and mentions some of the documents on which it will rest.

A Cohesive Body

The main part, or body, of your essay presents the results of your research, organized in such a way as to help convince the reader of the significance and validity of the thesis. The body should consist of clear, concise sentences grouped into coherent paragraphs.

Sentences: The Building Blocks of Writing

The most effective sentences are clear and concise, and they usually employ the **active voice**. In addition, writers in history need to pay special attention to verb tense.

Clarity.   Clear writing begins with clear sentences. A clear sentence leaves no doubt about the subject of the sentence. It also leaves no doubt about what the subject is doing.

UNCLEAR

On September 1, 1939, Germany was strong and Poland was weak, and so it attacked.

The subject of the above sentence is unclear. The reader cannot tell if the subject is Germany or Poland and therefore cannot tell who attacked whom.

CLEAR

On September 1, 1939, Germany attacked Poland.

In the revised sentence, the subject (*Germany*) is placed as close as possible to the verb naming the action (*attacked*), and the meaning becomes much more clear.

Conciseness.   A phrase can add information, but the wordiness that results from the indiscriminate use of phrases can obscure a sentence's meaning.

WORDY

Although his plane was loaded down with extra fuel, Lindbergh was still able to get off the muddy runway in New Jersey despite very bad weather that rainy morning in 1927 and the fact that several other people had been killed trying to become the first person to stay awake for the thirty-three hours it took to fly solo across the Atlantic Ocean.

In the above sentence, Lindbergh's flight is surrounded by so many phrases that the main point of the sentence is lost. Never attempt to pack into one sentence every fact you have learned. If some facts are not necessary, leave them out. If they are necessary, make room for them by creating additional sentences. For example, if the weight of the fuel and the muddy runway are important but the weather conditions and the failed attempts by others are not, writing two sentences instead of one would make the additional points and make them clearly:

CONCISE

Lindbergh's plane was so heavily loaded with fuel that it almost failed to get off the muddy runway in New Jersey. Once in the air, however, Lindbergh was able to stay awake for the thirty-three hours it took to fly across the Atlantic.

Active Voice versus Passive Voice.   The subject and verb are the core of any sentence. Active voice verbs describe what the subject of the sentence is doing; **passive voice** verbs describe what is being done to the subject.

PASSIVE VOICE

A vaccination against smallpox <u>was introduced</u> in 1796.

In the above example, the verb (*was introduced*) is passive. The subject (*vaccination*) is not the actor; it doesn't do anything. As a result, the sentence is vague, and we are missing a key piece of information: Who introduced the vaccination?

ACTIVE VOICE

In 1796, Edward Jenner introduced a vaccination against smallpox.

In the above example, the subject — *Jenner* — is the actor. The active voice verb *introduced* clarifies the subject and its action.

The passive voice may be needed when you want to emphasize what is being done to the subject.

PROPER USE OF THE PASSIVE VOICE

Three U.S. presidents were assassinated in the nineteenth century.

Past Tense versus Present Tense. When you are writing about historical events, use the past tense.

PAST TENSE

Thomas Jefferson wrote a draft of the Declaration of Independence.

Jefferson's action took place in the past, so it is best to use the past tense when writing about it.

When you are referring to the contents of a specific written document or to an object (such as an old building or a work of art) that still exists, use the present tense.

PRESENT TENSE

The Constitution guarantees equal protection under the law.

Cohesive, Connected Paragraphs

A paragraph consists of sentences that all relate to the topic of the paragraph. In a well-constructed paragraph, the paragraph's topic is clearly expressed in a *topic sentence*, and every other sentence in the paragraph sheds light on that topic. For example, if you are writing a paragraph about Islamic architecture, every sentence in your paragraph should say something about that subject. If you have something to say about Chinese architecture, those comments probably belong in a separate paragraph.

Each paragraph in an essay should provide new information or explanation and take your essay one step closer to substantiation of your thesis. Each paragraph should flow logically from the one that precedes it and lead smoothly into the one that follows it. As you begin each paragraph, consider how it supplements the previous one and whether it supports your thesis. A new paragraph that does not accomplish these goals needs to be rewritten or perhaps placed elsewhere in your essay.

Sometimes you will need to help your reader see the **continuity** or connection between paragraphs. A **linking sentence** at the end of one paragraph or at the beginning of the next one will inform the reader that your essay is moving from one important point to a new but related one.

LINKING SENTENCE

Therefore, changes in printing technology made newspapers cheaper and more available. <u>But new technology alone does not explain rising readership.</u> As immigrants poured into the country from Europe, it was the new look of the newspaper, especially the use of large illustrations and photographs, that attracted these new "readers."

The linking sentence indicates that a paragraph dealing with technological change is going to be followed by a discussion of a new topic: how changes in the look of newspapers attracted new readers.

In a long essay in which extended arguments are developed in support of the thesis, a **linking paragraph** might be needed to tell readers where your essay is heading, and why. Keep your readers in mind: if you think they might not be able to follow your line of thought, tighten the connections between paragraphs.

A Meaningful Conclusion

How do you know when to end your essay? You must not go over the page limit, of course. It is best to stop when you have made all of the points needed to support your thesis. You don't need to keep writing until you have included every point in your outline or noted every document you have read. Review the most important parts of your outline. Check your essay to see if each has been included.

How long should your conclusion be? The length of the paper determines the length of the conclusion: for a shorter paper (3–6 pages), write a conclusion of one or two paragraphs; write three or four paragraphs for a longer paper (7 or more pages).

What should you say in the conclusion? Reread your introductory paragraph. What did you tell the reader you intended to do? Summarize briefly the major points that took the reader from the statement of your thesis to this conclusion. A conclusion is also the place to remind the reader of the significance of the topic and of the way your thesis has examined it.

Here is the concluding paragraph of the essay on slavery in Virginia introduced on page 56:

While race was a factor in the origins of slavery in Virginia, the enslavement of African Americans did not occur at the founding of the colony or even with the arrival of the first Africans. The experience of African landowners such as Anthony

Johnson demonstrated that no group (white, black, or Native American) was enslaved while the tobacco economy was in its earliest stage. Not until a half century or so later were laws established that defined slavery as the status of African Americans. By that time, however, a mature tobacco economy was under the control of wealthy, white landowners. The white workers were unwilling to accept the harsh conditions of labor, so the landowners turned to blacks. The rights of blacks could (and would) be denied, and thousands of them were already enslaved in English colonies in the Caribbean. While race was clearly a factor in *who* was enslaved, the need for en-slaved labor of *any* kind was a result of the perceived economic requirements of the growing tobacco plantations. If Virginia had had a different economic base, the history of slavery in this colony, and perhaps of the entire country, might have been very different.

REVISING YOUR ESSAY

If, after writing your rough draft, you make significant additions to your research or changes to your writing outline, you must account for these in your revision. Otherwise, your task is to read your rough draft carefully to be sure that it has a proper thesis statement, a clear direction, adequate documentation, well-crafted paragraphs, and a meaningful conclusion. If you are asked to review a peer's paper, you should keep these same considerations in mind. For a list of questions to ask when revising a draft, see the guidelines below. For a list of revision guidelines for long research papers, see page 143 in Chapter 7.

PROOFREADING YOUR ESSAY

The last step in preparing a writing assignment is **proofreading**. Carefully read your entire paper, looking for misspellings, missing or incorrect punctuation, and layout issues (that is, how the text looks on the page). Read slowly to catch as many typos as you can. It may be helpful to read the paper out loud. A spell-checker is a terrific help in avoiding incorrect spellings, and you should always make use of one before turning in a paper. However, don't expect the spell-checker to catch every misspelled or misused word. It will not catch misspelled words that it reads as other words. For example, if you write "him" instead of "his," or "no" for "know," the spell-checker will not read it as a mistake. You must catch these kinds of errors yourself when you proofread

---

Guidelines for Revising Your Essay

ORGANIZATION

- Does the introductory paragraph give context for the topic? Does it contain a clear thesis statement?
- Is the thesis adequately supported in the body of the essay? Is any new evidence needed?
- Is any counterevidence introduced and addressed?
- Is the supporting evidence arranged in a logical order?
- Is each paragraph focused around a single main point? Does any existing material need to be removed?
- Is the direction of the essay made clear by tight, linked paragraphs? Are linking sentences used when needed for transitions?
- Does the conclusion effectively summarize the thesis and its supporting evidence?
- Are all major points documented with the proper format? (See Chapter 8.)

CLARITY

- Does each sentence clearly name its subject and state what the subject is doing (or saying, feeling, etc.)?
- Are any sentences too wordy?
- Are active verbs used whenever possible?
- Is the past tense used to describe past historical events? Is the present tense used only to describe documents or objects that still exist?

---

your paper. Also, the spell-checker flags any word that it does not recognize, including correctly spelled words not in its electronic dictionary.

Grammar-checkers are even less reliable. When you use a grammar-checker, consider its advice as a suggestion for revision. If the grammar-checker questions the way you have said something, think twice before deciding to make any changes to your original sentence, phrase, or word. Keep in mind that you, not your computer, are the author of your paper.

THE DANGER OF PLAGIARISM

When you prepare a written assignment from notes that you have taken from books or other course materials, be careful how you use those notes. Otherwise, you run the risk of including in your paper sentences or extended phrases that you copied word for word from your sources. Even if you do this copying accidentally, you are guilty of **plagiarism**. Unless the phrases or sentences written by other authors are placed in quotation marks and their sources are identified in **citations**, you have committed a very serious breach of academic honesty. Plagiarism can lead to failing a course and even to expulsion from school. Be sure to read the section on avoiding plagiarism in Chapter 6 (pp. 126–27).

CHAPTER
5

Preparing Specific
Writing Assignments

Instructors give many kinds of writing assignments — **book reviews**, papers that analyze historical sources, **research papers**. These papers range in length from a few pages to ten or twenty. This chapter helps you understand some of the relatively short writing assignments that you are likely to encounter in history courses. For detailed advice on writing full-length research papers, see Chapters 6 and 7.

WRITING ABOUT PRIMARY SOURCES

As noted in Chapter 3 (see pp. 25–28), **primary sources** are the raw materials of history. **Secondary sources** — written by professional historians — are *about* history; primary sources are *from* history. When you examine primary sources — for example, 10,000-year-old cave paintings or 1950s radio commercials — you are handling raw materials. You may not understand much about a thirteenth-century papal decree until you become familiar with the history of thirteenth-century Europe, until you know some of the **historical context** in which the decree was written. But even if much of the significance of a primary source is beyond your current grasp, examining it and thinking about it will lead you to a degree of familiarity with the past that can be arrived at in no other way.

Instructors often build assignments around the interpretation of primary sources. They do so to increase your interpretive abilities. You may be asked to draw connections between primary sources and some part of the historical context that you have learned about. Or you may be asked to respond to the source without much in the way of historical context. Even unsuccessful efforts to unravel the mystery of, say, a nineteenth-century love letter may draw you into the past in a way that a long essay on the origins of Hindu nationalism may not. Of course, Hindu nationalism has its own primary sources.

Two typical assignments involving the study of primary sources are single-source analysis and comparative analysis. We will examine each of them.

Single-Source Analysis

When you are given a writing assignment that requires you to analyze a single primary source, read the question carefully to make sure you understand what you are expected to do. Your instructor will usually include key verbs in the assignment, such as *describe* or *explain*, that will give you a clue as to what is expected. The assignment may also include an indication of the focus your analysis should take. You may be asked to look at the economic aspects of a speech, for example, or at the political implications of a treaty. Whatever the assignment, you may find it helpful to review the sections on reading primary texts (pp. 31–32, 33) and "reading" nonwritten sources (pp. 36–50) in Chapter 3 before you begin to write.

Below is an example of a single-source analysis assignment, followed by a sample student essay written in response to the assignment.

SAMPLE ASSIGNMENT: SINGLE-SOURCE ANALYSIS

As the nation awaited the Spanish Armada, Queen Elizabeth I visited the English army encamped at Tilbury on August 9, 1588. An eyewitness to the event, Dr. Leonel Sharp, transcribed her brief words to the troops years later in a 1623 letter. Although some historians doubt its complete authenticity, this speech is considered one of the great examples of English oratory. In a brief, two-page essay, consider the queen's speech (reprinted below), and describe how it reflects gender expectations in the Tudor-Stuart era.

Queen Elizabeth I's Spanish Armada Speech (1588)

My loving people, we have been persuaded by some, that are careful of our safety, to take heed how we commit ourselves to armed multitudes, for fear of treachery; but I assure you, I do not desire to live to distrust my faithful and loving people. Let tyrants fear; I have always so behaved myself that, under God, I have placed my chiefest strength and safeguard in the loyal hearts and good will of my subjects. And therefore I am come amongst you at this time, not as for my recreation or sport, but being resolved, in the midst and heat of the battle, to live or die amongst you all; to lay down, for my God, and for my kingdom, and for my people, my honor and my blood, even the dust. I know I have but the body of a weak and feeble woman; but I have the heart of a king, and of a king of England, too; and think foul scorn that Parma or Spain, or any prince of Europe, should dare to invade the borders of my realms: to which, rather than any dishonor should grow by me, I myself will take up arms; I myself will be your general, judge, and rewarder of every one of your virtues in the field. I know already, by your forwardness, that you have deserved rewards and crowns; and we do assure you, on the word of a prince, they shall be duly paid you. In the mean my lieutenant general shall be in my stead, than whom never prince commanded a more noble and worthy subject; not doubting by your obedience to my general, by your concord in the camp, and by your valor in the field, we shall shortly have a famous victory over the enemies of my God, of my kingdom, and of my people.

SAMPLE STUDENT ESSAY: SINGLE-SOURCE ANALYSIS

Eric Chin

History 100

October 15, 2008

A Woman at Tilbury

Queen Elizabeth's speech to the army at Tilbury might say a great deal about the strength of the English nation. It also speaks, however indirectly, to the limited roles designated to women in the Tudor-Stuart era and the limitations that might be applied even to a woman who ascended to the position of ruling monarch of England.

Perhaps the most obvious sign of Elizabeth's role is given when she says, "I know I have but the body of a weak and feeble woman; but I have the heart of a king, and of a king of England, too." Here, she seems to bow to contemporary beliefs that thought of women as the "weaker sex" — incapacitated by their physical makeup for anything but the simple tasks of the domestic sphere of home and family duties. She does not attempt to deny such a view of women, or excuse herself from stereotypes. Instead, she implies that her royalty, her royal blood, balances out her womanly weaknesses. She suggests that her royal heart gives her the soul and the honor of a male king — thus she can repeatedly identify herself as a "king" and a "prince." She is never merely the female equivalent, a "queen." Indeed, if it becomes necessary, she is fully capable of taking up arms herself in defense of her subjects.

What equally gives her strength is the love of her "faithful and loving people." She says that, though her advisers believe her to be in danger by presenting herself in public, perhaps because her advisers see her as a mere woman needing protection from the masses, she puts her faith and trust in her subjects. She asserts that only tyrants need fear their subjects, and, of course, she is not that. She is not, she says, a ruler who would come to speak to them only for sport or recreation; by implication, she is not a silly woman who might fail to understand the gravity of the situation or who might be there only to curry their favor. At the same time, she is not an unnatural woman, who does not care about the fate of her people or their love for her — it is their love which makes her strong, which moves her beyond the limitations of her body to be able to meet the responsibilities of a ruler. And, to prove it, she can and will take up arms if necessary to return that love; to do otherwise would only lead her to dishonor.

At the end of her speech, Elizabeth acknowledges that it is her lieutenant general — not herself — who will be leading the men into battle. But again, her words are chosen carefully. In commending her general, she equates herself with princes (men), and she calls England her "kingdom." So, in some ways, this primary source shows how even monarchs were subject to the limitations of gender roles in Tudor-Stuart England.

The student writer does a nice job of responding to the assignment, focusing on the question of gender and not simply repeating the general topics of the speech. He selects the most obvious quotes about women from the source and analyzes them, and he uses other parts of the speech to reinforce the claims he made about gender roles. The analysis is presented in a clear and logical fashion, without straying off **topic**, and it shows that the student read the source with the assignment in mind.

Comparative Analysis

Much like a single-source analysis, a comparative analysis requires close examination of primary sources (see Chapter 3, pp. 31–32, 33, 36–50). But when you are asked to compare two or more documents, you need to demonstrate that you can find and clearly explain similarities and differences between them. You must also relate the sources to their historical contexts in a way that distinguishes them from each other (or links them together). As with a single-source analysis, pay careful attention to the language used in the assignment. Look for key verbs such as *compare, contrast,* or *discuss the similarities.* Also, make sure you understand the focus of the assignment, the expected length, and the use of other sources or course material that you are expected to discuss.

Here is an example of a comparative analysis assignment, involving two contrasting images of the same political figure. Following the assignment is a sample student essay.

SAMPLE ASSIGNMENT: COMPARATIVE ANALYSIS

In a two-page essay, compare the two primary sources shown below. Describe the prominent features of each image of Mao Zedong. Be sure to include any aspects of the long history of China and of popular opinion of Mao in Cold War America that help to explain the less obvious aspects of these nonwritten primary sources.

Image 1: Sun Guocheng, "Reporting to Chairman Mao," 1971
SOURCE: *Collection International Institute of Social History, Amsterdam.*

Image 2: Edmund Valtman, "The New Religion," 1966
SOURCE: Library of Congress Prints and Photographs Division.

SAMPLE STUDENT ESSAY: COMPARATIVE ANALYSIS

Lauren Sagastume

History 100

December 2, 2008

Opposing Visual Images of Mao Zedong

Each of these primary sources is an example of political propaganda. They attempt to convince their audience that Mao Zedong was either a great or a terrible leader of China. We need to examine each one closely to see how it attempts to do so.

The Chinese artist portrays Mao as "father" of the nation. The readings we did on China described social hierarchy and obedience to elders as ancient aspects of Chinese civilization. The traditional Chinese ruler is not only father but also teacher. In the painting, Mao, the wise father, is surrounded by his adoring "family." His role as teacher is conveyed by the rapt attention paid by his "students" as he reads to them. The image of abundance (baskets of food, lush vegetation) in the background serves as a powerful symbol in an ancient peasant society in which food has been a precious commodity. All of these images would make a strong impression on a Chinese audience, especially a rural one.

If this painting was also distributed outside of China, it might be used for external propaganda as well. Perhaps in such a context its purpose might be to spread the image of Mao and Maoism as a way out of poverty and exploitation for Asian peasants in general. As with all propaganda, the viewer needs to be aware of the reality behind the image. This idyllic view of Mao's China was created at a time of great political upheaval, including a purge of the Communist Party leadership by Mao, an effort by military leaders to overthrow Mao, and assaults on "backward" elements by militant Red Guard youth.

The United States political cartoon pictures Mao as a cross between an emperor and Buddha. His brainwashed followers chant Maoist slogans as they carry him on his portable throne. Maoism, the cartoon is saying, is really a form of Eastern religious fanaticism. To make the image more threatening, the hammer and sickle — the symbol of the Soviet Union — is on the chain around Mao's neck and on top of the flags carried by the masses. The American audience is reminded that the power and ideology of the Soviet Union serve as vital support for Chinese communism. Such a strong anti-Communist statement is understandable in the historical context of mid-1960s America, which was engaged in intensifying conflict with Communist forces in Vietnam. The intended audience of this cartoon is clear: U.S. newspaper readers familiar with both Chinese government attacks on the United States as an "imperialist" power and U.S. government attacks on Chinese attempts to "enslave" the people of Asia. For this cartoon, the people of Asia are not an intended audience. Connecting Maoism to Buddhism and/or to the Soviet Union would not have been an effective way of improving the image of the United States.

This U.S. propaganda statement, like the Chinese painting, does not represent the reality of international politics in Asia. The idea that Moscow was the power behind Chinese communism is challenged by the growing ideological rift between the Soviet Union and China that had begun in the early 1960s. As we learned from our readings about the Vietnam War, Washington attempted to take advantage of that hostility to relieve its very difficult military position in Vietnam.

The student writer does a very good job of addressing the assignment. She clearly explains what each of the artists is saying about Mao, and she provides an analysis of the wider historical contexts within which the artists did their work.

WRITING ABOUT SECONDARY SOURCES

A secondary source is a work of history that is based on primary sources. Having no firsthand knowledge of the subject, the author of a secondary source conducts research using primary sources to gain insights from people with such knowledge. Professor Jones writes an article on Irish immigration to Canada in the years of the Great Potato Famine. He bases his **argument**, that many passengers died because of unsanitary conditions aboard the boats, on primary sources — official immigration records, the papers of the companies whose ships carried the immigrants, and the records of the Famine Museum in Ireland. His article is a secondary source. When published in a **scholarly journal**, Professor Jones's research becomes available for study by professional historians and student researchers. Student researchers might read his article to gain background knowledge on the subject. They might compare Jones's **thesis** to that of Professor Smith, who argues that the state of semi-starvation of the passengers when they boarded the ships better explains the level of mortality aboard what were known as "coffin ships." Student researchers might test both theses by examining similar primary documents themselves. (For a more thorough explanation of secondary sources, see pp. 28–36 in Chapter 3.)

Instructors often build assignments around secondary sources. Paying close attention to these secondary sources helps you to understand how historians interpret the significance of a body of primary sources and build a thesis around them. Some assignments might require you to write short papers that identify the thesis, **summarize** the **evidence**, and assess the **conclusions** of a secondary source, or to compare one source with another.

Book reviews, article critiques, and comparative reviews and critiques are typical assignments involving the study of secondary sources. We will examine each of them.

Book Reviews

A book review is not usually a summary. Unless your instructor asks you to summarize a book's content, devote most of your review to *analyzing* its content. Identify its thesis; then describe how the thesis is presented and how well it is defended. Were you persuaded by the author's arguments? Compare the book to other course materials if doing so is part of the assignment. Be sure that your review makes it clear that you read and understood the book, and always provide the kind of analysis asked of you.

Here is a student's review of the book *Colonial Habits: Convents and the Spiritual Economy of Cuzco, Peru,* by Kathryn Burns (Duke University Press, 1999).

SAMPLE STUDENT BOOK REVIEW

Chloe Bernard

History 100

October 15, 2008

Book Review of

Kathryn Burns, *Colonial Habits: Convents and the Spiritual Economy of Cuzco, Peru* (Duke University Press, 1999).

When considering the lives of cloistered nuns, you might think that it was the deliberate choice of these women to cut themselves off from the outside world. In her book *Colonial Habits: Convents and the Spiritual Economy of Cuzco, Peru,* Kathryn Burns demonstrates that this was not always the case. She argues in her introduction that "convents were vital" to the establishment of Spanish control over the native Incas that the Spanish conquered (p. 2). The seven chapters that follow trace the ways in which the nuns of Cuzco played a crucial part in the economic and political history of Spanish Peru from its founding in the 1550s through the creation of the Peruvian republic in the 1820s. The author argues that for nearly three centuries these cloistered women

---

dwelled not at the margins but at the center of one of South America's most significant colonial societies. Although there are some additional elements of her book that are not as clear as they could be, Burns's overall thesis, that convents created a "spiritual economy" that was essential to the development of Peru, is well grounded in evidence, is clearly articulated throughout the text, and is a great example of how the hidden history of women in colonization can be revealed through meticulous research and a careful reading of the sources.

Burns begins *Colonial Habits* with a description of the founding of a convent in Cuzco called Santa Clara, less than two decades after the arrival of Europeans in Peru. Although the Spanish dominated the Inca both militarily and politically, the process of conquering them included social and cultural programs as well. One important component of this ongoing conquest, Burns argues, was the creation of monasteries and convents to provide Christian education for the children of mixed (Spanish and Inca) parentage. After the foundation of Santa Clara, the *mestiza* — the daughters of the Spanish conquistadores and Inca women — arrived there to stay "off the marriage market while it was decided exactly what role they would play in the new society" (p. 31). The new convent also helped in the colonization of Peru by holding confiscated Inca lands and leasing them out to Spanish residents. Women entering Santa Clara also gave their family dowries to the convent, which added to its wealth. By the 1600s, then, the nuns of Santa Clara held enough land and cash that they could actually lend money to Spanish colonists. Here is where Burns's idea of a "spiritual economy" really takes center stage, as she describes how the convent bypassed church laws against collecting interest in order to provide *censo al quitar* — essentially a mortgage on land — to borrowers. "The monastery did not enter into loans," she writes, "but rather contracts of purchase and sale in which the nuns purchased the right to collect an annuity" (p. 64).

After explaining how Santa Clara played such a pivotal role in early Peru, Burns explains how nuns in Cuzco could remain individually poor but collectively powerful. In the 1600s, for example, Cuzco added two more convents, Santa Catalina in 1605 and Santa Theresa in 1673, although Burns really focuses on the first of the two. These convents soon integrated themselves into the Peruvian "spiritual economy" with assets of landholdings, dowries, and *censo* arrangements similar to those of Santa Clara. But in addition to their important economic role, Burns also describes daily life in these convents, which was quite interesting. Although some cloistered women technically took vows of poverty, many of them maintained apartments and "constructed their own complex, colonial households with infants and toddlers, adolescents, maids, and slaves — perhaps all at once — inside their capacious cells" (p. 116). Since the nuns were physically separated from the material world, the residents of Cuzco would ask for prayers, loans, and other favors of them through the *locutorio*, or a receiving room with iron bars that separated the cloistered and the outsiders.

Burns sometimes seems unclear as to whether the nuns used their position to reinforce or undermine Spanish patriarchy — she claims that they did both — so it is a bit difficult to understand just where these women stood in society. Perhaps this is because the complex arrangements of *censos* and other colonial financial instruments seem so strange to modern readers. In any case, a more detailed explanation of them might have made Burns's idea of a "spiritual economy" clearer.

As Cuzco's convents entered the 1700s, their spiritual and economic influence began to wane. According to Burns, "'enlightened' Spaniards were developing a forceful critique of the church as excessively worldly and unduly rich," and they began to fear that the Spanish economy as a whole would suffer if the church was allowed to continue acquiring property (p. 159). This shift in Spanish economic thinking, known as the *economía civil*, "threatened monastic livelihoods as far away as Cuzco" (p. 159) and weakened the "spiritual economy" just as the famous Inca rebellion led by Túpac Amaru hit Peru in 1780–1781. Spanish authorities enlisted the convents in putting down the rebels, but this further eroded their economic standing by forcing them to reorganize their finances. Cuzco's once-prosperous nuns, whose lives were supposed to be devoted to prayer, now found themselves "scrambling for an income" (p. 182).

Political events in Europe further undermined the structure of colonial society in South America, as Napoleon's invasion of Spain in 1808 left the Viceroy of Peru short of funds and administrative support from the home country. Nuns had a difficult choice to make. Either they could prop up colonial authorities with their rapidly diminishing resources, or they could try to reconcile themselves with the growing independence movement in Peru. They tried to side with the viceroy, but the Republic of Peru nonetheless arrived on the scene by late 1824. The new republican leaders confiscated the property of convents, secularized education, and took welfare agencies out of the exclusive hands of religious institutions. "Thus by the mid-1820s," Burns concludes, "the state had placed itself right in the middle of convent business, leaving the nuns of Cuzco little room to maneuver out of their difficulties" (p. 197).

Despite the secularization brought on by independence, Cuzco's convents survive to this day. This might be enough to signal the importance of *Colonial Habits,* but there is much more here that makes Kathryn Burns's work significant. Most notably, her depiction of cloistered women at the center of a colonial economy is a far cry from the traditional notion that Spanish patriarchal traditions cast women into the margins of public life. The fact that this economic power emerged from convents is even more surprising. Who would have thought that women living out their lives in prayer and meditation would cast such a strong shadow over colonial Peru? Even though their authority waned as the colonial order fell to more secular, republican ideas, the cloistered women of Cuzco persevered. Although her explanation of the day-to-day operations of the "spiritual economy" of colonial Cuzco is at times difficult to understand, Kathryn Burns's depiction of the influence enjoyed by the convents of Santa Clara and Santa Catalina provides fascinating and important examples of how women can affect history in unexpected ways that might be hidden in traditional narratives. Even though these women individually lived cloistered lives, Kathryn Burns successfully places their collective presence at center stage in colonial Peru.

Reviews can vary widely in content to accommodate the different kinds of work they discuss. Still, a good review, like this one, includes specific elements. The book under review here is identified at the very beginning, with all of the bibliographic data in the initial heading. Then the author's thesis (that the economic and social influences of the Cuzco convents were essential to the development of colonial Peru) is made clear, and the overall scope of the work (the period of Spanish colonial rule in Peru, from the 1530s through the 1820s) is described. The **introduction** also gives the reviewer's general assessment of the book's main argument, which in this case is positive.

Then the review takes a more extensive look at the book's content, being careful to include quotes that describe the author's points along with a summary of the book's narrative scope. A student reviewer should focus on the effectiveness of the thesis and assume that the evidence is accurate, for students are likely not as familiar with the sources or with the wider historical literature as a professional historian would be. However, if the course includes several related works or if students are doing primary research in this field, the review could evaluate the primary sources as well. In this case, the student reviewer is willing to limit her comments to the book's effectiveness as a stand-alone work.

If your instructor asks for a particular kind of review, be sure to follow his or her directions. You might be asked to mention some of the **counterevidence** — evidence that argues against the thesis — and to assess the author's ability to present it fairly and respond to it effectively. Or you might be asked to comment on the author's personal or academic background and reasons for writing the book. This last point should certainly be included if there is significant debate among historians about the thesis of the book or if the book's preface or introduction refers to such disagreements. With a book of this kind, your instructor may ask you to comment on the debate and perhaps also ask you how the book affects your views on the subject.

Guidelines for Writing a Book Review

- At the top of the first page, put the name of the author, the title of the work, the publisher's name, and the date of publication.
- State the author's topic and thesis.
- Describe the evidence presented to support the thesis.
- If possible, assess the arguments and evidence used. (Are they clear or unclear, strong or weak, convincing or unconvincing?)
- If appropriate, describe the author's background and reason for writing the book.
- If required, compare the work to related course materials. (Does it agree or disagree? Does it add a new perspective?)
- If expected, close with your own assessment of the book's assumptions, arguments, and conclusions.

It is usually unwise to emphasize your personal opinion in a review unless your instructor asks you to do so. If you are asked to express it, don't write simply, "I liked the way the author defended women's rights." Instead say, "I was impressed by the author's use of many concrete examples of actions by women to dramatize their demand for the right to vote. The fact that one day they chained themselves to the White House fence made clear how strongly they felt about their cause." Show that your opinion is the result of serious thought about the arguments made in the book.

If your assignment is a review that is longer than a few pages, you might want to quote a sentence or phrase from the book to support a point you are making. But don't use too many quotations. Your review should be written in your own words rather than those of the author.

Article Critiques

An article critique assignment asks you to make a very close examination of a scholarly article — a ten- to fifty-page, heavily documented essay normally published in an academic journal. Your instructor will likely give specific instructions about the kind of critique that is expected, but you will undoubtedly need to read the source carefully before you begin writing. For details on how to read and assess scholarly articles, see pages 32, 34–35 in Chapter 3 and pages 109–11 in Chapter 6.

In general, the goal of an article critique is similar to that of a book review, but you will be expected to treat your source in greater detail. Your assignment might also ask you to make connections between this article and related course materials. Mention any weaknesses in the author's efforts to support the thesis and any biases or unwarranted assumptions that you detect. Note any counterevidence you are aware of that the author has not mentioned.

Be sure that your critique covers the points that your instructor has asked for, and keep within assigned page limits. If you have been asked to express your own reaction to the article, do so. If not, confine your conclusions to the content of the article itself.

NOTE: As you read and take notes on the article in preparation for writing your critique, watch for any of the author's words that you might wish to quote. Leave no doubt in your notes as to whose words these are by placing them, unmistakably, within quotation marks.

Comparative Reviews and Critiques

If you have questions about writing single-source reviews and critiques, see the previous sections, "Book Reviews" and "Article Critiques." Here we take up an assignment in which you are expected to *compare* secondary sources to one another. Your instructor may point out any specific comparisons that you should make. The following is general advice about drawing comparisons.

Comparisons illustrate significant similarities and differences between the sources being examined, especially ones that are suggested in the assignment. If your instructor asks you to discuss the different views of two authors, then your comparisons are likely to be drawn from the theses and conclusions of each source. In a different kind of assignment it may be necessary to look as well at connections between subject matter, approach to subject (social, economic, political, etc.), writing style, kind of argument (the way the thesis is supported), and primary sources drawn from, as well as theses and conclusions.

Don't begin your comparison until you have read (or reread) each of the sources. Examine each one carefully, and pay special attention to the points of comparison mentioned above. Your ability to find and explain points of comparison will rest on a careful reading of each source.

When writing comparisons, don't look only for disagreements. Authors may come to similar conclusions yet differ in the kinds of arguments they make or the evidence they use. Two different authors may agree that the religious outlook of the founders of the nation of Saudi Arabia was Wahabism. Yet one might argue that Wahabism was an authentic expression of Arabian Islam while the other might argue that it was not. To take another example, two authors may study the same subject (say, the native peoples of California in the nineteenth century) and even use similar kinds of evidence (mission records) yet draw different conclusions from their research. One may study the mission records and conclude that the native population underwent a tremendous decline while the other concludes, from the same records, that basic cultural traits of these peoples survived well into the twentieth century. In this case, the difference between the two studies is the result of the very different kinds of information that each focused on from the same primary sources. One examined evidence of the size of populations (demographic history) while the other examined evidence of native ways of life (cultural history).

Examine each source for the basic components listed above: subject, thesis, approach, evidence, structure, sources, and conclusion. Introduce your general findings, and then build your essay around points of similarity or difference that are most relevant to the assignment, making sure to justify any comparisons you make. Make clear to your reader not only what the similarities and differences are, but why they are important. In your conclusion, summarize your main points, and, if possible, place your findings in a wider historical context.

WRITING SHORT ESSAYS

In many history courses, you will be expected to use your analytical skills to do more than write about one or two sources. You may be asked to write a full-fledged research paper of fifteen pages or more. (Conducting research, writing research papers, and documenting sources are covered in Chapters 6, 7, and 8.) Or, more commonly, you will be asked to write a short essay that requires some research and analysis, some synthesizing and persuading.

You might, for example, be asked to write an essay about a historic event after examining a scholarly article, a firsthand account, and several photographs. Considering those sources together, you would be expected to formulate a thesis, organize your evidence, and present your argument in an essay. Refer to Chapter 4 for detailed advice on how to build an effective essay.

NOTE: If your short essay assignment is part of an exam, you may want to refer to "Taking Exams" on pages 79–87 of this chapter.

GIVING PRESENTATIONS

Oral Presentations

Some instructors require students to give an oral presentation in class. Eloquence and effectiveness in public speaking cannot be mastered in a week or two, but you can make a start by taking such an assignment seriously and adequately preparing yourself for it. If you are allowed the option, reading from a prepared text is often the safest procedure. However, this type of delivery can lead to a dull presentation. It is usually better to speak from notes: your presentation will be livelier and more enjoyable for the class. To do a good job, you need to be fully familiar with your subject and pay close attention to getting your points across. Prepare your presentation outline as you would the outline for a short paper (see "Creating a Writing Outline" in Chapter 4, pp. 54–55). Be sure to cover all the important points and to present them in a logical manner.

Guidelines for Giving an Oral Presentation

- Use 3-by-5 note cards, each with one or (at most) two major points on it.
- Write neatly and use phrases, not whole sentences.
- Put a number in the corner of each note card so that the cards will not get out of order.
- If you have a time limit, rehearse your talk beforehand so that you won't need to rush. Pare down your notes to fit the time needed to present the material clearly.
- Visual aids (such as overhead projections, slides, or videos) can make your presentation much more interesting. (See also the next section, on PowerPoint presentations.) Make sure, however, that you have the resources you need beforehand and that you know how to integrate them easily and smoothly into your verbal remarks.
- Relax! Speak slowly and clearly, and make eye contact with your audience every few sentences.

Use short phrases rather than sentences in your presentation notes. Suppose you intend to tell the class the following: "Before 1848, most of the large landowners in California were Mexicans. In the decades after the United States annexed California, these Californios, as they were called, lost most of their lands to migrants from the eastern states." Your notes need only say:

(a) Until 1848 big landowners Californios.

(b) Cal. annexed in 1848.

(c) Lost land to easterners.

Once you are fully prepared, do a dry run of your presentation before a relative, friend, or roommate (or even in front of a mirror). Be sure that you exhibit knowledge of your subject because this is most likely to determine your grade. Effective public speaking is one of the most important tools for success in many fields of work, and giving a talk in class is a good opportunity to develop your skills in this area.

PowerPoint Presentations

PowerPoint, as you probably know, is a software program that enables you to make a presentation to the class in the form of a digital "slide show." Screens or "slides" can contain text in various fonts and colors, data organized into tables and graphs, artwork from a variety of sources, and much more. You also can animate and sequence your screens.

Don't underuse or overuse PowerPoint. If screen after screen is merely a series of bulleted lists, you might as well write them on the board. At the other extreme, don't turn your presentation into a Hollywood-style extravaganza — even if you know the program well enough to do so. Know what points you want to get across; then create just enough screens with just enough visual elements to do so clearly and effectively.

Be sure to proofread your screens to keep errors out of your presentation. Preview the screens for both content and sequence. Rehearse the presentation to make sure it fits into the time allotted. Make sure that the classroom has the necessary hardware for you to run your PowerPoint presentation.

Finally, don't expect the screens to do all of the work for you. Assist the class with each screen by explaining how the text, data, and images illustrate and advance your main points.

TAKING EXAMS

When a test is announced, try to find out what kind of exam it will be: essay, short answer, multiple choice, or a combination of those formats. Determine what topics will be covered and what portions of the reading material and lectures deal with those topics. If you have not done all of the necessary reading, do so immediately and record the important facts and interpretations as indicated in the "Keeping Up with Reading Assignments" section of Chapter 2 (pp. 12–15). If you missed any lectures, try to obtain lecture notes from someone who knows the rules of good note taking. Then gather together all the materials to be covered in the exam. Reread the parts of the texts that you underlined (or otherwise marked) as being important. Reread all of the relevant lecture notes, paying special attention to any points emphasized by the instructor. Sometimes it helps to do your rereading aloud. If an exam will cover visual materials — slides, films, maps — be sure to go over this information, even if you have to watch a video a second time.

If the test is to be an essay exam, compose sample questions based on the important topics in the readings and lectures. Many textbooks contain sample exam questions or topics for discussion at the end of each chapter. If you do not know how to answer any portion of a sample question, go over your study materials again and look for the information needed. If you are preparing for an objective exam — that is, one requiring short factual answers — pay special attention to the important facts (persons, places, events, changes) and key terms in your study materials. You must be precise in order to get credit for your answer. Make a list of outstanding people, events, and historical developments, and be sure that you can adequately identify them and explain their importance. Again, your textbook may help you by providing sample short-answer questions. Take the time you need to prepare adequately. If tests make you nervous, keep on studying until you master your sample questions and until the material to be covered makes sense to you.

Objective and Short-Answer Exams

Objective exams call for short, factual answers. The three most common objective exams are (1) short answer, (2) identification, and (3) multiple choice. Read each question carefully, and don't jump to conclusions. Answer short-answer and identification questions briefly (there is usually a time and space limit) and directly. Don't put anything in your answer that wastes space or time. If you are asked to identify John F. Kennedy, don't mention how he was killed (unless that is part of the question); instead talk about some aspect of his presidency that was stressed in class or in course readings. When you have so little room to show what you know, answers that stray from the core of the subject are as bad as wrong answers.

Example of a Short-Answer Question

QUESTION

Describe one of the motives that caused the European powers to explore Africa beginning in the late fifteenth century.

INCORRECT ANSWER

They wanted to dominate Africa and get all the gold for themselves. Columbus wanted to take slaves from Africa, but the Pope said it would start a war. But the war didn't start and the Europeans dominated Africa anyway because they were stronger.

CORRECT ANSWER

The wars between Christianity and Islam were an important factor. The Christian states wanted to weaken the hold of the Muslim religion on Africa and to convert the natives. They also hoped to break Muslim control of trade with Asia by finding a sea route around Africa.

(Check these two answers against the example of good note taking in Figure 2.3 [p. 18]. The notes presented there make clear why the second answer is satisfactory and the first one is not.)

Example of an Identification Question

QUESTION

Identify the "progressive" philosophy of historical interpretation.

INCORRECT ANSWER

Historians who believed that our country was always making progress because Americans were very hardworking people.

CORRECT ANSWER

The interpretation of history that holds that human beings and their condition are continually improving as each generation builds on the foundation laid by previous generations.

(See the "Philosophies of History" section in Chapter 1 on pp. 5–7 to find the basis for the correct answer.)

Example of a Multiple-Choice Question

The British monarch at the time of the American Revolution was:

a. George II
b. Charles I
c. James II
d. George III
e. Henry I

If you look up the reign dates of those five monarchs, you will discover that George III (who was king from 1760 to 1820) was the ruler of England at the time of the American Revolution.

In-Class Essay Exams

Of course, the best preparation for an essay exam is to be given the question in advance. Some instructors do this (usually in the form of a take-home test), but many give in-class essay exams and hand out in advance a number of possible topics or questions from which they will choose when making up the exam. (For more on take-home essay exams, see pp. 83–87.) If you face an in-class essay exam without *any* questions presented in advance, the key to successful preparation is to come up with potential questions on your own.

Composing Sample Questions

As your instructor probably will tell you, the essay questions will deal with the major topics covered in the course so far. Using your textbooks, lecture notes, and other course materials, determine what these topics are. Then compose your own questions.

Guidelines for Writing In-Class Essay Exams

- When you are given the exam, don't panic. Read the entire exam slowly, including all of the instructions. Gauge the amount of time you will need to answer each question. Then choose the question you know most about to answer first.
- Don't write the first thing that comes to mind. Read the question slowly, and be sure you understand it.
- Determine how you will answer the question and the central points you wish to make.
- Write these central points or even a full outline in the margin of the exam booklet. As you compose each sentence of your answer, make sure that it relates to one of these points.
- Model your answer on the question. Be as specific or general, as concrete or reflective, as the question suggests. Never allow your answer to wander away from the focus of the question. If the question asks you to "describe" or "trace" or "compare" or "explain," be sure that that is what you do.
- Don't repeat yourself. Each sentence should add new material or advance a line of argument.
- Where necessary, mention the facts that support the points you are making. But the mere relation of a series of facts is not enough. You also must give evidence that you have thought about the question in broad terms.
- Toward the end of an answer, you may wish to include your own opinion. Doing so is fine, even desirable, but be sure that your answer as a whole supports your opinion.
- If there is time, reread and fine-tune your answers. The pressure of an exam may cause you to write sentences that are not clear.

For example, if the material to be covered in the exam is reasons for the decline of the Roman Empire, list the major reasons mentioned in the course work. Among them may be civil war, military insubordination, the cost of defending distant frontiers, declining agricultural output, "barbarian" invasion, heavy tax burdens on the peasantry, the growth of central bureaucracy, the decline of the Roman senate, the cult of the Roman emperor, the rise of Christianity, and the rise of Islam. The exam question is likely to focus on one or more of these explanations. Be prepared to write about *each* of these factors and how they relate to one another.

Don't prepare for an essay exam by composing questions that are too broad. If the class spent six weeks examining the decline of the Roman Empire, don't expect a broad question such as "Discuss the decline of the Roman Empire." Don't prepare questions that are too narrow either. For example, "Who was the last Roman emperor in the West?" is a question for a short-answer or an identification exam.

Taking the Test

Even if you have prepared properly for an essay exam, you must stay calm enough to remember what you studied, you must understand the questions, you must answer them directly and fully, and you must not run out of time. None of this is easy, but here are a few pointers to follow until you gain the experience to overcome these problems.

Read over the exam slowly. Given the length and complexity of the questions asked, allot the proper amount of time to answer each question. Think about the central points you wish to make, and create a brief outline of these points in the margin of the exam booklet. Directly address the questions asked. If the questions are very specific, respond to them with the amount of detail required. Support the points you make with facts, but avoid composing an answer that is merely a series of facts. Think about the questions asked in broad terms, and pursue your central points. As you write, refer back to your outline and be careful not to repeat yourself. Each sentence should add new material to your answer or advance its line of argument. Finally, try to allow a few minutes to proofread your answers.

Take-Home Essay Exams

When you are writing take-home essay exam answers, all of the points made in Chapter 4 about clarity and continuity apply. A take-home essay exam question requires you to write an original essay of usually two to five pages. Of course, if your instructor asks for a specific length, topic, approach, or format, you need to follow those requirements even when they differ from the information provided here.

First, note the length requirements of the exam and the due date. Obviously, you will need more time to prepare a six-page essay answer than a three-page one. If your instructor allows you access to sources (which is common), you will need to review all course material that relates to the exam question.

If you have not yet outlined or taken notes on this material, do so now. Focusing on the portion of the course material that relates to the question, make a list of the most important points. Try to find from two to six main points for each question, depending on the length of the essay. Compose your answer by introducing and then supporting these points in logical order. Like all essays, your answer should have a clear, central thesis. In this case, your thesis is determined by — and should directly address — the exam question. (See the section on writing in-class essay exams on pp. 82–83.)

Your goal when taking any essay exam is to demonstrate (1) adequate knowledge of the subject, (2) clear thinking about the points covered, (3) clear and connected writing, and (4) clear understanding of the question. Read the following two answers to an exam question on Chinese history. Do they meet those four requirements?

QUESTION

Explain the origins of the Chinese civil war of 1945–1949. How did the differing political programs of the two contenders affect the outcome of that conflict?

POOR ANSWER

The Guo Mindang (Kuomintang) had a stronger army than the Communists, but the Communists won the civil war and took over the country. Their political program, communism, was liked by the peasants because they didn't own any land and paid high taxes.

China was based on the Confucian system, which was very rigid and led to the Manchu dynasty being overthrown. The Chinese didn't like being dominated by foreigners, and Sun Zhongshan (Sun Yat-sen) founded the Guo Mindang to unite China. He believed in the Three People's Principles. At first he cooperated with the Chinese Communists, but later Jiang Jieshi (Chiang Kai-shek) tried to destroy communism because he was against it. Communism was not in favor of the wealthy people.

The Communists wanted a revolution of the peasants and gave them land. They also killed the landlords. Jiang Jieshi worried more about the Communists than about the Japanese invasion. The Japanese looked to conquer China and make it a part of their empire. Jiang Jieshi wanted to fight the Communists first.

After World War II the Chinese Communists attacked Manchuria and took over a lot of weapons. They fought the Guo Mindang army. The Guo Mindang army lost the battles, and Jiang Jieshi was chased to Taiwan, where he made a new government.

The Communists set up their own country, and their capital was Beijing (Peking). That way the Communists won the Chinese civil war.

GOOD ANSWER

The origins of the 1945–1949 civil war can be traced back to the rise of Chinese nationalism in the late nineteenth century. Out of the confusion of the Warlord period that followed the overthrow of the Manchu dynasty in 1911, two powerful nationalist movements arose — one reformist and the other revolutionary. The reformist movement was the Guo Mindang (Kuomintang), founded by Sun Zhongshan (Sun Yat-sen). It was based on a mixture of republican, Christian, and moderate socialist ideals and inspired by opposition to foreign domination. The revolutionary movement was that of the Chinese Communist Party (CCP), founded in 1921, whose goal was a communist society but whose immediate program was to organize the working class to protect its interests and to work for the removal of foreign "imperialist" control.

Although these two movements shared certain immediate goals (suppression of the Warlords and resistance to foreign influence), they eventually fell out over such questions as land reform, relations with the Soviet Union, the role of the working class, and the internal structure of the Guo Mindang. (The CCP operated within the framework of the more powerful Guo Mindang during the 1920s.)

By the 1930s, when Jiang Jieshi (Chiang Kai-shek) succeeded Sun, the CCP was forced out of the Guo Mindang. By that time the CCP had turned to a program of peasant revolution inspired by Mao Zedong (Mao Tse-tung). A four-year military struggle (1930–1934) between the two movements for control of the peasantry of Jiangxi (Kiangsi) Province ended in the defeat but not destruction of the CCP.

The Japanese invasion of Manchuria (1931) and central China (1936–1938) helped salvage the fortunes of the CCP. By carrying out an active guerrilla resistance against the Japanese, in contrast to the more passive role of the Guo Mindang, which was saving its army for a future battle with the Communists, the CCP gained the leading position in the nationalist cause.

In the post–World War II period, the CCP's land reform program won strong peasant support, whereas the landlord-backed Guo Mindang was faced with runaway corruption and inflation, which eroded its middle-class following. The military struggle between 1945 and 1949 led to the defeat of the demoralized Guo Mindang army and the coming to power of the CCP.

Let's compare how well the two essays meet the requirements for a well-written answer.

1. *Adequate knowledge of the subject.* The writer of the poor answer omits many important facts, uses vague terms to describe the political programs of the two contending parties, and lists events out of chronological order. The well-written answer illustrates good knowledge of the subject matter. The origins, philosophies, leaders, and relationship of the two contending parties are clearly described, and the writer includes related issues such as nationalism, Warlords, guerrilla warfare against Japan, corruption, and inflation, thus indicating knowledge of the historical context in which the Chinese civil war developed. The chronology is clear: events are mentioned in proper time sequence, and the dates of all major events are given.

2. *Clear thinking about the points covered.* The poor answer is not well organized. The paragraphs do not make separate points, and each succeeding paragraph does not further develop the thesis of the essay. By contrast, the well-written answer uses each paragraph to make a separate important point, and each succeeding paragraph further develops the essay's thesis. The first paragraph sets out the political programs of the two groups and the historical context in which the movements originated. The second paragraph explains the beginning of the conflict in the 1920s. The third paragraph discusses that conflict in relation to the Chinese peasantry during the early 1930s. The fourth paragraph relates the development of the conflict to the Japanese invasion of the late 1930s. The final paragraph summarizes the effects of the conflicts and of postwar developments on the outcome of the civil war.

3. *Clear and connected writing.* Many sentences in the poor answer are badly constructed. Awkward and passive phrases, such as "communism was *liked by* the peasants," lead to unclear sentences that keep the student from getting his or her point across. In addition, repetitious and irrelevant sentences and phrases, such as "Jiang Jieshi (Chiang Kai-shek) tried to destroy communism *because he was against it*," add nothing to the answer. The sentences of the well-written answer are clear, and each adds new material to the essay.

4. *Clear understanding of the question.* The poor answer does not deal with the central issue of the question — the political programs of the Guo Mindang and the CCP. It notes that the Guo Mindang was founded on the Three People's Principles, but it does not explain what these were. Of the CCP, it says that there was a belief in communism (which is obvious) and in peasant revolution (which is vague). These are the only references to political programs in the entire answer! It is obvious that the writer of this answer failed to understand that the central focus of the question was on political philosophy. In contrast, the well-written answer is directed to the central issue of political programs and begins on that very point. The remainder of that answer makes clear the relationship of political programs to the origins and course of the Chinese civil war, as called for in the first sentence of the question.

The Dangers of Plagiarism

A problem that sometimes arises with take-home exams is **plagiarism**. Your instructor may allow you to **paraphrase** the sources you use in preparing your essay. Be sure, however, that you write these paraphrases totally in your own words. If you use sentences or even phrases from another source, you are plagiarizing whether you realize it or not. Most schools require instructors to penalize students severely for plagiarizing. This is a very serious matter. If you still have questions, turn to the discussion of summarizing, paraphrasing, and quoting without plagiarizing in Chapter 6 (pp. 118–21).

CHAPTER

6

Researching a History Topic

The assignment to write a **research paper** requires you to gather your own sources of information and draw your own **conclusions**. It is one of the most creative tasks you will do as a history student; the paper you write is uniquely your own. Because a lot of independent work is involved, research is often the most challenging history assignment. The skills you gain from this kind of project (gathering, evaluating, and organizing **evidence**) are invaluable. They will be of use to you in any career you pursue. The subjects of your research may fade from your memory in years to come, but the ability to investigate a complex **topic** is a skill you will always be able to call on.

This chapter surveys sources of historical information and explains how to use these sources most profitably. It will help you decide on a suitable topic, formulate a meaningful **research question**, and do the research necessary to propose an answer to your question. It will help you navigate your school library as well as the Internet in your quest for relevant sources, and it will help you evaluate those sources for relevance and reliability once you have tracked them down. Finally, it will explain how to record and organize information from your sources so that you will be ready to draft your paper. (For details on writing a research paper, see Chapter 7.)

BEGINNING THE RESEARCH PROCESS

A lengthy research paper takes many weeks of research and writing. If your instructor sets interim deadlines, meet them. Otherwise, break up the assignment into segments like those listed in the guidelines on page 89, and set a reasonable deadline for each segment.

Guidelines for the Research Process

- Browse the course materials and historical bibliographies, and find a topic that interests you.
- Do some initial reading to narrow your topic into one aspect that is manageable for the scope of your project.
- Come up with a debatable research question that is relevant to your topic and worthy of examination.
- Conduct initial research to explore possible answers to your question.
- Create a research strategy that helps you to determine which kinds of sources to read and in what order.
- Do extensive research to gather reliable and relevant sources, interpreting them and taking notes as you go.
- Settle on a tentative thesis that proposes an answer to your research question.
- Create a writing outline for your paper, and begin to organize your research in accordance with this outline.
- Conduct more research to fill out supporting evidence for your thesis. (Do not ignore counterevidence.)
- Write a rough draft that organizes the evidence in support of your thesis and documents your sources (see Chapter 7).
- Revise your draft to make sure it is well organized, clearly written, and properly formatted (see Chapter 7).
- Proofread your final draft for spelling mistakes and other typos.

Choosing a Topic

Most instructors offer a list of possible research topics. Choose carefully; work on a topic that raises your curiosity or builds on your established interests. Weeks of research and writing will seem much longer if your curiosity in the topic wanes. If, early in your research, you discover that you misjudged your interest in the topic, choose another.

Read through the course materials on a topic that seems of interest. Carry out some research in generalized **reference sources** to be sure of your interest in the topic. (For a list of useful reference works, see Appendix A, or check with your school's reference librarian.) As you explore, take on the role of an investigator. Ask yourself why this happened or how that happened. Most questions have more than one answer, and some answers may surprise you.

Also, carry out broader research on your tentative topic. Your goal is to become familiar with the **historical context** surrounding your topic. Some aspects of your topic will not be clear to you if you begin your research without this kind of knowledge.

Narrowing Your Topic

Once you have settled on a general topic, begin to narrow it to meet the needs of the assignment, especially those concerning form, length, and time limits. Within these constraints, look for some aspect of the topic that stimulates your curiosity — one that raises interesting questions in your mind. If your topic is Native Americans of the western United States, you may wish to explore some part of Native American life such as the practices of medicine men or the conflict between a particular tribe and European settlers. Further investigation might lead to an even more specific subject area, such as "the practice of magic among the Cheyenne" or "efforts of the Nez Perce to protect their native lands in Oregon."

If you know very little about your topic, conduct preliminary research. For example, if your topic is the Mexican Revolution of 1910, read a brief history of the subject in a good **historical dictionary** or **historical encyclopedia**. An encyclopedia article on the Mexican Revolution will mention its principal leaders — Francisco Madero, Pancho Villa, Emiliano Zapata, and Venustiano Carranza. From there, your interest in the Mexican Revolution might begin to focus on Zapata. Turn now to a **biographical dictionary**, where you will discover that Zapata led a peasant guerrilla army whose aim was to recover village lands seized by the owners of expanding sugar plantations. As you continue your initial research on this larger-than-life figure, you will find that Zapata was a highly respected military leader and a campaigner for land reform who even today inspires the Mexican peasantry. If Zapata's role in the Mexican Revolution of 1910 seems of interest, if it raises questions in your mind that you would like to pursue, then you have successfully narrowed your topic.

NOTE: Your narrowed-down topic will need to match the sources available to you. You cannot read sources in a language unfamiliar to you or sources that are located in an **archive** far from your school.

Formulating a Research Question

You have narrowed your topic and done enough broad research to become familiar with its historical context. The next step is to take your narrow topic — the role of land reform in the Mexican Revolution of 1910 — and focus it more tightly by turning it into a research question. This question will serve to direct your research toward the kinds of sources that will provide an answer to it. The research question "What caused the failure of Zapata's land reform program?" will enable you to write a paper tightly connected to this specific question. Rather than haphazardly examining several unrelated aspects of Mexican land reform, your research and your paper will focus on the reasons for its failure.

In order to guide your research effectively and pave the way for a success-ful, analytical paper, a research question must be *debatable* (not factual), *narrow* (not broad), *significant* (not unimportant), and *researchable* (not vague).

Debatable Questions

An effective research question is debatable rather than factual. It is not a simple "yes or no" question, but a question that can be answered in more than one way.

TOO FACTUAL

Who was the first person to sign the Declaration of Independence?

DEBATABLE

What factors might explain the historical inaccuracies in John Trumbull's famous painting *The Declaration of Independence*?

Narrow Questions

An effective research question is narrow rather than broad. A question that is too broad is unmanageable and cannot be answered adequately in an under-graduate research paper. A narrow question has boundaries; it asks about aspects of history that can be investigated and answered with a reasonable expenditure of time and effort.

TOO BROAD

Why did the Roman Empire fall?

NARROW

What aspects of the political system of the Roman Republic survived the rise of dictatorship and empire?

Significant Questions

An effective research question is significant rather than unimportant. The question has to be one that historians would take seriously, one whose an-swer would provide increased historical knowledge.

UNIMPORTANT

Why are Ping-Pong tables green?

SIGNIFICANT

What was the importance of "Ping-Pong diplomacy" to the relations between China and the United States?

Researchable Questions

An effective research question is researchable rather than vague. A question that is vague or aimless gives no clue as to how it might be answered. A researchable question makes clear what aspects of a historical topic need to be pursued.

TOO VAGUE

Why did Mexico have so many revolutions?

RESEARCHABLE

In the decade prior to the Mexican Revolution of 1910, in what ways were the buttresses of the Porfirio Diaz dictatorship undermined?

The **thesis** is the central argument of a research paper; it is the point the author is trying to convince the reader of. A good research question enables you to create a strong thesis for your paper. Suppose your research is directed by the following question:

In the decade prior to the Mexican Revolution of 1910, in what ways were the buttresses of the Porfirio Diaz dictatorship undermined?

This is a debatable, narrow, significant, and researchable question that could lead to an effective paper with the following thesis:

The dictatorship of Porfirio Diaz rested, to a great extent, on the support of the large landowners. The declining authority of landowners over peasant farmers seriously weakened the dictatorship in the years before the 1910 revolution.

Planning a Research Strategy

A **research strategy** is a plan for organizing your research tasks: what kind of sources to look for, which to read, and in what order.

Your early research helps you test the quality and availability of the evidence needed to answer your research question. It also helps you assess the amount and range of material you may need to examine. If advised by your instructor as to the number and kind of sources needed, be sure that they are available. Be sure, as well, to allow enough time to read and take notes from these materials. In assessing the time needed for specific tasks, keep in mind that there will be time lost pursuing false starts and coming upon dead ends.

Budgeting Your Time and Staying Focused

Plan ahead to manage your time and stay focused on your question. If you are interested in Zapata's land reform program, you might come up with this research question: "To what extent was Zapata's land reform program a factor in the success of the Mexican Revolution?" Your first research task will be to learn about the historical context of the 1910 revolution. You might divide your preliminary research tasks into the following broad subject areas:

- Background on the Mexican Revolution — historical encyclopedias, textbooks, Web sites (approximately 3 hours)
- Overview of prerevolution land reform efforts — historical encyclopedia or general history of nineteenth-century Mexico (approximately 3 hours)
- Zapata's life — biographies and books or articles on his home state of Morelos (approximately 8 hours)

After you have done some initial reading, you will need to do more in-depth research on more specific subject areas such as land reform in Mexico. Tracking down and working with these more specific sources is covered in the remainder of this chapter and will require a significant amount of time. To continue with the Zapata example, you might break down your remaining research tasks as follows:

- Information about land reform efforts in Morelos — books, articles, and documents, perhaps from online sources (approximately 8 hours)
- Zapata's role in the effort to regain village lands — various sources (approximately 8 hours)
- Zapata's role in the larger revolution — various sources (approximately 10 hours)
- Zapata's specific land reform proposals — **primary sources** (approximately 6 hours)
- The fate of Zapata, the revolution, and the land reform efforts — various **secondary sources** (approximately 6 hours)

Of course, a research strategy and timeline must be flexible. Certain tasks will take more time and others less than expected. Nevertheless, a research strategy will keep your research focused and will warn you if you begin to fall behind.

NOTE: Estimates should include the time needed to find a source, read it, and take notes from it. When searching the library's online catalog (see pp. 95–99), be sure to find out whether the material you want is on campus and readily available. Some items may be held in off-site storage facilities; other materials may need to be requested from another library through a process called **interlibrary loan.** Don't wait until it is too late to find out that a book you really need has to be tracked down from another location.

Keeping an Open Mind

In the early stages of your research, you may become aware that there is not enough information available to answer your proposed research question and that it has to be changed. Also bear in mind that you may find an answer to your question that is quite different from what you anticipated. Accept the fact that your thesis may turn out differently than you envisioned.

In addition, as you begin uncovering the evidence that relates to your research question, be aware of **counterevidence** — any respectable source that answers your research question in a way very different from yours. Don't ignore such evidence! Even if you decide that many more sources support your way of answering your question, you must acknowledge the challenging **arguments** in your research notes and in your written paper. Addressing counterevidence effectively will strengthen, not weaken, your paper. Don't expect to convince your reader that your argument is true and the other false. Rather, your goal is to convince your reader that, despite the counterevidence, your thesis remains strong and persuasive.

Maintaining a Working Bibliography

A **working bibliography** is a list of all the relevant sources you discover in the course of your research. These may be sources you read and take notes from, sources you skim and deem worthy of full examination, and sources that you only see references to but want to be able to find in case you decide to examine them. Of course, all of them should be (or be likely to be) relevant, available, and scholarly. Copy down the source information and enter it into your working bibliography. (If you have questions about what source information to include, see Chapter 8.)

Creating a working bibliography serves two important purposes. First, it provides the information about a source that you will need if you eventually use that source in your research paper. Second, it enables you to find the source if at a later point you wish to examine it again. A working bibliography is a valuable timesaver and organizational tool.

CONDUCTING RESEARCH

Begin your research efforts with both a virtual and real tour of the school library. No other place brings together all of the connections between your research project and the sources you will need to carry it out. Become familiar with both the online layout and physical layout of the library because you'll be exploring both realms during your research project.

To discover the resources available in the physical library, take a formal tour or ask a librarian to point them out to you. Find out, for example, where the **library stacks** are — the shelves where bound books and journals (and audio and video materials) are stored. You also should be able to find areas such as the section where reference books (historical encyclopedias, dictionaries, **atlases**, etc.) are shelved, the microprint section (**microfilms** and **microfiche**), and any "special collections" that are in the library.

You also should browse the library's home page, either on your own or at a terminal in the library with the help of a reference librarian. Although all library home pages are different, most include a variety of tools for finding books, journals, and other reliable sources. Most also include links to the library's digital collections, such as electronic databases and digital archives. Some home pages include special online help areas, such as tutorials and live chats with librarians. Find out how you can access your library's home page remotely and whether you need to register for a password or create a proxy server. Also, check for any limitations to see which resources can be used remotely and which are restricted to in-library use only. Figure 6.1 on page 96 shows an example of a typical library home page.

NOTE: Don't make the mistake of thinking that the immense amount of information on the Web will allow you to bypass the library. In many cases, access to the most useful online research material is possible only through your school library, which pays for many academic database subscriptions that are not available to the general public.

Using the Library's Online Catalog

Once you have a clear sense of how your library is organized, become familiar with its **online catalog**. In most cases, the catalog is accessed through a link on the library home page, although at small colleges the online catalog may be part of the home page. The online catalog allows you to search the library's entire collection by subject, keyword, author, or various other search parameters. When you perform a search, you receive a list of results — or hits — that match your criteria. Clicking on one of these links takes you to a catalog entry page with details about the source. For an example of a catalog entry page for a book, see Figure 6.2 on page 97.

Searching by Subject or by Keyword

Your search for sources will be most effective if you understand the difference between subject headings and keywords and if you choose your search terms wisely. **Subject headings** are the words or phrases that are assigned to materials in a library catalog or database in order to classify them. **Keywords** are the terms found in the descriptions of individual items in a library catalog or database. In many instances you will be able to search by both subject and keyword.

Subject Searches.   Searching the library catalog using a **subject search** calls for an understanding of what a **subject hierarchy** is. A subject hierarchy is a series of subjects that moves from the broadest to the narrowest category. The trick is to start with the broad category that is most likely to contain the narrower subject area that you are researching.

Most online catalogs follow the official set of headings compiled by the Library of Congress, which aren't always intuitive. If you set out to research the history of handgun ownership in the United States, you might be surprised to find that an initial subject search on the term "handguns" yields very few results, because "handguns" is not an official Library of Congress Subject Heading ("pistols" and "firearms" are). If you are having trouble finding the proper subject headings for your search, do not hesitate to ask the advice of the reference librarian. Doing so can save you a great deal of time.

NOTE: One way to discover the proper subject heading for your research topic is to look up a book that you know is relevant to your topic in the online catalog and then check to see what is listed for that book's "Subject" in its catalog entry (see Figure 6.2 on p. 97).

FIGURE 6.1   Example of a Library Home Page
Library home pages vary greatly in content, design, and layout, and your school's library home page will probably look quite different from this one. The numbered items listed here are some of the most common and useful features on many library home pages:

- ❶ Name of library; the sponsor of the site
- ❷ Links to the university home page and to other university libraries
- ❸ Searchable index of all features on the site
- ❹ Series of tabs that allow user to choose from popular search areas, including "Catalog" (the online catalog) and "E-Journals" (the electronic databases)
- ❺ Simple search box (with "Advanced Search" option) for the online library catalog
- ❻ Popular links for students, including online research help, a virtual librarian, and writing tips from the university writing center
- ❼ Links to the library's special collections

Keyword Searches. In keyword searching, instead of trying to figure out which *subject* your topic is under, you ask the computer to search its records of books and other materials for certain *words.*

Suppose you are researching "women workers in the Lowell, Massachusetts, textile mills, 1820–1850." Your most promising keywords will be the nouns in your topic: *women, workers, Lowell,* and *textile mills.* Don't search by using any of these words by themselves. They are too general and will generate a long

FIGURE 6.2   Example of a Catalog Entry Page for a Book

Although catalog entry pages vary from library to library, most will contain the important information listed here:

❶ Image of the cover and general information about the title.

❷ Tabs link to further details about the title, including its physical location, the table of contents, and a summary.

❸ The "Full Record" tab is highlighted, so the box below displays the complete list of details for the title.

❹ "Subject" refers to the official subject category for this title; subject categories are usually based on the system of subject headings created by the Library of Congress.

❺ The call number ("Call #") gives the title's exact location within the library stacks.

list of sources, most of them not related to your topic. It is always best to do an "advanced" or "complex" search, in which you can combine a series of keywords, asking to see only those sources that have several of the keywords in a certain order. In this case, you might use the following: *"women" AND "workers" AND "textile mills."* The rules for advanced keyword searching are usually available through a link from the search page.

NOTE: Keep in mind that older works might use antiquated or obsolete language in their titles. For example, a book on Russia that was published in the 1970s might have the term *Soviet Union* in the title. A work on Myanmar might be under "Burma." If you need assistance with keyword searches, ask a librarian.

Searching by Author and by Title

Author and title searches are fairly straightforward, but before you begin, you need to know the name of the author or book you are looking for. This is often not possible, especially in the early stages of research. For the most part, you will need to discover which sources by which authors are related to your topic. To do this, you must search the online catalog by subject or by keyword (see pp. 95–98).

To conduct effective author and title searches, you must spell author names and titles correctly. If you are uncertain about the spelling, ask the reference librarian for help. Sometimes the spelling of an author's name can be tricky, especially if the name is spelled differently in English than in its language of origin. Be especially careful when searching for ancient or foreign names.

Locating Materials by Using Call Numbers

Don't sit at the computer for long stretches trying to find that one subject heading or keyword that will give you everything you want. Once your searches have turned up a number of promising titles, record all of the information from the catalog entry page (see Figure 6.2 on p. 97). You will need this information for your working bibliography and, eventually, for the **bibliography** for your written paper. (For information about organizing a bibliography, see Chapter 8.) If the source on your list is a book or journal on the library shelves, be sure to take down the **call number**, which indicates an item's location in the library stacks. As you look over your list of call numbers, you will probably discover that many of the books and journals you listed have call numbers that begin with the same letters or numbers. Books with similar call numbers are usually on related topics. When you get to the stacks, don't look only for the specific books you found in your computer search. Look at all of the books on nearby shelves as well. You are likely to find additional works related to your topic. If they seem promising, add them to your working bibliography.

NOTE: As you begin to track down sources related to your topic, be sure to mine them for clues to finding other useful sources. The **notes** and especially the bibliographies will mention the books and articles that the author relied on, and many of them will be relevant to your topic. Whenever you find a good source, check its notes and bibliography for any promising items to add to your working bibliography.

Using Print and Electronic Reference Works

Reference works can be found in print form in the reference section of your library or in electronic databases. (Appendix A lists many of these sources, and additional resources can be found at <bedfordstmartins.com/benjamin>.) Nonprint reference sources will be linked to the library home page under "Electronic Reference Sources" or a similar name. Some electronic reference sources are also available on the Web, but access to many of the most helpful ones usually requires a password. Your reference librarian can help you to find trustworthy reference sources on the Web.

Reference sources can help you define your terms, gather background information on a topic, and locate specific facts, dates, and biographical and statistical material. Since many reference sources are large and have special ways of organizing their content, look for the place at the beginning of each source where advice is given about using the source. This will save you a lot of time. If you cannot find your way around one of these sources, ask a reference librarian for help.

The Problem of Wikipedia

Among the resources available on the Web is *Wikipedia*. This is an online encyclopedia with "open" architecture, which means *anyone* can write or revise *any* article in this huge reference work. Most instructors consider it unreliable, and many will not accept it as a legitimate source. Be sure to determine your instructor's rules on this subject.

Wikipedia has made an effort in recent years to enhance the reliability of its articles. If a reader raises a question about a particular entry, a warning appears cautioning other readers and asking those with knowledge of the subject to improve the entry by, for example, checking the facts, inserting notes to reliable sources, or correcting the text. Teams of volunteer editors (both scholars and nonscholars) police articles on related subjects, look for ways to improve them, and remove clearly false or malicious material.

In a surprising improvement on traditional encyclopedias, editorial changes to *Wikipedia* entries are transparent. Once you become familiar with the site, you can trace the history of each article: its original form, any changes made (when and by whom), the reasons for the changes, current discussions of the state of the entry, and so on. Readers are invited to become contributors and to join editorial teams that monitor entries. There is no academic experience quite like it.

Still, as of today, *Wikipedia* cannot meet the standard academic demands of quality, authorship, and reliability that this *Guide* and your instructor require. *Wikipedia* is an extremely useful reference tool, but, unless your instructor clearly indicates otherwise, use it only as an aid in finding scholarly material. *Do not use it as a source!*

Atlases, Dictionaries, and Encyclopedias

Atlases are collections of maps. Some atlases are very specialized, showing highly detailed maps of specific regions, towns, and so on. Some of these maps lay out topography (mountains, valleys, rivers, etc.); others display the economic, ethnic, weather, or navigational features of an area. Historical atlases display changes that have occurred in nations, regions, communities, and so on, over time. For example, a historical atlas of transportation might display the expansion of different railroad lines over a period of many decades.

You are already familiar with general dictionaries, but various historical dictionaries should also be available in your school library. They define terms of historical importance not usually found in a general dictionary. Suppose your research requires that you know a particular term from the history of China. A dictionary explaining this term (such as *China: A Historical and Cultural Dictionary*) might be available in your library. Important in the study of history are biographical dictionaries, which give brief descriptions of the lives of important individuals. Information about a Canadian explorer might be found in a source such as the *Dictionary of Canadian Biography*.

Some **encyclopedias**, such as *Encyclopaedia Britannica*, are general; others focus on historical topics. You could find, for example, a historical encyclopedia of slavery or of the French Revolution. Such an encyclopedia, whose entries might run from a few paragraphs to several pages, is a good place to begin research on a historical topic.

Subject Bibliographies

Subject bibliographies list various research materials — including books, book reviews, and journal articles — by subject. They may be available in print form in the reference section of your library, or in electronic form in the library's online catalog. Some subject bibliographies are openly available on the Web. A large number of print and electronic subject bibliographies are included in Appendix A and on this book's companion Web site at <bedfordstmartins.com/benjamin>.

Subject bibliographies are almost always the best sources to use when you are in the early stages of your research. Once you determine your research topic, seek out the subject bibliography that best fits. If you narrow your topic to an aspect such as "the role of journalists in the Vietnam War," the print subject bibliography *The Wars in Vietnam, Cambodia and Laos, 1945–1982: A Bibliographical Guide* might lead you to many useful sources. When using a subject bibliography, keep in mind that the sources it lists will be only as up-to-date as the bibliography itself. For print bibliographies, check the publication date; for online bibliographies, check the date of the most recent update.

Using Print and Electronic Periodical Databases

A **periodical** is a publication that appears on a regular basis — daily, weekly, monthly, quarterly. For example, newspapers usually appear daily, popular magazines weekly or monthly, and **scholarly journals** quarterly (don't overlook this valuable category of periodicals in your research).

Some "directories" of periodicals can be found in print form in the library's reference section, but in most cases, the best way to search for periodicals is through the library's electronic **periodical databases**. Most of these databases are searchable by author, title, or keyword. A list of periodical databases can be found on pages 210–12 in Appendix A and at <bedfordstmartins.com/benjamin>.

Locating Articles in Scholarly Journals

The periodicals most useful for historical research are scholarly journals. Although the articles in these journals are written for scholars, most are accessible to students. These articles are often based on primary sources, and they usually have a clear thesis or argument. (For details on distinguishing between popular and scholarly sources, see Chapter 3, pp. 32, 34–35.)

The articles in scholarly journals are **refereed**, which means that one or more scholars in the appropriate field read each article *before* it was accepted for publication. The process of refereeing provides a kind of quality control, helping to ensure that articles in scholarly journals can serve as reliable sources for scholarly research.

There are a great number of scholarly history journals, covering many areas, such as *China Quarterly, Film and History, History of Religions, Journal of Environmental History,* and *Russian History.* Your library has scholarly journals in its stacks, and its subscriptions to online databases such as *JSTOR, Project Muse, America: History and Life,* and *Historical Abstracts* will give you access to many others. Searching these databases is similar to searching the online catalog. Choose one of the **journal databases** that include a large number of history journals (or, if possible, search many simultaneously). Search these journals by subject or by keyword, paying attention to search rules, which may vary from database to database. For sample screens from an online database, see Figures 6.3 and 6.4, on pages 102–03.

Some journal databases contain "full text," which means that the entire article is available on the database. Other databases are "annotated" or "abstracted." Those databases do not have the articles themselves but contain summaries of their content that will help you decide whether or not to seek out the full text. Still other databases, often called "indexes," list only the basic information: author, title, journal, and date. Journal indexes usually organize articles by subject and period, and most indexes list articles from a very large number of journals, including many not covered by databases with abstracts or full texts.

FIGURE 6.3   Advanced Search Screen in a Periodical Database

Like online catalogs, the page design and layout of the electronic databases you use will vary significantly depending on which ones your library subscribes to. However, similar search fields, options, and limiters will appear on the "Advanced Search" pages for most electronic databases. This example shows an advanced search screen for the *Historical Abstracts* database at Ithaca College. The search screen is divided into three main areas:

❶ The top section of the search screen allows the user to type in search terms for various search fields — such as text, subject, author, and others. The student decided to search the words "ping pong diplomacy" in the text fields only.

❷ The second area provides options to qualify the search. "Boolean" searches allow the user to combine search terms with the directions "and," "or," and "not"; the other checkboxes allow the user to clarify how the search terms should be used. The student checked "Find all my search terms," which means the search will return only documents with all three words — "ping," "pong," and "diplomacy."

❸ The third area of the screen provides options to limit the search by factors such as date range, language, and document type. The student decided to search only for peer-reviewed articles in academic journals available in English. The "Linked Full Text" box would allow the student to search only for articles in the *Historical Abstracts* database that can be electronically accessed in full. The student decided not to select this feature because some relevant articles may not be available in that form in the library's databases.

SOURCE: *Ithaca College Library* / © *EBSCO Publishing Inc. 2009. All rights reserved.*

FIGURE 6.4   Search Results from a Database

Different databases display their lists of search results in different ways, but most provide a list of article titles with links to additional information, as in the top screenshot here. A link such as "Linked Full Text" (as shown under the first article in the list) typically leads to the full text of an article in a different database. A "PDF Full Text" link (as shown under the second article) usually opens the article in a format that displays actual images of print article pages, including page numbering. "HTML Full Text" links (as shown under the third article) typically lead to the complete text of the article within the same database, as shown in the bottom screenshot. Note that "HTML" links generally do not include original page numbering.

NOTE: Even databases with the word *Abstracts* or *Index* in their title may lead you to full-text articles. Depending on your library's subscription, a database such as *Historical Abstracts* may be able to provide you with links to full-text articles. See, for example, the top image in Figure 6.4, which shows a list of search results in the *Historical Abstracts* database at Ithaca College.

If your library has no full-text electronic access to the particular journal articles you want, the full text may be available in the library stacks or through interlibrary loan. Always seek out all the articles that you think will be most useful in your research. Don't discount articles that aren't immediately available, and don't download or print out articles just because they are available in full text.

Even very large databases that allow you to search for articles in hundreds of journals have limitations you should be aware of. Some have articles only from *recent* issues of the journals they contain. Others have articles published only in *older* issues. In history research, the **date range** of a database is important to know; it can tell you what is *not* there and save you a lot of searching time.

NOTE: Many scholarly journals have their own indexes. Printed indexes to specific journals are kept in the library's reference section or in the stacks next to the bound volumes of the journal. Once you have looked at general databases, you may discover that several articles related to your topic come from a small number of journals. If this is the case, find out if your library has

---

Guidelines for Using Periodical Databases

- Choose a database that includes a large number of history journals that deal with the general topic you are working within. For example, for the topic "apartheid in South Africa," choose a database that includes the *Journal of African History*.
- Determine the content and range of your chosen database. What years of the journals you are interested in does it cover? Date ranges that change regularly are called "moving walls."
- Carefully choose two or three keywords that express the most important aspects of your topic. To search by subject, choose the large category that includes your topic.
- Scan the list of articles generated in response to your search. If the article titles do not seem close enough, refine your search terms.
- If an abstract accompanies an article, be sure to read it.
- If an abstract seems promising, take down *all* the information about the article so that you can find the full text.
- If the full text of the article is contained in the database, read enough of it to be sure it is related to your topic. Don't waste time and money downloading or printing it until you have done this.

print copies of these journals. If it does, go to the reference section or into the stacks and seek out the indexes to these specific journals.

Locating Articles in Magazines and Newspapers

Search for magazine articles and newspaper articles in databases and indexes dedicated to magazines and newspapers, such as *Index to Early American Periodicals* and *Reader's Guide Retrospective*. Some magazine and newspaper databases are full text and contain every page, including advertisements; others list articles by title or by subject.

Popular magazines (such as *People, Time,* and *National Geographic*) and newspapers rarely contain serious historical studies. However, if your library has print copies of, or electronic access to, magazines and newspapers *from the period of your topic,* these can be valuable sources. For example, an 1830s newspaper article in the *Lowell Courier* that reports on women workers in the textile mills could prove to be a valuable primary source (see "Primary Sources" in Chapter 3, pp. 25–27). If you are seeking old issues of magazines and newspapers, make sure that the print copies or database goes back to the years encompassed by your topic. If your library does not have the particular newspaper or magazine you are looking for, try to find it on the Web or borrow it — via interlibrary loan — from another library.

Searching for Primary Sources

Primary sources are as close to history as you can get. Such sources help you to imagine what the past was like for those who lived it. Primary sources can be written, such as letters and laws, or nonwritten, such as photographs, artifacts, and audiovisual recordings. (For more details about the nature of primary sources, see Chapter 3.) To track down primary sources related to your topic, you can search in three main venues: the Web, published texts or collections, and museum or library archives.

NOTE: You need to have read a lot about your topic in order to understand primary sources. You won't know why the faces of the Italian family look so bewildered in the old photograph of immigrants arriving in America if you haven't learned about the mixture of confusion, fear, and excitement that was part of coming to the United States in the late nineteenth and early twentieth centuries. You won't know why the letters of Thomas Jefferson on the subject of slavery sound so uncertain unless you know about the battle going on in his mind about the place of Africans in a republic. Use primary sources if you can, but save them until you are well acquainted with your topic.

Primary Sources on the Web

Numerous archives of primary sources can be found on the Web. Entire sites are dedicated to making primary documents widely available. These sites include not only printed and handwritten documents but visual and audio materials such as sound recordings, historical maps, artwork, photographs, and motion pictures. The largest such site for U.S. primary sources is American Memory: <memory.loc.gov/ammem/index.html>. (A large number of primary source Web sites are included in the lists of general and specialized resources in Appendix A and on this book's Web site, <bedfordstmartins.com/ benjamin>.) To assist you in finding such sources, your instructors may list important Web sites in the course syllabus or elsewhere. If so, be sure to follow their advice.

In many cases, access to Web sites for primary sources is free. This is one instance in which using the Web for research is highly recommended. Also check the databases of historical documents to which your library may have subscribed. To see an example of this kind of database, examine *Alexander Street Press*: <www.alexanderst.com>. This site has a well-organized collection of letters, diaries, speeches, interviews, and so on.

Primary Sources in Published Collections

You can find published collections of both written and nonwritten primary sources in your library. These collections often revolve around a specific event, such as the Spanish civil war, or the collected works of a particular historical figure, like Christopher Columbus or Frederick Douglass. Edited collections are, of course, not as close to the historical event as an original manuscript or a contemporary source published in its own context, but they do provide you with the text of the original, and they usually give additional information about the source. For example, they often include **headnotes** that introduce each primary source, and they sometimes include notes that help make the document more accessible.

NOTE: When working with a primary source in a collection, read the headnote as well as any general **introduction** to the collection carefully to determine whether the source itself has been edited from its original version. Often, compilers of collections edit primary documents for length or perceived relevance to their theme. In addition, nonwritten works, such as photographs or illustrations, may have been cropped or otherwise altered from their original appearance.

Primary Sources in Museum Archives

Primary sources are also available in archives such as museums, historical societies, specialized libraries, and the private records of an institution or corporation, including the film and audiotape libraries of television and radio studios. Major university libraries also have large primary source collections, many of which are available through links on the home pages of such libraries. Finally, it may surprise you to learn that most colleges, perhaps including your own, have archives of documents that chronicle the history of the school. Could these materials serve as primary documents for your research?

Interviews as Primary Sources

If your topic concerns events that occurred within the last seventy or eighty years, you might be able to interview someone who lived through them. Members of your community or your own family can be sources of historical information. You might be able to gain access to people who have been leaders in local or national affairs and have personal knowledge of important historical events. Perhaps you can prepare a list of questions about past events in which they were participants. You can write to these individuals or perhaps speak with them. They may have personal papers they are willing to show you. This kind of historical research is exciting and satisfying, and it may enable you to use primary historical material that no other historian has uncovered.

Older adults can recall their years in another country (if they are immigrants) or describe the America in which they grew up. They may not have been important historical figures, but they reflect the experiences of countless others and are thus the stuff of which history is made. Their recollections of how they felt and of what they and others did and said when Pearl Harbor was attacked, when they first saw television, when John F. Kennedy was assassinated, or when the Berlin Wall came down are priceless pieces of the historical puzzle. For information about how to conduct interviews with older people, see "How to Research Your Family History" in Appendix B, pages 264–65.

Using Internet Search Tools

The Web offers countless sites with information for historical researchers. If you know how to explore it wisely, you can find primary and secondary sources as well as trustworthy references on the Internet. In order to find the most useful and reliable sources, begin with your course Web site, or ask your instructor for any good sites related to your topic. Next, you can check your school library's home page and look for links to reputable history sites (see pp. 94–99 of this chapter). In addition, you can find many online sources on a wide variety of historical subjects in Appendix A or on this book's companion Web site: <bedfordstmartins.com/benjamin>.

NOTE: When you track down a source on the Web, you should use extra caution when evaluating it. See "Special Problems of Evaluating Web-Based Sources" on pages 114–16.

Searching Efficiently

The key to online searching is knowing the best way to turn up the most relevant search results in the shortest amount of time. Unlike an online library catalog or a periodical database, the Web isn't very organized, and many unreliable sites can get in the way of your finding the reliable ones. When you set out on a Web search, try doing a subject search first. If all else fails, turn to a keyword search.

Searching the Web by Subject.   Most search engines, such as Google and Yahoo!, allow you to search by subject just as you would in a library online catalog. As noted earlier, a subject hierarchy is a long list of information sources that begins with the broadest subject category and allows you to narrow the choices on the screen until you reach a subject category that is close to your topic. For example, to get to information about Joan of Arc, the narrowing of subjects might go like this: *Humanities> History> Europe> France> Fifteenth Century.* The goal is to choose the most promising link or links at each stage. If your choices move away from your topic, backtrack and try a different route. Using the example of Joan of Arc, if you chose "Religion" after "France" instead of "Fifteenth Century," you might be led to sites about the building of cathedrals.

Searching the Web by Keywords.   Searching the Web by keywords should be seen as a last resort in your research efforts. It will likely yield many thousands of results, but a high percentage of them will be nonscholarly commercial or personal sites that aren't considered credible research sources. If you do conduct a keyword search on the Web, use "advanced search," and follow the same advice as that given on pages 97–98 for keyword searching in online library catalogs.

NOTE: Google Scholar (<scholar.google.com>) is a specialized area of Google that tries to filter out nonacademic sites. It allows you to do a more focused keyword search than the main Google and Yahoo! sites, but it is no substitute for the carefully organized and maintained catalogs and databases available through your library.

Previewing Search Results

If the result of a subject search or a keyword search of the Web brings to the screen more than, say, one hundred sites, narrow your search terms. Use "advanced search" whenever it is offered. To choose the best sites for your history research, look for the following characteristics.

- Check search results for "edu" or "gov" domains, which are restricted to educational and governmental institutions. Alternatively, look for site names that include the name of a major library, museum, or historical organization.
- Avoid results listed under "sponsored results," which are typically commercial in nature.
- If the brief description in the search results list sounds promising, go to the site to see if it is of an educational, noncommercial nature.
- When you reach a site, look for links to such areas as "digital archives," "electronic resources," or "research."
- If a site provides no links to relevant historical materials, abandon it and return to your search results list.

- Bookmark any promising sites, or keep a file of the best sites (including URLs and brief descriptions) so you can easily find them again later.

EVALUATING SOURCES

Chapter 3 provides an overview of various primary and secondary sources and how to approach them most effectively. The material in this section explains how to evaluate a source for reliability and relevance to your research topic.

There are many factors to consider when you evaluate a book or article, a primary text, a nonwritten source, or a Web-based source. You need to know if it is appropriate for college-level work and if it fits your topic. You need to figure out the perspective of the author or creator. You cannot make proper use of a source unless you understand the points the author is trying to make.

Evaluating Secondary Sources

Most history books and articles fall into the category of secondary sources because they are written by someone who did not observe or participate in an event but investigated primary evidence of it. (For more on secondary sources, see Chapter 3, pp. 28–36.) The following sections will help you determine the value of a secondary source to your research.

Reviewing Secondary Sources for Basic Information

The background of the author tells you much about the kind of sources you have uncovered. This information is normally recorded on the cover or the introductory pages. For more information, do an author search in your online catalog or on the Web. A scholar is likely to produce a reliable and research-oriented work. Other kinds of authors — journalists, professionals with a background on the subject, a highly respected author — may write books helpful in your research, but you need to examine their work closely. Look for notes and a bibliography as these are essential components of scholarly work. In addition, check to see who published the work. Is the publisher a university press or a commercial publisher such as Knopf or Penguin with a reputation for producing serious books?

Also consider the intended audience of the book or article. Scholarly journals contain scholarly articles. Popular magazines written for a general audience are not proper sources of information — unless your topic includes a study of such magazines. (For advice on distinguishing between popular and scholarly sources, see Chapter 3, pp. 32, 34–35.) Consider whether the source is meant to entertain or to inform. Often the title provides a clue. A scholarly book might have a title such as *Hindu Fundamentalism and the Destruction of the Mosque of Babur in Ayodya*, whereas a popular book on the same subject might be titled *Massacre at Ayodya: The True Story!* You should be able to distinguish *Changing Images of Female Beauty in Renaissance Art* from *How to Look like a Renaissance Beauty: Twelve Easy Steps.*

Once you feel confident that you have a serious source, you need to be sure that it deals with your topic. A book on Charles Lindbergh that you intend to use in your paper on "Charles Lindbergh's role in the isolationist movement" may be about his celebrity status in 1927 as a result of his solo flight across the Atlantic. The essay "The Kidnapping of Charles Lindbergh's Infant Son in 1932," which you found on a Lindbergh Web site, is unlikely to say much about his political views. The date of publication may determine the relevance of a source to your topic. A book published in 1950, even if it examines aspects of race in American history, cannot help you answer the research question "How did the Supreme Court ruling on school segregation in 1954 affect the integration of public schools?"

Evidence of a book's relation to your topic can also be found in the introduction and the table of contents. In the preface or introduction, the author may explain the background of the book, describe the kinds of questions it addresses, and preview some of its conclusions, and the chapter titles listed in the table of contents may indicate how broadly or narrowly a topic is covered. There is no substitute, of course, for reading sections of the text to see if the author directly addresses your topic.

Reading Secondary Sources for Signs of Bias

Any **bias** on the part of an author or work that you are considering will tell you a lot about a work's seriousness. Bias — an author's perspective on a topic — can be modest or very strong. Strong bias is indicated by an unwillingness to consider or acknowledge other interpretations and by the use of harsh language to characterize authors with different perspectives. A book with a strong bias is unlikely to be a useful source, unless your research requires an examination of biased works, as would a paper on the anti-Semitism expressed in nineteenth-century French accounts of the Dreyfus trial.

Moderate bias, however, is a characteristic of all scholars. Every author has a perspective on his or her subject and, like you, is making an argument in support of a thesis. A history of World War II written by an English author is likely to have a different viewpoint from one written by a German author. Many historical developments and their interpretation are topics of profound controversy, and it is almost impossible for a historian to investigate one of these controversial areas without being affected by his or her own biases. A particular attitude toward a topic is to be expected. Historical problems are highly complex, and without a sense of which aspects of a problem are most important, a historian will be unable to develop a thesis. It is important for you to become familiar with the biases and perspectives of the authors you read so that you do not unknowingly accept their viewpoints. If you agree with someone's point of view, it is natural for you to favor his or her work in your own research. If you do not understand the points of view of the authors

> ### *Guidelines for Evaluating Secondary Sources*
>
> - Is the author a scholarly writer or an expert on your topic? (If you're not sure, conduct a Web search to find out more about the author.)
> - To obtain an overview of the subject of the work, read the table of contents, preface, and other introductory materials. For this purpose, examine also the notes and bibliography.
> - Is the intended audience scholars, serious readers, and college-level students?
> - Who is the publisher? It is a good sign if the work is published by a major commercial publisher or a university press.
> - Is the bias (the perspective) of the author moderate or strong? Be careful when using the work of an author who uses strong language against people who disagree with him or her or who ignores other perspectives.
> - Is the source relevant enough to your topic to merit inclusion in your research bibliography? If your topic covers recent events, does the date of publication indicate that the source covers the period that you are focusing on?

whose work you read, you will not know why you agree with some authors more than with others. Furthermore, you will not be able to make a clear presentation of these points of view in your own written work.

Evaluating Primary Sources

As described in Chapter 3, a primary source is direct evidence of some part of the history of the time when it was created. It may be a handwritten document still in that form, or it may be a typeset version published at a later date. Or it may be an **artifact**, a physical object (building, pot, old camera, ancient coin, etc.) that has survived into the present.

Whether written or nonwritten, primary sources cannot simply be taken at face value. You must look behind them, so to speak. Whenever you intend to use a primary source as evidence, be sure to take the time to learn about the historical context in which it was created and the impact that it had on its original audience. In addition, primary sources, just like secondary sources, must be carefully evaluated to determine both their reliability and their relevance to your topic.

Written Primary Sources

Written primary sources were created at the time of the events that they describe. The author of a primary source is someone who took part in or who witnessed those events. The journal in which Ibn Battuta describes his travels

---

Guidelines for Evaluating Written Primary Sources

- If the author is known, check his or her background to see whether his or her position in society and political, religious, or cultural beliefs may suggest a particular point of view.
- If the author is unknown, determine when and where the source came from in order to consider who might have written it.
- Read very carefully, especially if the handwriting, spelling, grammar, or vocabulary is unfamiliar.
- Compare the source to other documents from the same period in order to determine reliability. Also consider what other scholars conclude about the source.
- Why and for whom was the document written?
- Why and how was the document preserved?
- Check for serious problems such as factual error, deception, or fabrication.

---

from North Africa to India and China in the fourteenth century is an example of a primary document. Written primary sources record the reaction of someone who lived through a particular event and felt its effects. Be aware, however, that recorded memories can be faulty.

Primary texts can be found in newspaper articles, written interviews, diaries, and letters. Official documents such as speeches, political platforms, statistics, and laws are also primary sources. When studied as evidence from a particular time period in history, literary works such as novels, poems, and stories are primary sources that can be particularly useful for understanding social or cultural history.

If you will be using written primary documents in your research, you need to become aware of their historical and cultural context — that is, the circumstances surrounding an author at the time a particular document was written. For example, to understand an American woman's diary from the nineteenth century, you need to know something about the world in which the writer lived. Was she an urban or a rural resident? How old was she? Was she married, divorced, or single? Was her family rich or poor? What was her religion, her attitude toward the subjects she mentioned in her diary, and so on? Understanding the meaning of her diary entries rests on knowing something about this woman, the society she lived in, and her position in that society.

As explained in Chapter 3, written primary evidence is not always reliable (see pp. 31–32, 33). The views of participants or observers (like the views of any author) may be biased; the writers may have misunderstood what they saw or experienced. Ancient eyewitness testimony may claim that the god of war spread great flames across the valley in what was actually the eruption of a volcano. Primary evidence can also be intentionally deceptive. The edict of a

Chinese emperor may have been intended to hide the truth from his subjects. Of course, a historian may want to study the influence of the emperor's edict even if it was intended to deceive. Primary sources may also be outright fabrications. The Protocols of the Elders of Zion, for example, were fabricated documents created in the early twentieth century to further an anti-Semitic agenda, yet many dubious works of history cite them as real primary sources.

Nonwritten Primary Sources

Nonwritten primary sources — such as physical objects, paintings, photographs, and sound or video recordings — raise additional evaluation issues. For these kinds of primary sources, you need to know something about the technical process by which they were produced as well as the intent of the maker. Changes in the size and weight of cameras and in the time it took to develop a picture in the nineteenth century affected the subject matter of photographs, for example. Nonwritten primary sources require kinds of interpretation that are different from those used to evaluate written sources, whether primary or secondary. Still, for certain topics, nonwritten primary sources may prove central to your argument.

Nonwritten primary sources are quite varied. Physical objects — artifacts — can take many forms. Some, such as clothing, jewelry, furniture, and tools, were made for personal use. Others are art objects such as paintings, drawings, and sculpture. Recorded pictures and sounds (photographs, films, records) constitute one of the major categories of nonwritten primary sources.

Guidelines for Evaluating Nonwritten Primary Sources

- Who created the source? What impact might the creator's political, religious, or cultural beliefs have had on the source?
- What was the creator trying to "say"? All artists, builders, performers, craftspersons, and so on, express something of themselves in their creations.
- When and where was the source created?
- How was the source created? By what technical, artistic, or natural process? (For modern chemical, electronic, or digital sources, it may also be necessary to know how sources were *reproduced*.)
- For what intended audience, if any, was the source created?
- If the source is a consciously artistic creation (whether "pure" or "commercial" art), what is its style, design, school, genre, and so on? What place does it have in the history of the art form?
- What is the source's relevance to your topic? How might it serve (eventually) to support your thesis?

See also the guidelines for "reading" nonwritten sources on page 36 in Chapter 3.

NOTE: Audio and video recordings are most often treated as primary sources in the sense that they convey artistic expressions — as paintings or sculptures do. *Gone with the Wind* is not a serious historical source, but it could be a proper primary source for anyone studying Hollywood films of the 1930s.

Nonwritten sources have to be analyzed for what they "say" even though many of them do not use words. (For more information, see "'Reading' Nonwritten Sources" in Chapter 3, pp. 36–50.) The creator — architect, photographer, potter, designer, composer — and the historical context in which the source was created need to be examined. For example, a jazz recording from the 1920s needs to be understood from a variety of perspectives: Who is playing? How, where, and when was it recorded? How popular was it? What style of jazz is it? How does it compare to other jazz styles in other periods? Any product of art or of popular culture needs to be examined in these kinds of ways.

Special Problems of Evaluating Web-Based Sources

Evaluating Web Sites

Before we discuss the evaluation of material you might access on the Web, some advice is in order about the evaluation of Web sites themselves. Sites recommended by your instructor or accessed from the library home page (as well as those listed in Appendix A) will for the most part contain sources appropriate for serious research. If you come across a site on your own, however, you must use extra caution to determine whether it can be trusted. The following guidelines indicate the major aspects to be examined.

Guidelines for Evaluating Web Sites

- Most sites sponsored by universities, libraries, museums, governmental bodies, and research organizations are reliable ones.
- Reliable sites have serious, documented content and reliable links, and they are regularly updated.
- A site for serious researchers does not have distracting visuals or advertisements. Links to the parts of the site where scholarly material is available should be clearly marked.
- To determine the degree of bias of a site, look for a formal statement by the sponsor. If sources seem one-sided, are not documented, or do not indicate who wrote them and where they originated, do *not* use this information without first checking with your instructor.
- If you decide to reproduce the source for your research, be sure that it is related to your topic and that you have proper documentation for it.

NOTE: Some online reference sources, most notably *Wikipedia,* allow anyone with Internet access to anonymously edit entries. These sites should not be considered authoritative sources for a research paper; in fact, many instructors specifically forbid them. See pages 99–100 for details.

Evaluating Material Found on Web Sites

Certain aspects of evaluating Web sources and printed sources are similar, but some special characteristics of Web documents make their evaluation more difficult. Authors of scholarly books and journal articles have had their work reviewed by editors and by experts in the field. Because of this process, much of what gets into print is of high quality. For the most part, the Web is unedited. *Anyone* can become the author of a Web document. This accessibility is one of the marvels of the Web, but it makes separating serious authors from less informed ones difficult. Nevertheless, if you take care to conduct your Web research in stable, scholarly sites, as explained above, you can minimize the problems noted below.

Before you download or print a possible source from a Web site, find out as much as you can about the author, either from the site itself or by conducting a Web search. If you cannot figure out who wrote the material you are interested in or how it got to the site, you would be wise not to use it.

If you can identify an author of the Web-based material, you then need to ascertain the author's bias. Examine the document and the site at which you found it to determine the author's perspective on your topic. Some sites and the authors whose work they include are as serious as any university publisher or scholarly journal, but many sites are created to disseminate the viewpoint of a particular group. In the latter case, all of the documents on the site as well as those on any linked sites are likely to share a similar perspective, and you will need to be aware of this bias. If you cannot find out much about the author or the origins of a Web document, show the document to your instructor before including it in your research.

You should also be aware of potential problems concerning the accuracy and authenticity of Web-based sources. Sometimes the fact that only part of a document is included on a site is not made clear. If a document has been translated, the translation may not be accurate. If a document is an early version of something that was later revised, you may be missing important changes made by the author. The text of a written document may have been altered. Similarly, a photograph can be altered and sound or video recordings may be edited. Your best assurance of accuracy is to confine your research to sites about whose seriousness you feel confident, and to inform your instructor about any questionable Web-based sources.

If you decide to use a source from the Web that was copied from an original print source, you should attempt to track down the print version, so you can cite it directly in your paper. Sometimes print documents are reformatted to fit the needs of the Web, in which case the "pages" of the electronic version are different from the pages of the original. If you cannot obtain the original

---

Guidelines for Evaluating Material Found on Web Sites

- Try to identify the author of the source. Do a Web search for any author or sponsor name that is on the site or on the source that interests you.
- Look for signs of bias on the site or in the document: dramatic presentation, one-sided arguments, lack of documentation for statements made.
- Check reliable resources such as the online library catalog to see whether there are more recent versions or translations of a source that may be more accurate than the version or translation you found on the Web.
- Try to ascertain whether any nonwritten materials — still photographs, sound recordings, films — that you found on the Web were altered in any way.
- If you cannot determine the seriousness of an author or a site sponsor, or the quality of the documents that interest you, discuss these issues with your instructor.

---

printed source, you should record the page numbers that appear in the Web document, taking care to make that fact clear in any notes you take from the document and in the notes to the document that you create for your paper. The reader must know both that the version of the document you used came from the Web and that the page numbers you cited are not those of the original print version.

Because of the unstable nature of Web-based documents, you must tell the reader what site a document came from (including its URL) and the title of the document. In addition, it is useful to provide (and many instructors require) the date that you accessed the material on the site. (For information on documenting sources from the Web, see pp. 192–93 in Chapter 8.)

INTERPRETING SOURCES
AND TAKING NOTES

As you gather reputable sources that are relevant to your topic, you need to carefully read them and interpret their meaning. When you interpret a source, you make judgments about its content. To make such judgments, you need to understand what you are reading. You also need to have a clear view of your topic so that you can take notes efficiently and effectively. In order to avoid **plagiarism**, your notes need to make clear when the words you are recording are those of your source and when they are your own.

Reading Your Sources

Reading scholarly books, journal articles, and Web documents can present challenges. Until you gain experience in reading serious historical studies, the going is likely to be slow. Some of the vocabulary may be new to you. A work on the French Revolution will contain words such as *Jacobin, Thermidor,* and *Girondin.* A study of the atom bomb will talk about *implosion* and *fission* and places such as Tinian and Eniwetok. If possible, keep a good dictionary (and an encyclopedia) handy. Another challenge is the academic or scholarly style of writing found in specialized works. Ease into your topic by reading the most general works first. Read difficult sentences slowly, and look up any unfamiliar words. As you become familiar with your topic, you will learn the meanings of terms that scholars use, and you will become increasingly comfortable with their style and terminology.

When you move on to more specialized sources, your main task is to understand the points an author is trying to establish. In particular, you need to identify the author's thesis. Good historical writing does more than lay out a series of historical events and then combine them into an understandable story of what occurred. Professional historians want to prove a point — a thesis — to show that a series of historical events means one thing rather than another.

A history of the rise of Adolf Hitler, for example, won't merely tell you that the National Socialist Party (Nazi), which he led, increased the number of its representatives in the German Reichstag (parliament) from twelve to 107 in the election of 1930. It will attempt to describe the conditions that led to such an outcome and to explain the impact of the election on later events. Among the many ways of approaching the subject, the author might discuss unemployment, German nationalism, the cartelization of German industry, the Treaty of Versailles, the growth of the German Communist Party, anti-Semitism, the structure of the German family, the philosophy of Nietzsche, or the insecurity of the lower middle class. The author will emphasize one or more of these subjects and will attempt to show how the emphasized factors offer a better explanation of the subject than the others. The argument for a particular explanation of the rise of Nazism will most likely be the author's thesis. Although almost all historians will agree on the number of National Socialist members of the 1930 Reichstag, each historian will construct the causes and effects of that fact in different ways — often as a result of his or her own philosophy or historical field (see Chapter 1) — and each will argue a somewhat different thesis to explain the outcome.

If you wish to understand a particular author's interpretation of an event, you must know how the author arrived at that interpretation and what significance he or she believes it to have. Only a careful reading of the entire work and close attention to its main arguments can give you such knowledge. Remember, history works are a selection of facts and interpretations constructed to explain a particular writer's understanding of a historical subject.

If your own research relies heavily on a particular book, you will need to know its perspective and its thesis. For more on working with historical sources, see Chapters 3 and 5.

Summarizing and Paraphrasing without Plagiarizing

Most notes that you take on your sources will fall into two categories: **summaries** and **paraphrases**. When you *summarize* information from a source, you are drawing upon ideas that spread across several pages in the source. You are restating these ideas briefly in your own words. When you *paraphrase* information, you are capturing the meaning of just a few sentences from a source. A third form of note taking is direct quotation, which is covered on pages 120–21.

Summarizing Your Sources

When you want to record an author's general arguments and conclusions, you will probably want to write a summary of particular points or even of an entire work. As stated above, a summary is a brief restatement, in your own words, of a point made by an author over the space of several pages.

Suppose an author spends several pages connecting the nineteenth-century decline in Spanish-Mexican trade to Mexican independence from Spain. You may want to summarize the findings simply by noting that the author feels that the diminishing economic tie between colony and mother country was one of the major factors leading to Mexican independence. If you wish to record some of the evidence itself, you may want to paraphrase the author's description of the decline in trade with several sentences of your own that include the main factors of this decline.

Paraphrasing Your Sources

A paraphrase directly reflects the ideas of an author. When you write your paper, you may use paraphrases as long as you footnote them. Even so, paraphrasing must be done carefully. Take care that your paraphrase does not come too close to being a loose quotation. If it does come that close and is not in quotation marks, you are guilty of plagiarism.

Here is a passage from J. Joseph Hutchmaker and Warren I. Sussman, eds., *Wilson's Diplomacy: An International Symposium* (Cambridge, MA: Schenkman, 1973), 13:

ORIGINAL TEXT

Wilson took personal responsibility for the conduct of the important diplomacy of the United States chiefly because he believed that it was wise, right, and necessary for him to do so. Believing as he did that the people had temporarily vested their sovereignty in foreign affairs in him, he could not delegate responsibility in this field to any individual. His scholarly training and self-disciplined habits of work made him so much more efficient than his advisors that he must have thought that the most economical way of doing important diplomatic business was for him to do it himself. Experience in dealing with subordinates who sometimes tried to defeat his purposes also led him to conclude that it was the safest method, for he, and not his subordinates, bore the responsibility to the American people and to history for the consequences of his policies.

Here is an ineffective attempt at paraphrasing, which plagiarizes the original source:

INEFFECTIVE PARAPHRASE (PLAGIARISM)

Wilson took personal responsibility for conducting diplomacy because he believed it was right for him to do so. Believing that the people had vested their sovereignty in foreign affairs in him, he couldn't delegate this responsibility. His scholarly training and self-discipline made him more efficient than his advisors. He thought that the most economical way of doing important business was to do it himself. Experience in dealing with subordinates who sometimes tried to defeat his purposes led him to conclude that it was the safest method because he bore responsibility to the American people for the consequences.

The "paraphrase" is too close to the original. The underlined phrases are almost the same as those of the source. If they were used in a paper without quotation marks, they would constitute plagiarism, even with a footnote or endnote. Rather than recording the main points of the passage, this paragraph repeats much of the text word for word. It is time-consuming to take such lengthy notes, and, more seriously, the unacknowledged use of the author's wording constitutes plagiarism.

Here is an improved version of the paraphrase:

EFFECTIVE PARAPHRASE

Wilson felt personally responsible for major diplomacy because he believed that the voters had entrusted him with such matters. He felt he was more capable than his advisors in this area. He, and not his advisors, was responsible to the people.

This paraphrase is effective because it records only the principal point of the passage — that Wilson decided major foreign policy issues on his own because he felt personally responsible to the people in such matters. It does not copy phrases from the original text. This type of note taking saves time, avoids plagiarism, yet conveys the central idea of the passage. Remember, however, that the effective paraphrase still needs to be footnoted in the research paper, because it incorporates ideas taken from a source.

Paraphrasing that reduces your readings to their essential points and uses your own words is not easy to do at first. But by mastering this technique, you will avoid plagiarism and produce a finished paper that is truly yours.

Quoting without Plagiarizing

As you go through a source, you may find passages that you want to repeat word for word in your own research paper. Although overreliance on **quotations** can be a weakness, if you feel that a quote is necessary to make a very important point, be careful to copy the words exactly *and to enclose them in quotation marks.* If you quote, be sure that the meaning of the words you take from the author will be clear when they appear in your paper. Also be sure that you do not alter the author's point by quoting it out of **context**.

Suppose you wish to use a quotation to demonstrate that Robert E. Lee was an excellent military strategist — a point that is important to your thesis. The quotation "Lee was more admired by the average soldier than any other commanding officer" would not make that point because it refers to Lee's popularity, not his generalship. Moreover, if the next sentence in the text you are quoting from were "However, his strategic decisions were not usually equal to those of Union army commanders," then you would have altered the author's point by ignoring the original context.

Before you use a quotation, make sure you understand the author's meaning. Do not quote more material than is necessary to convey the desired point clearly and accurately. Never quote something in your notes simply because you find it difficult to say in your own words. You will have to express the idea in your own words when you write your paper, and it is best to think about the meaning of your research material now, while you are taking notes.

Suppose the material you wish to quote from a source is itself a quotation from another text. You will need to make that clear in your own notes. If you think you might want to quote this material in your own paper, you should try to locate the original source that the quote comes from and quote that source directly.

Suppose a quotation is very long and some parts of it are not related to your thesis. You may omit portions of the original quote from your notes as long as you indicate the omission with the **ellipsis mark** — three spaced dots (. . .) — in the quoted material. Suppose the quotation is "Feudalism, despite later idealizations of it, was maintained by an oppressive social order." If you decide to omit "despite later idealizations of it," you must use the ellipsis mark and quote the sentence like this: "Feudalism . . . was maintained by an oppressive social order." If the portion you want to omit includes the end of a sentence, insert four dots — three to indicate the omission and the fourth to mark the end of the original sentence — and place the closing quotation mark after the fourth dot.

Never use the ellipsis mark if doing so will change the meaning of the author's words. Suppose the quoted sentence is "Feudalism in its later stages in Moravia was maintained by an oppressive social order." If you shortened it to "Feudalism . . . was maintained by an oppressive social order," the author's meaning would be seriously altered.

Organizing Your Notes

As you approach the end of your research, you will have taken a large number of notes. It is important for you to organize your notes effectively as you create them so that you can find the information you need when you are ready to write your paper. Be sure to give each **note card** or file a subject heading that indicates the aspect of your topic that it will help you to document and the part of your paper that it is most likely to appear in. When you complete your research, you will use these headings to help you place each note with other notes to which it is related.

Taking Notes on Note Cards

A long-established and effective system of note taking uses paper index cards. For an example, see Figure 6.5 (p. 122). For each source you take notes from, you create a series of cards. On the first card, called the **source card**, you record *all* of the information you will need to cite the work if you decide to use it in your paper — such as the author, title, publisher, and place and date of publication for a book. (For information about how to cite a variety of sources, see Chapter 8.) You may also want to include specific information that would help you locate the source again, if necessary, such as the library call number.

Each card in the series contains a quotation, paraphrase, or summary of information from the source that you might use in your paper and, if helpful, any comments of your own about the source. At the top left corner of the second and later cards will be the author's last name, a short version of the full title (which you recorded on the source card), and the page or pages where you found the information. The top right corner will contain a word or phrase — a subject heading — that describes the aspect of your topic to which the information on the card is related. Subject headings will prove crucial when you begin the process of arranging your notes as you prepare to write your paper (see "Organizing Your Evidence with a Writing Outline" in Chapter 7, pp. 131–35). If a source could relate to more than one aspect of your topic, be sure to note this as well.

Taking Notes on a Computer

Computerized note-taking programs allow you to write up digital note "cards" and create a folder for each of your sources. For an example of a digital source

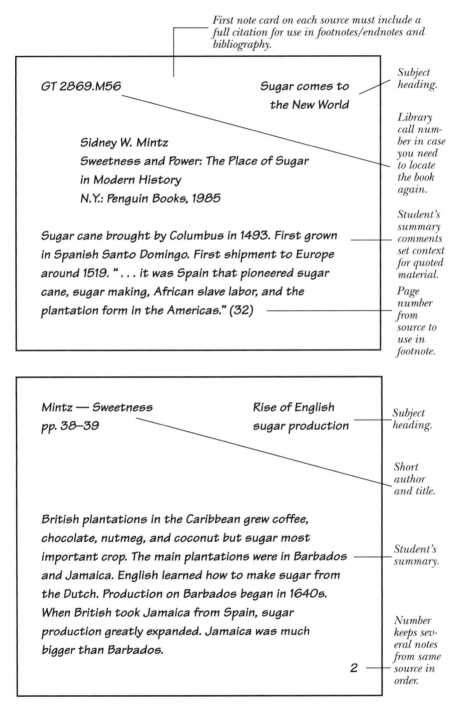

First note card on each source must include a full citation for use in footnotes/endnotes and bibliography.

GT 2869.M56

Sugar comes to
the New World

Subject heading.

Library call number in case you need to locate the book again.

Sidney W. Mintz
Sweetness and Power: The Place of Sugar
in Modern History
N.Y.: Penguin Books, 1985

Sugar cane brought by Columbus in 1493. First grown
in Spanish Santo Domingo. First shipment to Europe
around 1519. " . . . it was Spain that pioneered sugar
cane, sugar making, African slave labor, and the
plantation form in the Americas." (32)

Student's summary comments set context for quoted material.

Page number from source to use in footnote.

Mintz — Sweetness
pp. 38–39

Rise of English
sugar production

Subject heading.

Short author and title.

British plantations in the Caribbean grew coffee,
chocolate, nutmeg, and coconut but sugar most
important crop. The main plantations were in Barbados
and Jamaica. English learned how to make sugar from
the Dutch. Production on Barbados began in 1640s.
When British took Jamaica from Spain, sugar
production greatly expanded. Jamaica was much
bigger than Barbados.

Student's summary.

2

Number keeps several notes from same source in order.

FIGURE 6.5 **Example of Handwritten Note Cards for a Source**

folder, see Figure 6.6 (p. 124). Be sure that each source folder has all the information you will need in order to document the source if you decide to use it in your paper. Each digital note "card" that you file within the source folder should indicate whether the information it records is a quotation, paraphrase, or summary. An example of a digital note "card" appears on page 125 (Figure 6.7). Each note "card" also should have a subject header that describes its content. This is the essential arranging tool that will enable you to organize your notes by content and, eventually, by the part of your thesis to which they relate. If you need to reorganize your notes, the subject headers will make doing so relatively easy.

Be sure to keep all of your digital source folders and the note "cards" filed within them in a labeled folder separate from the folder you will create for the drafting of your paper. Be sure to give these folders different names that cannot be confused with one another so that you do not enter notes or draft text into the wrong folder.

If you copy and paste material from a digital source directly into a note "card" file, be sure to immediately add to the file the full source information of the pasted material. To prevent the possibility that you might later mistake the contents of this file and paste it into a draft of your paper, change the font or color of the pasted text and surround it with quotation marks.

A quick way to obtain text from some digital sources is to e-mail the text to yourself. Do not manually or digitally enter this text into a note "card" file without including the full source information and without placing the text itself within quotation marks. Although it is likely that if you use any of these notes in your paper you will change the quoted material into a paraphrase or summary, the presence of quotation marks will ensure that you never lose track of the fact that the notes contain quoted material. As with all computer files, save your notes regularly and create a backup file.

Figures 6.6 and 6.7 show how you might use a note-taking program to produce both a source "folder" that describes a source and a typical "card" for notes taken from that source.

Photocopying, Downloading, or Printing Sources

Whenever you come across a source that you feel may be very important to your research, photocopying it, downloading it, or printing it may seem preferable to note taking because it will save time. But don't fool yourself. At some point you will have to read and take notes on all those copied, downloaded, or printed pages. Also, don't copy, download, or print anything without reading enough of it to know that it contains material central to your topic. Finally, be sure that you have all of the source information for such documents. You may find it nearly impossible to track down the origin of an unmarked photocopy or downloaded passage of text at a later date.

Part of an advanced note-taking program.

Be sure to use proper note style.

URL & Path / Library Catalog #/ Name of Database / Etc.

Use "Search" and "Sort" to organize.

In advanced programs these would be live links.

TOOLBAR: [..FOLDER NAME..] [..SORT OPTION..] [..SEARCH OPTIONS..]

SOURCE: University of North Carolina, "Documenting the American South," "The Lives and Writings of Antebellum Students at the University of North Carolina," Chapter 6: 1860-69 (Primary Documents). SHORT SOURCE NAME: Letters of UNC students.

WHERE FOUND: http://docsouth.unc.edu/true/ (2/5/2006)

TOPIC: Anti-Secessionist Opinion in the American South, 1860-1861.

RESEARCH QUESTION: (Tentative) To what extent did Southerners oppose secession during this period?

LIST OF SUBJECT HEADERS FOR THIS SOURCE: Student Opinion. Reaction of Secessionists to Unionists. Backgrounds of Unionists.

COMMENTS ON THIS SOURCE:
An archive of letters by UNC students (1795-1869).

LINKS:
a. TO LIST OF CARDS FOR THIS SOURCE
b. TO LIST OF SOURCES
c. TO DRAFT BIBLIOGRAPHY
d. TO DRAFT OUTLINE
e. TO DRAFT FOLDER OF YOUR PAPER.

2/5/06   Date Created

FIGURE 6.6   Example of a Digital Source Folder
This source folder is for a collection of digital documents containing letters by students at the University of North Carolina. Note that these letters are part of a larger collection of documents called "Documenting the American South." The source folder page includes a series of "subject headers," one of which will appear on each digital note "card" so that cards with similar headers can be found through a search.

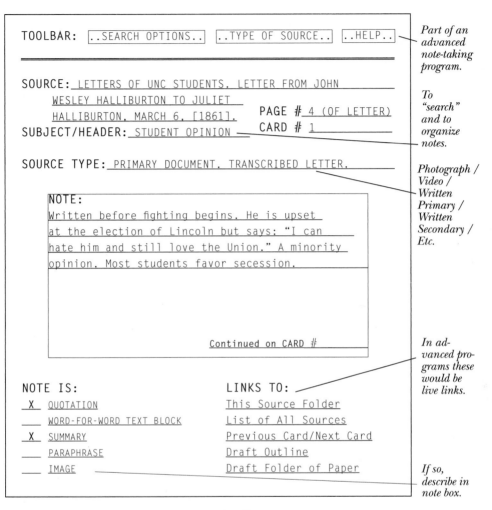

FIGURE 6.7 Example of a Digital Note "Card"
This digital note "card" identifies the source of the note, records the subject
header the note is related to, and indicates the source type. A note from a different letter in the *same* collection would be filed in the same source folder. A note
from a document in another part of the "Documenting the American South"
collection would require a new source folder.

AVOIDING PLAGIARISM

As a beginning researcher, you may be tempted to use the sophisticated language of the trained historians you are reading. In most cases, their expertise enables them to make their points clearly, and it is easy to fall into the dangerous habit of using their words instead of your own. Remember that your instructor is also a historian and can tell the difference between the language of someone who has spent years researching a topic and that of the average history student. Moreover, thinking is learning. If you substitute the simple task of copying the author's words for the more difficult but rewarding one of learning to understand the point she or he is making and then expressing it in your own words, you are doing yourself a disservice. Finally, plagiarism is cheating — a very serious violation of college rules. The penalty can be severe, sometimes leading to expulsion.

When taking notes, never copy an author's words unless you think you might need to quote them in your paper. In that case, be sure to put very clear quotation marks on your note card or digital note file at the beginning and end of each word-for-word passage. In all other instances, paraphrase or summarize the author's ideas and information *in your own words.* Moreover, your own words should not even come close to the words of the author, and all ideas taken from your sources must be documented when you write your paper, even if you are not using direct quotations. You will need to include footnotes or endnotes even for your summaries of an author's ideas in order to tell the reader where the ideas originally came from.

One of the very few times you can use information from a text without documenting it is when you are sure that the information is common knowledge that can be verified in a wide range of sources. Proper names, dates, and other very widely known facts can generally be used without documentation. If a source says, "Isaac Newton is well known as the discoverer of the law of gravitation but he was also a serious student of biblical prophecy," you can mention Newton's scientific work without including the source. However, mention of his surprising interest in biblical prophecy would need to be documented.

Of course, the points that you record from your sources and incorporate in your paper should accurately reflect your sources. However, all of the words in your paper that are not in quotation marks must be your own, and you must document any information that you take from your sources unless it is common knowledge.

Plagiarism and Working Online

The increasing use of computers in note taking and writing intensifies the difficulty of avoiding plagiarism. If you enter your research notes directly into a computer, be sure to put your notes into folders and files that are different from the folders and files that you are using (or will use) for drafts of your paper. Never cut and paste words from a source into any draft of your paper. In your note files, clearly distinguish words that you are quoting from words that you are paraphrasing or summarizing. Always put quotation marks around quoted material and fully document it. Also indicate the source of any paraphrase or summary, because you will have to acknowledge the origin of the ideas when you use them in your paper. When you create your notes, it is also wise to change the color or the font of material taken from your sources. (See "Organizing Your Notes," pp. 121–25.)

Plagiarism can be inadvertant, as described above, or deliberate, as when a student downloads an entire paper from the Web. People trying to make money and students overwhelmed by the task of conducting independent research and writing come together at Web sites where thousands of papers are available. Submitting such work as your own is dishonest and also fool-ish. Software that allows you to search the Internet for papers to plagiarize can also be used by your instructor to search for the source of "your" paper. Don't play this dangerous game. It has serious consequences.

Plagiarism and Group Work

Working with other students can be an enjoyable and rewarding experience. Still, group work can lead to forms of plagiarism different from those arising from individual research. If the work of your team is evaluated as a whole, each member of the group is responsible to see to it that no part of the group's work has been taken improperly from research sources. Do not let the fact that your work is a group product lessen your concern for this vital matter.

Guidelines for Avoiding Plagiarism

- When taking notes from sources, rarely use the exact words of the source. If you do use them, always place the words within quotation marks. It is best to paraphrase or summarize source material. Indicate in your notes whether the words are exact quotations, paraphrases, or summaries.
- If you enter research notes directly into a computer, be sure to put your notes in a folder separate from the folder you are using for draft versions of your paper.
- If you download quoted material from a source directly into your note files, change the color or font of the quotation to avoid confusion with your own words.
- When you paraphrase a source, do not use either the sentence structure or the exact words of the author.
- When writing your paper, be certain to acknowledge your sources and to correctly document paraphrased material as well as direct quotations.

CHAPTER

7

Writing a Research Paper

Here are three requirements to keep in mind as you approach the writing stage of your research project: (1) The **introduction** of your paper should contain a clear statement of your **thesis**. (2) The body of your paper should support your thesis with a series of logically connected, well-documented sections. (3) The **conclusion** of your paper should summarize the principal **arguments** in support of your thesis. Chapter 4 provides basic advice on writing historical essays, from drafting a thesis to creating a writing outline to writing the paper. Here in Chapter 7, we focus on specific requirements of full-length research papers and the challenges they represent.

ASSERTING YOUR THESIS

Chapter 6 explains how to choose and narrow a **topic** and formulate a **research question**. If your question was carefully chosen and if your research to seek an answer to the question was thorough, you now should be ready to state your thesis — a formal answer to your research question. This statement should take the form of an assertion that will be sustained by the **evidence** you present.

NOTE: Before you begin to write, examine your notes closely. If they don't provide enough support for your thesis, more research is necessary. Or if your notes point to a conclusion that is different from your thesis, you need to alter your thesis or come up with a new one.

Why Your Paper Needs a Thesis

Good history research papers always take a stand on an issue. Rather than meandering aimlessly among interesting pieces of information, a college-level research paper makes a serious argument based on evidence. Though not intolerant of other views, the writer makes his or her own point of view quite clear. That point of view, stated at the beginning of the paper, is the thesis.

Writing a paper is like presenting a case to a jury; that is why it is often referred to as "making an argument." You organize your evidence to demonstrate to your reader that your thesis is well documented. Don't claim that your thesis is the *only* correct one; argue that the evidence for it is strong.

The absence of a thesis prevents a paper from being a serious product. For example, having spent many months examining documents on the origins of postwar suburban shopping malls, a historian would not be content to write a paper on "What I learned about shopping malls." Such a paper would be a **summary**, without a point of view. Instead, the historian would organize her research around a serious question such as "What factors influenced the design of postwar shopping malls?" And the weight of her research might lead toward the conclusion that an especially important factor was the design of postwar automobiles — that their size and wide turning radius made necessary the construction of very large parking areas at malls. Her idea about the importance of automobile design is a claim that she will make in the form of a thesis statement: "One of the most significant factors affecting the size of suburban shopping malls was the design of postwar automobiles." The historian gets ready to present her conclusion in a tightly focused paper. Her conclusion could be a serious contribution to the subject, for many researchers had assumed that mall parking lots were large in order to accommodate the large number of people driving to the malls.

What Makes a Thesis Effective

Building your research around a specific question helps keep you focused on the aspect of the topic you wish to study in depth. An effective question is debatable, narrow, significant, and researchable (see Chapter 6, pp. 90–92). Such a question will lead to a thesis statement that takes a stand on a worthwhile issue. In the example that follows, you will see the steps that a student named Sarah takes to formulate an effective thesis for a research paper in her current course in U.S. history.

Like many Americans in December 1941, Sarah finds it difficult to understand the reasons for the Japanese attack on Pearl Harbor. (U.S. congressional committees, by the way, also were puzzled and held lengthy hearings, which Sarah will use as a **primary source**.) Sarah's curiosity about why the attack took place leads her to make the "why" question the topic of her research paper assignment.

Initial research gives Sarah enough familiarity with the **historical context** so that she is able to formulate a possible research question. Using the criteria set forth in Chapter 6, Sarah takes one of the points she is most curious about and poses this question: Since relations between Japan and the United States were clearly heading for a confrontation by 1941, why had Washington done so little to prepare Pearl Harbor for a possible Japanese attack?

Sarah's background research makes it clear that issues surrounding her question have been debated in the scholarly literature — in **secondary sources**. Historians, she discovers, have examined various answers to the question about the inadequacy of Pearl Harbor's defenses. For this reason, Sarah feels confident that her question is serious and is worthy of debate.

Armed with her research question, Sarah conducts further research and finds sources that examine various aspects of U.S.–Japanese relations in the years leading up to the attack. From some of these sources she is surprised to learn that what most concerned U.S. leaders during this period was not Japan but Germany. Quite a few sources, both primary and secondary, emphasize Washington's concern over the military successes of German forces beginning in September 1939. In 1940–1941, the Roosevelt administration was deeply involved in the effort to supply British forces (Britain was one of the few allies of the United States still able to resist the German attack). After examining primary documents concerning U.S. relations with Britain, Sarah feels confident that she can explain why the U.S. government considered Japan less menacing than Germany. She now has an answer to her question, and she states the answer in formal terms: "Concern about a growing threat

---

Guidelines for Developing an Effective Thesis

- Begin with a topic that is appropriate to the assignment, attracts your interest, is of manageable proportions, and is one about which you can find a significant amount of evidence.
- Focus your research on a worthwhile question that is *debatable* (more than one answer is possible), *narrow* (answerable within the scope of the assignment), *significant* (worthy of serious investigation), and *researchable* (enough serious evidence to answer it).
- Choose the answer to your question for which there is the strongest evidence.
- Rephrase this answer as a formal statement of the argument you intend to make in your paper. This formal statement of your argument is your thesis.
- Include a clear statement of your thesis at the beginning of your research paper. (Until you have organized your paper and written a rough draft, your thesis will remain in tentative form.)

from Germany was a major factor in the failure of the United States to adequately prepare Pearl Harbor for a possible Japanese attack." This statement is her thesis. Sarah begins her paper with the following paragraph (the thesis statement has been underlined):

> On December 7, 1941, Japan carried out a devastating surprise attack on the U.S. Naval Base at Pearl Harbor in Hawaii. A large number of U.S. ships were sunk or heavily damaged. This disaster led to a major investigation by the U.S. Congress and has long been a source of debate among historians. While my research examined several possible explanations for the disaster, it eventually led me to the conclusion that <u>failure to adequately defend Pearl Harbor against possible Japanese attack was due principally to intense concern in Washington over the growing threat from Nazi Germany</u>. This paper will present the principal evidence for this thesis.

Sarah's thesis satisfies all of the criteria of an effective thesis. Her original question results from significant research on a topic of interest to her. Further research enables her to answer that question. She states that answer in the form of her thesis at the beginning of her paper.

ORGANIZING YOUR EVIDENCE WITH A WRITING OUTLINE

A mass of facts and opinions concerning a subject does not constitute a historical study. Your main goal in writing a research paper is to arrange the material you have found so that it supports your thesis. If, as you begin to organize your evidence, you find that it doesn't entirely support your thesis, then you need to change your thesis or seek other evidence to support it.

Once you are satisfied that your research has uncovered sufficient evidence for your thesis, you need to present the evidence in a manner that clearly shows that the conclusion you've drawn is a proper one. If you uncover any **counterevidence** — evidence that leads to other conclusions — you have a responsibility to mention it. In doing so, you must explain why the evidence in support of your thesis outweighs the nonsupporting evidence. There are many ways to organize evidence in support of a conclusion. The pages that follow describe some possible approaches.

During the research process, your **research strategy** helped you to decide what sources to seek first and in which order to read them (see "Planning a Research Strategy" in Chapter 6, pp. 92–94). Now that your reading is mostly finished, it is time to prepare a writing outline, to give yourself an overall plan for your paper. Creating this outline helps you decide the order in which to present your evidence and how each section will build toward a conclusion that sustains your thesis. The outline will keep your writing headed in the proper direction.

In the course of your research you compiled a large number of notes or computer files. You created headings that identified similar kinds of evidence. For a relatively simple paper, you might have organized your notes chronologically, or by major characters or events. For a complex topic, such as the impact of the sixteenth-century revolution in print technology, your note categories might reflect the various impacts of the new technology that you examined in your readings — on universities, monasteries, libraries, literacy, bookbinding, and so on.

Here is a description of one way to organize your notes for a paper on the role of Great Britain in the Middle East after World War II. Your research question asks about Britain's motives in giving up its control of Palestine in 1947. Your research leads you to a tentative thesis arguing that *domestic* political and economic factors (rather than international ones) best explain British withdrawal. Your research also leads you to create note categories concerning the post–World War II future of Palestine for Arabs, Jews, and Britain. Within these large categories you create smaller ones: Arab nationalism, Zionism, British colonial policy. Those three topics present natural sections of your writing outline. You also read many sources that deal with the role of the United Nations and the role of the United States. Those two subjects become note categories and also should be sections of your outline. Because your research question asks about Britain's motives, your notes should have a lot of evidence in this area. It makes sense, then, to create an outline section for each of the British motives that you explain.

Of course no two outlines will be alike. Still, there are general frameworks for outlines of similar kinds of topics. If you are making an argument about a person, you might choose a chronological organization. There are many variations of this form. If you build your argument around a significant aspect of someone's life, each heading might describe the influences and events that led up to the point in that person's life that your thesis deals with. For example, an argument about some aspect of George Washington's career might have sections in chronological order, about his work as a surveyor, as an officer in the British army, as commander of the Continental forces fighting for independence from the British, and so on. But even a simple outline like that requires you to do more than narrate a life story. Human beings are one of the most complex elements of history.

Most research papers examine complex topics that cannot be reduced to a timeline. The argument here needs to be made from a variety of angles. An outline with a topical organization — sections drawn from a wide variety of factors — may or may not present its parts in chronological order. Its goal is not to narrate a life or to focus on the "what" of history but to explain the "why" of its topic. To argue that African Americans were ignored by New Deal legislation in the Great Depression of the 1930s, you might create note categories about economic discrimination, physical segregation, southern Democratic

Party politics, as well as the legislation itself. Each of these areas also would deserve its own section of an outline.

Arguments of an even broader kind require outlines of an analytical (that is, explanatory) nature. This kind of outline includes categories of evidence that can account for the ways in which one strand of history becomes entwined around another — as when Arab nationalism, eastern European Zionism, and British imperialism encounter one another in a place called Palestine.

NOTE: Different *kinds* of outlines can be most effective for different *parts* of the same paper. Chronological sections can be followed by analytical ones, and so on.

No particular format for an outline is best. Some students prefer this "down-the-stairs" model, in which each heading is indented more than the one above:

I.
  A.
    1.
      a.
        (1)
          (a)

Such a format is easily expandable. If you think of a new point, you enter a new heading and put it in the proper place. Changing one heading, however, may require changing others. A detailed outline is very difficult to create before you begin to write. (If, however, such an outline is a required stage of a research assignment, follow your instructor's guidance.) What many students need as they begin to write is merely a list of the major sections of the paper and a commonsense order in which to put them. This "list-type" outline is illustrated in Figure 7.1. The best outline is one that gives you enough guidance about organizing the evidence for your thesis yet allows you enough flexibility to change your mind about what should come next. Some writers need write-by-outline assistance; others require only gentle reminders. Choose the format that works best for you. Make sure you have enough evidence to flesh out the elements of your outline. If you discover a mismatch between a part of your outline and the evidence you need for it, alter that section or, if necessary, return to your sources to see if you can find such evidence. Notes and outline are rarely in perfect harmony at the outset, but don't wait until your paper is half written before you realize that an important part lacks the evidence it requires.

You must also make room in your outline for counterevidence — evidence that differs strongly with any argument you intend to make. Counterevidence should not be ignored. Rather than claiming that your views are the *only* valid ones, tell your reader about the counterevidence and explain why you have confidence in your thesis.

To summarize, a writing outline helps you organize your evidence and determine the order in which you will write about it. Note that the process of

<u>Tentative Thesis:</u> In the early years of the English colony in Virginia (1607–1665), Africans living there were not slaves. They were enslaved (only) when control over their labor was needed due to the growth of tobacco plantations. English racism was not the reason.

Will be put in final form when paper is written.

<u>Context:</u> (1530–1630) Idea of rights in England; treatment of Irish; treatment of Native Americans; view of Africans; religious justifications; English colonies in the Caribbean.

Background reading by student; will become introductory section of paper.

<u>Evidence:</u>

The evidence the student will use to support the thesis. Also, the tentative order in which it will appear.

1. No slavery in England.

2. No slavery in English colonies in the Caribbean until rise of plantations.

3. In Virginia laborers were not slaves but indentured servants.
    3a. Blacks and whites treated the same
    3b. Some evidence of friendships of blacks and whites

4. Evidence of black landowners.
    4a. Anthony Johnson
    4b. Others

5. Rise of large tobacco plantations.
    5a. White indentured servants less available as laborers
    5b. Whites want to be landowners

6. Need for a dependable labor force.
    6a. Reasons why Native Americans were not enslaved
    6b. Reasons why Africans begin to be enslaved

7. First slave laws in the colony.

<u>Counterevidence:</u>
1. English were early participants in slave trade.
2. English believe in social hierarchy; treatment of Irish.
3. Harsher penalties for black servants? (weak evidence)
4. English had a negative view of nonwhite peoples.

Ideas encountered by the student that challenge his thesis. He must be sure to address these.

<u>Conclusion:</u> Absence of slave laws; evidence of black landowners; changes in colony's economy and in its sources of labor.

Summary of the main evidence in support of thesis; still in rough form.

FIGURE 7.1   List-type Outline

creating an outline works two ways: while your outline helps bring order to your evidence, that evidence helps brings order to your outline. In either case, your goal is to organize your evidence in the way that best supports your thesis.

WRITING THE TEXT

As you prepare your paper, you may find it helpful to review the section "Drafting Your Essay" in Chapter 4 (pp. 55–60). Also, keep the following basic points in mind: Don't let parts of your paper drift away from your topic. Stick to your outline and stay focused on the central arguments that support your thesis. Be sure that you can provide evidence for the points you are making.

The Rough Draft

Your **rough draft** will change, perhaps several times, so don't worry too much about the exact wording when you begin to write it. Your thesis statement, too, will change. Many a thesis needs fine-tuning before a rough draft is finished. Nevertheless, even at this early stage, you need a direction for your writing, and that direction should be indicated in your writing outline. The introduction should help set the direction for your writing as well. Your introductory paragraphs will state your thesis and any historical context that might be of interest to your reader.

Suppose the rough draft you are writing is about the independence of Texas and your research question is "What was the role of Sam Houston in Texas independence?" You will of course need to focus tightly on Houston's role. If your thesis is that Houston's actions were vital to the success of Texas independence, you need to state this in your introduction. Of course, other people will appear in your paper (the Mexican general Antonio López de Santa Anna, for example), but a clear focus on Houston and his leadership role in your introduction will keep you from writing a long section on Santa Anna or saying too much about the defense of the Alamo (Houston was not there). As your writing proceeds, always use the test of relevance to the thesis so that you maintain the direction set out in your introduction.

Writing the central sections of your draft raises the practical question of how long each section should be. There is no correct length, of course, but each section should be long enough to present the evidence for one aspect of your thesis. Don't, however, feel obliged to include *all* of your evidence surrounding each claim. When you have made the case you intended to make, stop. Then begin the next section. Be sure to write a **linking sentence** — either at the end of one section or at the beginning of the next — that introduces the next claim you intend to make. Repeat the process in the next section of your paper, and in the next, until you reach your conclusion.

Keep the overall length of the paper in mind as well. If your paper is limited to twenty-five pages and your outline has seven main points, don't start out with ten pages of evidence on the first point. Of course, sections may be of unequal length; some claims are more important than others, and some evidence takes more space to document. Here is a very general guide: For a paper of about twenty-five pages, it is best to have no more than six to eight sections. You will need about two or three pages in each section to properly lay out your argument. You also need to leave about one page at the beginning for your introduction and another at the end for your conclusion. **Notes** and **bibliography** are not usually counted as part of page length, but it is best to clarify this point with your instructor.

The last section of your paper is, of course, the conclusion. Any fine-tuning of your thesis or **revising** of the central sections will necessitate fresh thinking about your conclusion. Keep in mind that the purpose of your conclusion is to summarize the arguments you have made concerning your thesis. In the paper about Sam Houston's leadership, for example, you would briefly refer to the evidence (both supporting and countering your thesis) about his leadership and explain why you concluded that it was vital to Texas independence.

Clear Writing: A Matter of Continuity

To achieve **continuity** in your paper, follow your outline and keep in mind the arguments you wish to make and the evidence you wish to include. Suppose your thesis is that "German aid to the forces of General Franco in the Spanish civil war was essential to victory over the Spanish republic." Your first section might focus on the reasons for German support. Here, you would explain in some detail Hitler's strategic and economic considerations as well as ideological and diplomatic factors, and you would conclude by relating these reasons to the evidence of later sections, such as the actual aid given and its effect on the course of the war. Your principal concerns as you construct each section of your paper should be: Does this argument follow logically from the one preceding it? Does it adequately support and develop the thesis? Does it establish the necessary background for the argument that follows?

As each section mirrors the overall structure of the paper by containing an introduction, a main body, and a transition to the next section, so each paragraph within a section contains a similar structure. A well-constructed paragraph begins with a sentence that introduces the evidence to be presented and concludes with a sentence that leads logically to the next paragraph. If each paragraph is developed in this way, and if sentences making clear the relationship between paragraphs appear where they are needed, then the paper as a whole becomes a tightly knit series of related statements. The key to tight construction is for each sentence to (1) be related to the one preceding it, and (2) advance the development of the thesis to which it is related. The closer you can come to this kind of organization, the better your paper will be.

What is the best way to ensure that there are no gaps in logic between your sentences? As you construct each paragraph, take into account the knowledge of the average person likely to read your paper. Very often, a set of sentences that seems clear to you because of your familiarity with your topic will raise questions in the mind of your reader, who probably is not familiar with your thesis and is entirely dependent on the words you write. If those words do not make your point clearly, you must revise until they do. Refer to Chapter 4 for detailed help on clear writing.

Quotations: When and How to Use Them

Paraphrasing and summarizing are usually the preferred methods of integrating information from your sources (see "Summarizing and Paraphrasing without Plagiarizing" in Chapter 6, pp. 118–20). However, there are instances in which a **quotation** will best serve the purpose of supporting your thesis. Here are some ground rules that will help you determine when to quote:

When to Quote Sources Directly

Three general rules are: (1) Don't quote too often. (2) Don't quote too much from any one source. (3) Use your own words unless there is a good reason for quoting those of your source. When is it appropriate to quote a source directly? There are really only a few special instances that call for direct quotation:

- *When a particularly authoritative source says something particularly important.* If an important figure in your research makes an important and relevant comment, it may make sense to quote his or her exact words:

  It is significant that a scholar as important as Professor Smith told the conference, "After my second trip to the site, I became convinced that Professor Rodriguez's claim of its pre-Roman origins was correct."[1]

- *When an author uses especially striking language that may be lost in a paraphrase.* If an author uses vivid language that you would have difficulty putting into your own words, a quotation may make sense:

  In an unusually strong remark, the leader of the sugar worker's union, his head still in bandages, referred to the president as "a wriggling insect."[2]

- *When an author makes a controversial claim.* If you want to make it perfectly clear to the reader that a controversial statement is that of your source, and is not a misinterpretation on your part, you may wish to use a quotation:

  Despite the French bishop's vigorous campaign to root out heresy, Professor Georgevsky insisted that "Jews fleeing Spain were actually welcomed."[3]

In those instances, direct quotation may be useful. When you quote, be sure to include enough of the original statement to make its meaning clear, but don't make a quote any longer than is necessary.

Finally, be sure that quotations actually support the point you intend to make. Suppose your thesis is that early European settlers in the Americas got along with the Native Americans. Notice that the first quotation below does *not* support the point but the second quotation does:

IMPROPER QUOTATION

The early settlers were not hostile to the Native Americans. As pointed out by the *Claxton Banner* in 1836: "Our Sioux neighbors are peaceable but only when they are penned up in closely guarded reservations."[1]

PROPER QUOTATION

The early settlers were not hostile to the Native Americans. As pointed out by the *Claxton Banner* in 1836: "We have always respected our Sioux neighbors. There has never been warfare between us."[2]

How to Format Quotations

Introduce every quotation by clearly identifying the speaker. The reader will always want to know who is speaking and in what **context**. Don't write: "The strikers were 'a dangerous mob.'" Instead, tell the reader whose words you are repeating: "According to D. H. Dyson, the plant manager, the strikers were 'a dangerous mob.'"

If you do not wish to quote a whole statement, be sure to insert an **ellipsis mark** — three spaced dots (. . .) — wherever words were omitted. You must always let your reader know when you leave out part of a quotation. Compare the two "short quotation" examples below. Of course, never omit part of a quotation if doing so would change its meaning. (See Chapter 6, "Quoting without Plagiarizing," pp. 120–21.)

If a quotation is brief, taking up no more than two or three lines in your paper, then it should appear within a paragraph of your text and be enclosed in quotation marks:

SHORT QUOTATION

The early settlers were not hostile to the Native Americans. As pointed out by the *Claxton Banner* in 1836: "Our Sioux neighbors, despite their fierce reputation, are a friendly and peaceable people."[3]

SHORT QUOTATION WITH ELLIPSIS MARK

As pointed out by the *Claxton Banner* in 1836: "Our Sioux neighbors . . . are a friendly and peaceable people."[4]

If your quotation will take up more than two or three lines in your paper, it should be set off from the sentences that precede and follow it. It should be indented ten spaces from the left margin and be single-spaced. Do not put quotation marks around a long, displayed quotation, even though you are quoting. Indenting identifies the words as a quotation, as in this example:

LONG QUOTATION

The early settlers were not hostile to the Native Americans. As pointed out by the *Claxton Banner* in 1836:

> Our Sioux neighbors, despite their fierce reputation, are a friendly and peaceable people. No livestock have been disturbed, and the outermost cabins are unmolested. We trust in God that our two peoples may live in harmony in this territory.[5]

Finally, remember that the source of every quotation must be cited in a note (either a footnote or endnote) and in your bibliography (see Chapter 8).

Incorporating Visual Materials into Your Paper

Ask your instructor about the usefulness of visual material. Be sure to find out if the space taken up by visuals will be counted as part of the assigned length of the paper or if it will be an addition to this limit. Also ask your instructor about the quantity that is appropriate; you do not want to pad your paper with too many visuals.

If visuals are acceptable, try to find ways to include them. Illustrating important points with maps, charts, tables, drawings, and photographs can strengthen your argument. Some points — the way something looks, a very important comparison between numbers (as in a chart) — can best be made by *showing* your reader a visual of it. Be sure that any visual you use will reproduce clearly.

You can place each visual on or near the page containing the text it illustrates, or you can group all visuals together at the end of the paper in an **appendix**. If you use an appendix, you need to place a note in the text that directs your reader to the page where the corresponding image is located — for example, "See Figure 3.2 on page 14." If your visuals are within the body of the paper, make sure that they are cleanly separated (perhaps by a top and bottom line) from the surrounding text. Even more important, be sure they are formatted so that they end up where you expect them when your paper is printed out.

Each visual, regardless of its position (within the text or in an appendix), should have a title above or below it that tells readers what it refers to. And, at the bottom of each visual, except for visuals that you created, be sure to provide a source note indicating where you found the map, chart, table, drawing, or photo. Doing this is as necessary as using notes and a bibliography to document printed sources.

For a thesis arguing the importance of Sam Houston's leadership to the success of Texas independence, a variety of visuals might be relevant. You could use a map showing his army's successful, strategic retreat before a large Mexican army in 1836. You could create a bar graph comparing the size of the two armies. (The Texans were often heavily outnumbered.) Or you could

---

Guidelines for Incorporating Visuals

- Look for visual materials on your topic when you do your research. They can strengthen your argument.
- Be sure that the visual actually is what you say it is and means what you say it means. You can misinterpret a visual just as you can misinterpret a printed source.
- Learn about your word processing program's ability to download, store, and insert visuals into your paper.
- Do not pad your paper with visuals.
- Format your visuals correctly by clearly separating them from the surrounding text. Identify them correctly, and make sure that in the final draft of your paper the visual appears where you want it to.
- In addition to a proper identification of a visual on the page where it appears, you need to document its source as you would any other source. You need to tell the reader where the visual came from.

---

use a dramatic painting of Houston at the Battle of San Jacinto, where a Texas army under his command defeated a much larger Mexican army. Indeed, Houston's forces captured the Mexican commander, López de Santa Anna, who was also the president of Mexico, and in doing so gained independence for Texas. Each visual would illustrate some aspect of Houston's leadership — that is, each would support the thesis that his leadership was important to achieving Texas independence.

Be sure that each visual is accurate and that it really does illustrate and support your thesis. Your map of the retreat of Houston's army must get the place-names and the movement of the armies correct. Your graph must be calibrated accurately. The painting of Houston at San Jacinto needs to be consistent with claims in your paper that Houston's generalship at the battle was excellent. A visual may seem "real" simply because it looks real. However, don't treat visuals as facts. Examine them as carefully as you would examine any other source used in your paper. (See pp. 36–50 in Chapter 3 and pp. 113–14 in Chapter 6 for advice on evaluating nonwritten sources.) For example, the painting may show Houston in the midst of the battle when, in fact, he was well behind the lines.

Again, be sure to document any visuals. (See model notes and bibliography entries for multimedia sources on pp. 192–96 in Chapter 8. Also see the documentation for the sample research paper on pp. 166–72 of this chapter.)

When to Use Footnotes and Endnotes

If you quote from, paraphrase, or closely summarize your research sources, you must include a **citation** telling your reader where the original information can be found. In this way, the reader can check the accuracy of your quotes and statements, judge the **bias** and credibility of your sources, or carry out research of his or her own.

Footnotes (which appear at the bottom of the page) or endnotes (which appear in a list at the end of the paper) are the preferred method that historians use to document their research. Footnotes and endnotes have the same format and provide the same information; they differ only in their placement. If your instructor has no preference, you can choose to put your **documentation** in either place, but you must be consistent throughout the paper. The following discussion uses the word *notes* to refer to both footnotes and endnotes. (For details on formatting notes, see Chapter 8, pp. 173–74. For a sample endnote page, see p. 166 of this chapter.)

The question that troubles students the most is: Which of the statements that I make in my paper needs documentation? There are only a few hard-and-fast rules to guide you. However, five types of statements must be accompanied by notes:

- Direct quotations
- Paraphrases
- Controversial facts or opinions
- Summaries of important points from your sources
- Statistics

NOTE: On occasion, you may want to use notes to make brief comments that qualify or supplement statements in your paper. These are called "explanatory" notes.

To review summarizing, paraphrasing, and quoting, see pages 118–21 in Chapter 6.

What is meant by "controversial facts or opinions"? Facts or opinions about which your sources disagree are considered to be controversial. So are facts or opinions that will surprise your readers. Suppose, in a paper on "the treatment of slaves on Mississippi plantations," you write that some slave owners were kind to their slaves. This statement may surprise some readers and thus must be documented. Suppose, while researching the topic "European discoverers of America," you find that all your sources agree that Vikings visited the New World long before Columbus. If you suspect that most of your readers believe that Columbus was the first European to see the New World, then you must include a note identifying the source of your information.

The number of notes to use is another thorny problem. If your paper goes on for several pages without any notes, you are not documenting as much as you should. If you are writing five or more notes per page, you may be overdoing it.

Here is a final point about using notes. Citing a source with a note does not give you permission to plagiarize. If the words in your paper are the same, *or very nearly the same,* as the words in your source, you have committed **plagiarism** even if you include a note. (For more on plagiarism, see Chapter 6, pp. 126–27.) You should not use sentences or even phrases from your sources unless you put them in quotation marks.

REVISING AND REWRITING

Leave time in your writing schedule for revising your paper. Before writing your final draft, put the paper aside for a day or two (another reason to allow extra time) and then reread it. This way, you will gain a fresh perspective and you may spot weaknesses that you hadn't noticed before.

A rough draft always needs smoothing out. As you reread your paper, check for continuity. Look for any places where it seems to wander away from a direct focus on the thesis. Be certain that the thesis is stated clearly at the outset and that each part of the paper contains information that supports the thesis. Does each part of the paper seem clearly connected to the part that follows it? Be sure that documentation appears wherever it is needed.

NOTE: When making large-scale revisions to your rough draft, it is usually best to work from a printout of your paper first and then transfer your changes to the computer file. In the screen-by-screen environment of the computer you may lose the larger context of your writing.

While you examine the overall structure of the paper for defects, you also need to look closely at the language itself. If you repeated yourself, eliminate the repetition. If you included material that is unrelated to your thesis, discard it. Check the connections between paragraphs to see whether the reader will be able to follow your argument. Make sure that you have accomplished what you set out to do in your introduction, that you have sufficiently supported your thesis, and that your conclusion makes it clear that you have done so. Check the notes and bibliography entries for proper style and accuracy.

Finally, examine your writing for errors in spelling and grammar. **Proofread** carefully and slowly. At normal reading speed your eyes can go right by major errors. You are so familiar with your paper that you may not see what is on the page. Reading your paper aloud will help you catch unclear phrases. (For more revising and editing advice, see Chapter 4, pp. 60–61, and the guidelines on p. 143 of this chapter.)

NOTE: Spell-checkers and grammar-checkers are *not* replacements for word-by-word proofreading. They catch only those spelling errors that are not actual words. Grammar-checkers balk at some words or phrases that may be fine. Only you know what you meant to say. Use the computer's tools, but also print out and carefully read each page for yourself.

Guidelines for Revising and Rewriting

- Revising a rough draft takes time. Be sure to include that time in your writing schedule.
- Wait a day or two after completing the rough draft to prepare the final draft. This will help you to look at your rough draft with a fresh perspective.
- Examine the overall structure of the rough draft. Is it clearly focused on your intended thesis?
- Be sure that the introduction states your thesis and that the major arguments behind your thesis are supported in the body of your paper.
- Check to see if the parts of the paper follow one another in a clear and direct way.
- Rewrite or eliminate any points that are weak, are repetitive, seem out of order, or are unrelated to your thesis.
- Examine the placement, form, and accuracy of the notes. Check the bibliography for form and accuracy as well.
- Proofread your paper carefully, looking for errors of grammar and spelling. Check the format of the paper, looking at margins, spacing, and the insertion of any visual material.

Sometimes **peer reviewing**, or reading a draft of another student's paper, is part of the work for the course. If your instructor gives specific guidelines for this assignment, follow them. (You may also find it helpful to refer to the peer-reviewing guidelines on p. 22 in Chapter 2.)

EXAMPLE OF A RESEARCH PAPER

As a final aid in preparing your research paper, this chapter ends with a full-scale example. The examination of the research paper begins with a discussion of how the topic, research question, and thesis were chosen and then moves on to the writing outline that the student developed. Finally, there is the paper itself, including endnotes and a bibliography, all of which follow the rules and suggestions made earlier in this chapter.

This sample research paper can help you in two important ways. First, reading the sample paper as a whole *before* you write your own will give you a clear sense of what your paper should look like, how it should be developed, and what kind of documentation it should have. Second, referring to the sample paper *while* you are writing your own will help you to answer specific questions about issues such as the introduction, continuity between paragraphs, paraphrases and quotations, the format of notes and bibliography entries, and the conclusion.

Annotations in the margin of the sample paper help you to see what the writer is trying to accomplish. Also in the margin are a series of explanatory phrases that identify stages in the unfolding story and are related to specific sections of the writing outline. Finally, a numbered comment in the margin of each endnote tells you what point in the paper is being supported. As you read the sample paper, ask yourself what point the author is making and whether she is accomplishing her goal. Pay special attention to the way in which the parts are put together and how each section advances the effort to describe and support the thesis. Read the endnotes to determine why a citation is full or shortened and to see the format used for citations. Notice also the format of the bibliography. If anything is unclear, review the discussions of writing in Chapter 4 and the "Writing the Text" section of this chapter (pp. 135–42).

How the Thesis Was Developed

The topic of this paper would fit a variety of courses: pre–Civil War U.S. history, American labor history, women's history, and the history of industrialization, among others. Within the framework of one such course, the student became curious about the lives of workers in the earliest factories. Her curiosity led to a narrower topic about industrialization in New England, where the student had grown up. Preliminary research indicated that textiles were the first goods to be made in factories, so the topic was narrowed further to workers in that industry. When the student discovered that many of the earliest workers were young women who were the same age as she was, she decided to look at their lives in particular. At this point, her broad topic, "early industrialization in New England," had been narrowed to "women workers in early industrialization in New England." The largest number of these women worked in mills in Lowell, Massachusetts, so that town was chosen. (The student's research also made it clear that there were numerous sources that discussed Lowell mill workers.) The time period to be covered was the one during which women workers were the principal workforce in Lowell. Finally, the student formulated a preliminary research question: How did American women respond to their experience with industrial labor in the early nineteenth century?

All of this background research and the eventual research question led the student to her thesis: Women workers in Lowell, though working under difficult material conditions, were able to put up with the rigors of factory work while at the same time gaining a new sense of independence in their lives. Finally, the student chose a title that introduced the reader both to her general topic, "women workers in the Lowell, Massachusetts, textile mills, 1820–1850," and to the question she intended to answer. (See the sections on coming up with a topic, a research question, and a thesis for your paper in Chapter 6, pp. 89–92.)

The Writing Outline for the Paper

During the research phase, the student uncovered several sources that gave detailed accounts of the experiences of the women workers, showing both positive and negative aspects of their working lives. It became clear that the trade-offs between hard work and independence should have an important place in the paper. Sections 4, 5, and 6 of the outline focus on this subject. Section 4 talks about work life in general, section 5 social life, and section 6 the independent attitudes that women began to embrace as a result of their new work experiences. Having decided on the importance of the work experience, the student found it necessary to give the reader an understanding of how these women came to be mill workers in the first place. Section 3 examines this subject. Showing how the women came to be mill workers required an explanation of where the mills themselves came from. This was necessary because the mills represent the first stage of industrialization in America. Sections 1 and 2 deal with industrialization. Section 7 covers the end of the period during which women workers predominated in textile work. The other two sections, of course, are the introduction and conclusion.

The subheadings within each section are divisions of the larger subject and indicate the order in which a section will be developed. For example, section 4, "Life on their own in a mill town," examines, in order, adjusting to life in a mill town, a typical workday, the work itself, and the pay received. Look at each part of the outline to see the function it serves and how the whole of the outline fully covers the important parts of the thesis. Try to be sure that your own outline sets the stage for writing your paper the way this one does.

SAMPLE WRITING OUTLINE

Wage Slavery or True Independence:
Women Workers in the Lowell, Massachusetts,
Textile Mills, 1820–1850

Introduction (thesis statement): Women were not merely exploited laborers, but were active participants in broadening their own lives.

1. Background on industrialization
   a. Early industrialization in England
   b. Attitudes toward industrialization in the United States

2. The origins of the textile industry in eastern Massachusetts
   a. The preindustrial economy in America
   b. Slater-type mills
   c. Plans for a textile mill in Lowell, Massachusetts
   d. The choice of a female workforce

3. Recruiting women workers
   a. The prejudice against women working outside the home
   b. Building a "moral" community

4. Life on their own in a mill town
   a. Adjusting to life in the mills
   b. Typical workday
   c. Nature of work
   d. Rate of pay

5. Social life
   a. Leisure hours
   b. Female companionship

6. Independent attitude gained from mill experience
   a. The *Lowell Offering*
   b. "Turn outs"
   c. Critics of female labor
   d. Saw themselves as "Daughters of Free Men"

7. Recession and declining conditions of work in the Lowell mills
   a. Many women left by choice
   b. End of paternalism
   c. The coming of the Irish workers

Conclusion: Young women experienced independence in early industrialization.

Formatting a Research Paper

The student research paper that follows illustrates generally accepted standards for formatting. Unless your instructor requires a special format, follow these guidelines:

- Use one-inch margins on all four sides of each page.
- Include a title page (which is *not* numbered) with your name, the course name and number, the name of your instructor, the date of your paper, and the title of your paper.
- Double-space the body of the paper.
- Single-space long (indented) quotations.
- Single-space footnotes or endnotes, but double-space between notes.
- Single-space bibliography entries, but double-space between entries.
- Consecutively number all pages following the title page — including pages with illustrations, maps, graphs, and anything else.
- If you include visuals, mention them by number in your text — for example, "See Figure 6." Immediately below each visual, place the number, a brief description, and the source.

Sample Student Research Paper

The following sample paper is documented according to the *Chicago Manual of Style* documentation system, which is explained in Chapter 8, "Documenting Your Paper."

Wage Slavery or True Independence:

Women Workers in the Lowell, Massachusetts,

Textile Mills, 1820–1850

Unless your instructor specifies a format, your title page should resemble this one. Whatever layout you choose, be sure to include paper title, course name and number (and section, if necessary), instructor name, your name, and the date.

American History 200

Section 4

Professor Kumar

Julianna Mathes

May 2, 2009

1

Introduction.

This paper will examine the development of the textile industry in Lowell, Massachusetts, and the young women who served as its principal workforce between 1820 and 1850. It will describe how these women came to accept what was for them an unusual and difficult form of labor, but it will argue that they shaped this experience to serve their own purposes. Such a story helps to explain much about early industrialization in America and particularly about the role of women in

Statement of thesis.

the early factory system. The paper argues that these women workers were not mere laborers exploited by the mill owners but were actively engaged in expanding the constricted opportunities for women.

Background information.

In the early part of the nineteenth century, while the vast majority of Americans were living on family farms, the industrial revolution was beginning to spread across England. One of the most rapid and noticeable changes in British manufacturing was the making of cloth. As late as the 1760s, English textile merchants were still making cloth by the age-old "putting out" system. They bought raw wool and hired women to spin it at home. When the wool had been spun into yarn, the merchant then sent it to weavers who also worked in their homes. In that decade, however, new machinery (the carding cylinder, spinning jenny, and, most important, the water frame) was developed that made possible the shift of spinning and weaving from homes to what were called "factories." By 1800, many such factories had been established in England, usually employing children to do most of the work. Many of these children were orphans or "paupers" from families so poor that they could not even afford to feed them. Conditions in these factories were very bad, and stories of these dark and dangerous

Superscript numbers refer to endnotes.

mills (some accurate, some exaggerated) filtered back to America.[1]

Rural Americans felt certain that the dark and dreary factory towns now dotting the English countryside should not arise in America. Political leaders Thomas Jefferson and James Madison both warned that large-scale manufacturing would lead to a class of propertyless wage

2

earners and would threaten the survival of republican government.
New Englanders watched the rise of industrialization in England with
special concern. In New England, which had been at the forefront of
the struggle against British rule, people were especially proud of their
independence and suspicious of anything that seemed to copy the ways
of the English. How could New England's men, let alone its women, be
expected to work in factories?[2]

Attitudes toward industrialization in the United States.

The reservations about factory labor persisted through the War of
1812, as Americans had little need for large factories to produce items
like textiles. While great changes in the production of textiles were
taking place in England, most New Englanders still spun yarn at home
and some also wove their own cloth. In most cases they were simply
making clothes for their families. Much of this work was done by women.
A spinning wheel was a possession of almost every household.[3] Despite
their anti-industrial prejudice, however, New England farmers witnessed,
in the first two decades of the nineteenth century, a slow shift in the
way cloth was made in America. Farm families began to adapt the old
English system of "putting out" — weaving prespun yarn at home for
sale in the market. Historian Thomas Dublin notes that young girls could
keep up with their duties such as watching over younger siblings,
preparing food, and cleaning house in addition to weaving yarn, and
thus "fit the demands of such work into the rhythms of their daily
lives."[4] Even though the girls were staying at home to perform this
work, known as "outwork," they were beginning to develop industrial-
type skills, and home production of textiles would gradually be replaced
by factory production.

The origins of the textile industry in eastern Massachusetts.

Samuel Slater and Francis Cabot Lowell, two leading New England
merchants, were impressed by the mechanization of English textile
production and began to think about an American textile industry. Men
like these noted the massive increase in productivity in the English
textile industry. At first, Slater, and others who followed his lead, built

small mills in rural villages and employed not children as in England but whole families. The building of Slater-type mills did not directly challenge the New England way of living. Most villages already contained small mills run by water power (streams pushing paddle wheels) that ground corn or wheat. Since the textile mills hired whole families who already lived in the villages, family and village life was not greatly altered. Early mills therefore did not really challenge the traditional division of labor in homes any more than outwork did.[5]

Transition sentence introduces discussion of new type of mill.

One new development in textile production, however, did raise troublesome questions about the impact of industrialization on America's rural way of life. This change came from a new type of mill. The first of its type was built in Waltham, Massachusetts, in 1813 by Francis Lowell and a small group of wealthy Boston merchants.[6] Three years earlier, Lowell had returned from a long trip to England. The British government would not allow the plans for the new power looms to be taken out of the country, but Lowell had paid close attention to their construction on his many tours of English mills and returned to America with enough knowledge in his head to eventually reproduce a machine comparable to the English power loom.[7]

In Waltham, Francis Lowell built a large mill that carried out both the spinning and the weaving processes. In fact, every step of the production process was done in a series of connected steps. Waltham was not a village with a textile mill in it; it was a "mill town" in which the factory dominated the economic life of a rapidly growing city. Most significantly, Lowell's system of production brought important changes in the lives of his workers. He hired them as individuals, not as families, and many came from great distances to live and work in the new mill town. When Lowell died in 1817, the small group of Boston businessmen who had invested in his mill at Waltham spread the new factory system to other places. Their biggest investment was in the small village of East Chelmsford about twenty-seven miles from Boston and lying along

4

the swift-flowing Concord and Merrimack Rivers. There they built what
was soon the biggest mill town in the nation, with more than a dozen
large integrated mills based upon mechanical looms. In honor of their
friend, they called the new town Lowell. (See Figure 1, a map of Lowell
in 1845.)[8]

The growth of Lowell between 1821 and 1840 was unprecedented.[9]
A rapidly developing textile industry like the one at Lowell needed
larger and larger numbers of people to work the mechanical looms and
other machines in the factories. Given the prejudice against factory
work in New England, how could large numbers of natives be drawn to
work in the mills? Could they draw upon female labor for their factories?
If so, would they pay them cash wages, or would they try to bring them
to Lowell as "servants"? These questions were carefully pondered by the
wealthy men who built the big textile mills at Lowell, Massachusetts.

The mill owners, aware of the negative view of English mill towns, *Recruiting women*
workers.
decided to confront the problem by creating a *planned* community where
workers would live in solid, clean housing rather than slums. Their
source of workers would also be different. The rapidly running rivers that
ran their mills were not near the major coastal cities. No large pool of
potential laborers lived near their new town. The mill owners had to
find a large group of people whose labor was not absolutely necessary
to the farm economy. The solution to their labor problem came in the
form of hundreds (later thousands) of young women who lived on the
farms of the region.[10]

Several developments in the social and economic history of New
England tended to make this group of workers available. Population
growth was making it more and more difficult for farmers to find land
close by for their sons (and their sons' families). Generations of the
same family had hoped to live near one another. By the 1820s, however, *Problems of the*
farm community.
many farms in New England, especially those on the less productive
land of Maine and New Hampshire, had run out of good land and had to

5

*Visual documen-
tation of location
of mills and
boarding houses.*

Figure 1.   Adapted from Map of Lowell, Massachusetts,
ca. 1845.
Source: *Lowell Historical Society.*

6

find sources of income outside of agriculture. While some farmers went west to find more fertile land and a less harsh climate, others sent their sons to work on neighboring farms, or as apprentices to craftsmen (shoemakers, blacksmiths, or leather workers). Extra cash was something that most farm families were in great need of, and outwork no longer provided enough.[11]

Another factor helped set the stage for the successful industrialization of textile production. This one was within the structure of the family itself and worked in favor of producing a new group of workers for the mills. The position of women (wives and, especially, daughters) in the family was an inferior one. Adult, property-holding males were citizens with full civil rights, but the same was not true for women *of any age*. The father of the family had the legal right to control most aspects of the lives of his wife and daughters. His wife could own no property. Her signature on a document meant nothing because only her husband could transact business. Daughters had even less independence. They were bound by social conventions to obey their fathers and rarely were able to earn money of their own. Even travel away from home was unusual. The idea that a woman's place was in the home was not merely a powerful concept; it was, with rare exceptions, a rule binding a woman's behavior. Although the work of daughters and wives was important to the family economy (it literally could not have functioned without their labor at field work, food preparation, cleaning, washing, etc.), they gained no independent income or freedom as a result. In fact, so strong was the belief that daughters' lives would be bound by decisions made by their fathers, their older brothers, and, eventually, their husbands, that many could not imagine for themselves a life of active, public involvement of the kind expected of men. For some women, however, their inferior position in family and society gave them an incentive to take hold of any opportunity to weaken their bonds of inferiority. So, when the opportunity knocked, many young and single New England

Subordinate status of women.

women chose to answer by going willingly to work in the textile factories.[12]

Women's motives were economic as well as social. Very few opportunities for employment outside the home existed; teaching in a local school was one of the most common, but that was very poorly paid and lasted for only a few months a year. The new mill work was steady work, and it paid more than any alternative available to women.[13] Young girls could thus contribute to their family's welfare by sending home a portion of their pay. This economic motive added to their desire to move outside the traditional sphere of the family. For many of them, the chance to live away from home and with other young women like themselves offered an independence that was otherwise impossible.[14]

Prejudice against women working outside the home.

Hiring young women, of course, ran up against strong Yankee resistance. As noted above, fathers rarely allowed their daughters to leave home when they were young. According to the prejudices of the period, young women were unprepared for a life among adult, male strangers. Their "innocence" and "purity" had to be protected by their family. The goal held out for these girls (almost the only respectable one) was eventual marriage. To prepare for that, they had to learn wifely duties and practical household skills. God-fearing New England fathers were very reluctant to let their daughters leave the farm to live and work among strangers in a faraway town.[15]

To confront this prejudice, the mill owners created boarding houses around the mills where groups of girls would live and take their meals under the care of a boarding housekeeper who was usually an older woman, perhaps a widow. Strict boarding-house rules were laid down by the company — rules that served the company's purposes but also reassured parents that their daughters' behavior would still be monitored even though they were away from home. For example, the young women could not have visitors in the late evening. (See Figure 2, a reproduction of boarding-house regulations.) Moreover, the girls would never grow

8

*Visual documen-
tation of boarding-
house life.*

REGULATIONS

FOR THE

BOARDING HOUSES

OF THE

MIDDLESEX COMPANY.

THE tenants of the Boarding Houses are not to board, or permit any part of their houses to be occupied by any person except those in the employ of the Company.

They will be considered answerable for any improper conduct in their houses, and are not to permit their boarders to have company at unseasonable hours.

The doors must be closed at ten o'clock in the evening, and no one admitted after that time without some reasonable excuse.

The keepers of the Boarding Houses must give an account of the number, names, and employment of their boarders, when required; and report the names of such as are guilty of any improper conduct, or are not in the regular habit of attending public worship.

The buildings and yards about them must be kept clean and in good order, and if they are injured otherwise than from ordinary use, all necessary repairs will be made, and charged to the occupant.

It is indispensable that all persons in the employ of the Middlesex Company should be vaccinated who have not been, as also the families with whom they board; which will be done at the expense of the Company.

SAMUEL LAWRENCE, Agent.

JOEL TAYLOR, PRINTER, Daily Courier Office.

Figure 2.   Rules for boarding houses where mill girls stayed.
Source: *American Textile History Museum, Lowell, Mass.*

into a permanent working class — something that no one wished to see — as it was expected that they would return to their homes for visits and after a year or two would go back to their villages. While they stayed in Lowell, their reputations (and thus their opportunity for marriage) would be protected by the town fathers.[16]

The mill owners did not advertise for help. They sent recruiters into the countryside to explain the special nature of Lowell and to soothe parents' fears. Because of the farmers' need for extra income, and the women's desire for independence, this effort was often successful.[17] Over the years, thousands of young women took the long trip by stagecoach or wagon from their rural homes to mill towns like Lowell.

Life in a mill town.

Upon first arriving in Lowell, the young girls were naturally nervous. They had not lived away from home or ever worked in a factory. They were not used to the atmosphere of a city. The boarding house was new also. Living with a strange woman (and probably her family), who might or might not be a caring mother-substitute, also required adjustment. The girls shared the home with a dozen or more other girls and usually roomed with three or four of them. While all this was happening, of course, the girls had to make the difficult adjustment to the rigorous rules and long hours at the mill. Making the transition from rural to industrial rhythms wore on these girls.[18] As Harriet Robinson wrote in her memoir entitled *Loom and Spindle,*

Indented quotation.

> And sorrowful enough they looked, even to the fun-loving child who has lived to tell the story; for they had all left their pleasant country homes to try their fortunes in a great manufacturing town, and they were homesick before they landed at the doors of their boarding-houses.[19]

Mill work and the workday.

Mill work was not only an opportunity; like so much of early factory labor, it was hard work. These girls were used to hard work on the farm, but industrial labor created an entirely new pattern of life. The typical workday began at five a.m. and did not end until seven in the evening, or later. Thus the women worked an average of twelve hours a

day. (See Figure 3, an image of a bobbin girl.) They were given only
thirty minutes for lunch and forty-five for dinner. Since they took their
meals at the boarding house, the thirty minutes for lunch had to include
a quick walk (perhaps a run) to and from the house, leaving only fifteen
or twenty minutes for the meal.[20] The mills operated six days a week so
that the only day off was Sunday, part of which was usually spent at
church. Thus free time was confined to two or three hours in the evening
(boarding-house rules required them to go to bed at ten) and to Sunday
afternoon.[21] For many, however, this was still more leisure (and more
freedom) than they would have had at home.

Despite a workday that, including meals, took up fourteen hours,
most of the young women did not find the work very strenuous or
particularly dangerous. As the mill owners had claimed, Lowell did not
resemble the grimy, packed mill towns of England.[22] Still, the work was
tedious and confining — doing the same operation over and over again
and under the watchful eye of the overseer. In the ideal plan for Lowell,
the overseer was to take the place of the absent father (just as the
boarding-house widow was to be the substitute mother), someone
responsible for seeing to the safety and welfare of the girls on the job.
Of course, the overseer was also hired by the company to ensure that
the mill ran smoothly and efficiently. He saw to it that the women
worked steadily and recorded their hours of labor; any possibility of
time off required his approval.[23]

The young women earned an average of three to four dollars a
week, from which their board of $1.25 a week was deducted.[24] At that
time no other jobs open to women paid as well. As noted above, rural
schoolteachers earned less than one dollar a week and taught for only
three months of the year.[25] Three or four dollars a week was enough to
pay their board, send badly needed money home, and still have enough
left over for new clothes once in a while. Many women workers even
established savings accounts, and some eventually left work with

11

*Visual of a mill
girl.*

Figure 3.   Image of a girl winding a shuttle bobbin, by Winslow
Homer, 1871.
Source: *Lowell National Historical Park.*

12

several hundred dollars, something that they could never have done
at home.[26]

In Lowell the women became part of a growing city that had shops,   *Social life.*
social events, and camaraderie that were absent in their rural villages
and farms. Most felt responsible to send part of their earnings home,
but enough was left over to give them consumer choices unavailable to
their rural sisters, cousins, and friends. Also, unlike farm and family
chores, mill work offered free time on Sundays and in the evenings.[27]

Even though their free time was very limited, the women engaged   *Leisure hours.*
in a wide variety of activities. In the evening they wrote letters home,
entertained visitors (though there was little privacy), repaired their
clothing, and talked among themselves. They talked of friends and relatives and also of conditions in the mill. They could go out to the shops,
especially clothing shops. The mill girls at Lowell prided themselves on
a wardrobe that, at least on Sunday, was not inferior to that of the
wives of prosperous citizens.[28] One of the most surprising uses of their
free time was the number of meetings attended by mill girls. There
were evening courses that enabled the young women to extend their
education beyond the few years of schooling they had received in the
countryside. They could also attend lectures by prominent speakers.
It was not unusual for the audience at serious presentations to be
composed mostly of mill girls. In their spare time, they also read novels
and essays. So strong was the girls' interest in reading that many mills
put up signs warning "No reading in the mills."[29] Perhaps the most
unusual pursuit of at least some mill girls was writing. Determined to
challenge the idea that mill girls were mindless drones of the factory
and lacked the refinement necessary to make them good wives, about
seventy-five mill girls and women contributed in the 1840s to a series
of publications that featured stories and essays by the workers themselves. Indeed, much of the editorial work was done by these women
as well.[30]

13

The Lowell
Offering.

The most well known of these publications was the *Lowell Offering*, which consisted exclusively of articles written and edited by women in the factories. Although many of the articles in the *Offering* reinforced traditional ideas and focused on noncontroversial subjects such as family, courtship, fashion, morality, and nature,[31] some writers used the publication to express a newfound sense of worldliness and independent thought. For example, one factory worker explains in a letter to the editor in 1840 that her boarding house is not like a domestic home at all, but is comprised of about a dozen young women of different backgrounds, faiths, and ideas. Of herself and her colleagues, she says, "we *need* not be ignorant upon the subjects which are agitating the world around us, nor of the transactions which excite the interest of others besides 'factory girls.'"[32]

Although they stayed away from outright criticism of working conditions, the women did manage to find a voice of opposition to factory life in their writings. According to historian Chad Montrie, the young writers typically expressed their disillusionment with factory life by "embrac[ing] a romantic version of nature, which they identified with the homes and the landscapes they had lost."[33] One writer in the *Lowell Offering*, for example, wrote in 1841:

> Those who have for any length of time been pent up in a cotton-mill and factory boarding-house . . . can appreciate the pleasures of a journey through the country, when the earth is dressed in her richest robes of green, bedecked with flowers, and all smiling with sunlight.[34]

During the early years of the mill towns, the owners had tried to keep up the image of the factory as a pleasant place. Buildings had many windows and much sunlight. The town had large green spaces and the atmosphere of a country village.[35] As time went on, however, the mill companies became more interested in profits and less concerned about their role as protectors of their young workers. By the 1830s, tensions in the mills had begun to rise. Factory owners, observing a decline in

14

the price of their cloth and the growth of unsold inventories, decided
to lower their workers' wages.[36] When the reduction was announced in
February 1834, the women workers circulated petitions among themselves pledging to stop work ("turn out") if wages were lowered.[37] When
the leader of the petition drive at one mill was fired, many of the women
protested. They left work and marched to the other mills to call out
their workers. It is estimated that one-sixth of all women mill workers
walked out as a result. The strikers wrote another petition, stating
that "we will not go back into the mills to work until our wages are
continued . . . as they have been."[38] In 1836, another effort to lower
wages led to an ever larger "turn out."[39]

Women workers' resistance to factory discipline.

Example of a quotation with an ellipsis mark.

Some critics of the Lowell system argued that girls could not
serve as successful factory operatives and that industrial labor would
deprive them of both their independence and their womanly virtue. One
critic, for example, wrote to the *New York Herald* in 1843 that the Lowell
factory girls earned "a very low position in society and very little weight
in the scale of virtue and the female ornaments" in the opinion of many
observers. After all, he argued, very few girls actually contributed to
the *Lowell Offering*, thus creating a "splendid illusion" of factory life
that was "got up by a clergyman on speculation and sustained by the
companies for effect."[40] Some southern newspapers, alert to challenge
northern claims of the superiority of free labor, doubted that the Lowell
girls could compare themselves favorably to African American slaves.
One Kentucky critic argued they were "in point of morals on a level with
the wretched females of a southern plantation — defencelessly exposed
and subjected to the brutality of master and overseer,"[41] and a corre-
spondent for the *Vicksburg Sentinel* argued, "The negroes of the South
could not be driven to do what those poor creatures are compelled to
submit to, to procure a subsistence."[42]

The preponderance of evidence, however, suggests that the
Lowell girls retained their moral and economic standing despite the

15

rigors of factory life and the stresses caused by strikes. They were not any less feminine, nor were they slaves. Although "turn outs" were brief and did not achieve their purposes, they demonstrated not only the independent attitude of many of the women workers but also their unique status among American workers. They did not accept the owners' view that they were minors under their benevolent care; nor did they consider themselves to be members of a permanent working class. The petitions prepared by the strikers indicate that they thought of themselves as the equal of their employers. The sense of independence gained by factory work and cash wages led them to reject the idea that they were mere factory hands. Petitions referred to their "unquestionable rights," and to "the spirit of our patriotic ancestors, who preferred

Example of a quotation with emphasis added.

privation to bondage. . . ." One petition ended, "we are free, we would remain in possession of what kind providence has bestowed upon us, and remain *daughters of free men still.*"[43] This language indicates that the women did not think of themselves as laborers complaining about low wages. They were free citizens of a republic and deserved respect as such. Because many of the women had relatives who had fought in the Revolutionary War, they felt that they were protecting not only their jobs but also their independence.

Although the strikes failed and these women did not really have complete "independence," this issue was so important to them that many left the mills and went home when it became clear that mill work would require a lessening of their status. As Harriet Robinson recalled, "the best portion of the girls left and went to their homes, or to the other employments that were fast opening to women, until there were very few of the old guard left."[44] They had originally accepted mill work because life away from home and good wages gave them greater freedom. When mill work came to seem less like independence and more like "slavery" (a comparison that also appeared in the petitions), many changed their minds. The willingness of these young women to challenge the authority

16

of the mill owners is a sign that their new lives had given them a feeling of mutual strength.[45]

Economic recession in the late 1830s and early 1840s led to the layoff of hundreds of the women workers. Many of the mills were forced to part-time schedules. In the 1840s and 1850s, the mill owners tried to maintain profits despite increased competition and lessened demand. They did so by intensifying the work process. The speed of the machinery was increased as was the number of machines tended by each worker. Historian David Zonderman argues that textile mill workers resented the so-called "speed-up and stretch out" because of "the physical toll of the intense labor, the constant reduction of piece rates, and the knowledge that their extra efforts were being exploited by the owners."[46] Paternalism was discarded. To save money, the companies stopped building boarding houses.[47] The look of Lowell changed as well. Mill buildings took up more of the green space that had been part of the original plan.

Declining conditions of work in the Lowell mills.

By 1850, Lowell did indeed look something like an English mill town. By then, however, the desire to pacify the fears of potential workers and their families was gone. Terrible famine in Ireland in 1845 and 1846 had caused a large number of Irish to immigrate to the United States.[48] As conditions in the mills declined and more and more young Yankee women left the mills for home or other work, their places were rapidly taken up by the very poor Irish for whom work of any kind in America was an opportunity, and who did not have the option of returning to their homes. Slowly, Lowell had become just another industrial city. It was dirty and overcrowded, and its mills were beginning to look run-down.

The coming of Irish workers.

By 1850, an era had passed. By then, most of the mill workers were recruited from newly arrived immigrants with backgrounds very different from those of the young New England women. During the period from the 1820s to the 1840s, however, young women from rural

Conclusion.

New England made up the majority of the textile workers in the area. At that time, an unusual era in the development of industrialization took place. Large textile mills with complex production systems were operated largely by young women who thought of themselves not as workers but as free citizens of a republic earning an independent existence for a few years before returning to their homes. These women gave the mill owners the workforce that was needed to make the U.S. textile industry large and profitable. Many fortunes were made for investors living in Boston and other major cities.[49] But the farmers' daughters profited as well. Not only did they earn more than earlier generations of women had been able to, but they did so outside the home.

Restatement of part of thesis.

A great debate had raged during the 1830s and 1840s about the impact of industrialization on American life. Because of the general belief that women were weak, it was presumed that they would be taken advantage of as workers, especially as they were away from the protection of the male members of their families. Further, it was feared that mill work would "defeminize" them and that young men would not marry them because they had not been brought up in an environment of modesty, deference to their fathers and brothers, and daily practice in domestic tasks such as cleaning, sewing, and cooking.[50] (Textile mill workers were known as "spinsters," a word that came to mean a woman who never married.) Seen from a longer perspective, however, the women showed these fears to be unfounded. Even more important, as effective workers they undermined the stereotype of women as frail and as thriving only in a domestic environment. While these young women helped make possible the industrialization of New England, at the same time they expanded their opportunities. Many women reformers and radicals in later years, as they raised the banner for equal rights for women in more and more areas of life, referred back to the example of the independent mill girls of the 1830s and 1840s who

Summary.

Restatement of thesis.

resisted pressures from their employers, gained both freedom and maturity by living and working on their own, and showed an intense desire for independence and learning.[51] Great fortunes were made from the textile mills of that era, but within those mills a generation of young women gained something even more precious: a sense of self-respect.

19

Endnotes

Endnotes begin on a new page. The numbered annotations correspond to the endnote numbers.

1. Barbara M. Tucker, *Samuel Slater and the Origins of the American Textile Industry: 1790–1860* (Ithaca, NY: Cornell University Press, 1984), 33–40.

1. The rise of industrialization in England.

2. Caroline F. Ware, *The Early New England Cotton Manufacture* (Boston: Houghton Mifflin, 1931), 4–8; Tucker, *Slater*, 38–41; Walter Licht, *Industrializing America: The Nineteenth Century* (Baltimore: Johns Hopkins University Press, 1995), 15; Robert F. Dalzell, *Enterprising Elite: The Boston Associates and the World They Made* (Cambridge, MA: Harvard University Press, 1987), 12–13; Allan Kulikoff, "The Transition to Capitalism in Rural America," *William and Mary Quarterly* 46 (1989): 129–30, 141–42.

2. American attitudes toward industrialization in England and mill work in general.

3. Thomas Dublin, *Women at Work: The Transformation of Work and Community in Lowell, Massachusetts, 1826–1860* (New York: Columbia University Press, 1979), 14; Adrienne D. Hood, "The Gender Division of Labor in the Production of Textiles in Eighteenth-Century Rural Pennsylvania," *Journal of Social History* 27 (Spring 1994): 542, http://www.searchbank.com/infotrac/session/4/0/82904/37xrn_7 (accessed January 16, 2009).

3. Home spinning in America.

Citation of an article from a database.

4. Thomas Dublin, *Transforming Women's Work: New England Lives in the Industrial Revolution* (Ithaca, NY: Cornell University Press, 1994), 30.

4. The origins of industrialization in America.

5. Tucker, *Slater*, 79, 85, 99–100, 111; Barbara M. Tucker, "The Family and Industrial Discipline in Ante-Bellum New England," *Labor History* 21 (Winter 1979–80): 56–60.

5. Slater-type mills and family production.

6. Dalzell, 26–30; Tucker, *Slater*, 111–16.

6. The creation of Waltham mills.

7. Dalzell, 5–6.

7. H. C. Lowell and power loom.

8. Tucker, *Slater*, 116–17.

8. The founding of Lowell.

9. Dublin, *Women at Work*, 19–21, 133–35.

9. The growth of Lowell.

10. Dublin, *Women at Work*, 26, 76; Benita Eisler, ed., *The "Lowell Offering": Writings by New England Mill Women (1840–1845)* (Philadelphia: Lippincott, 1977), 15–16; Peter Temin, "The Industrialization of New England, 1830–1880," in *Engines of Enterprise: An Economic History of New England*, ed. Peter Temin (Cambridge, MA: Harvard University Press, 2000), 96–101.

10. The owners' choice of a female workforce.

11. Christopher Clark, "The Household Economy: Market Exchange and the Rise of Capitalism in the Connecticut Valley, 1800–1860,"

11. Problems of the farm economy.

20

Journal of Social History 13 (Winter 1979): 175–76; Gail Fowler Mohanty, "Handloom Outwork and Outwork Weaving in Rural Rhode Island, 1810–1821," *American Studies* 30 (Fall 1989): 42–43.

12. Eisler, 16, 19, 62; Barbara Welter, "The Cult of True Woman-hood," *American Quarterly* 18 (1966): 155, 162–65; Dublin, *Transforming Women's Work*, 89.

13. Eisler, 16, 193; Clark, 178–79; Dalzell, 33.

14. Dublin, *Women at Work*, 40; Tucker, *Slater*, 255–56; Harriet H. Robinson, *Loom and Spindle* (1898), in *Women of Lowell* (New York: Arno Press, 1974), 194; Eisler, 61–63, 81–82.

15. On the influence of patriarchy, see Tucker, *Slater*, 25–26; Robinson, 61; Welter, 152, 170–71. Also see *Sins of Our Mothers*, video-cassette (Boston: WGBH/WNET/KLET/PBS, 1988).

16. Dublin, *Women at Work*, 77–79; Eisler, 19–24.

17. Eisler, 18–19. On the decline of New England agriculture, see Clark, 176; Ware, 14.

18. Dublin, *Women at Work*, 80; Eisler, 73–74.

19. Robinson, 64.

20. Dublin, *Women at Work*, 80; Robinson, 31; Lucy Larcom, "Among Lowell Mill Girls: A Reminiscence" (1881), in *Women of Lowell* (see note 14), 602; Eisler, 75–77.

21. See the table of mill hours printed in Eisler, 30. Boarding-house curfew is listed in "Regulations for the Boarding Houses of the Middlesex Company," in Figure 2 on page 8. For a very negative view of work hours and conditions, see A Citizen of Lowell, *Corporations and Operatives: Being an Exposition of the Condition [of the] Factory Operatives . . .* (1843), in *Women of Lowell* (see note 14), 15–19, 21.

22. Larcom, 599–602; Eisler, 56–66.

23. "Factory Rules from the Handbook to Lowell, 1848," *Illinois Labor History Society*, http://www.kentlaw.edu/ilhs/lowell.html (accessed January 19, 2009).

24. Dublin, *Women at Work*, 66, 183, 185; Ware, 239.

25. Ware, 240–42. For teachers' pay, see Eisler, 193.

12. The inferior position of women.

13. Limited opportunities for women in New England.

14. Women's desire for independence.

15. Early-19th-century rural attitudes toward women.

Example of a film citation.

16. Early Lowell paternalism.

17. Recruiting women workers.

18. Getting used to town life and the boarding house.

19. Firsthand account of mill-girl experience.

20. The nature of mill work and the workday.

21. Work hours and free time.

22. Lowell mill girls' favorable comments on mill work.

23. Role of the overseer. (Example of a Web citation.)

24. Rate of women's pay.

25. Low alterna-tive pay for women.

26. Savings accounts.

26. Elisha Bartlett, *A Vindication of the Character and Condition of the Females Employed in the Lowell Mills* . . . (1841), in *Women of Lowell* (see note 14), 21; Dublin, 188.

27. Free time.

27. Larcom, 599–600.

28. Leisure time and wardrobe.

28. Eisler, 49–50.

29. Reading and education.

29. Robinson, 91–93; Eisler, 113–32. For mill rules concerning reading, see Eisler, 31.

30. Women's writing.

30. Robinson, 97–102.

31. The Lowell Offering.

31. Eisler, 33–40; Dublin, *Women at Work*, 123–24, 129–30; Robinson, 114–20; Bertha Monica Stearns, "Early Factory Magazines in New England: The *Lowell Offering* and Its Contemporaries," *Journal of Economic and Business History* (August 1930): 690–91, 698.

32. Offering *quote demonstrates independent thinking.*

Online document.

32. H. T., "Our Household," *The Lowell Offering* (April 1841), in *The Lowell Offering: A Repository of Original Articles on Various Subjects, Written by Factory Operatives*, ser. 2, vol. 1 (Lowell, MA: Powers and Bagley, 1841–1842), 364–65, http://pds.lib.harvard.edu/pds/view/2669789?n=454&imagesize=1200&jp2Res=.25 (accessed January 15, 2009).

33. Significance of nature writing.

33. Chad Montrie, "'I Think Less of the Factory Than of My Native Dell': Labor, Nature, and the Lowell 'Mill Girls,'" *Environmental History* 9, no. 2 (April 2004): par. 45, http://www.historycooperative.org/journals/eh/9.2/montrie.html (accessed January 17, 2009).

34. Offering *quote demonstrates opposition to factory life.*

34. C. N., "Journey to Lebanon Springs," *The Lowell Offering* (September 1842), in *The Lowell Offering: A Repository of Original Articles on Various Subjects, Written by Factory Operatives*, ser. 2, vol. 2 (Lowell, MA: Powers and Bagley, 1841–1842), 221, http://pds.lib.harvard.edu/pds/view/2669789?n=699&imagesize=1200&jp2Res=.25 (accessed January 15, 2009).

35. The early Lowell setting.

35. Larcom, 598, 609; Eisler, 63–65.

36. Tensions of the 1830s; lowered wages.

36. Dublin, *Women at Work*, 87–90.

37. The 1834 "turn out."

37. Dublin, *Women at Work*, 89–91.

38. Strikers' petitions.

38. Dublin, *Women at Work*, 91.

39. The 1836 "turn out."

39. Dublin, *Women at Work*, 98–99.

22

40. "Lowell," *New York Herald*, November 5, 1843, http://find.galegroup.com/ (accessed February 2, 2009).

40. Criticism of female labor.

41. "Infamous Slander," *Boston Emancipator and Weekly Chronicle*, December 11, 1844, http://www.infoweb.newsbank.com/ (accessed February 21, 2009).

41. Comparison to slavery.

42. "White and Black Slavery," *Cleveland Daily Herald,* October 11, 1845, http://www.find.galegroup.com/ (accessed February 8, 2009).

42. Another comparison to slavery.

43. Dublin, *Women at Work*, 93 (emphasis added).

43. More quotes from petitions.

44. Robinson, 86.

44. Firsthand account.

45. Dublin, *Women at Work*, 44, 82–83, 103; Licht, 58–61.

45. Mutual support.

46. David Zonderman, *Aspirations and Anxieties: New England Workers and the Mechanized Factory System, 1815–1860* (New York: Oxford University Press, 1992), 33.

46. Reasons for resistance.

47. Dublin, *Women at Work*, 108, 134; Robinson, 204, 208–09; Eisler, 215.

47. Declining working conditions.

48. Dublin, *Women at Work*, 140, 156, 197. On the decline of Lowell, see Dalzell, 69.

48. The workforce after 1845; Irish immigration.

49. Dalzell, *Women at Work*, 60–61, 70–73.

49. Profits for owners.

50. Dublin, *Women at Work*, 32; Welter, 151–74. For the contemporary debate about the impact of factory work on women, see these pamphlets: Bartlett, *A Vindication of the Character and Condition*, and A Citizen, *Corporations and Operatives*.

50. The status of women.

51. Dublin, *Women at Work*, 127–29; Ware, 292.

51. Lowell women activists and later movements.

23

Bibliography begins on a new page.

Bibliography

Books

Citations are listed alphabetically under each heading.

Bartlett, Elisha. *A Vindication of the Character and Condition of the Females Employed in the Lowell Mills. . . .* 1841. Reprinted in *Women of Lowell*. New York: Arno Press, 1974.

Citizen of Lowell, A. *Corporations and Operatives: Being an Exposition of the Condition [of the] Factory Operatives. . . .* 1843. Reprinted in *Women of Lowell*. New York: Arno Press, 1974.

Second and following lines of each citation are indented.

Dalzell, Robert F. *Enterprising Elite: The Boston Associates and the World They Made*. Cambridge, MA: Harvard University Press, 1987.

Dublin, Thomas. *Transforming Women's Work: New England Lives in the Industrial Revolution*. Ithaca, NY: Cornell University Press, 1994.

Multiple sources by the same author.

————. *Women at Work: The Transformation of Work and Community in Lowell, Massachusetts, 1826–1860*. New York: Columbia University Press, 1979.

Eisler, Benita, ed. *The "Lowell Offering": Writings by New England Mill Women (1840–1845)*. Philadelphia: Lippincott, 1977.

Licht, Walter. *Industrializing America: The Nineteenth Century*. Baltimore: Johns Hopkins University Press, 1995.

Robinson, Harriet H. *Loom and Spindle; Or, Life among the Early Mill Girls*. 1898. Reprinted in *Women of Lowell*. New York: Arno Press, 1974.

Tucker, Barbara M. *Samuel Slater and the Origins of the American Textile Industry: 1790–1860*. Ithaca, NY: Cornell University Press, 1984.

Ware, Caroline F. *The Early New England Cotton Manufacture*. Boston: Houghton Mifflin, 1931.

Zonderman, David. *Aspirations and Anxieties: New England Workers and the Mechanized Factory System, 1815–1860*. New York: Oxford University Press, 1992.

Articles

Newspaper articles are not included in bibliography.

Clark, Christopher. "The Household Economy: Market Exchange and the Rise of Capitalism in the Connecticut Valley, 1800–1860." *Journal of Social History* 13 (Winter 1979): 169–89.

24

Hood, Adrienne D. "The Gender Division of Labor in the Production of
    Textiles in Eighteenth-Century Rural Pennsylvania." *Journal of
    Social History* 27 (Spring 1994): 537–61. http://www.searchbank
    .com/infotrac/session/4/0/82904/3?xrn_7 (accessed January 16,
    2009).

Kulikoff, Allan. "The Transition to Capitalism in Rural America." *William
    and Mary Quarterly* 46 (1989): 120–44.

Larcom, Lucy. "Among Lowell Mill Girls: A Reminiscence." 1881.
    Reprinted in *Women of Lowell.* New York: Arno Press, 1974.

Mohanty, Gail Fowler. "Handloom Outwork and Outwork Weaving in
    Rural Rhode Island, 1810–1821." *American Studies* 30 (Fall
    1989): 41–68.

Montrie, Chad. "'I think less of the Factory: Than of My Native Dell':
    Labor, Nature, and the Lowell 'Mill Girls.'" *Environmental History* 9,
    no. 2 (April 2004): 275–95. http://www.historycooperative.org/
    journals/eh/9.2/montrie.html (accessed January 17, 2009).

Stearns, Bertha Monica. "Early Factory Magazines in New England: The
    Lowell Offering and Its Contemporaries." *Journal of Economic and
    Business History* (August 1930): 685–705.

Temin, Peter. "The Industrialization of New England, 1830–1880." In
    Engines of Enterprise: An Economic History of New England, edited
    by Peter Temin, 109–52. Cambridge, MA: Harvard University
    Press, 2000.

Tucker, Barbara M. "The Family and Industrial Discipline in Ante-Bellum
    New England." *Labor History* 21 (Winter 1979–80): 55–74.

Welter, Barbara. "The Cult of True Womanhood." *American Quarterly* 18
    (1966): 151–74.

Documents

"Factory Rules from the Handbook to Lowell, 1848." *Illinois Labor History
    Society.* http://www.kentlaw.edu/ilhs/lowell.html (accessed
    January 19, 2009).

*The Lowell Offering: A Repository of Original Articles on Various Subjects,
    Written by Factory Operatives.* Ser. 2. 2 vols. Lowell, MA: Powers
    and Bagley, 1841–1842. Harvard University Page Delivery Service.
    http://nrs.harvard.edu/urn-3:FHCL:600480 (accessed January 15,
    2009).

Regulations for the Boarding Houses of the Middlesex Company.
    ca. 1850. American Textile History Museum, Lowell, MA. Sign.

Nonwritten Sources

Homer, Winslow. Image of a girl winding a shuttle bobbin. 1871. Lowell
    National Historical Park. http://library.uml.edu/clh/All/Mgi.htm
    (accessed January 20, 2009).

"Map of Lowell, showing the location of mills and boarding houses." In
    So Far from Home, by Barry Denenberg, 164b. New York: Scholastic,
    1997.

Sins of Our Mothers. Boston: WGBH/WNET/KCET/PBS, 1988. Videocassette.

CHAPTER

8

Documenting Your Paper: How to Cite Sources in *Chicago* Style

Documentation tells your reader where you found the material in your paper. Most undergraduate history professors require students to follow what is known as "*Chicago* style": documentation as described in *The Chicago Manual of Style*, 15th ed. (Chicago: University of Chicago Press, 2003) or Turabian's *A Manual for Writers of Research Papers, Theses, and Dissertations*, 7th ed. (Chicago: University of Chicago Press, 2007). *Chicago*-style documentation for history papers usually includes both **notes** (numbered footnotes or endnotes) and a **bibliography** that lists sources alphabetically.

The pages that follow include dozens of documentation models for a wide variety of sources, as well as detailed guidelines showing how to document some of the most common types of sources. For ease of reference, the model note and bibliography entries are displayed as paired examples on pages 176–200. An "**N**" in the margin signifies "note" examples, and a "**B**" indicates "bibliography entry" examples. A directory of models can be found on page 175.

FORMATTING FOOTNOTES AND ENDNOTES

The section "When to Use Footnotes and Endnotes" in Chapter 7 (pp. 140–42) explains the circumstances in which **citations** are required. If a note is necessary, place a raised (superscript) numeral at the end of the sentence that contains the information to be documented. Do not enclose the superscript note number in parentheses, and be sure to insert it *after* any punctuation except a dash.

According to Diamond, "Different rates of development on different continents, from 11,000 B.C. to A.D. 1500, were what led to the technological and political inequalities of A.D. 1500."[1]

---

1. Jared Diamond, *Guns, Germs, and Steel: The Fates of Human Societies* (New York: Norton, 1999), 16.

If you are documenting a general idea or opinion, place the number at the end of the paragraph or paragraphs in which you discuss it.

Footnotes are placed at the bottom of the page containing the text to which they refer. Endnotes are gathered together in numerical order in an "Endnotes" section, which is placed after the text of the paper. (See the "Endnotes" section of the sample student paper in Chapter 7, pp. 166–69.)

The example above shows the correct format for a note. The first line is indented five spaces or one-half inch; the other lines begin at the left margin. Both footnotes and endnotes are single-spaced, and an extra line of space separates individual notes. Notes should be numbered consecutively throughout your paper.

ORGANIZING A BIBLIOGRAPHY

A bibliography is an alphabetical listing of nearly all of the sources that appear in your paper's notes. (Some sources, such as personal interviews, are cited in notes but are not included in bibliographies. See individual models for details.) Your bibliography should *not* include all of the sources that you consulted in the course of your research.

Entries in a bibliography that is long may be arranged by category, such as books, articles, documents, and nonwritten sources (maps, photographs, audio and video recordings, etc.). See the bibliography for the sample paper in Chapter 7, pp. 170–72. Each section is alphabetized according to the *last* name of the author. If a work has more than one author, alphabetize according to the last name of the first author mentioned on the title page of the book or article. That name should be followed by the names of all of the other authors listed with their *first* names first. A work that has no author (or editor or translator) is alphabetized according to the first word of its title excluding "A," "An," and "The."

Begin each entry at the left margin, and indent any subsequent lines five spaces or one-half inch. Each entry in a bibliography is single-spaced, with an extra line of space between entries. You should notice that the parts of a note generally are separated by *commas* but the parts of a bibliography entry usually are separated by *periods*. For further details, see the documentation models that follow.

Directory of Documentation Models for Notes and Bibliography Entries

OVERVIEW OF NOTES
1. First reference to a source, *176*
2. Subsequent reference to a source, *176*

OVERVIEW OF BIBLIOGRAPHY ENTRIES
3. Typical bibliography entry, *176*
4. Multiple works by the same author, *176*

AUTHOR VARIATIONS
5. One author, *177*
6. Two authors, *177*
7. Three authors, *178*
8. Four or more authors, *178*
9. Author's name in title, *178*
10. Organization as author, *178*
11. Unknown author, *178*

BOOKS
12. Basic format for a book, *179*
    Guidelines for Citing Books, 180
13. Online book, *179*
14. Translated book, *179*
15. Book with one or more editors, *181*
16. Selection in an edited work or anthology, *182*
17. Letter in a published collection, *182*
    Guidelines for Citing Letters in Published Collections, 184
18. Edition other than the first, *182*
19. Multivolume work, *183*
20. Encyclopedia or dictionary, *183*
21. Book in a series, *186*
22. Sacred text, *186*

PERIODICALS
23. Basic format for a journal article, *186*
    Guidelines for Citing Articles in Print Journals, 188
24. Journal article accessed from a database, *187*
    Guidelines for Citing Articles in Electronic Databases, 189
25. Article in an online journal, *187*
26. Article in a magazine, *187*
27. Article in a newspaper, *187*
28. Article from an online news source, *190*

29. Editorial, *190*
30. Letter to the editor, *190*
31. Book or film review, *191*
32. Online review, *191*

PUBLIC DOCUMENTS
33. U.S. legislative branch committee report, *191*
34. U.S. treaty, *192*
35. U.S. Supreme Court decision, *192*
36. Canadian legislative branch committee report, *192*
37. Online government document, *192*

MULTIMEDIA SOURCES
38. Material from a Web site, *192*
    Guidelines for Citing Information from Web Sites, 194
39. DVD or videocassette, *193*
40. Broadcast interview, *193*
41. Recorded speech or reading, *195*
42. Musical recording, *195*
43. CD-ROM, *195*
44. Work of art, *195*
45. Slide, *196*
46. Map or illustration, *196*
47. Chart, graph, or table, *196*

OTHER PUBLISHED SOURCES
48. Pamphlet, *197*
49. Dissertation abstract, *197*
50. Published interview or transcript, *197*
51. Musical composition, *198*
52. Source quoted in another source, *198*

UNPUBLISHED SOURCES
53. Unpublished thesis or dissertation, *198*
54. Unpublished letter in a manuscript collection, *198*
55. Unpublished lecture, paper, or public address, *199*
56. Personal interview, *199*
57. Personal e-mail message or letter, *199*
58. Web forum or discussion list posting, *200*

DOCUMENTATION MODELS

Overview of Notes

1. FIRST REFERENCE TO A SOURCE

The first time you document any source in a note, include the author's full name, followed by a comma; the full title of the work; the publication information; and the page number or numbers that you cited (followed by a period).

N   1. Robert Darnton, *George Washington's False Teeth: An Unconventional Guide to the Eighteenth Century* (New York: Norton, 2003), 64.

2. SUBSEQUENT REFERENCE TO A SOURCE

If you cite the same work again in your paper, include only the author's last name and the page number in your note.

N   2. Darnton, 102.

If your citation of a source *immediately* follows a reference to the same source, you have the option of using the abbreviation "Ibid." (short for the Latin *ibidem*, meaning "in the same place") instead of repeating the author's name.

N   2. Ibid. 102.

NOTE: Some instructors prefer that students not use "Ibid." Check with your professor.

When your sources include *more than one* work by the same author, any second or later reference to every work by that author must include a shortened form of the title so that the reader will know which work you are citing. "Ibid." may never be used when your sources include more than one work by the same author.

N   2. Darnton, *George Washington's False Teeth*, 68.

Overview of Bibliography Entries

3. TYPICAL BIBLIOGRAPHY ENTRY

Bibliography entries generally include the same information as notes, but the information is listed slightly differently. The author's last name is listed first, for the purposes of alphabetizing, and page numbers usually are not included. Also, periods (not commas) are used to separate information.

B   Darnton, Robert. *George Washington's False Teeth: An Unconventional Guide to the Eighteenth Century.* New York: Norton, 2003.

4. MULTIPLE WORKS BY THE SAME AUTHOR

If your bibliography includes more than one work by the same author, give the author's complete name in only the first entry. Replace it with three hyphens in the second and any other entries. List the works in alphabetical order by title, ignoring "A," "An," and "The."

B   Darnton, Robert. *George Washington's False Teeth: An Unconventional Guide to the Eighteenth Century.* New York: Norton, 2003.

B   ———. *The Great Cat Massacre and Other Episodes in French Cultural History.* New York: Vintage Books, 1995.

Author Variations

The models below indicate how to format the names of authors in your notes and bibliography. In general, author names are followed by a comma in notes, and by a period in bibliography entries. Only author names and editor names are shown here.

5. ONE AUTHOR

When a source has a single author, list the name in normal order in the note, and follow the name with a comma.

N   5. Jules Benjamin,

In the bibliography entry, list the author's name last name first, insert a comma between the last and first names, and end with a period.

B   Benjamin, Jules.

NOTE: If "Jr.," "Sr.," or a numeral appears after the author's last name, put it after the first name in the bibliography entry, preceded by a comma. In the note entry, "Jr.," "Sr.," or a numeral need not be preceded by a comma.

N   5. Harvey C. Mansfield Jr.,

B   Mansfield, Harvey C., Jr.

N   5. Joseph M. Marshall III,

B   Marshall, Joseph M., III.

6. TWO AUTHORS

When a source has two authors, both names, separated by "and," appear in the note and in the bibliography entry in the order in which they appear on the title page.

N   6. Pat Nyhan and Helen Epstein,

In the bibliography entry, invert the name of only the first author; put a comma after the first author's last name; and use a comma and "and" to separate the first author name from the second.

B   Nyhan, Pat, and Helen Epstein.

7. THREE AUTHORS

When a source has three authors, all three names, separated by commas, appear in the note and in the bibliography entry in the order in which they appear on the title page.

N   7. Ronald Inden, Jonathan Walters, and Daud Ali,

B   Inden, Ronald, Jonathan Walters, and Daud Ali.

8. FOUR OR MORE AUTHORS

When a source has more than three authors, only the name of the author listed first on the title page appears in the note, and the abbreviation "et al." (from the Latin, meaning "and others") follows that name.

N   8. Thomas G. Weiss et al.,

In the bibliography, all names are usually included.

B   Weiss, Thomas G., David P. Forsythe, Roger A. Coate, and Kelly-Kate Pease.

9. AUTHOR'S NAME IN TITLE

In some cases, such as autobiographies and edited collections, the name of the author is part of the title of the book. The note for such a book may begin with the book title.

N   9. *Personal Memoirs of Ulysses S. Grant,*

The bibliography entry should begin with the last name of the author.

B   Grant, Ulysses S. *Personal Memoirs of Ulysses S. Grant.*

10. ORGANIZATION AS AUTHOR

When documenting a source with organizational authorship, use the name of the corporation, government agency, or other organization as the author name.

N   10. League of Women Voters,

B   League of Women Voters.

11. UNKNOWN AUTHOR

If the author of a work is unknown or is listed as "Anonymous" on the title page, begin both the note and bibliography entry with the title of the work.

N   11. "Australia's Aborigines: A Dispute over Mistake Creek,"

B   "Australia's Aborigines: A Dispute over Mistake Creek."

NOTE: In your bibliography, alphabetize anonymous works according to the title, ignoring "A," "And," and "The." For example, *A Woman in Berlin* would be alphabetized under "W."

Books

12. BASIC FORMAT FOR A BOOK

When citing a book, include the author's name; the complete book title (including subtitle after a colon), italicized; and publication information — place of publication (followed by a colon), publisher's name (followed by a comma), and date of publication.

In notes, commas separate the author name and book title, the publication information is enclosed in parentheses, and the page number or numbers you are citing are listed at the end.

N   12. Juliana Barr, *Peace Came in the Form of a Woman: Indians and Spaniards in the Texas Borderlands* (Chapel Hill: University of North Carolina Press, 2007), 112–16.

In bibliographies, the parts of the entry are separated by periods, publication information is not enclosed in parentheses, and page numbers usually are not listed.

B   Barr, Juliana. *Peace Came in the Form of a Woman: Indians and Spaniards in the Texas Borderlands.* Chapel Hill: University of North Carolina Press, 2007.

For a detailed illustration of a basic book citation, see page 180. For author variations, see items 5 through 11. For shortened forms for second and subsequent references to the same source, see item 2. For specific types of books and parts within books, see items 13 through 22.

13. ONLINE BOOK

To cite a printed book that has been digitized and stored on the Web, list all the information as you would for a printed book, along with the title of the collection of online books in which you found it, the URL, and the date on which you accessed it.

N   13. George Rawlinson, *History of Phoenicia* (London: Longmans, Green and Co., 1889), 116, Project Gutenberg, http://www.gutenberg.org/etext/2331 (accessed May 15, 2008).

B   Rawlinson, George. *History of Phoenicia.* London: Longmans, Green and Co., 1889. Project Gutenberg. http://www.gutenberg.org/etext/2331 (accessed May 15, 2008).

14. TRANSLATED BOOK

In the note, after the title of the work, put the name of the translator, preceded by the abbreviation "trans." In the bibliography, put the phrase "Translated by" before the translator's name.

N   14. Mohandas K. Gandhi, *An Autobiography: The Story of My Experiments with Truth,* rev. American ed., trans. Mahadev Desai (Boston: Beacon Press, 1993), 74.

B   Gandhi, Mohandas K. *An Autobiography: The Story of My Experiments with Truth.* Rev. American ed. Translated by Mahadev Desai. Boston: Beacon Press, 1993.

Guidelines for Citing Books

When citing a book, include the following information, found on the title page and copyright page:

1 Author
2 Title and subtitle
3 City of publication
4 Publisher

5 Date of publication
6 Page number or numbers (for notes but not bibliography entries)

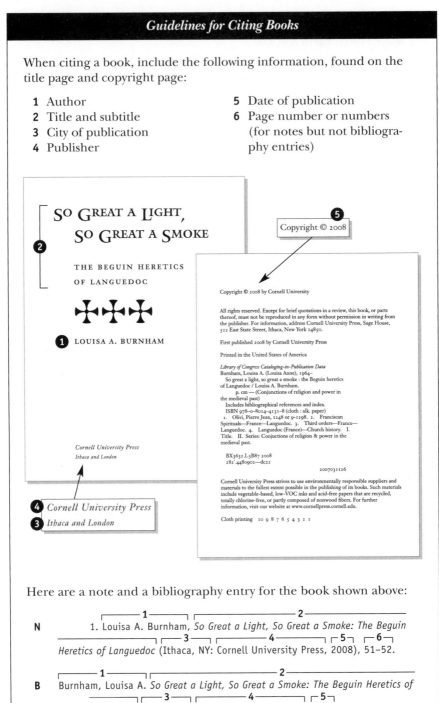

Here are a note and a bibliography entry for the book shown above:

N   1. Louisa A. Burnham, *So Great a Light, So Great a Smoke: The Beguin Heretics of Languedoc* (Ithaca, NY: Cornell University Press, 2008), 51–52.

B   Burnham, Louisa A. *So Great a Light, So Great a Smoke: The Beguin Heretics of Languedoc.* Ithaca, NY: Cornell University Press, 2008.

If the same person translated and edited the book, the abbreviated phrase "trans. and ed." follows the title in the note, but in the bibliography, "trans." and "ed." are spelled out.

N   14. Giovanni Boccaccio, *Famous Women*, trans. and ed. Virginia Brown (Cambridge, MA: Harvard University Press, 2001), 88.

B   Boccaccio, Giovanni. *Famous Women*. Translated and edited by Virginia Brown. Cambridge, MA: Harvard University Press, 2001.

15. BOOK WITH ONE OR MORE EDITORS

If a work has both an author and an editor, keep the author's name at the beginning of both the note and the bibliography entries, and put the name of the editor after the title. In the note, use the abbreviation "ed." before the name of either a single editor or multiple editors. In the bibliography, use the phrase "Edited by."

N   15. John Stuart Mill, *On Liberty*, ed. John Gray (Oxford: Oxford University Press, 2008), 62–63.

B   Mill, John Stuart. *On Liberty*. Edited by John Gray. Oxford: Oxford University Press, 2008.

If an edited work has a single editor and no author, the editor's name, followed by "ed.," takes the place of the author's name. If you are citing only one article from an edited work, see item 16, "Selection in an Edited Work or Anthology."

N   15. Nancy Shoemaker, ed., *Clearing a Path: Theorizing the Past in Native American Studies* (New York: Routledge, 2002), 51.

B   Shoemaker, Nancy, ed. *Clearing a Path: Theorizing the Past in Native American Studies*. New York: Routledge, 2002.

If a work has two or three editors and no author, use the format for two or three authors (see items 6 and 7), but follow the names with "eds."

N   15. Camron Michael Amin, Benjamin C. Fortna, and Elizabeth B. Frierson, eds., *The Modern Middle East: A Sourcebook for History* (Oxford: Oxford University Press, 2006), 326.

B   Amin, Camron Michael, Benjamin C. Fortna, and Elizabeth B. Frierson, eds. *The Modern Middle East: A Sourcebook for History*. Oxford: Oxford University Press, 2006.

If a work has four or more editors and no author, write the full name of only the first editor followed by "et al." to indicate the other editors, and conclude with "eds."

N   15. Esther Breitenbach et al., eds., *The Changing Politics of Gender Equality in Britain* (New York: Palgrave, 2002), 18–21.

B   Breitenbach, Esther, et al., eds. *The Changing Politics of Gender Equality in Britain*. New York: Palgrave, 2002.

16. SELECTION IN AN EDITED WORK OR ANTHOLOGY

If you are using only part of an edited work — for example, a chapter, an essay, one document — begin with the name of the author of that part, followed by the title of the selection, the title of the edited work (preceded by the word "in," which should be capitalized in bibliography entries), the name of the editor (preceded by "ed." in the note and by "edited by" in the bibliography), and publication information.

N   16. Paul R. Jones, "The Two Field System," in *Europe's First Farmers*, ed. T. Douglas Price (Chicago: University of Chicago Press, 2000), 26.

B   Jones, Paul R. "The Two Field System." In *Europe's First Farmers*, edited by T. Douglas Price. Chicago: University of Chicago Press, 2000.

17. LETTER IN A PUBLISHED COLLECTION

For letters and other forms of communication in published collections, begin with the names of the sender and recipient. If available, include the place of writing and the date that the letter was written. Next, include the title of the collection, name of the editor or compiler, and the publication information. Include the page number or numbers in the note but not in the bibliography entry.

N   17. Nicola Sacco to Bartolomeo Vanzetti, Dedham Jail, June 18, 1925, in *The Letters of Sacco and Vanzetti*, ed. Marion Denman Frankfurter and Gardner Jackson (New York: Penguin, 1997), 27–28.

If your paper refers to only one letter in a collection, list it individually in your bibliography, alphabetized by the name of the letter writer.

B   Sacco, Nicola. Nicola Sacco to Bartolomeo Vanzetti, Dedham Jail, June 18, 1925. In *The Letters of Sacco and Vanzetti*, edited by Marion Denman Frankfurter and Gardner Jackson. New York: Penguin, 1997.

If your paper references more than one letter from a collection, the bibliography should include a single entry for the entire collection, beginning with the editor's name, rather than the names of the individual letter writers.

B   Frankfurter, Marion Denman, and Gardner Jackson, eds. *The Letters of Sacco and Vanzetti*. New York: Penguin, 1997.

For a detailed illustration of how to cite a letter in a collection, see pages 184–85.

18. EDITION OTHER THAN THE FIRST

If you are using an edition other than the first edition of a work, place the number of the edition after the title.

N   18. John Charles Chasteen, *Born in Blood and Fire: A Concise History of Latin America*, 2nd ed. (New York: Norton, 2005), 225.

B   Chasteen, John Charles. *Born in Blood and Fire: A Concise History of Latin America*. 2nd ed. New York: Norton, 2005.

If you are using a revised edition, use the abbreviation "rev. ed." in the note and "Rev. ed." in the bibliography.

N   18. Carlton Jackson, *Who Will Take Our Children? The British Evacuation Program of World War II*, rev. ed. (Jefferson, NC: McFarland, 2008), 127.

B   Jackson, Carlton. *Who Will Take Our Children? The British Evacuation Program of World War II*. Rev. ed. Jefferson, NC: McFarland, 2008.

19. MULTIVOLUME WORK

When a work consists of more than one volume and the volumes all have the same title and were published in the same year, the volume number, followed by a colon, goes directly before the page number or numbers in a note. Notice that "vol." is not used and no space separates the colon from the page numbers.

N   19. Michael O'Brien, *Conjectures of Order: Intellectual Life and the American South, 1810–1860* (Chapel Hill: University of North Carolina Press, 2004), 1:193–97.

In the bibliography, the volume number, preceded by "Vol.," follows the title.

B   Michael O'Brien. *Conjectures of Order: Intellectual Life and the American South, 1810–1860*. Vol. 1. Chapel Hill: University of North Carolina Press, 2004.

When each volume of a multivolume work has its own title, the title of the volume you used follows the author's name, and the number of that volume precedes the general title.

N   19. Robert A. Caro, *Master of the Senate*, vol. 3, *The Years of Lyndon Johnson* (New York: Knopf, 2002), 85.

B   Caro, Robert A. *Master of the Senate*. Vol. 3, *The Years of Lyndon Johnson*. New York: Knopf, 2002.

When your bibliographic citation is to all of the volumes of a work, be sure to indicate in the entry the total number of volumes.

B   Schama, Simon. *A History of Britain*. 2 vols. New York: Hyperion, 2000–2001.

20. ENCYCLOPEDIA OR DICTIONARY

Well-known encyclopedias and dictionaries are usually cited in the notes but not in the bibliography. The facts of publication may be omitted, but the edition number is needed unless you are citing the first edition.

When a reference work is organized alphabetically, the title of the item being cited is preceded by "s.v." (short for the Latin *sub verbo*, meaning "under the word"). Volume and page numbers are not needed.

N   20. *The Columbia Dictionary of Quotations*, s.v. "Lincoln, Gettysburg Address."

If the author of an item in an encyclopedia is identified, list the author name at the end of your note, and include the work, alphabetized by the author's last name, in your bibliography.

Guidelines for Citing Letters in Published Collections

When citing a letter in a published collection, include the following information, found on the book's title page and copyright page as well as in the letter itself:

1 Author (sender) of the letter

2 Recipient of the letter, if given

3 Letter writer's location, if given

4 Date, if given

5 Title and subtitle of collection

6 Editor of collection

7 City of publication

8 Publisher

9 Date of publication

10 Page number or numbers (for notes but not bibliography entries)

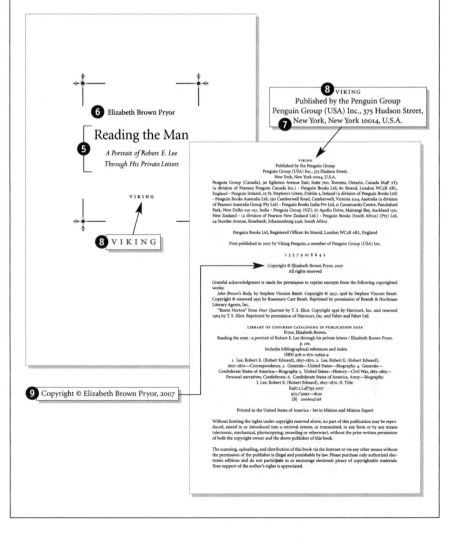

Citing Letters in Published Collections (continued)

10 *110*   Reading the Man

I spent last winter in W[ashington] partly on duty and partly not. Had a pleasant time with my friends in Virginia, and am now here working for my country—I have got through with my paper and have hardly commenced talking to you—We really must have a meeting Mackay, for this letter business is all a humbug. Your acct of the Cherokees &c., was very interesting to me. I hope you will be able to arrange matters peaceably. I see the Sav[annah] Papers are throwing out some commendations upon Genl Scott so I suppose his course is satisfactory to them—The Rumours of the disturbances on the N. Frontier you get from the papers. The boys in Wash. hold out hopes of the passage of the Army Bill and think it will go—I hope so but am dubious—I was glad to hear of all in Broughton Street. I think of them every day. The increase of the Gr^d ...ful but who is doing it Mackay—Mrs. L. joins me in much ...Your true friend RE Lee.^{1}

1

Chapter Seven

Pioneers

2 To—Lt John Mackay
Adjt 2nd Regt U.S. Artillery
Cherokee Agency near Calhoun
Tennessee

3   **4**

St. Louis 27th June 1838

Will you tell me my dear Jack, where the "Cherokee Agency near Calhoun Tenn." is? Is it in these United States, or to what country does it belong? Are all avenues of information closed, shut up and cut off; and is there no method of learning what is doing in the world? I tremble my friend least you have been smuggled off the continent, buried alive, and your days lost to you, yea and your nights too. Why you do not know that I am a sojourner in the "Western Metropolis"! Well! the whereabouts of the great can be but little noted in the "Agency", and a man can be better reconciled not to be famous. It is as true Jack as that I am living, that I am here: And what is more my dame and the little Lees are with me. It is a rough country to bring them to I acknowledge, but they smooth it to me most marvelously. You will now know why your letters have been so long reaching me. The first, March 11th must have nearly died of fatigue; as that of May 18th was treading closely on its heels. This last reached me just as I was on the eve of setting off to the Rapids, about a fortnight since; and I sat down and penned a note instantu to the Genl. to know what was the State of the App^t for the imp^t of the Savannah river; the intention of the Dept in regard to it; the prospect of the work going on &c and whether they wanted a good man & true like yourself to take charge of the business. This of course was done in [an] unofficial way, and I know the Genl will give me all the information in his power, which when rec^d I shall lose no time in handing over to you. But it will take time, Mackay, it will take time.

Why do you allow the "Sovereigns" to bother you? Don't spare them a thought. Do you recollect the Don's injunctions to Sancho, after he had slid

---

ROBERT E. LEE loved to banter with his West Point friend ... and the jocular tone of this message is so pleasing that it ...vs some revealing remarks about the emerging U.S. Army. ...army's work expanded in the Jacksonian period, yet mis...professional military force also grew during these years. ...t Lee casually mentions at the end of his letter did go ...g the army for the first time in two decades, but it was ...l highly politicized. The increased bureaucratization and ...g alienated the young soldier until, "fearing for his moral...rtedly told Mackay, he begged Charles Gratiot, the chief ...n escape Washington and aid in the improvement of west... ...items.^{2}

...cetiousness, it was an important period of maturation for ...uld also personally develop during this time, for he had ...great Western metropolis" to redirect the channel of the ...one of the most demanding engineering projects of the ...with the stubborn current offers a fascinating snapshot of ...ientist. Though later generations have seldom associated ...ental ecological engineering, Lee was in the very vanguard ...mpts to redesign nature. Reverence for innovation and ac...ire to exploit the continent's huge potential, was taking ...nal psyche. Lee and his colleagues in the army may have ...y pageantry and the valor of war, but they were destined to ...itical role on a different stage. With their technical educa-

---

Here are a note and a bibliography entry for the letter shown above:

N   1. Robert E. Lee to John Mackay, St. Louis, June 27, 1838, in *Reading the Man: A Portrait of Robert E. Lee through His Private Letters,* by Elizabeth Brown Pryor (New York: Viking, 2007), 108–110.

B   Lee, Robert E. Robert E. Lee to John Mackay, St. Louis, June 27, 1838. In *Reading the Man: A Portrait of Robert E. Lee through His Private Letters,* by Elizabeth Brown Pryor. New York: Viking, 2007.

N   20. *Handbook of American Women's History*, 2nd ed., s.v. "Willard, Frances E. (1839–1898)," by Anita M. Weber.

B   Weber, Anita M. "Willard, Frances E. (1839–1898)." In *Handbook of American Women's History*, 2nd ed., edited by Angela M. Howard and Frances K. Kavenik. Thousand Oaks, CA: Sage, 2000.

21. BOOK IN A SERIES

If a book you are citing is part of a series, the series title (not italicized) should be included after the book's title (and editor or editors, if applicable). Notice that the editor of the individual book is included, but not the editor of the entire series.

N   21. Sir Walter Ralegh, *The Discovery of Guiana: With Related Documents*, ed. Benjamin Schmidt, Bedford Series in History and Culture (Boston: Bedford/St. Martin's, 2008), 27.

B   Ralegh, Sir Walter. *The Discovery of Guiana: With Related Documents*. Edited by Benjamin Schmidt. Bedford Series in History and Culture. New York: Bedford/ St. Martin's, 2008.

22. SACRED TEXT

When documenting sacred religious works such as the Bible or the Qur'an, give the chapter and verse numbers (or their equivalents), separated by a colon. For the Bible, begin with an abbreviation of the book name ("Matt.," "Gen.," etc.), and end with the version you are referencing ("Revised Standard Version," "New American Bible," etc.). Page numbers are not necessary.

N   22. Rom. 2:1–4 (Revised Standard Version).

N   22. Qur'an 17:90–93.

Sacred texts are usually not included in bibliographies.

Periodicals

23. BASIC FORMAT FOR A JOURNAL ARTICLE

In a note for a journal article, include the author's full name followed by a comma; the title of the article followed by a comma, all in quotation marks; the title of the journal, italicized or underlined; the volume number (and issue number, if given) of the journal; the date of publication in parentheses, followed by a colon; and the page or pages cited, followed by a period.

N   23. Wendy Goldman, "Stalinist Terror and Democracy: The 1937 Union Campaign," *American Historical Review* 110, no. 5 (2005): 1435.

Bibliography entries include nearly the same information but presented differently. The author's name appears last name first, periods (not commas) separate items, and inclusive page numbers for the article are listed.

B   Goldman, Wendy. "Stalinist Terror and Democracy: The 1937 Union Campaign." *American Historical Review* 110, no. 5 (2005): 1427–53.

For a detailed illustration of a print journal citation, see page 188. For author variations, see items 5 through 11. For shortened forms for subsequent references to the same source, see item 2.

24. JOURNAL ARTICLE ACCESSED FROM A DATABASE

Cite a journal article that you accessed from an electronic database as you would cite an article from a printed journal (see item 23). Then add the URL of the database you used and the date on which you accessed the article.

N   24. Robert Finlay, "Weaving the Rainbow: Visions of Color in World History," *Journal of World History* 18, no. 4 (December 2007): 402–03, http://muse.jhu.edu/login?uri=/journals/journal_of_world_history/v018/18.4finlay.html (accessed January 20, 2009).

B   Finlay, Robert. "Weaving the Rainbow: Visions of Color in World History." *Journal of World History* 18, no. 4 (December 2007): 383–431. http://muse.jhu.edu/login?uri=/journals/journal_of_world_history/v018/18.4finlay.html (accessed January 20, 2009).

For a detailed illustration of a database article citation, see page 189.

25. ARTICLE IN AN ONLINE JOURNAL

Cite an article from an online journal as you would cite an article in a printed journal. If the journal was part of a database, include the title of the database, the creator of the database (if available), the URL of the article, and the date you accessed it. If you read the journal on the journal's own Web site, then use the URL of that site, as in the following example.

N   25. Scott Gac, "Jazz Strategy: Dizzy, Foreign Policy, and Government in 1956," *Journal of American Popular Culture* 4 (Spring 2005), http://www.americanpopularculture.com/journal/articles/spring_2005/gac.htm (accessed January 21, 2006).

B   Gac, Scott. "Jazz Strategy: Dizzy, Foreign Policy, and Government in 1956." *Journal of American Popular Culture* 4 (Spring 2005). http://www.americanpopularculture.com/journal/articles/spring_2005/gac.htm (accessed March 4, 2006).

26. ARTICLE IN A MAGAZINE

Reference to a popular magazine (rather than to a scholarly journal) requires author, title of article, title of magazine, date, but no volume or issue number. Include the cited page number or numbers in the note, preceded by a comma, but do not include any page numbers in the bibliography entry.

N   26. Greg Grandin, "Latin America's New Consensus," *Nation*, May 1, 2006, 24.

B   Grandin, Greg. "Latin America's New Consensus." *Nation*, May 1, 2006.

27. ARTICLE IN A NEWSPAPER

Individual articles from daily newspapers usually are not listed in a bibliography, but they are cited in notes. Reference to a newspaper article requires issue date (day, month, year), as well as author name (if available), article title,

When citing a journal article that you accessed in print, include the following information, found on the journal's title page as well as in the article:

1 Author

2 Title of article

3 Title of journal

4 Volume number

5 Issue number, if given

6 Date of publication

7 Page number or numbers

---

3 **The Journal of American History**
Published by the Organization of American Historians

4 **5** **6**
Vol. 95   No. 1   June 2008

© 2008 by the Organization of American Historians

The *Journal of American History*, formerly the *Mississippi Valley Historical* quarterly by the Organization of American Historians.

Manuscript submissions, books for review, and correspondence concerning editorial matters should be addressed to the **Editorial Office: Journal of** **1215 East Atwater Ave., Bloomington, Indiana 47401-3703, USA** (teleph fax: 812-855-9939; e-mail: jah@indiana.edu).

Guidelines for manuscript submission can be found at the *Journal W* .journalofamericanhistory.org/.

Please do not submit a manuscript that has been published or that is curre ation for publication elsewhere in either article or book form. The *Journal w* missions that duplicate other published works in either wording or substanc

The Organization of American Historians disclaims responsibility for sta fact or of opinion, made by contributors.

Changes of address, returned or undeliverable copies, and correspondence c ship, dues, subscriptions, back issues, advertising, the annual meeting, and al ters should be addressed to the **Executive Office: Organization of Americ** North Bryan Ave., P.O. Box 5457, Bloomington, Indiana 47407-5457, 855-7311; fax: 812-855-0696; e-mail: oah@oah.org; Web site: http://www.c

Printed in March, June, September, and December by Edwards Brothers, In Carolina 27546.

The Organization of American Historians promotes excellenc teaching, and presentation of American history and encourag historical questions and equitable treatment of all practitioner

The *Journal of American History*: ISSN 0021-8723. Individual members of American Historians ($35–$190 per year) receive the *Journal* or the *OAH* Institutional subscribers ($110–$400 per year) receive the *Journal* and the *tory*. All members and institutional subscribers receive the *OAH Newsletter* and Program. To become a member or institutional subscriber, go to http://w icals class postage paid at Bloomington, Indiana, and at additional maili 278180.

Postmaster: Send address changes to Executive Office address above.

---

2 **Warming the Poor and Growing Consumers: Fuel Philanthropy in the Early Republic's Urban North**

1 Sean Patrick Adams

Residents of Boston, New York, and Philadelphia at the turn of the nineteenth century had every reason to be optimistic, as their cities blossomed as centers of commerce, culture, and industry in a young, growing nation. But no matter how rosy the future might appear, the winters of the early republic seemed to get worse and worse. Take the southernmost city of the three, Philadelphia. In the winter of 1805, when snow drifts reached thirty inches high, the price of a cord of oak wood—traditionally defined as a stack four feet high, four feet wide, and eight feet long—shot up to $12. That was more than double the price per cord earlier that year. The city's working poor suffered the most under such conditions. The *Philadelphia American Daily Advertiser* reported that one family, "having expended all their wood, was under the direful necessity, in order to keep themselves from perishing, to burn their table, washing-tub, and many other articles of household furniture." Many froze to death in their own homes. "Scenes like these proclaim the uncertainty of human possessions & enjoyments & the incapacity of man to protect himself against adversity," the Philadelphia merchant Thomas P. Cope wrote in his diary that winter. "It is during these seasons of suffering that the voice of omnipotence is heard & confessed." During February of 1809 Charles Peirce, an amateur historian of Philadelphia weather, estimated the average temperature at twenty-six degrees Fahrenheit and recorded three consecutive days when the thermometer remained below zero. The poor suffered the brunt of the bitter season as firewood shortages caused the price of fuel to spike yet again. In this most temperate of the major northern cities of the early republic—in which the physician, geologist, and amateur meteorologist James Mease bragged that "our winters are less uniformly cold, and more variable" than those of other cities and that the Delaware River froze solid for only two weeks at a time by 1811—the pinch of cold weather coupled with fuel shortages made urban life more and more difficult in the winter.[1]

Sean Patrick Adams is associate professor of history at the University of Florida. The author would like to thank Juliana Barr, Matt Gallman, Dan Graff, Howell Harris, Karl Jacoby, Richard John, Cathy Matson, Larry Peskin, Conrad Edick Wright, and the anonymous readers for the *Journal of American History* for their comments on earlier versions of this essay. The author would also like to thank the National Endowment for the Humanities, the Program in Early American Economy and Society in Philadelphia, and the Gilder Lehrman Institute of American History for their generous financial support for this project and the Library Company of Philadelphia for support and also for permission to use illustrations from its collection.
Readers may contact Adams at spadams@history.ufl.edu.

[1] *Philadelphia American Daily Advertiser*, Jan. 25, 28, 1805; Eliza Cope Harrison, ed., *Philadelphia Merchant: The Diary of Thomas P. Cope, 1800–1851* (South Bend, 1978), 178; Charles Peirce, *A Meteorological Account of the Weather in Philadelphia, from January 1, 1790 to January 1, 1847, Including Fifty-Seven Years* (Philadelphia, 1847) 37–38; James Mease, *The Picture of Philadelphia, Giving an Account of Its Origin...se in Improvements in Arts, Science, Manufactures, Commerce and Revenue with a Compendious View of Its So...benevolent, Patriotic*

June 2008   The Journal of American History   **7** 69 ▶ 69

Here are a note and a bibliography entry for the article shown above:

N   1. Sean Patrick Adams, "Warming the Poor and Growing Consumers: Fuel Philanthropy in the Early Republic's Urban North," *Journal of American History* 95, no. 1 (June 2008): 73.

B   Adams, Sean Patrick. "Warming the Poor and Growing Consumers: Fuel Philanthropy in the Early Republic's Urban North." *Journal of American History* 95, no. 1 (June 2008): 69–94.

When citing a journal article that you accessed from an electronic database, include the following information:

1 Author
2 Title of article
3 Title of journal
4 Volume number
5 Issue number, if given

6 Date of publication
7 Page number or numbers (often visible in PDF file)
8 URL of database
9 Access date

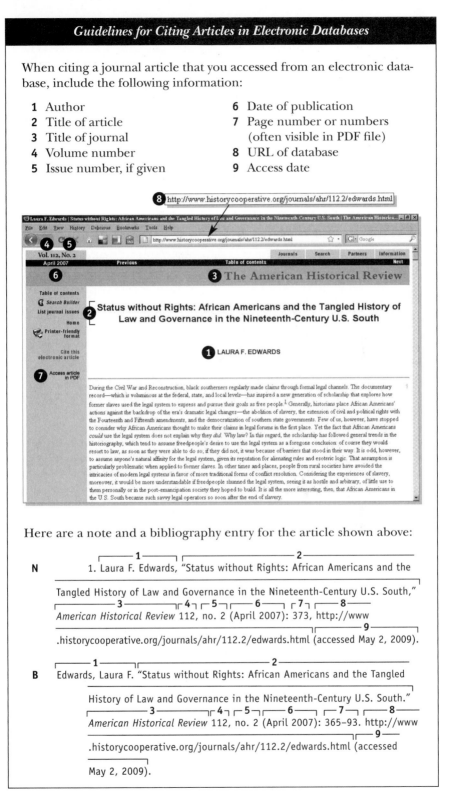

Here are a note and a bibliography entry for the article shown above:

N   1. Laura F. Edwards, "Status without Rights: African Americans and the Tangled History of Law and Governance in the Nineteenth-Century U.S. South," *American Historical Review* 112, no. 2 (April 2007): 373, http://www .historycooperative.org/journals/ahr/112.2/edwards.html (accessed May 2, 2009).

B   Edwards, Laura F. "Status without Rights: African Americans and the Tangled History of Law and Governance in the Nineteenth-Century U.S. South." *American Historical Review* 112, no. 2 (April 2007): 365–93. http://www .historycooperative.org/journals/ahr/112.2/edwards.html (accessed May 2, 2009).

and newspaper name. If the newspaper has separate sections, add the number, letter, or name of the section in which the article begins. Use the abbreviation "sec." Page numbers can be omitted, as they may vary from one edition of a daily paper to the next.

N   27. Steven R. Weisman, "South Korea, Once a Solid Ally, Now Poses Problems for the U.S.," *New York Times*, January 2, 2003, sec. A.

28. ARTICLE FROM AN ONLINE NEWS SOURCE

Include author name (if given), article title, name of the online newspaper or service, date of publication, URL, and date of access.

N   28. Adam Nagourney, "Obama Wins Election; McCain Loses as Bush Legacy Is Rejected," *New York Times*, November 4, 2008, http://www.nytimes.com/2008/11/05/us/politics/05campaign.html?_r=1 (accessed March 12, 2009).

B   Nagourney, Adam. "Obama Wins Election; McCain Loses as Bush Legacy Is Rejected." *New York Times*, November 4, 2008. http://www.nytimes.com/2008/11/05/us/politics/05campaign.html?_r=1 (accessed March 12, 2009).

29. EDITORIAL

The editorial page of a newspaper generally has short articles written by a member of the paper's editorial board as well as by invited columnists. If the name of the writer accompanies the editorial, then cite the editorial as you would an article in a newspaper. If the editorial is unsigned, write "Editorial" in the position usually reserved for an author's name. Newspaper editorials are not included in the bibliography.

N   29. Editorial, "Saving Detroit from Itself," *New York Times*, November 15, 2008, sec. A.

Editorials from magazines are listed in the bibliography. When you cite an editorial from a magazine, list the name of the editorial writer (if known), the title of the editorial, the name of the magazine, and the issue date. If the editorial is unsigned, write "Editorial" in the author position.

B   Winfrey, Carey. "Standing Tall: Niger's Giraffes and Our 16th President." *Smithsonian* 39, no. 8 (November 2008): 8.

30. LETTER TO THE EDITOR

To cite a letter to the editor of a magazine or a journal, list the author's name, followed by the identifier "letter to the editor," then the publication information.

N   30. Andrew Morriss, letter to the editor, *The Economist* 389, no. 8605 (2008): 20.

B   Morriss, Andrew. Letter to the editor. *The Economist* 389, no. 8605 (2008): 20.

For notes citing letters to the editor of a newspaper, use the same identifier after the writer's name and then provide publication information. Such letters are not listed in the bibliography.

N   30. Eric Chivian, letter to the editor, *Boston Globe*, January 21, 2003, sec. A.

31. BOOK REVIEW OR FILM REVIEW

In a reference to a book review or a film review, include the author of the review, the title (if any) of the review followed by the phrase "review of," the title of the book or film being reviewed, the name of the author or director of the reviewed work, and the relevant publication information.

N   31. Harold Kinkaid, "Scientific Historiography and the Philosophy of Science," review of *Our Knowledge of the Past: A Philosophy of Historiography*, by Aviezer Tucker, *History and Theory* 45 (2006): 125.

B   Kinkaid, Harold. "Scientific Historiography and the Philosophy of Science." Review of *Our Knowledge of the Past: A Philosophy of Historiography*, by Aviezer Tucker. *History and Theory* 45 (2006): 124–133.

32. ONLINE REVIEW

For a review accessed online, include the URL and, if required by your instructor, the date you accessed the review.

N   32. Bruce Heydt, review of *The King's Reformation: Henry VIII and the Remaking of the English Church*, by G. W. Bernard, HistoryNet, June 12, 2006, http://www.historynet.com/reviews (accessed January 31, 2009).

B   Heydt, Bruce. Review of *The King's Reformation: Henry VIII and the Remaking of the English Church*, by G. W. Bernard. HistoryNet. June 12, 2006. http://www.historynet.com/reviews (accessed January 31, 2009).

Public Documents

For government publications, begin the citation with the name of the national, state, city, county, or other government entity that issued the document you used as a source. If subdivisions of that entity, such as a committee of the U.S. House of Representatives (see item 33), are listed on the title page, they should come next, followed by the document title in italics. If the author or editor of the document is identified, list that person's name. Then provide a document or report number to help other researchers locate the document. The name of the publisher is necessary only if it differs from the issuing body. The Government Printing Office (GPO) publishes many U.S. government documents. Finally, include the publication date and (for a note) page numbers. If the government document is online, include the URL and date of access.

The following items are models for different kinds of government documents. They are intended not to be exhaustive but to give a sense of how to cite some types of public documents.

33. U.S. LEGISLATIVE BRANCH COMMITTEE REPORT

N   33. U.S. Congress, House, Select Committee on Assassinations, *Report of the Select Committee on Assassinations* (Washington, DC: GPO, 1979), 84.

B   U.S. House of Representatives. Select Committee on Assassinations. *Report of the Select Committee on Assassinations*. Washington, DC: GPO, 1979.

34. U.S. TREATY

N   34. U.S. Department of State, "The Paris Peace Accords," January 27, 1973, *United States Treaties and Other International Agreements* 24, pt. 1.

B   U.S. Department of State. "The Paris Peace Accords." January 27, 1973. *United States Treaties and Other International Agreements* 24, pt. 1.

35. U.S. SUPREME COURT DECISION

N   35. U.S. Supreme Court, *Brown v. Board of Education of Topeka, Kansas*, Case # 347US483, May 17, 1954.

B   U.S. Supreme Court. *Brown v. Board of Education of Topeka, Kansas*. Case # 347US483. May 17, 1954.

36. CANADIAN LEGISLATIVE BRANCH COMMITTEE REPORT

N   36. Canada, House of Commons, Standing Committee on Canadian Heritage, *Interim Report on the Canadian Film Industry* (Ottawa: June 2005), 24.

B   Canada. House of Commons. Standing Committee on Canadian Heritage. *Interim Report on the Canadian Film Industry*. Ottawa: June 2005.

37. ONLINE GOVERNMENT DOCUMENT

N   37. U.S. Congress, House, Committee on Government Reform and Oversight, *National Drug Policy: A Review of the Status of the Drug War* (Washington, DC: GPO, 1996), 6, http://frwebgate.access.gpo.gov/cgi-bin/getdoc.cgi?dbname=104_cong _reports&docid=f:hr486.104.pdf (accessed April 4, 2009).

B   U.S. Congress, House. Committee on Government Reform and Oversight. *National Drug Policy: A Review of the Status of the Drug War*. Washington, DC: GPO, 1996. http://frwebgate.access.gpo.gov/cgi-bin/getdoc.cgi?dbname=104_cong _reports&docid=f:hr486.104.pdf (accessed April 4, 2009).

Multimedia Sources

38. MATERIAL FROM A WEB SITE

Much of the material you find online is a specific type of source (a government document, an article, a book) that you can cite by following the style for that particular item, then adding a URL and access date. Some online material, however, is unique to the Web. When citing original material from a Web site, refer to the models below.

If the author is known, include his or her name, the title of the document, the title or owner of the Web site, the URL, and the date of access.

N   38. E. L. Skip Knox, "The Papacy," *Europe in the Late Middle Ages*, http://www.boisestate.edu/courses/latemiddleages/papacy/ (accessed February 8, 2009).

B   Knox, E. L. Skip. "The Papacy." *Europe in the Late Middle Ages*. http://www.boisestate .edu/courses/latemiddleages/papacy/ (accessed February 8, 2009).

If you are citing a Web document whose authorship is unknown, begin with the owner of the site.

N   38. National Park Service, "Ancestral Puebloans and Their World," *Mesa Verde National Park*, https://imrcms.nps.gov/meve/forteachers/upload/ancestral _puebloans.pdf (accessed October 15, 2008).

B   National Park Service. "Ancestral Puebloans and Their World." *Mesa Verde National Park*. https://imrcms.nps.gov/meve/forteachers/upload/ancestral _puebloans.pdf (accessed October 15, 2008).

For a detailed illustration of how to cite original material from a Web site, see page 194.

NOTE: *Chicago Manual of Style* does not provide specific advice for how to handle exceptionally long URLs. If the URL of your source is very long, you may choose to provide your source's home-page URL along with a series of links that lead to the specific source. For example, the note below has a very long URL:

N   38. Wilbur Roberts, "Alphabet Song," in "Florida Folklife from the WPA Collections," *American Memory*, http://memory.loc.gov/cgi-bin/ampage?collId=afcflwpa &fileName=tt0001/afcflwpatt0001page.db&recNum=0&itemLink=S?ammem/flwpabib: @filreq(@field(TITLE+@od1(Alphabet+Song++Textual+Transcription+))+@field (RESOURCETYPE+@od1(text))) (accessed February 16, 2009).

You may prefer to cite it this way:

N   38. Wilbur Roberts, "Alphabet Song," in "Florida Folklife from the WPA Collections," *American Memory*, http://memory.loc.gov/ammem/collections/florida/index .html → browse collection by → manuscript → "Wilbur Roberts Alphabet" → Alphabet Song [Textual Transcription] → view page images (accessed February 16, 2009).

39. DVD OR VIDEOCASSETTE

The citation for a DVD or a videocassette includes the title of the film or episode, followed by the name of the series (if applicable), the type of medium, the name of the director, and the publication information.

N   39. "The Challenge of Freedom," *Slavery and the Making of America*, DVD, directed by Leslie D. Farrell (New York: Ambrose Video, 2005).

B   "The Challenge of Freedom." *Slavery and the Making of America*. DVD. Directed by Leslie D. Farrell. New York: Ambrose Video, 2005.

40. BROADCAST INTERVIEW

For a broadcast interview, include the name of the person interviewed, the title of the interview (if any), the name of the interviewer, the name of the show and network on which the interview appeared, and the date. If the broadcast was retrieved from an online archive or from some other source (such as a DVD or a museum archive), include that information as well.

N   40. Saddam Hussein, interviewed by Dan Rather, *CBS News*, CBS, February 24, 2003, http://www.cbsnews.com/htdocs/iraq/framesource_interview.html (accessed March 17, 2009).

Guidelines for Citing Information from Web Sites

When citing original material that you found on a Web site, include as much of the following information as possible:

1 Author or sponsoring institution

2 Title of the document or selection

3 Title of the site

4 URL

5 Access date

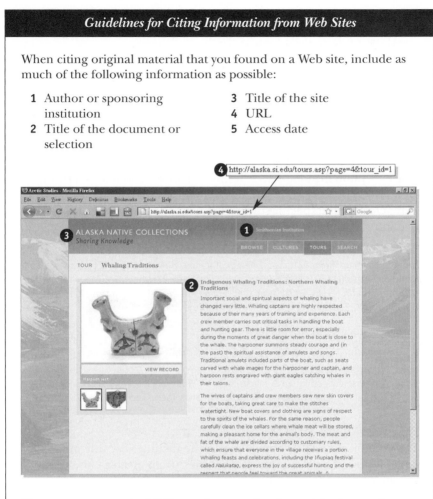

Here are a note and a bibliography entry for the article shown above:

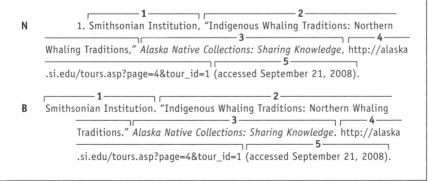

N   1. Smithsonian Institution, "Indigenous Whaling Traditions: Northern Whaling Traditions," *Alaska Native Collections: Sharing Knowledge*, http://alaska.si.edu/tours.asp?page=4&tour_id=1 (accessed September 21, 2008).

B   Smithsonian Institution. "Indigenous Whaling Traditions: Northern Whaling Traditions." *Alaska Native Collections: Sharing Knowledge*. http://alaska.si.edu/tours.asp?page=4&tour_id=1 (accessed September 21, 2008).

Broadcast interviews are not included in bibliographies. For information on citing a published transcript of an interview, see item 50. For personal interviews, see item 56.

41. RECORDED SPEECH OR READING

List the speaker, the title of the recording (italicized), the publication information, and the medium.

N 41. Martin Luther King Jr., *I Have a Dream* (London: Open Source Studios, 2005), MP3.

B King, Martin Luther, Jr. *I Have a Dream*. London: Open Source Studios, 2005. MP3.

To cite an unrecorded lecture or public address, see item 55.

42. MUSICAL RECORDING

For a recorded musical composition, list the name of the composer, the title of the piece (italicized), the performer or performers, the recording company, the number of the recording, and the medium.

N 42. Bernard Rands, *Le Tambourin, Suites 1 and 2*, Philadelphia Orchestra, New World Records 80392, compact disc.

B Rands, Bernard. *Le Tambourin, Suites 1 and 2*. Philadelphia Orchestra. New World Records 80392. Compact disc.

For information on citing a printed musical composition, see item 51.

43. CD-ROM

To cite a CD-ROM, list the title, the name of the production company, the location of the company, and the date.

N 43. *U.S. History: The American West*, CD-ROM (San Jose: Fogware Publishing, 2001).

B *U.S. History: The American West*. CD-ROM. San Jose: Fogware Publishing, 2001.

44. WORK OF ART

If you found an illustration or a photograph in a printed work, begin with the name of the artist, followed by the title of the work of art, the title of the book or article in which you found it, and the publication information. Include the page number at the end of the note.

N 44. Alexis Preller, "Hieratic Women," in *A History of Art*, rev. ed., ed. Sir Lawrence Gowing (Ann Arbor: Borders Press, 2002), 973.

B Preller, Alexis. "Hieratic Women." In *A History of Art*. Rev. ed. Edited by Sir Lawrence Gowing. Ann Arbor: Borders Press, 2002.

If the artist is unknown, begin with the title or description of the work.

N 44. "A Chavin Hammered Gold Plaque," in *A History of Art*, rev. ed., ed. Sir Lawrence Gowing (Ann Arbor: Borders Press, 2002), 479.

B   "A Chavin Hammered Gold Plaque." In *A History of Art*. Rev. ed. Edited by Sir Lawrence Gowing. Ann Arbor: Borders Press, 2002.

If you saw the photograph, painting, or sculpture in a museum, an archive, or a private collection, tell the reader where you saw it. Include the name of the artist, the title of the work, the type of medium, the date the work was created, and where it can be found.

N   44. Ansel Adams, *The Golden Gate before the Bridge, San Francisco, California,* gelatin silver print, 1980, National Gallery of Art, Washington, DC.

B   Adams, Ansel. *The Golden Gate before the Bridge, San Francisco, California.* Gelatin silver print. 1980. National Gallery of Art, Washington, DC.

45. SLIDE

A citation for slides should include the compiler of the collection, the title of the collection, the name of the editor (if any), the publication information, and the identifier "slides."

N   45. Elizabeth Hammer, *The Arts of Korea: A Resource for Educators*, ed. Judith G. Smith (New York: Metropolitan Museum of Art, 2002), slides.

B   Hammer, Elizabeth. *The Arts of Korea: A Resource for Educators.* Edited by Judith G. Smith. New York: Metropolitan Museum of Art, 2002. Slides.

46. MAP OR ILLUSTRATION

Treat a map or an illustration that you found in a printed work as you would treat any other printed visual. Include the name of the map designer or illustrator (if one is recorded), the title of the map or illustration followed by "in," then the title of the work in which the visual was found, the author or editor of the work, and the usual publication information. Include the page number at the end of the note.

N   46. "Francophone France in 1863," in *The Discovery of France: A Historical Geography from the Revolution to the First World War*, by Graham Robb (New York: Norton, 2007), 54.

B   "Francophone France in 1863." In *The Discovery of France: A Historical Geography from the Revolution to the First World War*, by Graham Robb. New York: Norton, 2007.

47. CHART, GRAPH, OR TABLE

If a chart is in a printed work, treat it as you would a map or an illustration. Include the title of the chart, graph, or table, usually found beneath it, and the publication information for the work in which it appeared. Include the page number at the end of the note.

N   47. "Reich Elections, 1919–1933," in *The Weimar Republic*, 2nd ed., by Eberhard Kolb (New York: Routledge, 2005), 224–25.

B   "Reich Elections, 1919–1933." In *The Weimar Republic*, 2nd ed., by Eberhard Kolb. New York: Routledge, 2005.

Other Published Sources

48. PAMPHLET

Cite a pamphlet as you would a book.

N   48. United Nations, *Report of the United Nations High Commissioner for Refugees* (New York: United Nations Press, 2008), 25.

B   United Nations. *Report of the United Nations High Commissioner for Refugees.* New York: United Nations Press, 2008.

49. DISSERTATION ABSTRACT

To cite a dissertation abstract, list the work as you would list a dissertation (see item 53), but indicate where you found the abstract, including volume number and date (if applicable) before the page number.

N   49. David Charles Engerman, "America, Russia and the Romance of Economic Development" (PhD diss., University of California, Berkeley, 1999), abstract in *America since 1607* 678 (1999): 308t.

B   Engerman, David Charles. "America, Russia and the Romance of Economic Development." PhD diss., University of California, Berkeley, 1999. Abstract in *America since 1607* 678 (1999): 308t.

If you accessed the abstract in an electronic database, include the name of the database, the URL, and the date of access.

N   49. Catherine Yoonah Bae, "All the Girl's a Stage: Representations of Femininity and Adolescence in Japanese Girls' Magazines, 1930s–1960s" (PhD diss., Stanford University, 2008), abstract in *Proquest Dissertations and Theses Online*, http://proquest.umi.com/pqdweb?did=1539272921&sid=1&Fmt=2&clientId=20179&RQT=309&VName=PQD (accessed January 21, 2009).

B   Bae, Catherine Yoonah. "All the Girl's a Stage: Representations of Femininity and Adolescence in Japanese Girls' Magazines, 1930s–1960s." PhD diss., Stanford University, 2008. Abstract in *Proquest Dissertations and Theses Online*. http://proquest.umi.com/pqdweb?did=1539272921&sid=1&Fmt=2&clientId=20179&RQT=309&VName=PQD (accessed January 21, 2009).

50. PUBLISHED INTERVIEW OR TRANSCRIPT

If an interview has been published, cite it by listing the person interviewed, the title of the interview, the name of the interviewer, the name of the publication, the date, and the page number.

N   50. Herman J. Viola, "Viola Records the View of the American Indian," interview by Stephen Goode, *Insight on the News*, January 3, 2000, 37.

B   Viola, Herman J. "Viola Records the View of the American Indian." Interview by Stephen Goode. *Insight on the News*, January 3, 2000.

For personal interviews that you conducted yourself, see item 56. For broadcast interviews, see item 40.

51. MUSICAL COMPOSITION

To cite a printed musical score, list the composer, the title of the piece, the editor or arranger (if applicable), and the publication information. If the score is part of a series, list the volume number and title of the series after the title of the score.

N   51. Luciano Berio, *Alternatim: per clarinetto, viola e orchestra* (Vienna: Universal Edition, 2001).

B   Berio, Luciano. *Alternatim: per clarinetto, viola e orchestra.* Vienna: Universal Edition, 2001.

If you are citing a musical recording rather than a score, see item 42.

52. SOURCE QUOTED IN ANOTHER SOURCE

You should try to track down every original source you wish to cite, but you may not always be able to do so. When citing a source (such as a long quotation) that you discovered in another person's work, begin with the information about the original source, and then provide details of the secondary source where you found it.

N   52. *Baltimore Herald*, July 3, 1903, quoted in Edmund Morris, *Theodore Rex* (New York: Random House, 2002), 257.

B   *Baltimore Herald*, July 3, 1903. Quoted in Edmund Morris, *Theodore Rex*. New York: Random House, 2002.

Unpublished Sources

53. UNPUBLISHED THESIS OR DISSERTATION

After the name of the author, give the title of the dissertation in quotation marks. For a note, indicate within parentheses the type of thesis ("master's thesis," "PhD diss.," etc.), the university at which the paper was written, and the date, all separated by commas, and provide the page number or numbers outside the parentheses.

N   53. Daniel R. Magaziner, "From Students to Prophets: Writing a Political Faith in South Africa, 1968–1977" (PhD diss., University of Wisconsin–Madison, 2007), 143–48.

B   Magaziner, Daniel R. "From Students to Prophets: Writing a Political Faith in South Africa, 1968–1977." PhD diss., University of Wisconsin–Madison, 2007.

54. UNPUBLISHED LETTER IN A MANUSCRIPT COLLECTION

As with published letters (see item 17), begin with names of the sender and recipient, followed by the place of writing and the date the letter was written (if available). Also include identifying information about the manuscript collection, such as the name and location of the collection and the number of the file, box, or container where the letter reposes.

N 54. John Potts to Robert E. Hobard, December 5, 1805, Alexandria, Virginia, letter box 1, folder 1, John Potts Business Papers, Hagley Museum and Library, Greenville, DE.

If your paper refers to only one letter in a collection, list it individually in your bibliography, alphabetized by the name of the letter writer.

B Potts, John. John Potts to Robert E. Hobard. December 5, 1805. John Potts Business Papers. Hagley Museum and Library, Greenville, DE.

If your paper references more than one letter from a collection, your bibliography should list the entire collection rather than the individual letters.

B Potts, John. Business Papers. Hagley Museum and Library, Greenville, DE.

55. UNPUBLISHED LECTURE, PAPER, OR PUBLIC ADDRESS

To cite a lecture, paper, or public address that has not been published, list the name of the speaker and the title of the presentation. Then, in parentheses, identify the type of program, the sponsoring organization, the location, and the date.

N 55. Eva Bremner, "From Heldenkaiser to Hausvater: Wilhelm I as the King of Christmas" (paper presented at Young Scholars Forum, "Gender, Power, Religion: Forces in Cultural History," at the German Historical Institute, Washington, DC, March 31, 2001).

B Bremner, Eva. "From Heldenkaiser to Hausvater: Wilhelm I as the King of Christmas." Paper presented at Young Scholars Forum, "Gender, Power, Religion: Forces in Cultural History," at the German Historical Institute, Washington, DC, March 31, 2001.

For a recorded speech or reading, see item 41. For a published lecture, follow the format for the source in which it was published (book, journal article, etc.).

56. PERSONAL INTERVIEW

To cite an interview that you conducted yourself, start with the name of the person you interviewed. Then describe the nature of the interview ("telephone interview by author"; "in-person interview by author"), the place of the interview (if applicable), and the interview date. Do not list personal interviews in your bibliography.

N 56. Sandra Thurlow, telephone interview by author, April 7, 2009.

For broadcast interviews, see item 40. For published transcripts of interviews, see item 50.

57. PERSONAL E-MAIL MESSAGE OR LETTER

Be sure to obtain permission to use the content of an e-mail message or a letter from the person who wrote it. In the citation, begin with the author's name, the type of message ("e-mail message to author"; "letter to author"), and the date on which it was sent. Do not include the author's e-mail address in your citation. Do not list personal letters or e-mail messages in your bibliography.

N   57. Heidi Hood, e-mail message to author, March 26, 2009.

58. WEB FORUM OR DISCUSSION LIST POSTING

Give the author's name, the thread title if there is one, the name of the forum or discussion list, the date when it was posted, and the date on which you read the posting. Do not include the author's e-mail address in the citation. Do not include online forum and list postings in your bibliography.

N   58. Eva Swidler, "RE: Peasant resistance and agricultural degradation," posting to H-Environment Discussion Log, December 4, 2008, http://h-net.msu.edu/cgi-bin/logbrowse.pl?trx=vx&list=H-Environment&month=0812&week=a&msg=fN/9gq3Bz0qmc6LRsAZs2w&user=&pw= (accessed January 14, 2009).

APPENDIX

A

Resources for History Research

The resources in Appendix A will assist you in choosing a **topic**, narrowing a topic, and conducting research on a topic. Different kinds of resources lead you to different kinds of information. Some are most useful at the beginning of your research when you are choosing or refining the topic. Others are necessary later, when you are gathering the information that will support your **thesis**. **Historical dictionaries**, **historical encyclopedias**, and **historical atlases**, for example, will be especially useful in the early stages of your research. More specialized resources in world and U.S. history should be consulted once you have chosen your topic and become familiar with the basic information about it.

The categories of resources described in this appendix are as follows:

- Historical dictionaries, encyclopedias, and atlases (p. 202)
- Biography collections (p. 207)
- Newspaper indexes and databases (p. 209)
- Periodical indexes and databases (p. 210)
- Public documents (p. 212)
- Historical statistics (p. 215)
- General resources in world history (p. 218)
- Specialized resources in world history (p. 221)
- General resources in United States history (p. 242)
- Specialized resources in United States history (p. 245)

Each category begins with a brief description of the kinds of information the listed resources contain and at what stage of your research they are likely to be most helpful. Within each category, individual items are listed alphabetically by title. In most cases, the title is followed by the name of the person or organization that compiled the resource and then by the publication information or the URL.

The resources listed in Appendix A are available in most college libraries. If a particular resource is not available to you, try another. A more complete list of resources is included in "A Student's Online Guide to History Reference Sources" at this book's Web site: <bedfordstmartins.com/benjamin>.

Because print sources are generally easier to find and to evaluate than online sources, Appendix A emphasizes Web sites. Online material varies greatly in quality, and care must be taken when using sources from Web sites. The sites included here are reliable sources of high-quality research material. As noted in Chapter 6, full-text digital resources are often available only by library subscription. If your school has not purchased access to a particular resource, you will need to search out an alternative.

Resources on CD-ROM or **microfiche** should be included in your library's **online catalog**. As always, the reference librarian is the best guide to your library's information resources.

HISTORICAL DICTIONARIES, ENCYCLOPEDIAS, AND ATLASES

The resources included here will be most useful when you are choosing and refining a topic. Once you have begun research on a particular topic, they also may be helpful by explaining any unusual terms you may encounter.

A *historical dictionary* will help you define a term such as "Austro-Hungarian Empire." The brief description of this term will tell you when the empire existed, what lands it encompassed, the names of its rulers, and several of its major characteristics. This information will let you know if the term falls within the subject area of your course, and if it seems of interest to you as a possible topic. At later stages of your research, you can use a historical dictionary to obtain a brief description of a term you came across in your reading.

In most cases a *historical encyclopedia* treats a term in greater depth than a historical dictionary. It might describe how the Austro-Hungarian Empire was formed, the forces that enabled it to expand, its alliances and conflicts with neighboring states and empires, the tensions among the different peoples who were part of the empire, and the forces that worked to break up the empire. An encyclopedia article can be of assistance in choosing a topic, and in determining which aspects of the topic you wish to pursue.

A *historical atlas* contains a series of maps showing geographical changes over time or lays out in spatial form the location of different kinds of information. In the case of the Austro-Hungarian Empire, a historical atlas would likely picture the territories of the empire, when they were acquired, and what groups of people lived in those territories. A good historical atlas would include information about those peoples — for example, the population size of each group, the percentage of Catholics and Protestants in different parts of the empire, and the languages they spoke.

It is important to remember that historical dictionaries, encyclopedias, and atlases are most valuable at the beginning stages of research. They do not contain extended examinations or interpretations of historical subjects. You should not depend on them for the substance of your paper. For more highly specialized reference works, see "Specialized Resources in World History" (p. 221) and "Specialized Resources in United States History" (p. 245) later in this appendix. Additional reference works are included in this book's Web site: <bedfordstmartins.com/ benjamin>.

NOTE: If your topic concerns recent history, or if important new facts and interpretations have arisen in recent years, be sure to use the latest edition of any historical dictionary, encyclopedia, or atlas that covers your topic.

Historical Dictionaries — World

The Blackwell Dictionary of Modern Social Thought. Ed. William Outhwaite. Malden, MA: Blackwell, 2003.

The Cambridge Historical Dictionary of Disease. Ed. Kenneth F. Kiple. New York: Cambridge University Press, 2003.

Dictionary of Contemporary History, 1945 to the Present. Ed. Duncan Townson. Oxford: Blackwell, 1999.

Dictionary of Race and Ethnic Relations. By Ernest Cashmore. London: Routledge, 1994.

Historical Dictionary of Judaism. Ed. Norman Solomon. Lanham, MD: Scarecrow Press, 1998.

Historical Dictionary of Mexico. 2nd ed. By Marvin Alisky. Lanham, MD: Scarecrow Press, 2008.

Historical Dictionary of United States–Middle East Relations. By Peter L. Hahn. Lanham, MD: Scarecrow Press, 2007.

New Dictionary of the History of Ideas. Ed. Maryanne Cline Horowitz. 6 vols. New York: Scribner, 2004. Also online at **etext.virginia.edu/DicHist/dict.html**, available by subscription only.

The New Grove Dictionary of Music and Musicians. 2nd ed. Ed. Stanley Sadie and John Tyrrell. 29 vols. New York: Macmillan, 2001. Also see the online database *Grove Music Online.*

The New Penguin Dictionary of Modern History, 1789–1945. Ed. Duncan Townson and Alan W. Palmer. Baltimore: Penguin Books, 1994.

The Oxford Dictionary of Philosophy. Comp. Simon Blackburn. Oxford: Oxford University Press, 1994.

The Oxford English Dictionary. 2nd ed. 20 vols. Oxford: Clarendon Press, 1989. This is the most complete English-language dictionary. If you are tracing the historical development of the meaning of a word, it is an essential reference. If, however, you wish to determine the contemporary spelling or definition of a term, other general dictionaries are better sources. If the term is colloquial or is a recent derivation, be sure to use the most recent edition. The *Oxford English Dictionary* is now on CD-ROM and online by subscription.

Historical dictionaries for specific regions or nations are listed separately, on pages 221–42.

Historical Dictionaries — United States

Dictionary of American Diplomatic History. Ed. John E. Findling. Westport, CT: Greenwood Press, 1989.

Dictionary of American History. Ed. James T. Adams and Roy V. Coleman. New York: Scribner, 1942–1961. Revised, 1976. Supplement, 1996.

Dictionary of American History. 3rd ed. Ed. Stanley I. Kutler. 10 vols. New York: Thomson Learning, 2003.

Dictionary of United States Economic History. Ed. James S. Olson. Westport, CT: Greenwood Press, 1992.

The Penguin Dictionary of Contemporary American History, 1945 to the Present. Ed. Stanley Hochman and Eleanor Hochman. New York: Penguin Books, 1997.

Historical dictionaries for specific topics in U.S. history are listed separately, on pages 245–62.

Historical Encyclopedias — World

Colonialism: An International Social, Cultural and Political Encyclopedia. Ed. Melvin E. Page. 3 vols. Santa Barbara, CA: ABC-CLIO, 2003.

Companion Encyclopedia of the History of Medicine. New York: Routledge, 1997.

Encyclopaedia Britannica. 15th ed. 32 vols. Chicago: Encyclopaedia Britannica Educational Corp., 2001. This is one of the best encyclopedias. It is also available on the Web at **www.britannica.com**, but only by subscription.

Encyclopedia Judaica. Ed. Cecil Rovhand and Geoffrey Wigoder. 16 vols. Jerusalem: Keter Publishing, 1972. Reprint, New York: Coronet Books, 1994.

Encyclopedia of the Age of the Industrial Revolution, 1700–1920. Ed. Christine Rider. 2 vols. Westport, CT: Greenwood Press, 2007.

Encyclopedia of Bioethics. Rev. ed. Ed. Warren Thomas Reich. 5 vols. New York: Macmillan Library Reference, 1995.

Encyclopedia of Children and Childhood: In History and Society. Ed. Paula S. Fass. New York: Macmillan Reference USA, 2003.

Encyclopedia of Early Cinema. Ed. Richard Abel. New York: Routledge, 2005.

Encyclopedia of the History of Science, Technology, and Medicine in Non-Western Cultures. Ed. Helaine Seline. 2 vols. Berlin: Springer, 2008.

Encyclopedia of the Middle Passage: Great Milestones in African American History. Ed. Toyin Falola and Amanda Warnock. Westport, CT: Greenwood Press, 2007.

Encyclopedia of Nationalism. Ed. Alexander Motyl. New York: Academic Press, 2000.

Encyclopedia of Religion. Ed. Mircea Eliade. 16 vols. New York: Macmillan, 1993.

Encyclopedia of Religion. 2nd ed. Ed. Lindsay James. Detroit: Macmillan Reference USA, 2005.

Encyclopedia of the Scientific Revolution: From Copernicus to Newton. Ed. Wilbur Applebaum. London: Routledge, 2008.

Encyclopedia of Social History. Ed. Peter N. Stearns. New York: Scribner, 2000.

Encyclopedia of Western Colonialism since 1450. Ed. Thomas Benjamin. Farmington Hills, MI: Macmillan Reference USA, 2007.

Encyclopedia of World Environmental History. Ed. Shepard Krech, John R. McNeill, and Carolyn Merchant. 3 vols. New York: Routledge, 2004.

Film Encyclopedia. 4th ed. Ed. Ephraim Katz. New York: HarperCollins, 2001.

Greenwood Encyclopedia of Global Medieval Life and Culture. Ed. Joyce Salisbury. 3 vols. Westport, CT: Greenwood Press, 2008.

The Harper Encyclopedia of Military History: From 3500 B.C. to the Present. Ed. Ernest R. Dupuy and Trevor N. Dupuy. New York: Harper & Row, 1993.

Historical Encyclopedia of Natural and Mathematical Sciences. Ed. Ari Ben-Menzhem. 5 vols. Berlin: Springer, 2009.

The Historical Encyclopedia of World Slavery. Ed. Junius P. Rodriguez. 2 vols. Santa Barbara, CA: ABC-CLIO, 1997.

New Catholic Encyclopedia. 2nd ed. Detroit: Gale, 2003.

New Encyclopedia of Islam. Ed. Cyril Glasse. Walnut Creek, CA: Alta Mira Press, 2001.

The Oxford Companion to the History of Modern Science. Ed. J. L. Heilbron. Oxford: Oxford University Press, 2003.

Oxford Encyclopedia of the Modern World: 1750 to the Present. Ed. Peter N. Stearns. Oxford: Oxford University Press, 2008.

Routledge Encyclopedia of Philosophy. Ed. Edward Craig. 10 vols. New York: Routledge, 1998.

Women's Studies Encyclopedia: History, Philosophy, and Religion. Ed. Helen Tierney. 2 vols. Westport, CT: Greenwood Press, 1999.

Specialized encyclopedias for specific regions or nations are listed separately, on pages 221–42.

Historical Encyclopedias — Europe

Ancient Europe, 8000 B.C. to A.D. 1000: An Encyclopedia of the Barbarian World. Ed. Peter Bogucki and Pam Crabtree. New York: Scribner, 2003.

Encyclopedia of Barbarian Europe: Society in Transformation. By Michael Frassetto. Santa Barbara, CA: ABC-CLIO, 2003.

Encyclopedia of the Enlightenment [Eighteenth-century French intellectual history]. Ed. Alan C. Kors. Oxford: Oxford University Press, 2003.

Encyclopedia of European Social History [1350–2000]. Ed. Peter N. Stearns. 6 vols. New York: Scribner, 2005. Print and e-book versions.

Encyclopedia of the Holocaust. Ed. Israel Gutman. 4 vols. New York: Macmillan, 1995.

Encyclopedia of the Renaissance. Ed. Paul F. Grendler. New York: Scribner, 1999.

Europe 1450–1789: Encyclopedia of the Early Modern World. Ed. Jonathan Dewald. New York: Scribner, 2003.

Europe 1789–1914: Encyclopedia of the Age of Industry and Empire. New York: Scribner, 2006.

Europe since 1945: An Encyclopedia. Ed. Bernard A. Cook. 2 vols. New York: Garland, 2001.

The Oxford Encyclopedia of the Reformation. Ed. Hans J. Hillerbrand. 4 vols. New York: Oxford University Press, 1996.

Specialized encyclopedias for specific eras or nations are listed separately, on pages 221–34.

Historical Encyclopedias — United States

Encyclopedia of American Agricultural History. By Edwin I. Schapsmeier and Frederick H. Schapsmeier. Westport, CT: Greenwood Press, 1975.

Encyclopedia of American Economic History. Ed. Glen Porter. 3 vols. New York: Scribner, 1980.

Encyclopedia of American History. 7th ed. Ed. Richard B. Morris. New York: HarperCollins, 1996.

Encyclopedia of American History. Ed. Gary B. Nash. 11 vols. New York: Facts on File, 2003.

Encyclopedia of the American Military. Ed. John E. Jessup. 3 vols. New York: Scribner, 1994.

The Encyclopedia of American Political History. Ed. Paul Finkelman and Peter Wallenstein. Washington, DC: CQ Press, 2001.

Encyclopedia of American Religious History. 6th ed. Ed. J. Gordon Mellon. Detroit: Gale, 1999.

Encyclopedia of American Social History. Ed. Mary K. Cayton, Elliott J. Gorn, and Peter W. Williams. 3 vols. New York: Scribner, 1993.

Encyclopedia of the United States in the Nineteenth Century. Ed. Paul Finkelman. 3 vols. New York: Scribner, 2001.

Encyclopedia of the United States in the Twentieth Century. Ed. Stanley Kutler. 4 vols. New York: Scribner, 1996.

Encyclopedia of United States Foreign Relations. Ed. Bruce Jentleson and Thomas Patterson. Oxford: Oxford University Press, 1997.

Encyclopedia of Urban America. Ed. Neil L. Shumsky. Santa Barbara, CA: ABC-CLIO, 1998.

Encyclopedia of Women in American History. Ed. Joyce Appleby et al. 3 vols. New York: M. E. Sharpe, 2002.

Specialized U.S. encyclopedias for specific topics are listed separately, on pages 245–62.

Historical Atlases — World

Atlas of the Roman World. Comp. Tim Cornell and John Matthews. New York: Facts on File, 1982.

The Complete Atlas of World History. 3 vols. New York: M. E. Sharpe, 1997.

David Rumsey Map Collection. **www.davidrumsey.com/collections/cartography.html**. Emphasis is on North and South America in the eighteenth and nineteenth centuries. Hosted by *Visual Collections,* a portal to a wide range of online art, architecture, and cartography archives.

Historical Atlas of the Islamic World. By David Nicolle. London: Mercury Books, 2004.

National Geographic Atlas of the World. 7th ed. Washington, DC: National Geographic Society, 1999.

The Penguin Historical Atlas of Ancient Civilizations. Ed. Andrew Jotischky and Caroline Hull. London: Penguin Books, 2005.

The Penguin Historical Atlas of the Medieval World. Ed. John Haywood. London: Penguin Books, 2005.

The Perry-Castañeda Library Map Collection. University of Texas. **www.lib.utexas.edu/maps/index.html**. An extensive collection of historical maps covering many areas of the world.

The Routledge Atlas of Jewish History. 6th ed. Ed. Martin Gilbert. London: Routledge, 2003.

The Times Atlas of the World: Comprehensive Edition. 10th ed. London: Times Publishing, 1999.

Historical Atlases — United States

Atlas of American History. Rev. ed. By Robert H. Ferrell and Richard Natkiel. New York: Facts on File, 2007.

Digital Sanborn Maps. See next item.

Map Collections of the Library of Congress, 1500–2003. Library of Congress, American Memory. **memory.loc.gov/ammem/gmdhtml/gmdhome.html**. A large collection from many eras and areas.

Mapping America's Past. By Mark C. Carnes. New York: Henry Holt, 1996. Emphasis on social and cultural maps.

Omni Gazetteer of the United States of America. Ed. Frank R. Abate. 11 vols. Detroit: Omnigraphics, 1991. A gazetteer is a list of place-names, including insignificant ones. This volume organizes places by region and state.

Osher Map Library. Smith Center for Cartographic Education, University of Southern Maine. **www.usm.maine.edu/maps/web_exhibit.html**. Over 600 maps and related documents, essays, and annotated bibliographies.

BIOGRAPHY COLLECTIONS

The resources in this section will provide background information about a particular individual whose name you have come across in your research. An article in a biography collection will give you a brief (or in some cases a fairly comprehensive) description of an individual's life and will usually end with a list of sources to consult for further information. Each biography collection has its own criteria for determining which individuals to include. Take care to select the collection most likely to include the individuals on whom you are seeking information. More highly specialized biography collections for some countries are listed in the "Specialized Resources in World History" section of this appendix, which starts on page 221.

International Biography Collections

Biographical Encyclopedia of Ancient Natural Sciences. Ed. Paul Keyser. London: Routledge, 2009.

Biography and Genealogy Master Index. Ed. Miranda C. Herbert and Barbara McNeil. 8 vols. Detroit: Gale, 1980–. Supplements issued annually. Also available on CD-ROM and online.

Biography and Genealogy Master Index. Thomson Gale. A database containing multiple indexes to a wide range of biographical resources. By subscription only.

Biography Index: A Cumulative Guide to Biographical Material in Books and Magazines. New York: H. W. Wilson, 1949–. Now in database form as *Biography Index: Past and Present* (see next item).

Biography Index: Past and Present. H. W. Wilson. An updated, searchable database of the yearly *Index* since its initial edition. By subscription only.

Biography Resource Center. Thomson Gale. Combines a large number of Marquis *Who's Who* publications with other biographical databases. Some biographies include related articles, images, and links. Fully searchable. By subscription only.

Current Biography. New York: H. W. Wilson, 1940–. A cumulative index was published in 2000. Also see database above, *Biography Index: Past and Present.*

Dictionary of Scientific Biography. Ed. Charles C. Gillispie. 16 vols. New York: Scribner, 1970–1980.

International Who's Who. London: Europa, 1935–. Now part of the Thomson Gale online database *Biography Resource Center,* available by subscription.

New York Times Obituary Index, 1858–1968, 1969–1980. New York: New York Times, 1970, 1980. Current volumes are published by Meckler, 1990–.

Oxford Dictionary of National Biography: Earliest Times to 2000. 61 vols. Oxford: Oxford University Press, 2004.

Who's Who in the World. Chicago: Marquis, 1971–. Now part of the Thomson Gale online database *Biography Resource Center,* available by subscription.

Who Was Who. Vol. 1, 1897–1915; vol. 2, 1916–1928; vol. 3, 1929–1940; vol. 4, 1941–1950; vol. 5, 1951–1960; vol. 6, 1961–1970; vol. 7, 1971–1980; vol. 8, 1981–1990; vol. 9, 1991–1995; vol. 10, 1996–2000. A cumulative index for 1897–1990 was published in 1991. These collections of biographies are now part of the Thomson Gale online database *Biography Resource Center,* available by subscription.

United States Biography Collections

African-American National Biography. Ed. Henry Louis Gates and Evelyn Brooks Higgenbothom. 8 vols. Oxford: Oxford University Press, 2008.

American Men and Women of Science. New York: Bowker, 1906–. The twenty-third edition is now online from Thomson Gale. By subscription only.

American National Biography. Ed. John A. Garraty and Mark C. Carnes. 24 vols. New York: Oxford University Press and American Council of Learned Societies, 1999. Supplement, 2002. The newest and most extensive print collection of U.S. biographies. Also available online by subscription only.

American Reform and Reformers: A Biographical Dictionary. Ed. Randall M. Miller and Paul A. Cimbala. Westport, CT: Greenwood Press, 1996.

Biographical Dictionary of American Business Leaders. Ed. John Ingham. 4 vols. Westport, CT: Greenwood Press, 1983.

Biographical Dictionary of American Journalism. Ed. Joseph P. McKerns. Westport, CT: Greenwood Press, 1989.

Biographical Dictionary of American Labor. Rev. ed. Ed. Gary Fink. Westport, CT: Greenwood Press, 1984.

Biographical Dictionary of American Sports. Ed. David L. Porter. Westport, CT: Greenwood Press, 1998.

Biographical Directory of the United States Congress, 1774–2005. U.S. Congress. **bioguide .congress.gov/biosearch/biosearch.asp**. Print and Web editions. Member biographies and information concerning the papers of U.S. senators and representatives.

Biographical Directory of the United States Executive Branch, 1774–1989. Westport, CT: Greenwood Press, 1990.

Dictionary of American Biography. New York: Scribner, 1928–1996, including supplements. When using older editions or volumes of a print biography collection, note the date of publication because it will indicate which individuals might be included. A one-volume work containing shortened versions of these biographies is published under the title *Concise Dictionary of American Biography*, 5th ed., 1997. An index to the multivolume collection was published in 1996.

Notable American Women, 1607–1950: A Biographical Dictionary. Ed. Edward T. James. 3 vols. Cambridge, MA: Harvard University Press, 1971. Supplemented by *Notable American Women: The Modern Period*, 1980. The supplement covers women who died between 1951 and 1975.

Who Was Who in America: Historical Volume, 1607–1896. Chicago: Marquis, 1967. If you are uncertain about your subject's date of death, check *Who Was Who in America: Index* (2002). These volumes are now part of the Thomson Gale online database *Biography Resource Center*, available by subscription.

Who Was Who in America, with World Notables, 1897–2002. 14 vols. Chicago: Marquis, 2002. The years covered in each volume indicate the dates of death of those included in it.

NEWSPAPER INDEXES AND DATABASES

If you need to find newspaper articles from the time period you are writing about, a newspaper **index** will tell you where copies of a particular newspaper can be found. Newspaper **databases** contain the full text of newspaper articles — but only for certain newspapers and only for a particular span of years. Most full-text newspaper databases are searchable, but they are usually available only by subscription. If your library does not have access to the online database that you want, check the **library catalog** for newspapers on **microfilm,** microfiche, or CD-ROM. Only English-language newspapers are included here.

Newspaper Indexes and Databases — General

Canadian Online Historical Newspapers. Chadwyck-Healey. Fully searchable collections of the *Toronto Star* and the *Globe and Mail.* Coverage begins in the mid-to-late nineteenth century. By subscription only.

LexisNexis Academic Universe. **www.lexisnexis.com/academic/**. Full text of articles in newspapers and magazines from the late 1980s on. Emphasis is on current developments in law, business, and government.

Official Index to the Times [of London]. London: 1907–. See next item.

Palmer's Index to the Times [of London], *1790–1905*. Succeeded by the CD-ROM *Official Index to the Times, 1906–1980*. Chadwyck-Healey. Chadwyck-Healey also has an *Index Online* from 1790 to 1905 and the full text from 1800 to 1870. Both are searchable. By subscription only.

Newspaper Indexes and Databases —
United States

Early American Newspapers. NewsBank. **www.readex.com/readex/?content=96**. A searchable archive of hundreds of newspapers from 1690 to 1922. By subscription only.

Historical Newspaper Project. Wisconsin Historical Society. **wisconsinhistory.org/ libraryarchives/aanp/**. A fine collection of nineteenth-century northern newspapers, emphasizing African American newspapers and periodicals.

New York Times Index. New York: New York Times, 1913–. This is usually the best source for beginning students. Most libraries have files of the *New York Times*, and the index has been extended back to 1851. Some libraries have Internet access to all of the articles themselves. In this case you can search by keyword. Also see below, *ProQuest Historical Newspapers*.

Nineteenth Century Masterfile. ProQuest. A large online database featuring a wide range of media on a variety of subjects, including history. Also contains a large newspaper database. By subscription only.

ProQuest Historical Newspapers. Available are the *New York Times*, 1851–2001; the *Wall Street Journal*, 1889–1987; the *Washington Post*, 1877–1988; the *Christian Science Monitor*, 1908–1991; and the *Los Angeles Times*, 1881–1984; among others. Fully searchable. By subscription only.

PERIODICAL INDEXES AND DATABASES

Articles in **periodicals** can be grouped into two categories: *magazine articles* written at the time of the events being discussed (usually **primary documents**) and *articles in scholarly journals* analyzing a variety of historical themes (**secondary sources**). Resources for finding articles of each type are in the next two lists.

Magazine indexes and databases help you to find contemporary articles in popular magazines concerning events, persons, or issues that are part of your topic. Some print indexes to magazine articles are in the reference section of your library. Most searchable magazine databases are online, and those available to you will be included in the library's online catalog under a heading such as "electronic," "digital," or "online" resources. Be sure that the database you are searching includes the kind of magazines most likely to have articles related to your topic. .

Journal indexes and databases contain citations, abstracts, or full-text articles from scholarly journals. These articles are among the most important sources of secondary evidence for history research; however, many will be available to you only if your school or public library has paid for a subscription. Often, when a library has several subscriptions, each covering different journals, these groups of journals are "linked" so that you can search several of them at once. If your library does not subscribe to the most promising journal database listed below, try a different database.

NOTE: Journal databases also store book reviews that appear in scholarly journals. If you wish to know more about a particular book before deciding to use it in your research, use these databases to seek out book reviews written by scholars.

Magazine Indexes and Databases

LexisNexis Academic. This database covers journals, magazines, news providers, and legal materials. It is particularly useful for researching current events. Online by subscription only.

Nineteenth Century Masterfile. ProQuest. A large online database featuring a wide range of media on a variety of subjects, including history. Also contains a large newspaper database. By subscription only.

Nineteenth-Century Periodicals: 1815–1900. Library of Congress, American Memory. **memory.loc.gov/ammem/ndlpcoop/moahtml/snchome.html**. A searchable collection of periodicals. Years of coverage of each periodical are indicated. Many articles are full text.

Poole's Index to Periodical Literature, 1802–1881. Boston: Houghton Mifflin, 1891. Now available online. See above, *Nineteenth Century Masterfile.*

Readers' Guide Full Text, Mega Edition. Wilson Web. Searchable full text of magazines but only for articles published since 1994.

Readers' Guide to Periodical Literature. New York: H. W. Wilson, 1900–. Annual updates still available in print. Beginning with articles published in 1983, this *Guide* began to appear in online form by subscription only. The annual volumes for the period before 1983 are now in digital form in *Readers' Guide Retrospective: 1890–1982.*

Readers' Guide Retrospective: 1890–1982. H. W. Wilson. This database allows you to search for articles among several hundred popular magazines going back to 1890. Note that many of the periodicals included were written for a popular rather than a scholarly audience. These magazines are valuable as records of popular opinions and interests.

Ulrich's International Periodicals Directory. 41st ed. New York: Bowker, 2003.

Journal Indexes and Databases

Academic Search Premier. EBSCOhost EJS. A large multidisciplinary database. By subscription only.

America: History and Life [United States and Canada]. A large database with abstracts of articles in 2,000 scholarly journals published since 1964. All topics in U.S. and Canadian history are covered. The print edition has been published since 1965 by ABC-CLIO. The latest print edition is 1995. Now online by subscription as part of EBSCOhost.

American Periodical Series. (Formerly by Chadwyck-Healey on microfilm.) Replaced by the following item.

American Periodical Series Online. ProQuest. Full-text archive of over 1,000 periodicals: scholarly, literary, scientific, and popular. Beginning in 1741. By subscription only.

Historical Abstracts: World History since 1450. This database offers abstracts of articles from a great number of scholarly journals in all areas except the United States and Canada. Those two areas are covered by *America: History and Life.* Both of these are now online by subscription as part of EBSCOhost.

Historical Periodicals Directory. Ed. Eric H. Boehm, Barbara H. Pope, and Marie Ensign. Vol. 1, *United States and Canada.* Vol. 2, *Europe (West).* Vol. 3, *Europe (East).* Vol. 4, *Latin America.* Vol. 5, *Australia and New Zealand.* Santa Barbara, CA: ABC-CLIO, 1981–1986.

History Cooperative. Full text of recent articles in twelve major history journals. Complements *JSTOR.* By subscription only.

Humanities Index. New York: H. W. Wilson, 1974–. Covers a wide range of journals in the humanities. Annual volumes. See also *Humanities Index Retrospective, 1907–1974.* Now available in online form.

JSTOR. Fully searchable database includes the full text of articles in over 200 academic journals, including many prominent historical journals. The most current articles are not available in *JSTOR.* For more current articles in scholarly journals see *Project Muse* (below) and *History Cooperative* (above). All by subscription only.

Periodicals Archive Online. ProQuest. Full-text articles from a large number of international journals in history and social science. Database articles run from 1802 to 1995. By subscription only.

Project Muse. Searchable database of full-text of recent articles in over 200 journals across many academic disciplines, including history. Some of the journals in this database are interlinked with the *JSTOR* database, so searching the full **date range** is possible. By subscription only.

PUBLIC DOCUMENTS

These general resources lead you to documents created by official bodies such as national governments. Only English-language documents are included here. More specialized public document collections are listed by region or nation, on pages 221–42 and 245–62.

Public Documents — Britain and Canada

Ancestry Library Edition. ProQuest. Searchable genealogical information from the United States and the United Kingdom taken from census, church, court, immigration, and other records. Online, by subscription only.

British History Online. Institute of Historical Research. **www.british-history.ac.uk/ subject.asp**. Documents relating to British history concerning local, national, and international affairs. Searchable by subject or place.

British Official Publications Collaborative Reader Information Service. **www.bopcris.ac .uk/bopcris/digbib/home**. A search facility for a wide range of British government documents, 1801–1995. Access to abstracts but not to documents themselves.

Government of Canada. See under the heading "**Canada**": *Library and Archives Canada* (p. 242). Government of Canada for a large number of searchable topics on Canadian history.

U.K. National Archives. **www.nationalarchives.gov.uk/documentsonline**. Major categories of documents are "Family History" (including military records and wills), "Society and Law," "Home and Foreign Affairs," and "Military and Defense." There is a download fee for most documents.

Public Documents — International

International Governmental Organizations. Library of Northwestern University. **www.library.northwestern.edu/govinfo/resource/internat/igo.html**. Contains links to a large number of international organizations.

League of Nations. Library of Northwestern University. **www.library.northwestern .edu/govinfo/collections/league/search.html**. Several hundred League documents online.

Permanent Court of International Justice. League of Nations. **www.icj-cij.org/ homepage/index.php?lang=en**. Decisions and documents of the court from 1922 to 1946. Predecessor to the Court of International Justice, a body of the United Nations.

United Nations. UN Documentation Centre. **www.un.org/documents/**. The UN site is a large and complex one. If you are not familiar with searching for UN documents, begin with a portal at the Library of Northwestern University, **www.library.northwestern.edu/govinfo/resource/internat/igo.html**, and scroll down to "United Nations" for links to the major bodies of the United Nations (Security Council, General Assembly, Economic and Social Council, etc.). Official documents of these bodies begin in 1946.

Public Documents — United States

American State Papers, 1789–1838. Readex–Newsbank. **www.readex.com/readex/ product.cfm?product=6**. A searchable database of printed material from the legislative and executive branches of government. By subscription only.

ARC. Archival Research Catalog. **www.archives.gov/research/arc/**. This site allows users to search for U.S. government documents housed in regional archives. Only a small fraction of these documents are online.

CQ Supreme Court Collection. CQ Electronic Library. Historical analysis and commentary on U.S. Supreme Court decisions, biographies of justices, and links to additional resources. By subscription only.

Foreign Relations of the United States. U.S. Department of State. Washington, DC: Government Printing Office, 1861–. These volumes are issued regularly and contain actual diplomatic correspondence. These are primary sources. Some documents for the period after 1945 are online at **www.state.gov/www/about_state/history/frus.html**.

House and Senate Journals, 1789–1817. Readex–Newsbank. Records of the sessions of the U.S. Congress. By subscription only.

LexisNexis Congressional. An online archive of congressional hearings, legislation, and background to legislation. By subscription only.

LexisNexis U.S. Serial Set Digital Collection. An online archive of congressional publications covering the period 1789–1969. Searchable. By subscription only.

List of National Archives Microfilm Publications, 1947–1974. Washington, DC: National Archives and Records Administration, 1974. Supplemented by *Supplementary List of National Archives Publications, 1974–1982.* Washington, DC: National Archives and Records Administration, 1982.

National Archives and Records Administration. **www.archives.gov/research/topics.html**. A portal to an enormous collection of U.S. government documents. It contains an extensive searchable catalog. Only a small fraction of this huge collection of materials is available online.

Oyez: U.S. Supreme Court Multimedia. Jerry Goldman, Northwestern University. **www.oyez.org/oyez/frontpage**. Audio files, abstracts, transcriptions, oral arguments, and written opinions. Covers 3,300 Supreme Court cases, selected cases starting in 1955, and all cases since 1995. Keyword searching of fourteen broad categories.

Presidential Libraries and Museums. **www.archives.gov/presidential-libraries/**. Every president since Herbert Hoover has his own library of presidential papers. This site contains links to each of the libraries. Many primary documents are available at the libraries. As yet, only a small number of these documents have been placed online.

Public Documents Masterfile. Paratext. A large database of U.S. government documents covering 1774 to the present. By subscription only.

Supplementary List of National Archives Publications, 1974–1982. Washington, DC: National Archives and Records Administration, 1982.

United States Congressional Committee Hearings Index, 1833–1969. Washington, DC: Congressional Information Service, 1981. Also available as part of *LexisNexis Congressional.*

United States Congressional Committee Prints Index from Earliest Publications through 1969. 5 vols. Washington, DC: Congressional Information Service, 1980. Now available on microfilm and online from LexisNexis. By subscription only.

United States Congressional Documents and Debates, 1774–1875. Library of Congress, American Memory. **memory.loc.gov/ammem/amlaw/lawhome.html**. The largest collection of online documents of the legislative branch of the U.S. government. Among many others, it contains pre-Constitution documents, House and Senate documents and debates, and the official publications of Congress.

United States Serial Set Indexes: American State Papers . . . 1789–1969. Washington, DC: Congressional Information Service, 1975. Now available online. See *LexisNexis U.S. Serial Set Digital Collection.*

U.S. Supreme Court Opinions. **www.findlaw.com/casecode//supreme.html**. This site allows you to search Supreme Court opinions. Full text from 1893.

University of Michigan Documents Center. **www.lib.umich.edu/govdocs/index .html**. Information, statistics, legislation, and news relating to each level of government.

HISTORICAL STATISTICS

These resources lead you to a wide range of numerical data useful to research in such areas as political, economic, and social history.

Historical Statistics — General

Historical Tables, 58 B.C.–A.D. 1990. By Sigfrid H. Steinberg. New York: Tuttle, 1991.

Index to International Statistics. Part of *LexisNexis Statistical.* By subscription only.

International Historical Statistics. Ed. Brian R. Mitchell. 3 vols. New York: Palgrave Macmillan, 2008. See individual volume entries under the heading "Historical Statistics — National and Regional" for specific coverage areas.

League of Nations Statistical Yearbook. Northwestern University. **www.library .northwestern.edu/govinfo/collections/league/stat.html**. Full text of the **yearbook** from 1926 to 1944.

Statistical Resources on the Web. University of Michigan. **www.lib.umich.edu/govdocs/ stats.html**. Statistics from the United States and from around the world. Links to many of the most important compilers of statistical information. Some sources are free; others are by subscription only.

United Nations Demographic Yearbook. **unstats.un.org/unsd/demographic/products/ dyb/dyb2.htm**. Statistical publications beginning in 1946.

United Nations Statistical Division. **unstats.un.org/unsd/methods/inter-natlinks/ sd_natstat.asp**. Links to national statistical Web sites.

Historical Statistics — National and Regional

Annual Abstract of Statistics. London: Office of National Statistics. Available in print and online. Earlier statistics are accessed through the link "Time Series" and are free to search and download.

The Arab World, Turkey and the Balkans, 1878–1914: A Handbook of Historical Statistics. Ed. Justin McCarthy. Boston: G. K. Hall, 1982.

Australian Historical Population Statistics. Australian Bureau of Statistics. **www.abs .gov.au/ausstats/abs@.nsf/mf/3105.0.65.001**.

British Historical Statistics. Ed. B. R. Mitchell. Cambridge: Cambridge University Press, 1988.

British Labour Statistics: Historical Abstract, 1886–1968. London: Great Britain Department of Employment and Productivity, 1971.

The British Voter: An Atlas and Survey since 1885. By Michael Kinnear. London: Batsford, 1981.

Census Finder. U.S. Census Bureau. Links to census records for the United Kingdom, Canada, Sweden, and Norway available at **www.censusfinder.com/**. For U.S. data see "Historical Statistics — United States" (pp. 216–18).

The Gallup International Public Opinion Polls: Great Britain, 1937–1975; France, 1939, 1944–1975. By George H. Gallup. Westport, CT: Greenwood Press, 1976–1977.

Heritage Quest Online. ProQuest. A large database of nineteenth- and twentieth-century census statistics, most from the United States but also from the United Kingdom and Canada. By subscription only.

Historical Statistics of Canada. By M. C. Urquhart. Ottawa: Statistics Canada, 1983. Available on the Web.

Historical Statistics of Canada. Statistics Canada. Ed. F. H. Leacy. **statcan.gc.ca/bsolc/olc-cel/olc-cel?lang=eng&catno=11-516-X**. Searchable online version of printed volume. Over 1,000 tables drawn from historical data for the period 1867 to 1970s.

International Historical Statistics: Africa, Asia, and Oceania: 1750–2005. 5th ed. Vol. 2. Ed. Brian R. Mitchell. New York: Palgrave Macmillan, 2008.

International Historical Statistics: The Americas: 1750–2005. 6th ed. Vol. 3. Ed. Brian R. Mitchell. New York: Palgrave Macmillan, 2008.

International Historical Statistics: Europe, 1750–2005. 6th ed. Vol. 1. Ed. Brian R. Mitchell. New York: Palgrave Macmillan, 2008.

Introduction to the Censuses of Canada, 1665 to 1871. Statistics Canada. [Printed: Ottawa, 1876.] Online version is at **statcan.gc.ca/bsolc/olc-cel/olc-cel?lang =eng&catno=98-187-X**.

Oxford Latin American Economic History Database. **oxlad.qeh.ox.ac.uk/**. Statistical information on the economies and societies of Latin America in the twentieth century.

Statistical Abstract of Latin America. Ed. James W. Wilkie. Los Angeles: UCLA Center of Latin American Studies, 1955–.

Statistical Accounts of Scotland. University of Edinburgh Library. **edina.ed.ac.uk/StatAcc**. By subscription only.

Twentieth-Century British Political Facts, 1900–2000. By David Butler and Gareth Butler. New York: Palgrave Macmillan, 2000.

United Kingdom Census Online: 1840–1911. **www.nationalarchives.gov.uk/census/**. Holds indexes to the census records of the United Kingdom. In some cases it describes document collections, but it does not give access to them. For this, readers are directed to commercial databases. See Appendix B.

Historical Statistics — United States

American Statistics Index: A Complete Guide and Index to the Statistical Publications of the United States Government. Washington, DC: Congressional Information Service, 1973–. Now part of *LexisNexis Statistical.* By subscription only.

Datapedia of the United States: American History in Numbers. 4th ed. Ed. George Thomas Kurian and Barbara A. Chernow. Lanham, MD: Bernan Press, 2007. A one-volume compilation of U.S. statistics covering the nineteenth and twentieth centuries.

Election Statistics. U.S. House of Representatives. **clerk.house.gov/member_info/ electionInfo/index.html**. Federal election returns since 1920.

Federal Population Censuses 1790–1890: A Catalogue of Microfilm Copies of the Schedules. Washington, DC: National Archives and Records Administration. Catalogs of the 1900, 1910, 1920, and 1930 census have also been created. Note that these catalogs contain no online data; they are to assist researchers who go to the sites where the records are kept. Gradually, digitized census data is becoming available. Most of the individual data is on subscription sites such as those listed in Appendix B. For census "statistics" online, see sites such as *Heritage Quest Online* below.

The Gallup Poll. By George H. Gallup. New York: Random House and Scholarly Resources, 1935–.

The Gallup Poll Cumulative Index: Public Opinion, 1935–1997. Wilmington, DE: Scholarly Resources, 1999. Also available online, by subscription, at **brain.gallup.com**.

Gallup Polls. Gallup Organization. **brain.gallup.com**. Gallup polls beginning in the 1930s. By subscription only.

Heritage Quest Online. ProQuest. A large database of nineteenth- and twentieth-century census statistics, most from the United States but also some from the United Kingdom and Canada. By subscription only.

Historical Statistics of the United States, Colonial Times to 1970. Washington, DC: Bureau of the Census, 1976, and Government Printing Office, 1989. Also available on CD-ROM and online.

International Historical Statistics: The Americas: 1750–2005. 6th ed. Vol. 3. Ed. Brian R. Mitchell. New York: Palgrave Macmillan, 2008.

National Archives Publications. **www.archives.gov/publications/microfilm-catalogs/ census/1790-1890/part-01.html**. These are *descriptions* of census data. The actual census information is in the National Archives. Some federal census data has been digitized and now covers censuses up to 1930. The digitized material is usually on subscription databases.

National Historical Geographical Information System. University of Minnesota. **www .nhgis.org**. The site allows the user to aggregate and analyze U.S. census data for the period 1790 to 2000. Data is available for the national, state, county, census tract, and boundary files. Sophisticated interpretation is possible, but the site is complex and special software may be needed.

Roper Center for Public Opinion Research. University of Connecticut. **www.ropercenter .uconn.edu**. This site offers access to data gathered from Roper opinion polls, archived collections, and the Roper magazine.

Statistical Abstract of the United States. Washington, DC: Government Printing Office, 1878–. Annual. Also available on the Web (see next entry).

Statistical Abstract of the United States. U.S. Census Bureau. **www.census.gov/prod/ www/abs/statab1878-1900.htm**. Yearly collection of statistics. Files for most years are downloadable but are very large. Files are available for most years from 1878 to the present.

Statistical Resources on the Web. University of Michigan. **www.lib.umich.edu/govdocs/ stats.html**. Statistics from the United States and from around the world. Links to many of the most important compilers of statistical information. Some sources are free; others are by subscription only.

Visit bedfordstmartins.com/benjamin *for links to online resources.*

U.S. Census Bureau. **www.census.gov/compendia/statab/**. This site contains a limited number of historical statistics gathered by the Census Bureau since the mid-nineteenth century. Individual census data online is available at subscription sites. (See Appendix B.)

United States Historical Census Data Browser. University of Virginia. **fisher.lib.virginia .edu/collections/stats/histcensus/**. Allows searching of nonpersonal census data from 1790 to 1960, with links to more recent population statistics and census information. Online use only. A range of topics can be searched and plotted by overlay of census data on a base map.

U.S. Presidential Election Maps: 1860–1996. University of Virginia Library. **fisher .lib.virginia.edu/collections/stats/elections/maps/**. Popular and electoral vote totals mapped by state for each presidential election since 1860.

GENERAL RESOURCES IN WORLD HISTORY

Before examining the general resources in world history listed in this section and the specialized resources described on pages 221–42, you should consult the historical dictionaries, encyclopedias, and atlases listed at the beginning of this appendix (pp. 202–07). They will enable you to choose and narrow a topic.

The general resources in this section consist of bibliographies and Web sites that cover large areas and many periods of world history. The specialized resources described later will be useful once you have chosen a topic and have a clear understanding of the kind of research you will need to do to develop and support your thesis. Even if you have already narrowed your topic, you should not ignore the following general resources, because many of them include sections on or links to specialized topics.

Reference Works and Bibliographies

Academic Info: World History Links and General Resources. **www.academicinfo.net/ histaalibrary.html**. This site categorizes and annotates links to history Web sites and allows you to search by **keyword.**

Best of History Web Sites. **www.besthistorysites.net/index.shtml**. This annotated site uses a ranking system to guide users through Internet resources in history.

A Dictionary of Twentieth-Century History, 1914–1990. Ed. Peter Teed. Oxford: Oxford University Press, 1992.

The Oxford Dictionary of Byzantium. Ed. Alexander P. Kazhdan. 3 vols. New York: Oxford University Press, 1991.

Reference Sources in History: An Introductory Guide. 2nd ed. Ed. Ronald H. Fritze. Santa Barbara, CA: ABC-CLIO, 2003.

Slavery and Slaving in World History: A Bibliography, 1900–1991. Ed. Joseph C. Miller. New York: M. E. Sharpe, 1997–1998.

Web Sites

Academic ASAP. InfoTrac. A very large database of newspapers, biographies, reviews, references, and primary and secondary sources covering both world and U.S. history. By subscription only.

Advanced Papyrological Information System. APIS. **www.lib.umich.edu/pap/apis** (also **www.columbia.edu/cu/lweb/projects/digital/apis/index.html**). A consortium of academic institutions share this site, which displays originals and translations of some of the earliest written documents.

Archive for the History of Economic Thought. **socserv2.socsci.mcmaster.ca/~econ/ ugcm/3113/index.html**. The full text of several hundred works on economic theory, third century B.C. to mid-twentieth century.

ArchNet. MIT School of Architecture and Planning, University of Texas School of Architecture, and Aga Kahn Development Network. **archnet.org/library**. Covers urban planning and design throughout the Muslim world: emphasis is on Islamic architecture. Large photograph collection organized by country, century, usage, style, and type. A site with great depth.

ARCL: Women's Studies. Oregon State University. **wss.library.oregonstate.edu/ history.htm**. A large collection of links to serious sites. Covers many aspects of women's history in the United States and around the world.

Berkeley Digital Library SunSITE. **sunsite.berkeley.edu/**. Texts and images, including classical and medieval works, the Emma Goldman papers, and a strong collection relating to California.

Dead Sea Scrolls. **www.ibiblio.org/expo/deadsea.scrolls.exhibit/intro.html**. Essays and brief translations.

Directory of Historical Resources. History Database, Los Angeles. **www.history.la.ca .us/hddirect.htm**. An extensive database of Web sites relating to history and historical research.

Dissertation Abstracts International. ProQuest Dissertations and Theses Database. A database of non-U.S. dissertations. Abstracts available.

Film Index International. Chadwyck-Healey. A searchable database of information on 115,000 films from 170 countries. By subscription only.

Getty Digitized Library Collections. The J. Paul Getty Trust. **www.getty.edu/research/ conducting_research/digitized_collections/**. Digitized collections of decorative arts, manuscripts, paintings, drawings, photographs, and sculpture. Covers many eras and regions. One of the largest collections of this type in the world.

Historical Text Archive. **historicaltextarchive.com**. A searchable database of articles, books, and links.

The History Guide. **historyguide.org/resources.html**. A gateway to a large number of online history sources.

History Studies Centre. Chadwyck-Healey. A large collection of print and image resources. Nine separate collections. By subscription only.

Humanities E-Book. American Council of Learned Societies. **www.humanitiesebook .org**. Collection of digitized history books.

Index of Medieval Medical Images. UCLA Digital Library. **digital.library.ucla.edu/ immi**. Drawn from manuscripts created between 1250 and 1500. Five hundred medical-related images. Date, provenance, topic, physical characteristics, and annotation of the image.

InfoMine. University of California, Riverside. **infomine.ucr.edu/**. A large database of links to history and other Web sites. A nonsubscription database.

International Mission Photography Archive. University of Southern California. **digarc .usc.edu/impa/controller/index.htm**. A searchable collection of 12,000 photographs covering images of mission work in many countries.

Internet History Sourcebooks. Paul Halsall, Fordham University. **www.fordham.edu/ halsall/index.html**. Features full text of scholarly works organized by period, area, and, in a few cases, subject. Works appear without annotation. Some offsite links are no longer live.

Internet Public Library. **www.ipl.org/div/subject/browse/hum30.00.00/**. This site offers free access to magazines, newspapers, and over 20,000 books through the Web.

Intute Arts and Humanities. **intute.ac.uk/artsandhumanities**. Database containing a large number of links to a wide range of history Web sites. Emphasizes but is not confined to British resources. A nonsubscription database.

Librarians' Internet Index. **www.lii.org/pub/topic/reference**. Organized by California librarians. Annotates Web sites of interest to historians.

Paratext Reference Universe. A large collection of databases including this one of reference works. By subscription only.

Project Gutenberg. **www.gutenberg.org/catalog/**. A very large, searchable database of books. Access to most of the books is unrestricted. Search by author, title, or subject.

ProQuest Research Library. A group of several databases including "History Studies Center" and "Reference Works." By subscription only.

Questia. Questia Media America Inc. **www.questia.com/library/history**. A large database of books and articles on many areas and aspects of history. Fully searchable. By subscription only.

SAGE. Selected Archives at Georgia Tech and Emory Digital Archive Project. **sage.library.emory.edu/**. This site displays online multimedia exhibits.

Slave Studies Net: European Studies Project. World Wide Web Virtual Library. **www .slave-studies.net/**. Access to resources on the study of slavery. Global in scope.

Swarthmore Peace Collection. Swarthmore College. **www.swarthmore.edu/library/ peace**. A large library of links on the topic of peace.

Tennessee Tech History Web Site. **www2.tntech.edu/history/**. A great number of history links on most subjects and areas.

University of Pennsylvania Digital Library. **onlinebooks.library.upenn.edu/**. This site's Online Books page features over 25,000 books. It highlights banned books, female writers, and foreign-language texts.

Voice of the Shuttle History Page. **vos.ucsb.edu/browse.asp?id=2713**. Organizes a great number of links in an easily searchable format.

World History Archives. **www.hartford-hwp.com/archives/**. Organizes links geographically and topically, presenting a balance to Western-centered history.

World History Compass. **www.worldhistorycompass.com/**. Organizes annotated links geographically and by subject, and includes countries often underrepresented on such sites.

World History Matters. **worldhistorymatters.org**. A large index that gives thoughtful evaluations of Web sites in many areas and eras of history except for the United States. U.S. Web sites are evaluated at *History Matters:* **historymatters.gmu.edu/ browse/wwwhistory/**.

WWW Virtual Library. **vlib.iue.it/history/index.html**. A very large collection of links to history Web sites organized by topic, area, and era. Some materials not in English. Links not always reliable.

SPECIALIZED RESOURCES IN WORLD HISTORY

Once you have chosen your topic with the aid of the historical dictionaries, encyclopedias, and atlases listed at the beginning of this appendix (pp. 202–07), you are ready to seek out primary and secondary sources that you will use to develop and support your thesis.

The world history resources in this section are organized by time period ("Ancient") and by region ("Africa"). The sources for each specialized period or region are separated into two groups. The first group contains reference works and bibliographies available in print form. The second group contains a list of Web sites organized alphabetically by the name of the site. Additional specialized print and digital resources in world history are available on this book's Web site: <bedfordstmartins.com/benjamin>.

Ancient History

Ancient Europe 8000 B.C.–A.D. 1000: Encyclopedia of the Barbarian World. Ed. Peter I. Bogucki and Pam J. Crabtree. 2 vols. New York: Thomson Gale, 2004.

Biographical Encyclopedia of Ancient Natural Sciences. Ed. Paul Keyser. London: Routledge, 2009.

The Cambridge Ancient History. Cambridge: Cambridge University Press. First edition, 12 vols., 1924–1939. Second edition, 14 vols., 1970–2005. A multivolume work with extensive bibliographies.

A Dictionary of Ancient History. Ed. Graham Speake. Oxford: Blackwell, 1994.

The Encyclopedia of Ancient Civilizations of the Near East and Mediterranean. Ed. John Heywood. New York: M. E. Sharpe, 1997.

Encyclopedia of the Crusades. Ed. Alfred J. Andrea. Westport, CT: Greenwood Press, 2003.

Encyclopedia of Early Christianity. Ed. Everett Ferguson et al. New York: Garland, 1998.

Encyclopedia of the Roman Empire. Rev. ed. Ed. Matthew Bunson. New York: Facts on File, 2002.

The Oxford Classical Dictionary. 3rd ed. Ed. Simon Hornblower and Antony Spawforth. Oxford: Oxford University Press, 1999.

The Oxford Encyclopedia of Ancient Egypt. Ed. Donald B. Redford. Oxford: Oxford University Press, 2001.

ABZU: Guide to Resources for the Study of the Ancient Near East. **www.etana.org/abzu/**. A searchable catalog with links to Internet resources relating to the ancient Near East.

Academic Info: Ancient History. **www.academicinfo.net/histanc.html**. Annotated links to materials on ancient Greece, Rome, India, Mesopotamia, China, and Egypt, as well as information on archaeology.

Academic Info: Classical Studies. **www.academicinfo.net/classicsmeta.html**. Annotated links to materials on the languages, literatures, art, cultures, and histories of ancient Greece and Rome.

The Ancient Greek World. University of Pennsylvania Museum of Archaeology and Anthropology. **www.museum.upenn.edu/Greek_World/Index.html**. Text and images that explore the history and culture of ancient Greece.

Ancient Mesopotamia: This History, Our History. University of Chicago, Oriental Institute Museum. **mesopotamia.lib.uchicago.edu/**. A small number of artifacts, photographs, and archaeological sites. Emphasis is on daily life. Also deals with elements of this civilization that were the basis for important aspects of modern civilizations.

Ancient Treasures and the Dead Sea Scrolls. CMC Online Exhibits. **www.civilization.ca/cmc/exhibitions/civil/israel/isrele.shtml**. Examines the Dead Sea Scrolls and insights they offer on the peoples of that time, especially the Jewish people.

Centre for the Study of Ancient Documents. Oxford University. **www.csad.ox.ac.uk/index.html**. Presents information on and links to the materials and scripts of ancient writing.

Diotima: Materials for the Study of Woman and Gender in the Ancient World. Ross Scaife, editor in chief. **www.stoa.org/diotima**. Large number of current translations of Greek, Latin, Egyptian, and Coptic texts, as well as bibliographies and links to other sources.

Duke Papyrus Archive. Duke University. **scriptorium.lib.duke.edu/papyrus/**. Texts and images of 1,300 papyri. These are summarized but not translated.

Egyptology Resources. Cambridge University. **www.newton.cam.ac.uk/egypt/**. Texts, images, and links to organizations, publications, archaeological digs, and museums about Egypt.

Electronic Antiquity: Communicating the Classics. Virginia Polytechnic Institute and State University. **scholar.lib.vt.edu/ejournals/ElAnt/**. Articles and book reviews relating to ancient Greece and Rome.

Electronic Text Corpus of Sumerian Literature. The Oriental Institute, Oxford University. **www-etcsl.orient.ox.ac.uk/**. Important texts, in transliterations and translations, from ancient Mesopotamia. Texts cover culture, history, poetry, and prayers.

Encyclopedia Coptica. Coptic Network. **www.coptic.net/EncyclopediaCoptica/**. A scripture-based history of the Christian Church.

Eternal Egypt. Supreme Council of Antiquities, Egyptian Center for Documentation of Cultural and Natural Heritage (CultNat), and IBM. **www.eternalegypt .org**. Fifteen hundred objects from the Pharaonic era. Also covers Roman, Byzantine, and Islamic periods. A very well organized site with sophisticated multimedia and interactive presentations and a collection of scholarly articles on early Egypt.

Historic City: Jerusalem. Hebrew University of Jerusalem. Al Quds University. **jerusalem-library.org/frameset.php**. A well-organized collection on the history of Jerusalem. Contains maps, plans, photographs, inscriptions, among others.

Illustrated History of the Roman Empire. **www.roman-empire.net/**. An extensive text with chronologies, forums, and maps.

LacusCurtius: Into the Roman World. William P. Thayer. **penelope.uchicago.edu/ Thayer/E/Roman/home.html**. Online exhibitions of Roman archaeological sites. Primary and secondary sources and photographs of buildings and monuments. Latin and Greek primary texts with translations. Searchable by keyword.

Mohenjo Daro. Dr. Jonathan Mark Kenoyer, University of Wisconsin, Madison. **www.mohenjodaro.net**. A small collection of images and secondary sources from excavations at Mohenjo Daro in the Indus Valley (2600 to 1900 B.C.E.). Emphasis is on daily life. Each image is accompanied by a detailed explanation. Unfortunately, this Web site includes advertisements.

Oriental Institute of Oxford University — Electronic Text Corpus of Sumerian Literature. **www-etcsl.orient.ox.ac.uk/**. Translations of portions of 400 Sumerian texts from ancient Mesopotamia.

Perseus Digital Library. Gregory Cane, editor in chief. **www.perseus.tufts.edu/**. Excellent collection of literature and archaeology for ancient Greek and Roman culture. Includes several hundred primary texts, plus images from museum collections and archaeological sites. English translations seem to be out of date.

Vindolanda Tablets Online. Center for the Study of Ancient Documents, Oxford University. **vindolanda.csad.ox.ac.uk/**. Hundreds of wooden tablets in Latin found at a Roman fortress at Vindolanda behind Hadrian's Wall in Britain. Written by German soldiers serving in the Roman Army in England (ca. second century C.E.). Each document is presented in both Latin transcription and English translation.

Worlds of Late Antiquity. University of Pennsylvania. **ccat.sas.upenn.edu/jod/wola .html**. Covers several areas between 200 and 700 C.E.

Europe — General

Celtic Culture: A Historical Encyclopedia. Ed. John T. Koch. 5 vols. Santa Barbara, CA: ABC-CLIO, 2005.

Dictionary of Scandinavian History. Ed. Byron J. Nordstrom. Westport, CT: Greenwood Press, 1986.

Encyclopedia of the Age of Imperialism, 1800–1914. Ed. Carl Hodge. Westport, CT: Greenwood Press, 2008.

Encyclopedia of European Social History [1350–2000]. Ed. Peter N. Stearns. 6 vols. New York: Scribner, 2005. Print and e-book versions.

Encyclopedia of the Industrial Revolution. Ed. Thomas Heinrich. 3 vols. New York: M. E. Sharpe, 2002.

Historical Dictionary of Germany. Ed. Wayne C. Thompson, Susan L. Thompson, and Juliet S. Thompson. Metuchen, NJ: Scarecrow Press, 1994.

Scandinavian History: 1520–1970. Comp. Stewart P. Oakley. London: Historical Association of London, 1984.

Women in Western European History: A Select Chronological, Geographical and Topical Bibliography from Antiquity to the French Revolution. Ed. Linda Frey, Marsha Frey, and Joanne Schneider. Westport, CT: Greenwood Press, 1982. Supplement, 1986.

AdHoc [History of Christianity]. Yale University, Yale Divinity School. **research .yale.edu:8084/divdl/adhoc**. Images and documents from all eras of the history of Christianity.

EuroDocs: Primary Historical Documents from European History. Brigham Young University. **eudocs.lib.byu.edu/index.php/Main_Page**. Covers all European countries. Legal documents, local history, eras from classical to present. Translations from both primary and secondary sources are usually not the latest. A very large site. Some links may not be scholarly ones.

European History Project: Slave Studies Net. **slave-studies.net/**. A worldwide index to resources.

Gallica. National Library of France. **gallica.bnf.fr/?lang=en**. A very large national collection of thousands of digitized titles covering all eras and regions. You can search in English, but many of the documents are in French.

History Guide. **www.historyguide.de/**. Links, bibliographies, journals, and materials relating primarily to American and European history.

Library of Iberian Resources Online. **libro.uca.edu/**. Several hundred digitized works in English on the histories of Spain and Portugal.

United States Holocaust Memorial Museum. **www.ushmm.org/**. Multimedia exhibits and historical information relating to the Holocaust, World War II, and genocide.

Web Gallery of Art. **www.wga.hu/index.html**. Images and information about the history of European art from 1100 to 1850. The database is searchable. Extensive annotation of artists and eras.

Europe — Medieval

Atlas of Medieval Europe. Ed. Angus Konstern and Roger Kean. New York: Facts on File, 2000.

Dictionary of the Middle Ages. Ed. Joseph R. Strayer. 13 vols. New York: Scribner, 1998. Supplement, 2003.

Encyclopedia of the Crusades. By Alfred J. Andrea. Westport, CT: Greenwood Press, 2003.

Medieval France: An Encyclopedia. Ed. William W. Kibler et al. New York: Garland, 1995.

Medieval Germany: An Encyclopedia. Ed. John M. Jeep. New York: Garland, 2001.

Medieval Italy: An Encyclopedia. Ed. Chris Kleinhenz. London: Routledge, 2004.

Medieval Jewish Civilization: An Encyclopedia. Ed. Norman Roth. New York: Routledge, 2002.

De Re Militari: Online Resources for Medieval Warfare. Society for Medieval Military History. **www.deremilitari.org/onlineresources.htm**. Excellent source for the study of medieval warfare: military, social, economic, political, religious, and geographic. Covers the late Roman period (fifth century C.E.) to the seventeenth century C.E. Several hundred primary and secondary sources arranged by region and subject.

Early Manuscripts at Oxford University. Oxford University. **image.ox.ac.uk/**. Downloadable images "for personal study only." Eighty manuscripts.

Epistolae: Medieval Women's Latin Letters. Joan Ferrante, Columbia University, and Columbia Center for New Media, Teaching and Learning. **epistolae.ccnmtl .columbia.edu/**. The lives of important women are examined through their letters. Covers fourth to thirteenth centuries C.E. Historical notes and biographical sketches accompany each letter.

Florilegium Urbanum. Stephen Alsford. **www.trytel.com/~tristan/towns/ florilegium/flor00.html**. This site is dedicated to the study of medieval English towns. Two hundred short primary sources and excerpts from longer texts. Translations are accompanied by **historical context.**

Index of Medieval Medical Images. UCLA Digital Library. **digital.library.ucla.edu/ immi**. Drawn from manuscripts created between 1250 and 1500. Five hundred medical-related images. Date, provenance, topic, physical characteristics, and annotation of the image.

ITER: Gateway to the Middle Ages and Renaissance. University of Toronto. **www .itergateway.org/**. A large, searchable database of journal articles on topics relating to Europe from 400 to 1700. By subscription only.

The Labyrinth: Resources for Medieval Studies. Georgetown University. **www .georgetown.edu/labyrinth/**. This site allows you to search bibliographies, discussion groups, images, and primary and secondary works by category.

Libro: Medieval Spain. **libro.uca.edu/**. A modest archive of full-text scholarly works in (or translated into) English. Covers the Iberian Peninsula from the fifth to the seventeenth centuries.

Medici Archive Project. Medici Archive Project. **www.medici.org**. Medici family archive beginning in the sixteenth century. A very large database of three million letters is searchable by word, topic, place, date, and person. Only summaries of the documents are available in English.

NetSERF: The Internet Connection for Medieval Resources. **www.netserf.org/**. An extensive and well-organized collection of annotated links to research sites.

Online Medieval and Classical Library (OMACL). Douglas B. Killings. **omacl.org**. Thirty-four premodern European texts covering post-Homeric, preclassical Greek, Icelandic sagas, and others up to the sixteenth century C.E.

ORB: The Online Reference Book for Medieval Studies. **www.the-orb.net**. Translations of medieval texts.

Visit **bedfordstmartins.com/benjamin** *for links to online resources.*

Europe — Early Modern

Encyclopedia of Witchcraft: The Western Tradition. Ed. Richard M. Golden. 4 vols. Santa Barbara, CA: ABC-CLIO, 2006.

The Oxford Encyclopedia of the Reformation. Ed. Hans J. Hillerbrand. New York: Oxford University Press, 1996.

Renaissance and Reformation: Reference Library Cumulative Index. Detroit: U.X.L., 2002.

CERES. Cambridge English Renaissance Electronic Service. **www.english.cam.ac.uk/ceres/links.htm**. A large database of links to Renaissance documents online.

Columbus and the Age of Discovery. Millersville University. **www.millersville.edu/~columbus/**. Over 1,100 articles about Columbus and cross-cultural encounters.

European Voyages of Exploration. University of Calgary. **www.ucalgary.ca/applied_history/tutor/eurvoya**. A tutorial with maps and documents describing these sea voyages.

ITER: Gateway to the Middle Ages and Renaissance. University of Toronto. **www.itergateway.org/**. A large, searchable database of journal articles on topics relating to Europe from 400 to 1700. By subscription only.

PreColumbian Portfolio. Foundation for the Advancement of Mesoamerican Studies. **research.famsi.org/kerrportfolio.html**. A database of 2,000 artifacts from several pre-Columbian cultures in Central and South America. Mythology, daily life, religion.

Renaissance Forum: An Electronic Journal of Early-Modern Literary and Historical Studies. **www.hull.ac.uk/renforum**. This e-journal features historical and literary articles and book reviews relating to early modern Europe.

Renascence Editions [Renaissance]. **darkwing.uoregon.edu/~rbear/ren.htm**. Provides online access to texts printed in English between the late fifteenth century and the end of the eighteenth century.

The Revolt of the Netherlands. Leiden University. **dutchrevolt.leidenuniv.nl/English/default.htm**. A large collection of documents on the history of the Dutch struggle for independence (1568–1648). This site is an English-language one.

Witchcraft Collection. Cornell University. **historical.library.cornell.edu/witchcraft/browse.html**. A collection of digitized books on witchcraft, principally in Europe.

Europe — Modern

Dictionary of Modern Italian History. Ed. Frank J. Coppa. Westport, CT: Greenwood Press, 1985.

Encyclopedia of the Age of Imperialism and Empire: Europe, 1787–1914. Ed. John Merriman and Jay Winter. 5 vols. New York: Scribner, 2006.

Encyclopedia of European Social History [1350–2000]. Ed. Peter N. Stearns. 6 vols. New York: Scribner, 2005. Print and e-book versions.

Encyclopedia of the Industrial Revolution. Ed. Thomas Heinrich. 3 vols. New York: M. E. Sharpe, 2002.

Visit **bedfordstmartins.com/benjamin** *for links to online resources.*

The European Powers in the First World War: An Encyclopedia. Ed. Spencer C. Tucker. New York: Garland, 1999.

Europe since 1945: An Encyclopedia. Ed. Bernard A. Cook. 2 vols. New York: Garland, 2001.

French Culture, 1900–1975. Ed. Catharine Savage Brosman and Tom Conley. Detroit: Gale Research, 1995.

German Women in the Nineteenth Century: A Social History. Ed. John Fout. New York: Holmes & Meier, 1984.

Historical Dictionary of the French Fourth and Fifth Republics, 1946–1991. Ed. Wayne Northcutt. Westport, CT: Greenwood Press, 1992.

A Historical Dictionary of Germany's Weimar Republic, 1918–1933. Ed. C. Paul Vincent. Westport, CT: Greenwood Press, 1997.

Historical Dictionary of Modern Spain, 1700–1988. Ed. Robert W. Kern. Westport, CT: Greenwood Press, 1990.

Historical Dictionary of the Spanish Civil War, 1936–1939. Ed. James W. Cortada. Westport, CT: Greenwood Press, 1982.

Historical Dictionary of the Third French Republic, 1870–1940. Ed. Patrick H. Hutton, Amanda S. Bourque, and Amy J. Staples. 2 vols. Westport, CT: Greenwood Press, 1986.

The Longman Handbook of Modern European History, 1763–1997. Ed. Chris Cook and John Stevenson. New York: Longman, 1998.

Modern Germany: An Encyclopedia of History, People and Culture, 1871–1900. Ed. Dieter K. Buse. New York: Garland, 1998.

Modern Italian History: An Annotated Bibliography. Comp. Frank J. Coppa and William Roberts. Westport, CT: Greenwood Press, 1990. A companion to *Dictionary of Modern Italian History.*

Nazism, Resistance, and the Holocaust in World War II: A Bibliography. Ed. Vera Laska. Metuchen, NJ: Scarecrow Press, 1985.

Women in Western European History: A Select Chronological, Geographical, and Topical Bibliography; The Nineteenth and Twentieth Centuries. Ed. Linda Frey and Marsha Frey. Westport, CT: Greenwood Press, 1984.

Anarchism Pamphlets. Labadie Collection of the University of Michigan. **www.hti .umich.edu/l/labadie/**. A searchable database of several hundred anarchist books and pamphlets.

Cold War International History Project. Woodrow Wilson International Center for Scholars. **www.wilsoncenter.org/index.cfm?topic_id=1409&fuseaction=topics .home**. Publications and documents relating to the study of international relations during the Cold War. Many documents from former Soviet archives.

Einstein Archives Online. Hebrew University of Jerusalem. **www.alberteinstein.info/**. A large collection of Einstein's nonscientific writings, many in German, some in English.

Encyclopedia of the Revolutions of 1848. **www.cats.ohiou.edu/~chastain**. Online encyclopedia with the author of each article noted.

Exploring the French Revolution. Center for New Media, George Mason University History Project, CUNY. **chnm.gmu.edu/revolution/allfr.html**. A collection of over 500 texts, images, and other kinds of resources on various aspects of the Revolution.

German History in Documents and Images. German Historical Institute. **germanhistorydocs.ghi-dc.org/Index.cfm?language=english**. A moderately sized, self-contained site. It presents many aspects of German history, from 1500 to the present, with a series of well-organized exhibits each containing an introduction, documents, images, and maps. Exhibits integrate each of these elements. All sources are documented. Some parts of the collection are not yet completed.

Italian Life under Fascism. University of Wisconsin, Madison. **www.library.wisc.edu/ libraries/dpf/Fascism/Home.html**. This online exhibit features materials from the Fry Collection, organized thematically.

Liberty, Equality, Fraternity. CHMN, George Mason University, and ASHP, City University of New York. **chnm.gmu.edu/revolution**. Overview of the French Revolution in more than 600 images, texts, maps, and songs. Generally excellent context provided along with some in-depth scholarly essays.

The Nuremberg War Crimes Trials. Avalon Project at Yale Law School. **avalon.law .yale.edu/subject_menus/imt.asp**. A large number of online documents from the official records of the trials.

The Siege and Commune of Paris, 1870–71. Northwestern University. **www.library .northwestern.edu/spec/siege/index.html**. A database of a wide range of documents and images from besieged Paris.

Southworth Spanish Civil War Collection. University of California, San Diego. **libraries .ucd.edu/locations/mscl/collections/southworth-spanish-civil-war-collection .html**. Propaganda posters, children's drawings, newspapers, poems, and other primary resources.

Spartacus Educational. **www.spartacus.schoolnet.co.uk/**. Short hyperlinked essays focusing mostly on modern European political history. Degree of documentation for essays varies. Separate collections for many aspects of modern European history and also for some non-European topics.

WWI: The World War I Document Archive. Brigham Young University. **www.lib.byu .edu/~rdh/wwi/**. Government documents, maps, photographs, and biographies.

Britain — General

British Trials, 1660–1900. Chadwyck-Healey. Index of thousands of trials. Descriptions range from brief outlines to verbatim transcripts. Microfilm. By subscription only.

Dictionary of National Biography [United Kingdom]. Ed. Leslie Stephen and Sidney Lee. Oxford: Oxford University Press, 1908–. A summary of this large multi-volume collection can be found in *A Concise Dictionary of National Biography, from Earliest Times to 1985.* The book is now online. See below, *Oxford Dictionary of National Biography.*

English Poor Laws, 1639–1890. UMI. A collection of contemporary books, pamphlets, and public papers from England, Scotland, and Ireland focusing on the poor and the unemployed as public issues. Microfiche. By subscription only.

Historical Atlas of Britain. Ed. Malcolm Falkus and John Gillingham. New York: Crescent Books, 1987.

The Routledge Atlas of British History: From 45 BC to the Present. 4th ed. By Martin Gilbert. London: Routledge, 2007.

British Cartoon Archive. British Cartoon Archive at the University of Kent. **opal.ukc .ac.uk/cartoonx-cgi/ccc.py**. An archive of 120,000 newspaper cartoons covering 200 years. It has a searchable artist index with a collection of each one's work. Little historical context.

British History — BBC. BBC. **bbc.co.uk/history/british**. Short scholarly essays with images for a series of exhibits such as Anglo-Saxons, Normans, Middle Ages, Civil War, Tudors, Empire, Victorian era, World War I, World War II, and Modern Britain.

British History Online. Institute of Historical Research. **www.british-history.ac.uk/ subject.aspx?subject=**. Primary and secondary documents from the medieval to the modern periods and for a wide array of subjects. Searchable by subject or by place.

British Library. **www.bl.uk/onlinegallery/index.html**. Thirty thousand resources, especially on the history of Britain. Also contains a pathbreaking exhibit, "Turning the Pages," where the viewer can "turn" the leaves of the original volume of, for example, the Notebooks of Leonardo Da Vinci, Magna Carta, and other such treasures of the library.

Hansard: Official Reports of Parliamentary Debates, 19th & 20th c. **hansard/ millbanksystems.com/**. Reports of the business of the House of Lords and the House of Commons. Searchable by date.

History of Parliament. British Online History. **www.histparl.ac.uk/**. This collection contains studies of parliamentary elections, the lives of members, and Parliament as an institution. It includes records of the House of Commons (1386–1832) and House of Lords (1660–1832).

Oxford Dictionary of National Biography. Oxford University Press. **www.oup.com/ oxforddnb/info/online/**. Fully searchable, regularly updated United Kingdom online biography collection. By subscription only.

Parliamentary Publications. Parliamentary Archives. **www.parliament.uk/ publications/archives.cfm**. Contains the archives of the UK Parliament.

Royal Historical Society Bibliography. **www.rhs.ac.uk/bibl/dataset.asp**. A large, searchable database of books and articles related to British history. Articles on British history are drawn from 570 journals.

U.K. National Archives. **www.nationalarchives.gov.uk/documentsonline/?source =ddmenu_search5**. Click "Documents Online" for digitized records. There is a download fee for most documents. Major categories of documents are "Family History" (military records, wills), "Society and Law," "Home and Foreign Affairs," and "Military and Defense."

Britain before 1800

The Blackwell Encyclopedia of Anglo-Saxon England. Ed. Michael Lapidge. New York: Blackwell, 2000.

The Kings of Medieval England, c. 560–1485: A Survey and Research Guide. Ed. Larry W. Usilton. Lanham, MD: Scarecrow Press, 1996.

Medieval England: An Encyclopedia. Ed. Paul E. Szarmch et al. New York: Garland, 1998.

Tudor England: An Encyclopedia. Ed. Arthur F. Kinney et al. New York: Garland, 2000.

Women in Early Modern England, 1500–1700. Ed. Jacqueline Eales. New York: Garland, 1998.

Bodleian Library, Broadside Ballads. Bodleian Library, University of Oxford. **www .bodley.ox.ac.uk/ballads/**. Printed texts of 30,000 song-sheets. Searchable by topic. Includes thirteen sound files as examples of popular tunes.

Britannia History Index: The Age of Empire. **www.britannia.com/history/h80.html**. Documents, chronologies, articles, biographies, and links relating to Great Britain during the Age of Empire (1689–1901).

Britannia History Index: Reformation and Restoration [England, 1486–1689]. **www .britannia.com/history/h70.html**. Documents, chronologies, articles, biographies, and links relating to England during the Reformation, Civil War, and Restoration.

British History Online. University of London and the History of Parliament Trust. **www.british-history.ac.uk/subject.aspx**. Thousands of primary and secondary documents from the medieval, early modern, and modern periods of British history. These cover such subjects as government, church, economy, local history, Parliament, London, and maps, among others.

The British Library. **www.bl.uk/onlinegallery/index.html**. This site offers online access to historical newspapers and a variety of special exhibits.

CERES. Cambridge English Renaissance Electronic Service. **www.english.cam.ac .uk/ceres/links.htm**. A large database of links to Renaissance documents online.

Civil War and Revolution. BBC. **www.bbc.co.uk/history/british/civil_war_revolution**. A series of segmented essays by scholars with images and bibliographies.

Cobbetts Parliamentary History, 1700–1806. Oxford Digital Library. **www.odl.ox.ac .uk/collections/cobbett.htm**. Part of a large collection of works on the history of Parliament.

Early Manuscripts at Oxford University. Oxford University. **image.ox.ac.uk/ list?collection=all/omacl.org**. Eighty digitized manuscripts that can be viewed for personal use only.

Eighteenth Century Collections Online [1701–1800]. Thomson Gale. A large full-text database of eighteenth-century materials printed in Britain. By subscription only.

Eighteenth Century Entertainment Ephemera. Oxford Digital Library — Scholarly Editions. **www.odl.ox.ac.uk/collections/**. (then scroll down and click on "18th century Entertainment Ephemera). A large collection of newspaper articles, advertisements, and handbills, organized into topics such as theater, circuses, exhibits, "freaks," and wax museums. Some are open to view, others not.

Eighteenth-Century Resources — History. Rutgers, Newark. **andromeda.rutgers.edu/ ~jlynch/18th/history.html**. A large number of annotated links; particularly strong in American and British history but covers related areas as well.

The Middle Ages. BBC. **www.bbc.co.uk/history/british/middle_ages**. A series of segmented essays by scholars, with images and bibliographies.

The Normans. BBC. **www.bbc.co.uk/history/british/normans/**. A series of segmented essays (and linked images) by scholars.

Proceedings of the Old Bailey, London, 1674 to 1834. **www.oldbaileyonline.org/**. A searchable collection of 100,000 criminal trials at London's central criminal court.

The Rolls of Parliament: 1272–1507. Oxford Scholarly Editions. **www.sd-editions.com/ PROME/index.html**. These documents are available only by subscription.

Tudor History. **tudorhistory.org/files/texts.html**. A small archive of texts and documents from the Tudor period as well as commentaries on it.

The Tudors. BBC. **www.bbc.co.uk/history/british/tudors**. A series of segmented essays by scholars, with images and bibliographies.

Britain since 1800

British Economic and Social History: A Bibliographical Guide. 3rd ed. Ed. W. H. Chaloner and R. C. Richardson. Manchester, UK: Manchester University Press, 1995.

The Cambridge Historical Encyclopedia of Great Britain and Ireland. Ed. Christopher Haigh. Cambridge: Cambridge University Press, 1990.

Modern England, 1901–1984: A Bibliographical Handbook. Comp. Alfred F. Havighurst. Cambridge: Cambridge University Press, 2002.

The Oxford History of England: Consolidated Index. Comp. Roger Raper. Oxford: Clarendon/Oxford University Press, 1995.

Victorian Britain: An Encyclopedia. Ed. Sally Mitchell. New York: Garland, 1988.

Bodleian Library. Internet Library of Early Journals. **www.bodley.ox.ac.uk/ilej**. Full text of eighteenth- and nineteenth-century British journals. Browsable by journal, date, and page.

Britannia History Index: The Age of Empire. **www.britannia.com/history/h80.html**. Documents, chronologies, articles, biographies, and links relating to Great Britain during the Age of Empire (1689–1901).

British and Irish Women's Letters and Diaries. Alexander Street Press. A large collection of personal writings from the sixteenth to the twentieth centuries. By subscription only.

British Empire. BBC — History. **www.bbc.co.uk/history/british/empire_seapower**. A series of essays (with linked images) written by named scholars. Many aspects of the subject, covering several periods.

British Empire and International Relations. Victorian Web. **www.victorianweb.org/ history/index.html**. A well-organized set of documents and commentary covering nineteenth-century British imperialism with an emphasis on India.

Nineteenth Century Parliamentary Papers. Chadwyck-Healey. Covers 1801 to 1900. Searchable. Will eventually be extended up to the present. By subscription only.

Spartacus Educational. **www.spartacus.schoolnet.co.uk:80/Britain.html**. Short hyperlinked essays focusing mostly on modern European political history. The degree of documentation for the essays varies. This section deals with the modern United Kingdom.

Victoria Research Web. Patrick Leary. **victorianresearch.org**. A wide-ranging research-oriented site.

Victorian Census Project. University of Staffordshire. **www.staffs.ac.uk/schools/ humanities_and_soc_sciences/census/downcen.htm**. Databases from the 1831 and 1861 censuses.

The Victorian Web. **www.victorianweb.org/history**. Site content and links relating to Victorian-era culture, history, art, economics, science, politics, and imperialism. Resources include contemporary periodicals, cartoons, and bibliographies.

The Workhouse. Oxford University. **users.ox.ac.uk/~peter/workhouse/index.html**. An archive of linked resources examining the legal and actual treatment of the poor in England, Ireland, Scotland, and Wales in the eighteenth, nineteenth, and twentieth centuries. A small but excellent site.

Ireland and Scotland

A Bibliography of Works Relating to Scotland, 1916–1950. Ed. P. D. Hancock. Edinburgh: Edinburgh University Press, 1959–1960.

Celtic Culture: A Historical Encyclopedia. Ed. John T. Koch. Santa Barbara, CA: ABC-CLIO, 2006.

A Chronicle of Irish History since 1500. Ed. J. E. Doherty and D. J. Hickey. Savage, MD: Rowman and Littlefield, 1990.

Encyclopedia of Irish History and Culture. Ed. James S. Donnelly Jr. New York: Macmillan Reference USA, 2004.

Bibliography of Irish History. Royal Historical Society. **www.rhs.ac.uk/bibl/ireland .asp**. Sources on Irish history.

British and Irish Women's Letters and Diaries. Alexander Street Press. A large collection of personal writings from the sixteenth to the twentieth centuries. By subscription only.

CELT: Corpus of Electronic Texts [Irish studies]. University College Cork. **www.ucc .ie/celt/links.html**. Links to journals, bibliographies, and archives for research in Irish studies.

Enhanced British Parliamentary Papers on Ireland, 1801–1922. Bibliography of Irish History. **www.eppi.ac.uk/eppi/digbib/home**. A selection of parliamentary acts and publications relating to Ireland.

Great Hunger Collection Online [Ireland]. Quinnipiac University. **www.quinnipiac .edu/x912.xml**. A modest collection of full-text documents.

The Highland Clearances [nineteenth-century Scotland]. **www.theclearances.org/ clearances/main.php**. A large number of well-organized, annotated documents concerning the nineteenth-century displacement of Scottish farmers and the emigration of many.

Irish Resources in the Humanities. **www.irith.org/index.jsp**. A collection of links to archives and other academic resources in Irish history.

National Archives of Ireland. **www.nationalarchives.ie/research/archives.html**. A description of each collection of documents is available. Some documents are online but not a great number.

National Library of Scotland — Map Library. **www.nls.uk/maps**. Selected from a very important collection of maps covering Scotland and other areas. Historical context offered. Display of maps excellent.

Scottish History: Ancient to Modern. **www.bbc.co.uk/history/scottishhistory/index .shtml**. A ten-part TV series.

Stormont Papers: Parliamentary Debates of Questions Concerning Northern Ireland, 1921–1972. **stormontpapers.ahds.ac.uk/index.html**. Searchable by keyword or subject. In some cases full text is available.

The Word on the Street: Broadsides at the National Library of Scotland. **www.nls.uk/ broadsides/index.html**. A searchable database of broadsides from 1650 to 1910. Many are transcribed and downloadable.

Writings on Irish History. Royal Historical Society. **www.irishhistoryonline.ie/projhist .php**. A project to place online the very large bibliography published in print since the 1930s. The material since 1995 is now going online.

Eastern Europe

Encyclopedia of Eastern Europe. Ed. Richard Frucht. New York: Garland, 2000.

Historical Atlas of East Central Europe. Ed. Paul R. Magocsi and Geoffrey J. Matthews. Seattle: University of Washington Press, 1993.

Ukraine: A Bibliographic Guide to English Language Publications. Ed. Bohdan Wynar. Englewood, CO: Ukrainian Academic Press, 1990.

Yugoslavia: A Comprehensive English-Language Bibliography. Ed. Francine Friedman. Wilmington, DE: Scholarly Resources, 1993.

ABSEES Online. EBSCO, American Association for the Advancement of Slavic and East European Studies. A bibliography of books, journal articles, online resources, and so on. Includes many disciplines. The online version is available by subscription only.

Bulgaria's History. Aumda Gallery. **www.omda.bg/engl/common/history.htm**. A series of short hypertext essays on a variety of historical topics.

Czech and Slovak History: An American Bibliography. Ed. George J. Kovtun. **www.loc .gov/rr/european/cash/cash1.html**. An extensive bibliography of books and articles in English. Contains works written before 1994.

Radio Prague's History Online Virtual Exhibit. Radio Prague. **archiv.radio.cz/history/ history00.html**. A short essay on Czech history with images.

Russia and the Soviet Union

The Blackwell Encyclopedia of the Russian Revolution. Ed. Harold Shukman. Cambridge, MA: Blackwell Reference, 1994.

Encyclopedia of Russian History. Ed. James R. Milar. 4 vols. New York: Macmillan Reference USA, 2004.

The Russian Revolution, 1905–1921: A Bibliographic Guide to the Works in English. Ed. Murray Frame. Westport, CT: Greenwood Press, 1995.

Soviet Foreign Policy, 1918–1945: A Guide to Research and Research Materials. Ed. Robert H. Johnston. Wilmington, DE: Scholarly Resources, 1997.

The Soviet Union: A Biographical Dictionary. Ed. Archie Brown. New York: Macmillan, 1991.

ABSEES Online. EBSCO, American Association for the Advancement of Slavic and East European Studies. A bibliography of books, journal articles, online resources, and so on, covering many disciplines. The online edition is available only by subscription.

Revelations from the Russian Archives. **www.loc.gov/exhibits/archives/intro.html**. Documents from the Soviet era focusing on repression and espionage.

Russia Engages the World: 1453–1825. New York Public Library. **russia.nypl.org/**. A collection of documents on Russia and the West (and also Asia) in the fifteenth to nineteenth centuries.

Seventeen Moments in Soviet History. James von Geldern and Lewis Siegelbaum. **www.soviethistory.org/**. Extensive introductory essays, hundreds of audio and video clips, and thousands of archival documents. Written material is translated into English. Free registration is required to access some resources.

Africa

Africana: The Encyclopedia of the African and the African American Experience. 2nd ed. Ed. Kwame Anthony Appiah and Henry Louis Gates Jr. 5 vols. New York: Oxford University Press, 2005.

Dictionary of African Biography. New York: Reference Publications, 1977–1995.

Encyclopedia of African Nations and Civilizations. Ed. Keith Lye. New York: Facts on File, 2002.

Encyclopedia of Africa South of the Sahara. Ed. John Middleton. 4 vols. New York: Scribner, 1997.

Encyclopedia of Twentieth-Century African History. Ed. Tiyambe Zeleza. New York: Routledge, 2002.

Historical Dictionary of Pre-Colonial Africa. Ed. Robert O. Collins. Lanham, MD: Scarecrow Press, 2001.

New Encyclopedia of Africa. 2nd ed. Ed. John Middleton and Joseph Calder Miller. New York: Scribner, 2008.

African National Congress: Historical Documents. **www.anc.org.za/ancdocs/history**. A collection of documents by and about the ANC and about organizations that supported the ANC struggle.

African Posters. Melville J. Herskovitz Library, Northwestern University. **www.library.northwestern.edu/africana/collections/posters/index.html**. Three hundred fifty posters focusing primarily on South Africa and the struggle against apartheid. The collection covers domestic and international aspects of the movement.

African Studies. Columbia University Libraries. **www.columbia.edu/cu/lweb/indiv/ africa/cuvl/index.html**. A collection of links to sources of research on Africa including its "History and Culture."

African Voices. Smithsonian, National Museum of Natural History. **www.mnh.si .edu/africanvoices/**. Historical and contemporary images and text for African history and culture. Modest number of maps, photographs, drawings, and paintings. Subsections organized chronologically and thematically. Emphasis on material culture.

Africa South of the Sahara: Selected Internet Resources. Stanford University. **library .stanford.edu/depts/ssrg/africa/**. Links relevant to African cultures and history by country and topic.

Afriterra, The Cartographic Free Library. Afriterra Foundation Library. **www.afriterra .org/**. More than 1,000 maps of Africa by European mapmakers from the late fifteenth century to the twentieth century. Images can be examined in a variety of ways.

Atlantic Slave Trade and Slave Life in the Americas: A Visual Record. Jerome S. Handler, Virginia Foundation for the Humanities, and Michael L. Tuite Jr. **hitchcock .itc.virginia.edu/Slavery/index.php**. One thousand images emphasizing a pan-Atlantic perspective. Topics include culture, politics, economics, geography, military. Easily searchable by keyword or by subject. Images accompanied by annotations, but some are very brief.

Digital Image Project of South Africa: South African Freedom Struggle. DISA University of Natal. **www.disa.ukzn.ac.za/**. Digital images of forty-four South African publications, 1950–1994.

National Archives of the Republic of South Africa. **www.national.archives.gov.za/ index_content.htm**. Search facilities only.

National Museum of African Art. Smithsonian Institution. **africa.si.edu/collections/ index.htm**. An online permanent exhibit. A large number of annotated images organized by three categories: "diversity," "use," and "imagery."

Middle East and North Africa

Encyclopedia of the Arab-Israeli Conflict: A Political, Social and Military History. Ed. Spencer C. Tucker. 4 vols. Santa Barbara, CA: ABC-CLIO, 2008.

Encyclopedia of the Modern Middle East and North Africa. 2nd ed. Ed. Philip Hatter et al. 4 vols. Detroit: Macmillan Reference USA, 2004.

Encyclopedia of the Ottoman Empire. Ed. Gabor Agustan and Bruce Masters. New York: Facts on File, 2008.

Grove Encyclopedia of Islamic Art and Architecture. Ed. Jonathan Bloom and Sheila Blair. 3 vols. Oxford: Oxford University Press, 2009.

The Oxford Encyclopedia of the Modern Islamic World. Ed. John L. Esposito. New York: Oxford University Press, 1995. Covers the eighteenth century to the present.

* * *

Visit **bedfordstmartins.com/benjamin** *for links to online resources.*

Index Islamicus: Index to the Literature on Islam. Cambridge University Library. A large database of literature on Islam, the Middle East, and the Muslim world. By subscription only.

The Islamic World of 1600. University of Calgary. **ucalgary.ca/applied_history/tutor/islam**. A well-crafted tutorial examining many aspects of Islamic societies.

Middle East Studies Internet Resources. Columbia University Libraries. **www.columbia.edu/cu/lweb/indiv/mideast/cuvlm/index.html**. This site organizes resources by subject.

Question of Palestine: History. United Nations. **www.un.org/Depts/dpa/ngo/history.html**. This UN multimedia document discusses the history of Palestine since 1917.

The Topkapi Palace Museum. Bilkent University. **www.ee.bilkent.edu.tr/~history/topkapi.html**. More than 100 objects of Islamic art from the collections of the Ottoman dynasty.

Asia — General

Bibliography of Asian Studies. Ann Arbor: Association for Asian Studies, 1956–1991. Succeeded by *BAS Online* (see below).

Encyclopedia of Asian History. Ed. Ainslie T. Embree. 4 vols. New York: Scribner, 1988.

Southeast Asia: A Historical Encyclopedia. Ed. Ooi Keat Gin. 3 vols. Santa Barbara, CA: ABC-CLIO, 2004.

Vietnam Studies: An Annotated Bibliography. Ed. Carl Singleton. Lanham, MD: Scarecrow Press, 1997.

Asian Division, Area Studies. Library of Congress. **www.lcweb.loc.gov/rr/asian**. Information on the Library of Congress's Asian studies collections, as well as a Korean bibliography and a Japanese Documentation Center with a searchable database.

Asian Studies Search Engines. T. Matthew Ciolek. **www.ciolek.com/SearchEngines.html**. Onsite access to a series of offsite search engines including H-Nets. Also a database of images.

BAS Online. Association for Asian Studies. A fully searchable database of journal articles and other scholarly resources on Asia. By subscription only.

Formosa. Reed College. **academic.reed.edu/formosa/formosa_index_page/Formosa_index.html**. An archive of U.S. writings on "Formosa" in the nineteenth century. Also maps, art, photographs, and so on.

Huntington Archive of Buddhist and Related Art. Ohio State University. **kaladarshan.arts.ohio-state.edu**. A searchable database of photographed images of art from Asia and South Asia.

Indonesia: Society and Culture, World Wide Web Virtual Library. Australian National University. **coombs.anu.edu.au/WWWVLPages/IndonPages/WWWVL-Indonesia.html**. Annotated links to resources in Indonesian studies, including information on Islam in Indonesia.

Philippine Bibliography. Library of Congress. **lcweb2.loc.gov/asian/philhtml/bib9.html**. An online bibliography of the Library of Congress's Philippine history collection.

Portal to Asian Internet Resources. University of Wisconsin Library. **digicoll.library .wisc.edu/PAIR/directory/history.html**. An annotated list of sites on Asian studies. This URL brings you to resources in Asian history.

Southeast Asian Archive. University of California, Irvine. **www.lib.uci.edu/libraries/ collections/sea/sasian.html**. Virtual exhibits and annotated links to Southeast Asian resources.

SouthEast Asian Images and Texts. University of Wisconsin Digital Collections. **digicoll.library.wisc.edu/SEAiT/About.html**. Focuses on the Philippines and Laos. Collection of primary and secondary resources; 3,600 photographs from the early 1900s to the 1940s. Contains a series of short scholarly articles.

Viettouch. **www.viettouch.com**. Essays covering Vietnamese history with internal links to art, chronology, and so on. Especially strong in ancient Vietnam.

South Asia — India, Pakistan, and Sri Lanka

The Cambridge Encyclopedia of India, Pakistan, Sri Lanka, Nepal, Bhutan and the Maldives. Ed. Francis Robinson. Cambridge: Cambridge University Press, 1989.

Encyclopedia of India. Ed. Stanley A. Wolpert. 4 vols. New York: Scribner, 2005.

A Historical Atlas of South Asia. Ed. Joseph E. Schwartzberg. New York: Oxford University Press, 1992.

Digital South Asia Library. University of Chicago. **dsal.uchicago.edu**. Categorizes resources useful in South Asian research, including documents, books, newspapers, references, journals, bibliographies, and maps.

Harappa: Glimpses of South Asia before 1947. **www.harappa.com/index.html**. Text and images from early Indus Valley civilizations. Also, images, sound, and film from the decades prior to independence and partition.

Mahatma Gandhi Research and Media Service. Gandhi Serve Foundation. **www .gandhiserve.org**. A searchable archive of Gandhi's correspondence, published writings, and so on.

Mohenjo Daro. Dr. Jonathan Mark Kenoyer, University of Wisconsin, Madison. **www.mohenjodaro.net**. A small collection of images and secondary sources from excavations at Mohenjo Daro in the Indus Valley (2600 to 1900 B.C.E.). Emphasis is on daily life. Each image is accompanied by a detailed explanation. Unfortunately, Web site includes advertisements.

Primary Documents for the Study of Indian History, c. 1890–2000. **www.sscnet.ucla .edu/southasia/History/Independent/Histbiblio_indepindia.html**. A series of linked essays and annotated documents. Part of a larger site on the history of India.

South Asia Resource Access on the Internet [SARAI]. Columbia University. **www .columbia.edu/cu/lweb/indiv/southasia/cuvl/**. Links to journals, organizations, and topical guides on South Asian history.

China

China: A Historical and Cultural Dictionary. Ed. Michael Dillon. Richmond, Surrey, UK: Curzon, 1998.

Modern China: An Encyclopedia of History, Culture, and Nationalism. Ed. Wang Kewen. New York: Garland, 1998.

Academic Info: Chinese History. **www.academicinfo.net/chinahist.html**. Selected, annotated links to chronologies, databases, bibliographies, journals, and dictionaries. Site has some advertisements.

Chinese History Research Site. University of California, San Diego. **orpheus.ucsd .edu/chinesehistory**. A primary source guide, archives, links, book reviews, and a bibliography (after the Qing period), as well as information on contemporary research by scholars worldwide.

Chinese Propaganda Posters. Leiden University. **www.iisg.nl/~landsberger**. Hundreds of Chinese propaganda posters covering 1949 to 2000. Organized by theme.

The Gate of Heavenly Peace. Long Bow Group. **www.pbs.org/wgbh/pages/frontline/ gate/**. Digital material organized around a PBS documentary on the Tiananmen Massacre of June 4, 1989. Includes background material and a variety of perspectives on the event. Articles, essays, audio, video, and artwork.

John Fairbank Memorial Chinese History Virtual Library. CND. **www.cnd.org/fairbank/**. Information about the Qing period, the Republican era, and the People's Republic of China.

Japan and Korea

The Cambridge History of Japan. Ed. John Whitney Hall. 6 vols. Cambridge: Cambridge University Press, 1988–.

Concise Dictionary of Modern Japanese History. Ed. Janet Hunter. Berkeley: University of California Press, 1984.

Japan and Korea: A Critical Bibliography. Ed. Bernard Silberman. Westport, CT: Greenwood Press, 1982.

Japanese History and Culture from Ancient to Modern Times: Seven Basic Bibliographies. Ed. John Dower and Timothy George. New York: M. Wiener, 1997.

Modern Japan: An Encyclopedia of History, Culture and Nationalism. Ed. James Huffman. New York: Garland, 1998.

Studies on Korea: A Scholar's Guide. Ed. Han-kyo Kim. Honolulu: University of Hawaii Press, 1980.

Asian Division, Area Studies. Library of Congress. **www.loc.gov/rr/asian/**. Information on the Library of Congress's Asian studies collections.

Harvard Korean Studies Bibliography. **www.fas.harvard.edu/~korbib/**. This site, which covers the late sixteenth century to the present in a searchable online database, features over 80,000 references.

Japanese Studies Resources. East Asian Collection, Duke University Libraries. **library .duke.edu/research/subject/guides/japan**. An extensive compilation of bibliographies, journals, dictionaries, reference works, materials, and listservs useful to the study of Japan.

J Guide: Stanford Guide to Japan Information Resources. **jguide.stanford.edu/**. Covers all aspects of Japanese culture and history, with extensive links.

Korean Bibliography. Library of Congress. **lcweb2.loc.gov/misc/korhtml/ korbibhome.html**. A searchable database of books on Korea in English.

Korean History: A Bibliography. University of Hawaii. **www.hawaii.edu/korea/biblio/ BiblioOpen.html**. An online bibliography organized by period.

Kyoto National Museum. **www.kyohaku.go.jp/eng/syuzou/index.html**. An extensive online collection of pre-1800 Japanese art.

Australia and New Zealand

Australian Dictionary of Biography. Ed. Douglas Pike et al. 16 vols. Carlton, Victoria: Melbourne University Press, 1966–.

Australian Federation Full Text Database. University of Sydney. **setis.library.usyd .edu.au/oztexts/fed.html**. Transcribed debates and related writings on the Federation movement.

Australian Studies Resources. University of Sydney. **setis.library.usyd.edu.au/oztexts/ index.html**. A large digital collection of Australian literary and historical texts and journals.

National Library of Australia. **www.nla.gov.au/app/eresources/browse**. A list of serious Web sites on Australian history.

National Library of New Zealand: Papers Past. **paperspast.natlib.govt.nz/cgi-bin/ paperspast**. A digital collection of nineteenth-century New Zealand newspapers and periodicals.

Latin America and the Caribbean

Encyclopedia of Brazilian History and Culture. Ed. E. Riedinger. London: Routledge, 2009.

Encyclopedia of Latin American History and Culture. 2nd ed. Ed. Barbara A. Tenenbaum. 5 vols. New York: Scribner, 2008.

Handbook of Latin American Studies. Cambridge, MA: Harvard University Press, 1936–1947; and Gainesville: University of Florida Press, 1948–. Annual volume. Also a searchable database on the Web site of the Library of Congress at **rs6 .loc.gov/hlas**.

Hispanic Culture of South America. Ed. Peter Standish. Detroit: Gale Research, 1995.

Historical Dictionary of the Spanish Empire, 1402–1975. Ed. Sam L. Slick. Westport, CT: Greenwood Press, 1991.

The History Atlas of South America. Ed. Edwin Early. New York: Macmillan, 1998.

Mexico: An Encyclopedia of Contemporary Culture and History. Ed. Don Coerver, Robert Buffington, and Susanne B. Pasztor. Santa Barbara, CA: ABC-CLIO, 2004.

The Oxford Encyclopedia of Mesoamerican Cultures: The Civilizations of Mexico and Central America. Ed. David Carrasco. Oxford: Oxford University Press, 2001.

Ancient Mesoamerican Civilizations. University of Minnesota. **www.angelfire.com/ ca/humanorigins/**. Ancient Mesoamerican politics, culture, writing, government, and astronomy, with links to other sites of interest.

Castro Speech Database. University of Texas. **lanic.utexas.edu/la/cb/cuba/castro .html**. English translations of Fidel Castro's speeches.

Central American Archives. ProQuest. Primary documents from the national archives of several Central American nations. Mostly in Spanish, for the period 1519 to 1898. By subscription only.

Columbus and the Age of Discovery. Millersville University. **www.millersville.edu/ ~columbus/**. Over 1,100 articles about Columbus and cross-cultural encounters.

Cuban Heritage Collection. University of Miami. **www.library.miami.edu/chc/ collections/manuscript.html**. Mostly twentieth-century documents in Spanish, some with English summaries.

Frontera Collection of Mexican American Music. UCLA, Archoolie Foundation, Los Tigres Del Norte Foundation. **digital.library.ucla.edu/frontera**. Thirty thousand phonograph recordings in Spanish representing Mexican American vernacular music. A browsable list of subjects. Except for users on the UCLA campus, only 50-second sound clips are available.

Hispano Music and Culture from the Northern Rio Grande: The Jan B. Rael Collection. Library of Congress, American Memory. **memory.loc.gov/ammem/rghtml/ rghome.html**. Religious and secular music of southern Colorado and northern New Mexico. One hundred forty-six sound recordings with brief annotations for each. Songs can be searched by title and performer. Site includes research notes and publications by renowned folklorist Jan B. Rael.

Internet Resources for Latin America. **lib.nmsu.edu/subject/bord/laguia/#pub**. Open databases on Latin American studies.

Latin American Network Information Center. University of Texas. **lanic.utexas.edu/ la/region/history/**. This site organizes online history resources on Latin America.

Mexico: From Empire to Revolution. Getty Research Institute. **www.getty.edu/research/ conducting_research/digitized_collections/mexico/**. A photographic archive of Mexico covering the years 1857 to 1923.

The Perry-Castañeda Library Map Collection. University of Texas. **www.lib.utexas.edu/ maps/index.html**. An extensive collection of maps covering many areas of the world.

Realms of the Sacred: Early Written Records of Mesoamerica. University of California, Riverside. **www.lib.uci.edu/libraries/exhibits/meso/sacred.html**. An annotated collection of "Codices" — documents in the native "languages" of the Aztec, Maya, and Mixtec people of Mexico and Central America.

Templo Mayor Museum. **archaeology.asu.edu/tm/index2.htm**. This site guides you through the halls of the museum, dedicated to ancient Mexican history and artifacts.

Vistas: Visual Culture in Spanish America, 1520–1820. Dana Leibsohn, Smith College, and Barbara Mundy, Fordham University. **www.smith.edu/vistas**. Focuses on art and architecture of the Spanish colonial period in the Americas. One hundred fifty images of objects, buildings, sculptures, drawings, and maps. Each image includes an explanation of its use, origin, and significance.

Canada

Bibliography of Ontario History, 1867–1976: Cultural, Economic, Political and Social. By Olga B. Bishop. 2 vols. Toronto: University of Toronto Press, 1980. Supplement, 1976–1986. Toronto: Dunburn Press, 1989.

The Canadian Encyclopedia, 2000. Ed. James H. March. Toronto: McClelland and Stewart, 2000.

Canadian Reference Sources. Ed. Mary E. Bond and Martine M. Caron. Vancouver: University of British Columbia Press, 1996.

Canadian Who's Who. 37 vols. Toronto: University of Toronto Press, 2002.

Dictionary of Canadian Biography. Toronto: University of Toronto Press, 1966–. A print index covers *Volumes I to XII, 1000 to 1900.* See also below, *Dictionary of Canadian Biography Online.*

Historical Atlas of Canada. Ed. R. Cole Harris and Donald Kerr. Toronto: University of Toronto Press, 1987.

American Journeys. Wisconsin Historical Society. **www.americanjourneys.org/**. One hundred eighty texts written by explorers, traders, missionaries, settlers, and Native Americans. Documents range from works by early Viking explorers to the journals of nineteenth-century North Americans. All documents in English translation. Site includes a large number of drawings, maps, photographs, and paintings.

Canada's Digital Collections. Government of Canada. **collections.ic.gc.ca/**. An alphabetical index to a large number of online sites concerning many aspects of Canadian history.

Canadian Archival Resources on the Internet. University of Saskatchewan. **www.archivescanada.ca/car/menu.html**. This site allows you to search archives and historical Internet resources relating to Canada.

The Canadian Encyclopedia. **www.thecanadianencyclopedia.com/**. This site allows you to search 50,000 articles, many relating to Canadian history. Created for beginning researchers.

Canadian Native Law Cases, 1763–1978. University of Saskatchewan. **library.usask.ca/native/cnlc/index.html**. Documents for the study of court cases of this kind.

The Canadian West. Library and Archives Canada. **collectionscanada.ca/05/0529/052901_e.html**. A broad-ranging essay with links and images concerning the experience of Natives and Europeans on the Canadian "frontier."

Civilization Canada: The Last Best West, Advertising for Immigrants to Western Canada, 1870–1930. Canadian Museum of Civilization. **www.civilization.ca/cmc/exhibitions/hist/advertis/adindexe.shtml**. Text and images concerning the effort to attract European immigrants to western Canada.

Dictionary of Canadian Biography Online. **www.biographi.ca/index-e.html**. A searchable database of Canadians who lived or were well known before 1930. This date will move forward as the database is updated.

Early Canadiana Online. **www.canadiana.org/eco/english/collect.html**. A centralized, rapidly growing collection of documents relating to Canadian history through the early twentieth century. Some collections available to subscribers only.

Visit **bedfordstmartins.com/benjamin** *for links to online resources.*

First Peoples of Canada. Canadian Museum of Civilization, Online Exhibits. **www .civilization.ca/cmc/exhibitions/aborig/fp/fpindex.shtml**. Many subsections to the topic, each with its own introduction. Maps, bibliographies, and illustrations. Other online exhibits include "Gateway to Aboriginal History."

Library and Archives Canada. Government of Canada. **www.collectionscanada.gc .ca/index-e.html**. Wide-ranging collections of primary-source materials and research guides. Includes monographs and periodicals.

Library and Archives Canada. Collections Canada. Government of Canada. **www .collectionscanada.gc.ca/collection/index-e.html**. A large number of links to online collections of Canadian history.

The Urban Past. University of Guelph. **www.uoguelph.ca/history/urban/citybibV04 .html**. A series of bibliographies on urban history emphasizing Canadian cities from the eighteenth to the twentieth centuries. Other urban history links. Based on a course in urban history.

GENERAL RESOURCES IN UNITED STATES HISTORY

Before examining the general resources in U.S. history listed in this section and the specialized resources described on pages 245–62, you should consult the historical dictionaries, encyclopedias, and atlases listed at the beginning of this appendix (pp. 202–07). They will enable you to choose and narrow a topic.

The general resources in this section consist of bibliographies and Web sites that cover large areas and many periods of U.S. history. The specialized resources described later will be useful once you have chosen a topic and have a clear understanding of the kind of research you will need to do to develop and support your thesis. Even if you have already narrowed your topic, you should not ignore the following general resources, because many of them include sections on or links to more specialized topics.

Reference Works and Bibliographies

The American Historical Association's Guide to Historical Literature. 3rd ed. Ed. Mary Beth Norton. 2 vols. Ithaca, NY: Cornell University Press, 1995. This guide contains a large section on U.S. history.

Directory of Oral History Collections. Ed. Allen Smith. Phoenix: Oryx, 1988.

Encyclopedia of the American Constitution. 2nd ed. Ed. Leonard Levy. 6 vols. New York: Macmillan, 2000.

Encyclopedia of American Cultural and Intellectual History. Ed. Mary Kupiec Cayton and Peter W. Williams. New York: Scribner, 2001.

Encyclopedia of American History. Ed. Gary B. Nash. 11 vols. New York: Facts on File, 2003.

New York Times Book Review Index, 1896–1970. 5 vols. New York: New York Times, 1973.

The Reader's Companion to American History. Ed. Eric Foner and John A. Garraty. Boston: Houghton Mifflin, 1991.

Web Sites

Academic Info: United States History Resources. **www.academicinfo.net/histus.html**. This site includes gateways, reference materials, and topical sites with annotated links.

Amdocs. World Wide Web Virtual Library. **vlib.us/amdocs/**. A large collection of primary documents relating to North America and covering the large span from 800 C.E. to 2005.

American Journeys. Wisconsin Historical Society. **www.americanjourneys.org/**. One hundred eighty texts written by explorers, traders, missionaries, settlers, and Native Americans. Documents range from works by early Viking explorers to the journals of nineteenth-century North Americans. All documents in English translation. Site includes a large number of drawings, maps, photographs, and paintings.

American Memory. Library of Congress. **memory.loc.gov/ammem/index.html**. This site features more than 7 million documents relating to American history. This URL will take you to the main page of the site. It is a good place to start your research into a wide variety of topics in U.S. history.

American Studies at the University of Virginia. **xroads.virginia.edu**. A variety of multimedia and hypertext sources, exhibits, timelines, and other resources of use for studying American history, with a special section on the 1930s.

Archives USA. Chadwyck-Healey. **archives.chadwyck.com**. A searchable directory of over 5,000 archives of primary-source material. By subscription only. Updates and supersedes *Directory of Archives and Manuscript Repositories in the United States* (Phoenix: Oryx, 1988).

Avalon Project: Documents in Law, History and Diplomacy. Yale Law School. **avalon .law.yale.edu/default.asp**. Documents in law, history, and diplomacy from many periods in American history, organized by century.

Berkeley Digital Library SunSITE. **sunsite.berkeley.edu/**. Texts and images, including classical and medieval works, the Emma Goldman papers, and a strong collection relating to California.

Broadsides and Printed Ephemera: 1600–2000. Library of Congress, American Memory. **memory.loc.gov/ammem/rbpehtml**. A searchable collection of 10,000 posters, advertisements, leaflets, propaganda pieces, and business cards.

Core Historical Literature of Agriculture. Cornell University. **chla.library.cornell.edu/**. A collection of primary and secondary documents on agriculture in the nineteenth and twentieth centuries, including over 800 monographs.

Duke University Rare Book, Manuscript, and Special Collections Library. **library.duke .edu/specialcollections/**. Highly specialized and in-depth collections of digital materials on a variety of subjects but especially in the areas of advertising, the history of women, African American history, and Native American history.

The Great Chicago Fire. **www.chicagohs.org/fire/intro/gcf-index.html**. Essays, images, and primary documents about the fire of 1871.

History Matters. George Mason University. **historymatters.gmu.edu**. An annotated list of over 700 sites for serious research in U.S. history on the Web.

History Resource Center: U.S. Gale Group. **www.gale.cengage.com/HistoryRC/index .htm**. This site requires a subscription to use its integrated text and commentary.

H-Reviews. **www.h-net.org/reviews**. A searchable online collection of full-text book reviews in all fields of history.

In the First Person. Alexander Street Press. A searchable index to a large database of oral history collections in English.

Making of America. University of Michigan. **quod.lib.umich.edu/m/moa/**. Scanned images of books and magazine articles (over 10,000 books and 50,000 journal articles) from nineteenth-century America. The focus is on social history in the period 1850 to 1876. Searchable, full-text access. See also the next item.

Making of America. Cornell University Library. **library8.library.cornell.edu/moa/**. Complements coverage by the University of Michigan site (preceding item) with its own collection of nineteenth-century books and articles. Full-text access.

National Gallery of the Spoken Word. Michigan State University. **www.historical voices.org/**. A searchable database of oral history archives throughout the United States.

The National Union Catalog of Manuscript Collections. Washington, DC: Library of Congress, 1959–1993. **www.loc.gov/coll/nucmc/**. A searchable catalog, with complex search rules, of manuscript materials held by universities, libraries, archives, historical associations, and so on.

The Nineteenth Century in Print. Library of Congress, American Memory. **memory .loc.gov/ammem/ndlpcoop/moahtml/mnchome.html/**. A large, searchable collection of nineteenth-century books and periodicals.

ProQuest Dissertations and Theses Database. Citations to all U.S. dissertations (since 1861). Abstracted after 1980. Full text available on microfiche or for purchase from U.M.I.

ProQuest History Studies Center. A large database of reference works, media, journals, and so on. All by subscription. Find out which of the individual information collections can be accessed from your library.

Questia Net Library. Questia. **www.questia.com/library/history/united-states-history**. A large database of digitized research sources on all eras and aspects of U.S. history. By subscription only.

Reviews in American History. Johns Hopkins University Press. Full-text reviews of recent books. Back issues through *JSTOR.* Also available in print.

WestWeb: Western History. CUNY. **scholar.library.csi.cuny.edu/westweb/**. Primary sources, links, timelines, and bibliographies relating to the history of the American West.

WWW-VL History: United States. **vlib.iue.it/history/USA/**. This site categorizes links and materials by media, topic, and era. A very large site, some of whose links are not available and others not reliable.

SPECIALIZED RESOURCES IN UNITED STATES HISTORY

Once you have chosen your topic with the aid of the historical dictionaries, encyclopedias, and atlases listed at the beginning of this appendix (pp. 202–07), you are ready to seek out primary and secondary sources that you will use to develop and support your thesis. The U.S. history resources in this section are organized by subject, and the resources listed for each subject are divided into two groups. The first group contains reference works and bibliographies available in print form. The second group contains a list of Web sites organized alphabetically by the name of the site. Additional specialized print and digital resources in U.S. history are available on this book's Web site: <bedfordstmartins.com/benjamin>.

Regional, State, and Local

A Bibliography of American County Histories. Comp. P. William Filby. Baltimore: Genealogical Publishing, 1985.

Directory of Historical Organizations in the United States and Canada, 2002. 15th ed. Comp. Mary Bray Wheeler. Nashville: American Association for State and Local History, 2002.

Encyclopedia of the American West. 4 vols. New York: Simon and Schuster/Macmillan, 1996.

Encyclopedia of Local History. Ed. Carol Kammen. Walnut Creek, CA: Alta Mira Press, 2000.

Encyclopedia of Southern Culture. Ed. Charles Reagan Wilson and William Ferris. Chapel Hill: University of North Carolina Press, 1989.

Genealogical and Local History Books in Print. 5th ed. 4 vols. Washington, DC: Genealogical Books in Print, 1996–1997.

Center for the Study of Southern Culture. University of Mississippi. **www.olemiss.edu/ depts/south/#.** A series of documentary collections on southern popular culture. Contains a large media archive.

Directory of State Archives and Records Programs. **www.statearchivists.org/states .htm.** A linked list of state archives throughout the United States.

Documenting the American South. University of North Carolina. **docsouth.unc.edu/.** A wide array of primary sources relating to the American South before 1940, especially North Carolina.

The Handbook of Texas Online. Texas State Historical Society with the University of North Texas. **www.tshaonline.org/handbook/online/index.html.** Thousands of full-text articles and essays on Texas history, especially the Spanish and Mexican periods. Searchable by county, town, subject, and era.

History of the American West, 1860–1920. Library of Congress, American Memory; Denver Public Library. **memory.loc.gov/ammem/award97/codhtml/ hawphome.html.** About 30,000 photos taken between 1860 and 1920 of Colorado towns, mining industry, and Indian communities. Keyword searchable.

Maritime Westward Expansion: 1820–1890. Library of Congress, American Memory. **memory.loc.gov/ammem/award99/mymhihtml/mymhihome.html**. A searchable collection of documents, images, and other resources in a multimedia format.

Ohio River Valley: 1750–1820. Library of Congress, American Memory. **memory .loc.gov/ammem/award99/icuhtml/fawhome.html**. A searchable collection of documents, images, and other resources in a multimedia format.

Online Archive of California. California Digital Libraries. **www.oac.cdlib.org/about/ oacprojects.html**. Digital resources relating to the history of California. Several collections are more broad in scope.

State Archives Collections Online. Archives Resource Center. **www.statearchivists.org/ arc/education/online_coll.htm**. A linked list of online materials on state archive Web sites.

Texas Tides. **tides.sfasu.edu/home.html**. Timelines and documents of the five major ethnic groups in Texas history.

Colonial, Revolutionary, and Early National, 1607–1800

The American Revolution, 1775–1783: An Encyclopedia. New York: Garland, 1993.

The Blackwell Encyclopedia of the American Revolution. Ed. Jack P. Greene. Cambridge, MA: Blackwell, 1994.

Colonial Wars of North America, 1512–1763: An Encyclopedia. Ed. Alan Gallay. New York: Garland, 1995.

Encyclopedia of the North American Colonies. Ed. Jacob E. Cooke. 3 vols. New York: Scribner, 1993.

James Madison and the American Nation, 1751–1836: An Encyclopedia. Ed. Robert A. Rutland. New York: Scribner, 1994.

American Journeys: Eyewitness Accounts of Early American Exploration and Settlement. Wisconsin Historical Society. **www.americanjourneys.org/index.asp**. A collection of documents drawn from the library and archives of the Wisconsin Historical Society.

Calendar of State Papers, Colonial [America and the West Indies, 1574–1738]. **www .british-history.ac.uk/subject.aspx?subject=3&gid=123**. British government records on relations with its colonies in America.

Classics of American Colonial History. Dinsmore Documentation. **dinsdoc.com/ colonial-3.htm**. A full-text collection of journal articles and book chapters. About twenty different aspects of life during the colonial era are covered.

Continental Congress and Constitutional Convention: 1774–1789. Library of Congress, American Memory. **memory.loc.gov/ammem/collections/continental/**. A searchable collection of documents.

Doing History: Martha Ballard's Diary Online. Film Study Center, Harvard University. **DoHistory.org**. The diary of an eighteenth-century midwife.

Early Americas Digital Archive. University of Maryland. **www.mith2.umd.edu/eada/**. A very good source for early material on North America between 1492 and 1826. Mostly full text.

Early American Newspapers, Series 1, 1690–1876. NewsBank. **www.readex.com/readex/product.cfm?product=10**. A searchable archive of over 600 newspapers, most from the eighteenth century. By subscription only.

Early American Web Gateway. Maryland Institute for Technology in the Humanities. **www.mith2.umd.edu/eada/search.php**. Collection of documents and links covering the sixteenth and seventeenth centuries. Not all links are of high quality; not all sites are free.

Early Encounters in North America. Alexander Street Press. A large collection of primary materials by and about the Native and European American peoples in the early years of their contact. By subscription only.

Eighteenth-Century Resources — History. Rutgers, Newark. **newark.rutgers.edu/~jlynch/18th/history.html**. Annotated links; particularly strong in American and British history.

George Washington Papers at the Library of Congress, 1741–1799. Library of Congress, American Memory. **rs6.loc.gov/ammem/gwhtml/gwhome.html**. This URL brings you to a number of Washington-related documents.

James Madison: 1723–1836. Library of Congress, American Memory. **memory.loc.gov/ammem/collections/madison_papers/index.html**. A searchable collection of papers.

Omohundro Institute for Early American History and Culture. **oieahc.wm.edu/**. Access to the papers of John Marshall and links to other resources relating to early American history.

The Papers of John Jay. Columbia University Libraries. **www.columbia.edu/cu/web/digital/jay**. One of the largest collections of documents relating to the U.S. chief justice.

Pennsylvania Gazette. Accessible Archives. This database on CD-ROM includes the full range of the publication — 1728 to the early 1800s. A wide range of search options is available.

Plimoth-on-Web: Plimoth Plantation's Web Page [colonial America, 1620–1692]. **www.plimoth.org**. Multimedia educational materials about colonial America and the Plymouth Colony.

Plymouth Colony Archive Project. Patricia Scott Deetz, Christopher Fennell, and J. Eric Deetz, University of Virginia. **www.histarch.uiuc.edu/plymouth/index.html**. Documents and analytical essays; social history of Plymouth Colony from 1620 to 1691.

Religion and the Founding of the American Republic. Library of Congress. **lcweb.loc.gov/exhibits/religion/religion.html**. Documents and visual images; significance of religion for early American history; manuscripts, letters, books, prints, paintings, artifacts, and music.

Salem Witch Trials. University of Virginia. **etext.virginia.edu/salem/witchcraft/home.html**. Trial transcripts, contemporary narratives, pamphlets, and sermons. Also a historical overview and links to relevant organizations and archives.

The Thomas Jefferson Digital Archive. University of Virginia. **etext.virginia.edu/ jefferson**. A very large collection of writings about Jefferson, covering 1826 to 1997. Also included are extracts from Jefferson's writings and a large number of his letters. These are organized by topic. Also some papers for Alexander Hamilton.

Thomas Jefferson Papers. Library of Congress, American Memory. **memory.loc.gov/ ammem/collections/jefferson_papers/**. About 27,000 documents including Jefferson's letters, notes, and official writings. Reading the handwriting can be slow going.

Native American

American Indian Religious Tradition: An Encyclopedia. Ed. Suzanne J. Crawford and Ennis F. Kelly. Santa Barbara, CA: ABC-CLIO, 2005.

Atlas of American Indian Affairs. Ed. Francis Paul Prucha. Lincoln: University of Nebraska Press, 1990.

Encyclopedia of the American Indian. Ed. Bruce Johansen and Barry Pritzker. 4 vols. Santa Barbara, CA: ABC-CLIO, 2007.

Encyclopedia of the Great Plains Indians. Lincoln: University of Nebraska Press, 2007.

The Gale Encyclopedia of Native American Tribes. Ed. Sharon Malinowski. 4 vols. Detroit: Gale, 1998.

Handbook of North American Indians. Ed. William C. Sturtevant. 17 vols. Washington, DC: Smithsonian Institution, 1978–2001.

Native American Periodicals and Newspapers, 1828–1982: Bibliography, Publishing Record, and Holdings. Comp. Maureen Hardy. Westport, CT: Greenwood Press, 1984.

Native Americans: An Encyclopedia of History, Culture and Peoples. 2 vols. Santa Barbara, CA: ABC-CLIO, 1998.

Early Encounters in North America. Alexander Street Press. Primary sources describing the relationship between Native and European Americans from 1534 to 1850. By subscription only.

NativeWeb. **www.nativeweb.org**. This site, which is updated and expanded regularly, features information about Native American studies.

Slavery and the Civil War
(See also "African American," pp. 250–51.)

Dictionary of Afro-American Slavery. Ed. Randall M. Miller and John David Smith. Westport, CT: Greenwood Press, 1997.

Encyclopedia of the Confederacy. Ed. Richard N. Current. 4 vols. New York: Scribner, 1998.

Abolition and Reconstruction. Rutgers University. **www.libraries.rutgers.edu/rul/ rr_gateway/research_guides/history/civwar.shtml**. Many full-text documents from the period of the 1830s to the 1890s. Site includes many links to serious Civil War sites.

The Abolition Movement. Library of Congress. **www.loc.gov/exhibits/african/afam005.html**. A multimedia exhibit guiding users through African American history, particularly the abolition movement. Part of the "African American Mosaic" at the Library of Congress.

Abraham Lincoln: 1850–1865. Library of Congress, American Memory. **memory .loc.gov/ammem/alhtml/malhome.html**. A searchable collection of papers.

Abraham Lincoln Newspaper Archive. Newspaper Archives.com. **www.abraham lincolnarchive.com/**. Twenty-five thousand pages of Lincoln and Lincoln-related newspaper articles. Searchable by keyword, date, and so on. Searching is free but not all articles are. The articles are difficult to read in some cases as the picture of the page is not clear.

American Civil War Letters and Diaries. Alexander Street Press. A 100,000-page collection, indexed and searchable. By subscription only.

American Civil War Reference Library. Gale Reference Library. Detroit: U.X.L., 2003. A searchable e-book.

American Civil War Resources. Virginia Tech, Digital Libraries and Archives. **spec .lib.vt.edu/civwar**. Links to manuscript collections, dissertation information, print collections, and a guide to manuscript resources.

Amistad. Mystic Seaport Library. **amistad.mysticseaport.org/library/welcome .html**. A searchable collection of newspaper and personal accounts, official transcripts and records, maps and illustrations.

The Anti-Slavery Literature Project. Arizona State University and Iowa State University. **antislavery.eserver.org/**. A broad variety of texts and images can be found on this site. Very good documentation. Well-maintained site. Free registration required.

Born in Slavery: Slave Narratives from the Federal Writer's Project, 1936–1938. Library of Congress, American Memory. **lcweb2.loc.gov/ammem/snhtml/snhome.html**. Over 2,000 firsthand accounts of slavery; introductory essay discusses the significance of slave narratives.

Civil War Resources on the Internet: Abolitionism to Reconstruction, 1830's–1890's. Rutgers University. **www.libraries.rutgers.edu/rul/rr_gateway/research_guides/history/civwar.shtml/**. Selected and partially annotated links to documents, bibliographies, studies, images, and other sites relating to the Civil War.

The Coming of the Civil War. World Wide Web Virtual Library. **www.vlib.us/eras/war.htm**. Links to 80 documents and 40 longer works.

The Dred Scott Case. Washington University Libraries. **www.library.wustl.edu/vlib/dredscott**. This site features the papers of the Dred Scott case, as well as a chronology and information about the papers.

Freedmen's Bureau Online. **www.freedmensbureau.com**. Freedmen's Bureau records: supervision of relief and education activities for refugees and freedmen; issuing rations, clothing, medicine; issues concerning confiscated land; labor contracts; a variety of other records and reports.

Geography of Slavery in Virginia. Virginia Center for Digital History and University of Virginia. **www2.vcdh.virginia.edu/gos**. Several thousand runaway slave newspaper advertisements between 1736 and 1777.

Gilder Lehrman Center for the Study of Slavery, Resistance and Emancipation. Gilder Lehrman Institute. **yale.edu/glc**. A searchable database of 60,000 documents. Summaries but not full text are online. (Institute is closed for renovations until 2011.)

Journal of the Congress of the Confederate States of America. Library of Congress, American Memory. **memory.loc.gov/ammem/amlaw/lwcc.html**.

Mapping Virginia's Slave Migrations, 1790–1863. University of Virginia Library. **fisher.lib.virginia.edu/collections/stats/slavetrade/migrmaps.html**. An imaginative combination of maps and statistics uncovers facts about the local and regional slave trade.

North American Slave Narratives, Beginnings to 1920. William Andrews, University of North Carolina, Chapel Hill. **docsouth.unc.edu/neh/**. Over 200 full-text documents; all known published slave narratives; many published biographies of slaves.

Reconstruction Era Reference Library. 3 vols. Detroit: U.X.L., 2005.

Samuel J. May Anti Slavery Collection. Cornell University Library. **digital.library .cornell.edu/m/mayantislavery**. A rich collection of antislavery and Civil War materials. Over 10,000 pamphlets, leaflets, broadsides, local antislavery society newsletters, sermons, and essays. Slave trade and emancipation; 300,000 full-text pages. Searchable. Many links to other collections.

Slaves and the Courts, 1740–1860. Library of Congress, American Memory. **memory .loc.gov/ammem/sthtml/sthome.html**. Pamphlets, books, and primary documents illustrate the treatment of slaves and slavery by the U.S. courts prior to emancipation.

The Trans-Atlantic Slave Trade. Ed. David Eltis. Cambridge University Press. A database on CD-ROM. Records of slave ship voyages between 1595 and 1866. Interactive multimedia capabilities.

Uncle Tom's Cabin and American Culture. University of Virginia. **www.iath.virginia .edu/utc**. An excellent multimedia archive created around Harriet Beecher Stowe's famous novel. Draws on a wide range of documents to trace the origins of the book, its reception, and the evolution of the debate about slavery and race in America.

Valley of the Shadow: Two Communities in the American Civil War. Edward Ayers et al., University of Virginia. **valley.vcdh.virginia.edu/**. Documents from a northern county and a southern county throughout the Civil War, offering primary sources and secondary narrative and analysis.

African American

Africana: The Encyclopedia of the African and the African American Experience. 2nd ed. Ed. Kwame Anthony Appiah and Henry Louis Gates Jr. 5 vols. New York: Oxford University Press, 2005.

Black Women in America: An Historical Encyclopedia. Bloomington: Indiana University Press, 1994.

Encyclopedia of African-American Culture and History. Ed. Jack Salzman, David L. Smith, and Cornel West. 5 vols. New York: Simon and Schuster/Macmillan, 1996. Supplement, 2000.

Encyclopedia of African-American History, 1619–1895: From the Colonial Period to the Age of Frederick Douglass. Ed. Paul Finkelman. 3 vols. New York: Oxford University Press, 2006.

Encyclopedia of African-American Religions. Ed. Larry G. Murphy et al. New York: Garland, 1993.

Encyclopedia of the Harlem Renaissance. Ed. Cary D. Wintz and Paul Finkelman. 2 vols. New York: Routledge, 2004. E-book, Taylor & Francis, 2004.

The African-American Mosaic. Library of Congress. **www.loc.gov/exhibits/african/ afam001.html**. This online multimedia exhibit guides the reader through annotated images of many aspects of African American history.

African American Newspapers: Nineteenth Century. Accessible Archives. Full text of articles from major nineteenth-century African American newspapers. Searchable online. By subscription only.

African-American Perspective, 1818–1907. Library of Congress, American Memory. **memory.loc.gov/ammem/aap/aaphome.html**. The database of the Daniel A. P. Murray Pamphlet Collection, which focuses on the late nineteenth and early twentieth centuries in America.

African-American Religion: A Documentary History Project. Amherst College. **www .amherst.edu/~aardoc/menu.html**. Materials span 1441 to the present. Includes limited information and sample documents. The project eventually will be published in print form.

African-American Women. Duke University, Special Collections Library. **library .duke.edu/specialcollections/collections/digitized/african-american-women/**. Published and unpublished writings, most from the nineteenth century.

African American Women Writers of the 19th Century. New York Public Library. **digital .nypl.org/schomburg/writers_aa19/**. Fifty-two digitized books, novels, pamphlets, and poetry from the period before 1920.

Africans in America. PBS Online. **www.pbs.org/wgbh/aia**. Complements a four-part television series covering the seventeenth to the nineteenth centuries. Contains several hundred documents, images, and maps, as well as comments by a large number of historians.

Afro-Louisiana History and Genealogy, 1719–1820. Gwendolyn Hall. **www.ibiblio.org/ laslave/**. A searchable database of the genealogy and life of slaves in the Gulf of Mexico region.

Black Thought and Culture. Alexander Street Press. A large database of publications and documents written by leaders of the black community. Covers the eighteenth to the twentieth centuries. By subscription only.

In Motion: The African-American Migration Experience. New York Public Library. **www.inmotionaame.org/home.cfm**. An excellent collection of texts, maps, and images examining the many migrations of Africans and African Americans from the era of the slave trade to the late twentieth century.

Schomburg Center for Research in Black Culture. New York Public Library. **www.nypl .org/research/sc/sc.html**. Oral histories and online exhibits.

W. E. B. Du Bois Institute for Afro-American Research. Harvard University. **dubois.fas .harvard.edu/**. Links to recent projects and research, including databases, bibliographies, and other materials.

Visit **bedfordstmartins.com/benjamin** *for links to online resources.*

Women's

The Female Experience in Eighteenth- and Nineteenth-Century America: A Guide to the History of American Women. Ed. Jill K. Conway. New York: Garland, 1982.

The Female Experience in Twentieth Century America: A Guide to the History of American Women. Ed. Jill K. Conway. New York: Garland, 1991.

Handbook of American Women's History. 2nd ed. Ed. Angela M. Howard and Frances M. Kavenik. Thousand Oaks, CA: Sage, 2000.

Women's Studies Encyclopedia: History, Philosophy, and Religion. Vol. 3. Ed. Helen Tierney. Westport, CT: Greenwood Press, 1999.

American Women's History: A Research Guide. **www.mtsu.edu/~kmiddlet/history/ women.html**. A large collection of links to sites related to the study of women.

Civil War Women. Duke University, Special Collections Library. **library.duke.edu/ specialcollections/collections/digitized/civil-war-women/**. Diaries, letters, and other writing by women during the Civil War.

Documents from the Women's Liberation Movement. Duke University, Digital Scriptorium. **scriptorium.lib.duke.edu/wlm**. A searchable database of primary texts from the 1960s and 1970s.

The Emma Goldman Papers. University of California, Berkeley. **sunsite3.berkeley .edu/Goldman**.

North American Women's Letters and Diaries. Alexander Street Press. A large collection of primary sources by women from a variety of backgrounds and circumstances. Excellent searching facilities. By subscription only.

Trails of Hope: Overland Diaries, 1846–1869. Brigham Young University. **overland trails.lib.byu.edu/**. Background essays and about 60 full-text diaries of the westward migration.

Votes for Women: Selections from the National American Woman Suffrage Association Collection, 1848–1921. Library of Congress, American Memory. **memory.loc .gov/ammem/naw/nawshome.html**. A searchable collection of books and pamphlets.

Women's History. Library of Congress, American Memory. **memory.loc.gov/ ammem/awnhtml/index.html**. A large number of links to Library of Congress records related to American women. Many of these are full text; some are not. An important collection is *Votes for Women* (see preceding item).

Women Working, 1800–1930. Harvard University Library. **ocp.hul.harvard.edu/ww/**. A large archive of manuscripts, pamphlets, and photographs on the role of women in the U.S. economy. Several of the subcollections examine social, cultural, "racial," and gender issues.

Immigrant and Ethnic

American Immigrant Cultures. Ed. David Levinson and Melvin Ember. 2 vols. New York: Macmillan, 1997.

Asian American Studies: An Annotated Bibliography and Research Guide. Ed. Hyung-Chan Kim. Westport, CT: Greenwood Press, 1989.

Dictionary of Asian American History. Ed. Hyung-Chan Kim. Westport, CT: Greenwood Press, 1986.

Dictionary of Mexican American History. Ed. Matt S. Meier and Feliciano Rivera. Westport, CT: Greenwood Press, 1981.

Encyclopedia of American Immigration. Ed. James Ciment. 4 vols. New York: M. E. Sharpe, 2001.

Encyclopedia Latina: History, Culture and Society in the United States. Ed. Ilan Stavans and Harold Augenbraum. 4 vols. Danbury, CT: Grollier Academic Reference, 2005.

European Immigration and Ethnicity in the United States and Canada: A Historical Bibliography. Ed. David L. Brye. Santa Barbara, CA: ABC-CLIO, 1983.

Harvard Encyclopedia of American Ethnic Groups. Ed. Stephen Thernstrom et al. Cambridge, MA: Harvard University Press, 1980.

The Italian-American Experience: An Encyclopedia. Ed. Salvatore J. LaGumina et al. New York: Garland, 1999.

American Family Immigration History Center. The Statue of Liberty-Ellis Island Foundation. **www.ellisisland.org/**. Much useful advice about conducting family history. Search of passenger lists beginning in 1892. Full access requires "membership."

California History Online. California Historical Society. **www.californiahistory.net/**. Texts and images dealing with the Spanish and Mexican eras of California history.

The Chinese in California: 1850–1925. Library of Congress, American Memory. **memory.loc.gov/ammem/award99/cubhtml/cichome.html**. A searchable collection of documents, images, and other resources in a multimedia format.

Columbia River Basin Ethnic History Archive. Washington State University. **www.vancouver.wsu.edu/crbeha/browse.htm**. A searchable multimedia database of materials relating to each of the many ethnic groups that live in the portions of Oregon, Washington, and British Columbia (in Canada) surrounding the Columbia River.

Frontera Collection of Mexican American Music. UCLA, Archoolie Foundation, Los Tigres Del Norte Foundation. **digital.library.ucla.edu/frontera**. Thirty thousand phonograph recordings in Spanish representing Mexican American vernacular music. A browsable list of subjects. Except for users on the UCLA campus, only 50-second sound clips are available.

Immigration: The Changing Face of America. Library of Congress, American Memory. **memory.loc.gov/ammem/ndlpedu/features/immig/oldflash.html**. A multimedia exhibit of immigration to America from many different parts of the world.

Immigration History Research Center. University of Minnesota. **www.ihrc.umn.edu/**. A searchable archive of personal papers and images of immigrants, with a brief abstract for each collection. No full text online.

Japanese American Relocation Digital Archive. JARDA. **www.calisphere.universityofcalifornia.edu/jarda/**. A large collection of primary sources and images concerning the World War II internment of Japanese Americans.

Japanese American Relocation Digital Archive. USC Libraries Digital Archive. **digarc .usc.edu/search/controller/collection/jarda-m4.html**. Over 200 newspaper photos and captions from the period 1941 to 1946.

Japanese Immigrants in America. Brigham Young University. **abish.byui.edu/ specialCollections/fhc/Japan/index.asp**. A collection of biographical data on Japanese in the west. Searchable by name only.

Korean American Archive Photo Set. USC Libraries Digital Archive. **www.usc.edu/ libraries/archives/arc/findingaids/kaaphotos/index.php**. Primary materials, mostly photographs, related to Koreans living in the United States from 1903 to 1965.

North American Immigrant Letters and Diaries. Alexander Street Press. A large collection of primary sources by immigrants covering the period from 1840 to the present. By subscription only.

Puerto Rico and the Dawn of the Modern Age. Library of Congress, American Memory. **memory.loc.gov/ammem/collections/puertorico/**. This site also contains a searchable collection of books and pamphlets for the American Memory topic "Puerto Rico Books and Pamphlets, 1831–1929."

Social and Cultural

The Cambridge History of American Theater. Ed. Don B. Wilmeth. 3 vols. Cambridge: Cambridge University Press, 1998–2000.

Encyclopedia of American Education. 3rd ed. Ed. Harlow G. Unger. 3 vols. New York: Facts on File, 2007.

Encyclopedia of American Social History. Ed. Mary K. Cayton, Elliott J. Gorn, and Peter W. Williams. 3 vols. New York: Scribner, 1993.

Encyclopedia of Early Cinema. Ed. Richard Abel. New York: Routledge, 2005.

Encyclopedia of Lesbian and Gay Histories and Cultures. New York: Garland, 1999.

Encyclopedia of Social Welfare History in North America. Ed. John M. Herrick and John H. Stuart. Thousand Oaks, CA: Sage, 2005.

Historical Dictionary of American Education. Ed. Richard J. Altenbaugh. Westport, CT: Greenwood Press, 1999.

History of the Mass Media in the United States: An Encyclopedia. Ed. Margaret A. Blanchard. Chicago: Fitzroy Dearborn, 1998.

The New Grove Dictionary of Jazz. Ed. Barry Kornfeld. New York: Oxford University Press, 2001.

Social Reform and Reaction in America: An Annotated Bibliography. Santa Barbara, CA: ABC-CLIO, 1984.

Ad*Access. Duke University, Special Collections Library. **library.duke.edu/ digitalcollections/adaccess/**. Newspaper advertisements between 1911 and 1955; 7,000 examples in fields: beauty, hygiene, radio, television, transportation, and World War II.

American Film Institute Catalog. Chadwyck-Healey. A catalog of (almost) every American film from 1893 to 1970; 45,000 films, plot summaries, director and actor entries, and so on. By subscription only.

Americans' First Look into the Camera: Daguerreotype Portraits and Views, 1839–1864. Library of Congress, American Memory. **memory.loc.gov/ammem/daghtml/ daghome.html**. Over 700 early photographs, primarily daguerreotypes. A short introduction to the daguerreotype medium.

American Variety Stage: Vaudeville and Popular Entertainment, 1870–1920. Library of Congress, American Memory. **memory.loc.gov/ammem/vshtml/vshome .html**. Scripts, theater programs, playbills, motion pictures, ten sound recordings, 143 photos.

Broadsides and Printed Ephemera, 1600–2000. Library of Congress, American Memory. **memory.loc.gov/ammem/browse/listsome.php?**. A large collection of "street" news for the entire range of U.S. history.

Clash of Cultures in the 1910s and 1920s. Ohio State University. **ehistory.osu.edu/ osu/mmh/clash/default.htm**. Explains the cultural turmoil of the early twentieth century by focusing on the Scopes trial, Prohibition, immigration restriction, the Ku Klux Klan, and the "New Woman."

Dime Novels and Penny Dreadfuls. Stanford University. **www-sul.stanford.edu/depts/ dp/pennies**. Over 2,000 images of covers, nine full-text selections, weekly story papers, and essays. Searchable by subject.

Emergence of Advertising in America, 1850–1920. Duke University, Digital Scriptorium. **library.duke.edu/digitalcollections/eaa/**. Over 9,000 advertising items and publications from the period 1850 to 1920. Advertising ephemera, trade cards, calendars, almanacs, postcards, broadsides, and advertising cookbooks. Searchable by keyword or ad content.

Film Literature Index Online. **webapp1.dlib.indiana.edu/fli/index.jsp**. A collection of links.

Helios: The Smithsonian American Art Museum Photography Collection. Smithsonian American Art Museum. **AmericanArt.si.edu/helios**. Three hundred photos; 175 daguerreotypes. Scholars discuss images, landscape photos, and the history of daguerreotypes, among other topics.

Historic American Sheet Music. Duke University, Special Collections Library. **library .duke.edu/digitalcollections/hasm/**. Digital images of 3,000 examples of sheet music from the period 1850 to 1920. Background essays.

Medicine and Madison Avenue. Duke University, Digital Scriptorium. **library .duke.edu/digitalcollections/mma/**. Traces the evolution and complexity of twentieth-century health-related marketing. Over 600 health-related ads from 1910 to 1960. Also, transcripts of 1,930 radio commercials, plus medical journal articles.

New Deal Stage: Selections from the Federal Theater Project, 1935–1939. Library of Congress, American Memory. **memory.loc.gov/ammem/fedtp/fthome.html**. Over 13,000 images; 71 play scripts; 168 documents from Federal Theater Project records.

Performing Arts in America, 1875–1923. New York Public Library for the Performing Arts. **digital.nypl.org/lpa/nypl/sitemap/sitemap.cfm**. Over 16,000 items relating to the performing arts in the late nineteenth and early twentieth centuries: documents, photographs, clippings, films, theater programs, and sheet music.

Radio Program Archive. University of Memphis. **umdrive.memphis.edu/mbensman/ public/**. Transcripts of several thousand radio programs, most from the 1930s to the 1950s.

Visit **bedfordstmartins.com/benjamin** *for links to online resources.*

Red Hot Jazz Archive: A History of Jazz before 1930. Scott Alexander. **www.redhotjazz .com**. Biographical information, photos, and audio and video files for more than 200 jazz bands and musicians active from 1895 to 1929; biographical essays, discographies, and short jazz films.

September 11 Digital Archive. Center for History and New Media, George Mason University; American Social History Project, City University of New York. **www.911digitalarchive.org**/. Annotated resources connected with 9/11: firsthand accounts, e-mails, digital images, posters, press releases, brochures, and newsletters.

Social Welfare and Visual Politics: The Story of the Survey Graphic. **newdeal.feri.org/ sg/index.htm**. A series of articles from this journal. Includes a collection of online resources in U.S. social history.

Southern Mosaic: The John and Ruby Lomax 1939 Southern States Records Trip. Library of Congress, American Memory. **memory.loc.gov/ammem/lohtml/lohome .html**. In 1939, John Lomax, curator of the Library of Congress Archive of American Folk Songs, and his wife Ruby took a 6,500-mile journey and recorded 700 folk tunes, available in these audio files.

Southern Oral History Project. University of North Carolina, Chapel Hill. **www.sohp .org**/. Index to a large collection of interviews. A small selection online.

Temperance and Prohibition. K. Austin Kerr, Ohio State University. **prohibition .osu.edu**/. A collection of images, speeches, newspaper and journal articles, advertisements, reports, and statistics.

TV News Archive. Vanderbilt University. **tvnews.vanderbilt.edu**/. Major network news programs since 1968. By subscription only.

Vaudeville and Popular Entertainment [1870–1920]. Library of Congress, American Memory. **lcweb2.loc.gov/ammem/vshtml/vshome.html**. Library of Congress digital multimedia holdings about vaudeville in America.

Political

Dwight D. Eisenhower: A Bibliography of His Times and Presidency. Comp. R. Alton Lee. Wilmington, DE: Scholarly Resources, 1991.

Encyclopedia of the American Left. Ed. Mari J. Buhle. Oxford: Oxford University Press, 1998.

Encyclopedia of American Political History: Studies of the Principal Movements and Ideas. Ed. Jack P. Greene. 3 vols. New York: Scribner, 1984.

Encyclopedia of the American Presidency. New York: Simon and Schuster, 1994.

Encyclopedia of the Cold War. Ed. Ruub van Dijk. New York: Routledge, 2008.

The Great Depression and New Deal: A Thematic Encyclopedia. Ed. Steven Danver et al. Santa Barbara, CA: ABC-CLIO, 2009.

The Great Depression in America: A Cultural Encyclopedia. William H. Young and Nancy K. Young. 2 vols. Westport, CT: Greenwood Press, 2007.

Historical Dictionary of the Gilded Age. Ed. Leonard Schlup. Armonk, NY: M. E. Sharpe, 2003.

Historical Dictionary of the Progressive Era, 1890–1920. Ed. John D. Buenker. Westport, CT: Greenwood Press, 1988.

Political Parties and Elections in the United States: An Encyclopedia. Ed. L. Sandy Maisel. 2 vols. New York: Garland, 1991.

Protest, Power and Change: An Encyclopedia of Non-Violent Action. New York: Garland, 1997.

Abraham Lincoln Historical Digitization Project. Drew VandeCreek, Northern Illinois University. **lincoln.lib.niu.edu**. Illinois history focusing on Lincoln's years there (1831–1860).

Abraham Lincoln Papers. Library of Congress, American Memory; Lincoln Studies Center, Knox College. **memory.loc.gov/ammem/alhtml/malhome.html**. Twenty thousand documents relating to Lincoln's life and career.

America in the 1930's. American Studies Program, University of Virginia. **xroads .virginia.edu/~1930s/DISPLAY/displayframe.html**. Offers audio, visual, and textual sources to survey the culture and politics of the time.

The American President Project. University of California, Santa Barbara. **www .presidency.ucsb.edu/index_docs.php**. An archive of presidential documents: speeches, press conferences, party platforms, election data, and so on. A wide range of public documents for each presidency.

Brooklyn Daily Eagle [1841–1902]. Brooklyn Public Library. **eagle.brooklyn publiclibrary.org/Default/Skins/BEagle/Client.asp?Skin=BEagle&**. A well-organized long run of an important newspaper. Full text available.

Civil Rights Documentation Project: A Bibliography of Oral History Interviews. University of Southern Mississippi. **www.usm.edu/crdp/**. This site features an oral history bibliography, oral history transcripts, and a civil rights timetable. Organized by topic, by holding institution, and by name of person interviewed.

Documents on the History of Radicalism. Michigan State University. **www2.lib.msu .edu/branches/dmc/digital.jsp#bdc**. Covers twentieth-century issues such as AIM, birth control, Black Panthers, Hollywood Ten, KKK, Rosenberg case, Sacco and Vanzetti, SDS, Wounded Knee.

Franklin D. Roosevelt Presidential Library and Digital Archives. Franklin D. Roosevelt Library and Museum, Marist College. **www.fdrlibrary.marist.edu**. Ten thousand documents from FDR's presidency: correspondence, reports, memoranda, and so on.

Free Speech Movement. University of California, Berkeley. **www.fsm-a.org/**. An archive of documents concerning student activism at the university in the early 1960s.

The Gilded Age. Alexander Street Press. A large archive of primary and secondary works on this period. By subscription only.

The Gilded Page. Scott Nelson. **srnels.people.wm.edu/gildage/giltext.html**. Documents and links to materials relating to the American Gilded Age (1870–1898).

HarpWeek. Harpweek LLC. **http://elections.harpweek.com/introduction.htm**. Sources concerning U.S. elections from 1860 to 1921. Includes overview essays, cartoons, biographies, campaign issues, among others.

Living Room Candidate: A History of Presidential Campaign Commercials, 1952–2004. American Museum of the Moving Image. **www.ammi.org/livingroomcandidate**. Over 188 political TV commercials.

Martin Luther King Jr. Papers Project. Stanford University. **mlk-kpp01.stanford .edu/**. This site features materials relating to the life and works of Dr. King and includes his writings, speeches, and sermons, and audio files, chronologies, and analysis.

A New Deal for the Arts. National Archives. **archives.gov/exhibits/new_deal_for _the_arts/**. A description of the various government programs for artists. Describes and displays their art.

The New Deal Network. Franklin and Eleanor Roosevelt Institute/Columbia University. **newdeal.feri.org**. An online library of 900 documents and 5,000 images, as well as bibliographies and other aspects of the era.

Newspaper Collection. The State Historical Society of Missouri. **shs.umsystem.edu/ newspaper/index.shtml**. A growing collection of Missouri newspapers including those from small towns as well as cities.

Populism. Missouri State University. **history.missouristate.edu/wrmiller/Populism/ Texts/populism.htm**. A modest but useful site containing a text by the site's author along with a group of related documents and links.

Posters from the WPA, 1936–1943. Library of Congress, American Memory. **memory .loc.gov/ammem/wpaposters/wpahome.html**. A searchable collection of posters.

Presidential Elections, 1860–1912. Harpweek LLC. **elections.harpweek.com/**. Annotated political cartoons, campaign overviews, and biographical sketches.

The President John F. Kennedy Assassination Records Collection. National Archives. **www .archives.gov/research_room/jfk/index.html**. Documentation of the assassination and its investigation.

Prosperity and Thrift: The Coolidge Era and the Consumer Economy, 1921–1929. Library of Congress, American Memory. **memory.loc.gov/ammem/coolhtml/ coolhome.html**. A collection of documents illustrating the economic and political forces at work in the 1920s.

Radicalism in the Great Depression. University of Michigan. **www.lib.umich.edu/ spec-coll/radicaldepression/**. Part of a large collection of documents concerning American radicalism.

Red Scare, 1918–1921. Baruch College, CUNY. **newman.baruch.cuny.edu/digital/ redscare/default.htm**. A searchable image database.

Senate Executive Journals, 1789–1980. Readex–Newsbank. **www.readex.com/ readex/product.cfm?product=8**. Records of the nonlegislative sessions of the U.S. Senate. By subscription only.

Truman Presidential Museum and Library. Harry S. Truman Library. **www.truman library.org/library.htm**. An archive of hundreds of government documents from Truman's presidency.

Woodrow Wilson eLibrary. Woodrow Wilson Presidential Library. **woodrowwilson .org/learn/learn_show.htm?doc_id=321375**. Five thousand online documents and 1,000 images drawn from the Woodrow Wilson Library. Transcribed documents can be downloaded or printed.

Foreign Relations, International, and War

American Naval History: A Guide. Ed. Paolo E. Coletta. Lanham, MD: Scarecrow Press, 1998.

The Cambridge History of American Foreign Relations. Ed. Bradford Perkins et al. 4 vols. New York: Cambridge University Press, 1995. Also available on CD-ROM.

The Encyclopedia of United States Foreign Relations. Ed. Bruce Jentleson and Thomas Patterson. Oxford: Oxford University Press, 1997.

Encyclopedia of United States–Latin American Relations. Ed. Thomas Leonard. London: Routledge, 2009.

Encyclopedia of the Vietnam War: A Political, Social, and Military History. Ed. Spencer Tucker. New York: Oxford University Press, 2001.

Guide to American Foreign Relations since 1700. 2nd ed. Ed. Robert Beisner. Santa Barbara, CA: ABC-CLIO, 2001.

Guide to the Sources of United States Military History. By Robin Higham. Hamden, CT: Archon Books, 1975. Supplements, 1981, 1986, 1993, 1998.

Reference Guide to United States Military History, 1607–1815. Ed. Charles R. Shrader. New York: Replica Books, 1999.

The United States in the First World War: An Encyclopedia. New York: Garland, 1999.

CIA Electronic Reading Room. Central Intelligence Agency. **www.foia.cia.gov/**. The CIA has digitized thousands of formerly secret documents. These documents were declassified to comply with requests made under the Freedom of Information Act. Keyword searchable.

Cold War International History Project. Woodrow Wilson International Center for Scholars. **wilsoncenter.org/index.cfm?fuseaction=topics.home&topic_id=1409**. Lists publications and information relating to the study of international relations during the Cold War.

The Decision to Drop the Bomb. Truman Presidential Library. **trumanlibrary.org/ whistlestop/study_collections/bomb/large/index.php**. A series of documents on this topic selected from the Truman Library collection. Documents cover March 1945 to the end of the Truman presidency.

Experiencing War: Stories from the Veterans History Project Library. Library of Congress, American Folklife Center. **www.loc.gov/folklife/vets/stories/ex-war-home .html**. Oral histories from American veterans of twentieth-century wars; memoirs, letters, diaries, photo albums, scrapbooks, poetry, artwork, and official documents.

Foreign Relations of the United States. U.S. Department of State, Office of the Historian. **www.state.gov/r/pa/ho/frus/**. Contains foreign policy primary documents covering 1963 to 1976. Earlier documents (dating to the 1860s) are in the print version.

Iraqgate: Saddam Hussein, U.S. Policy and the Prelude to the Persian Gulf War, 1980–1994. Digital National Security Archive. Declassified U.S. government documents concerning U.S. relations with Iraq. By subscription only.

The Mexican-American War and the Media. **www.history.vt.edu/MexAmWar/INDEX .HTM**. A digital archive of newspaper articles related to the war.

National Security Archive. George Washington University. **www.gwu.edu/~nsarchiv/**. Declassified U.S. government documents relating to many countries and to many aspects of U.S. foreign policy since 1945. Contains several different collections of documents, some open and others by subscription through Chadwyck-Healey at **nsarchive.chadwyck.com**.

The Stars and Stripes: The American Soldiers' Newspaper of World War I, 1918–1919. Library of Congress, American Memory. **memory.loc.gov/ammem/sgphtml/ sashtml/sashome.html**. Searchable collection of all issues.

Terrorism and U.S. Policy, 1968–2002. Digital National Security Archive. A collection of declassified U.S. government documents, with introductory essay and bibliography. Searchable. Partly open and partly by subscription.

The U.S. and Its Territories, 1870–1925: The Age of Imperialism. University of Michigan. **quod.lib.umich.edu/p/philamer/**. Four thousand publications and 2,000 photographs. Emphasis is on the Philippines but Cuba, Puerto Rico, U.S.-Pacific relations, and U.S.-Caribbean relations are also included. Searchable by subject.

U.S. Nuclear Nonproliferation Policy, 1945–1991. Digital National Security Archive. Declassified U.S. government documents along with annotations and a bibliography. By subscription only.

Veterans History Project. Library of Congress. **lcweb2.loc.gov/diglib/vhp/html/ search/search.html**. A growing collection of digitized interviews with veterans.

Vietnam Center. Vietnam Center and Archive, Texas Tech University. **archive.vietnam .ttu.edu/vietnamcenter/**. Over 200 recorded oral histories. More than 63,000 documents.

Vietnam War Bibliography. Clemson University. **www.clemson.edu/caah/history/ FacultyPages/EdMoise/bibliography.html**. A list of books and articles relevant to the study of the Vietnam War.

Vietnam War Internet Project. **www.vwip.org/**. Documents about, images of, newsgroups on, and links to the events and debates surrounding the Vietnam War.

WWI: The World War I Document Archive. Brigham Young University. **www.lib .byu.edu/~rdh/wwi/**. Government documents, maps, photographs, and biographies.

Science, Technology, Environment, and Medicine

Encyclopedia of Environmental Issues. Ed. Craig Allin. Pasadena, CA: Salem Press, 2000.

The History of Science and Technology in the United States: A Critical and Selective Bibliography. Ed. Marc Rothenberg. New York: Garland, 1993.

The History of Science in the United States: An Encyclopedia. Ed. Marc Rothenberg. New York: Garland, 2001.

ECHO: Exploring and Collecting History Online — Science and Technology. Center for History and New Media, George Mason University. **echo.gmu.edu/**. History of science and technology; 800 firsthand accounts from Memory Bank. A directory of history of science Web sites; has 2,700 entries.

Environmental History. Tennessee Technological University. **www2.tntech.edu/ history/envir.html**. Links relating to environmental history.

Evolution of the Conservation Movement: 1850–1920. Library of Congress, American Memory. **lcweb2.loc.gov/ammem/amrvhtml/conshome.html**. A searchable collection of documents, images, and other resources in a multimedia format.

National Library of Medicine: History of Medicine Division. **www.nlm.nih.gov/hmd/ index.html**. Images, texts, and exhibits relating to all aspects of the history of medicine.

Nature Transformed: The Environment in American History. National Humanities Center. **www.nationalhumanitiescenter.org/tserve/nattrans/nattrans.htm**. Historical documents and related commentary in three exhibits: "Native Americans and the Land," "Wilderness and American Identity," and "The Use of the Land."

Seeing Is Believing: 700 Years of Scientific and Medical Illustration. New York Public Library. **seeing.nypl.org**. Traces the impact of illustrative technique on progress in medicine.

Whole Cloth: Discovering Science and Technology through American History. Smithsonian Institution. **invention.smithsonian.org/centerpieces/whole_cloth/**. Information relating to the history of American textiles in a multimedia format.

Labor, Business, Economic, and Urban

American Economic History: An Annotated Bibliography. Ed. John Braeman. Englewood Cliffs, NJ: Salem Press, 1994.

Class in America: An Encyclopedia. Ed. Robert Weir. 3 vols. Westport, CT: Greenwood Press, 2007.

Encyclopedia of American Urban History. Ed. E. David Goldfield. Thousand Oaks, CA: Sage, 2007.

Encyclopedia of U.S. Labor and Working-Class History. Ed. Eric Arnesen. London: Routledge, 2006.

A Financial History of the United States [to 1900]. Ed. Jerry W. Markham. New York: M. E. Sharpe, 2002.

Gale Encyclopedia of United States Economic History. 2nd ed. Ed. Thomas Carson. Detroit: Gale, 2005. Also available in e-book format as part of *Gale Virtual Reference Library.*

Labor in America: A Historical Bibliography. Santa Barbara, CA: ABC-CLIO, 1985.

Urban History. Ed. John D. Buenker. Detroit: Gale, 1981.

The Emergence of Advertising in America: 1850–1920. Library of Congress, American Memory. **memory.loc.gov/ammem/collections/advertising/**. A searchable collection of documents, images, and other resources in a multimedia format.

Haymarket Affair: 1886–1887. Library of Congress, American Memory. **memory .loc.gov/ammem/award98/ichihtml/hayhome.html**. A searchable collection of documents, images, and other resources in a multimedia format.

Like a Family: The Making of a Southern Cotton Mill World. University of North Carolina, Chapel Hill. **www.ibiblio.org/sohp/laf**. A selection of oral histories. Life in southern textile mill towns from 1880s to 1930s. Mill work, company towns, labor protests, and audio clips.

The Triangle Factory Fire. Cornell University — ILR. **www.ilr.cornell.edu/ triangle fire/**. A collection of essays connect documents and images relating to immigrant sweatshop labor in the early twentieth century.

Religious

Atlas of American Religion: The Denominational Era, 1776–1990. Ed. William Newman. Walnut Creek, CA: Alta Mira Press, 2000.

Encyclopedia of American Religious History. Ed. Stephen Prothero. 2 vols. New York: Facts on File, 2009.

Encyclopedia of Fundamentalism. Ed. Brenda E. Brashau. New York: Routledge, 2001.

Encyclopedia of Protestantism. Ed. J. Gordon Melton. New York: Facts on File, 2005.

Encyclopedia of Religion in the South. 2nd ed. Ed. Samuel S. Hill and Charles H. Lippy. Macon, GA: Mercer University Press, 2005.

New Historical Atlas of Religion in America. Ed. Edwin Scott Gaustad. New York: Oxford University Press, 2001.

Adhoc [History of Christianity]. Yale University, Yale Divinity School. **research .yale/edu:8084/divdl/adhoc/**. A large collection of images and a few texts drawn from the history of Christianity.

ATLA-CDRI. American Theological Library Association and Cooperative Digital Resource Initiative. **www.atla.com/digitalresources/browsecoll.asp**. An extensive online archive of texts and images concerning many religious topics, including the history of Christian missionary work.

ATLA Religious Database. EBSCO Publishing. A large index of journal articles, book reviews, and essays. Includes an online collection of religion and theology journals. By subscription only.

Divining America: Religion in American History. National Humanities Center. **national humanitiescenter.org/tserve/divam.htm**. A site for teachers but also useful for student researchers. Essays and a series of links on religion and U.S. culture. Covers seventeenth to twentieth centuries. Includes essays by scholars.

International Mission Photography Archive. University of Southern California. **digarc .usc.edu/impa/controller/index.htm**. A searchable database of 12,000 photographs, with emphasis on U.S. missionary activity.

APPENDIX

B

Historical Sources in Your Own Backyard

The history that surrounds you is local history. Wherever you live, that place has its own historical record, and you can research it as you would any other historical research **topic**. Local history is something that you can, literally, reach out and touch. The documents and **artifacts** recording local history are easily within reach. Just about every town (or city, or county, or region) has its own historical **archive**. This repository usually has a name such as "Anytown Historical Society." Whatever the official name, it houses old books, documents, illustrations, artifacts, and photographs, among other historical items. You begin your research by walking in the door. Unless the items you want to see are very rare or delicate, you can hold many of them in your hands. These are the **primary sources** for the history of this particular place. The research skills set out in this book will enable you to make sense of those primary sources and to relate them to whatever you have learned about "Anytown" from traditional historical resources.

Wherever you live, or wherever your school is located, you are probably not more than a short drive from a local history archive. Find the address and make a visit. Ask the archivist to see, say, a hundred-year-old photograph of the town or the deed to the very building you have walked into. You can hold in your hand a token used to pay "car fare" on the trolleys that took people around the town and to nearby towns before most people owned automobiles. You can open a box filled with letters written by a mother to her son fighting in France in World War I. If you know something about "Anytown," and about the era in which the deed, the token, and the letter were parts of daily life, you can begin to draw in your mind a picture of the town of a hundred years ago. Those primary sources could become part of a research project just as valid and just as serious as a study of town transportation in 1900 or of the impact of World War I on people's lives. In fact, the token and the letter would be vital **evidence** in supporting a **thesis** on either of these topics.

Some of the most rewarding historical research focuses on the people, events, and places that provide the **historical context** for your own life. The experiences of your parents and grandparents are pieces of history that have touched you more than any other aspect of the past — even if you are not aware of those experiences. The more you discover about the history of your family, the more you will learn about yourself. The primary documents of your family's history (even if yours is not a "traditional" family) exist. They may lie in an old trunk in "grandma's" attic or be stuffed into a shoe box at the back of a closet. Family papers may consist of old photograph albums; birth, marriage, and death records; letters; old newspaper articles; report cards; and everything else that someone in the family decided to keep or didn't have the heart to throw out. You might discover a dozen neat boxes with clear labels, or you might find only a worn envelope with faded directions to a cemetery. Most likely, you will find a range of clues to your family's past: a dress that your grandmother told your mother had belonged to her own mother; a postcard in Chinese mailed to someone in your family and dated "Hong Kong, October 24, 1938"; a photograph of a house in Cincinnati, Ohio, with a note on the back saying "Uncle Boris's house." Not much to go on. Still, you have more than you may think. Armed with nothing more than your family's name, a place where family members once lived (in this or another country), the postcard from Hong Kong, and the photo of the house in Cincinnati, you can search public records (held by governments, towns, organizations, and businesses, among others) to find evidence of your ancestors' existence. Even if family members themselves kept no records, "Anytown" and the state and federal governments kept records of them.

HOW TO RESEARCH YOUR
FAMILY HISTORY

The effort to reconstruct your family's history is very personal, and each discovery an exciting event. Each discovery also is evidence of the connection between the members of your family and the world around them. Your ancestors' lives were touched — perhaps deeply — by the events of their day. The postcard from Hong Kong, when translated, says that your great uncle was desperate to leave China for America because of the growing civil conflict in China. Uncovering the history of your family makes you aware of the ways, however indirect, in which your own life has been touched by large historical events. Knowledge of your family's history and its meaning can give you a sense of your social and cultural roots — something that will strengthen you throughout your lifetime.

The private evidence of your family's past (however slight) and the public records of its existence can be fleshed out by the most important kind of evidence: the memories of your living relatives. Once you are as familiar as you can be about the relationships, places, and events of your family's history, you are ready to interview as many of your older relatives as you can find.

The interview is the core of a family history because, in most instances, it provides the only way of uncovering the day-to-day nature of your family's life. Without the recollections of your relatives, you would not be able to discover more than a handful of names, dates, and places — only the barest outline of your family's history.

In preparing for this crucial aspect of family research, you must familiarize yourself with the basic history of your family so that you can place in proper historical context the information you obtain from the people you interview. You will need to prepare your questions beforehand, focusing on important aspects of family life and of the larger social and political life surrounding your family. Be sure that your questions establish the basics: the names, relationships, and principal home and workplace activities of each member of the family in each generation, going as far down the trunk and out on the limbs of the family tree as possible given the scope of your project and the memories of your relatives. Look for information that will enable you to make comparisons between generations of your family and between your family and other families. Investigate such topics as types of dwelling and neighborhoods, parent-child and husband-wife relationships, authority and status patterns, and income and social mobility. When you come across major family events — immigration, military service, job and residence changes, involvement in political movements — probe the reasons for these events because the reasons will illuminate the ties between your family and the nation's history.

When actually conducting the interview, use your research questions, taking care to make them as open-ended as possible — for example, "What was the neighborhood like when you lived there?" not "What was your address in 1956?" When you get an answer that seems to lead in the direction of important material, ignore your prepared questions temporarily and probe further. Don't interrupt an answer even when the point seems unimportant. Your informants are the experts on their own lives, and their memories, even if not always factually correct, are essential ingredients of family history. Finally, because the intricate web of your relatives' feelings is as important as the milestones of their lives, it is best to record (audio or video) the interview rather than rely on written notes. Record it all, and then collect from your tapes the information that, on the one hand, best reflects your informants' testimony about their lives and, on the other, enables you to say something of importance about those lives and the times in which they were lived. If you have the needed skills and software, you can incorporate your recordings into a PowerPoint presentation or a Web site, or you can produce your own feature on CD or DVD. Such a document would itself be an important part of your family's history.

If important pieces of the story are still missing — your great-grandfather's birthplace, for instance, or the age at which your grandmother married — you can supplement your own family's records and memories with official sources. Listed below are the best sources both for county and local history and for family history research. As more and more public records are placed online, the World Wide Web becomes increasingly important to family history research.

SOURCES FOR COUNTY AND LOCAL HISTORY

Census Finder. **censusfinder.com/**. This site has a large collection of free census data, although its links often go to commercial sites. At this site, you can access historic state census data, county maps, other census sites, and more.

Directory of Historical Organizations in the United States and Canada. American Association for State and Local History. A large list of historical organizations in all states and provinces. Print edition, 2001. A larger list of state and regional historical offices, organizations, museums, and so on, appears on the organization's Web site: **www.aaslh.org/rlinks.htm**.

Directory of State Archives and Records Programs. Council of State Archivists. **www.statearchivists.org/statearchivists.htm**. Links to each of the state archives.

Encyclopedia of [U.S.] Local History. Walnut Creek, CA: Alta Mira Press, 2000.

Genealogical and Local History Books in Print. Comp. and ed. Marian Hoffman. 4 vols. Baltimore, MD: Genealogical Publishing, 1996–1997.

Historical Museum Guide. CensusFinder. **www.censusfinder.com/guide_to_historical_museums.htm**. Links to history museums and historical sites in all states.

National Register of Historic Places. National Park Service. **www.nps.gov/nr/**. Links to national historic preservation sites throughout the United States.

State and Local History. Tennessee Technological University. **www.tntech.edu/history/state.html**. A large collection of links.

State Censuses: An Annotated Bibliography of Censuses of Population Taken after 1790 by States and Territories of the United States. New York: Burt Franklin, 1969.

United States Local History. Library of Congress. 5 vols. Baltimore, MD: Magna Carta, 1974.

U.S. Census Bureau. **www.census.gov/population/www/censusdata/hiscendata.html**. A source for data from historical censuses by year and state. Contains Census Bureau reports on census data across time.

SOURCES FOR FAMILY HISTORY AND GENEALOGICAL RESEARCH

American Family Immigration History Center. **ellisisland.org/**. Much useful advice about conducting family history research. You can search ships' passenger lists beginning in 1892. Full access requires "membership."

Ancestry Library Edition. ProQuest. Genealogical information for the United States, United Kingdom, and Canada taken from census, church, court, immigration, and other records. Searchable. By subscription only.

Census Finder. **www.censusfinder.com/**. General census information is available here as are many good links. But information on specific individuals is on the commercial genealogical sites, which require fee-based membership of some kind.

Encyclopedia of American Immigration. Ed. J. Ciment. 4 vols. New York: M. E. Sharpe, 2001.

European Immigration and Ethnicity in the United States and Canada: A Bibliography. Ed. David L. Brye. Santa Barbara, CA: ABC-CLIO, 1983.

Family History Center. Brigham Young University. **lib.byu.edu/fslab/list.html**. A large number of digital collections centering on local and family history.

Family Search. The Church of Jesus Christ of Latter-Day Saints. **www.familysearch .org/**. A very large surname database including the 1880 U.S. Census. Access to most elements of the site is free. An excellent resource.

Guide to Federal Records in the National Archives. **www.archives.gov/research/ guide-fed-records/**.

Heritage Quest Online. ProQuest. A very large database of sources on family history. By subscription only.

Immigrant Ships. Immigrant Ships Transcribers Guild. **www.immigrantships.net/ index.html/**. A nonprofit group of transcribers has placed on this site passenger lists (most from Europe to the United States) from several thousand ships. Where the records are complete, searches are by name of person or name of ship. It takes some work but is worth it.

Immigration History Research Center. University of Minnesota. **www.ihrc.umn.edu/ research/familyhistory.php**. A valuable set of links to immigrant history. The center's own collection of family history resources is impressive.

NARA — Genealogists/Family Historians. U.S. National Archives. **www.archives.gov/ research/arc/topics/genealogy**. There are several important NARA (National Archives and Records Administration) records of interest to family historians. The online catalogs are an important aid in family history research. However, most NARA records themselves are not online except for summaries. The records must be seen at regional depositories.

The USGenweb Census Project. **www.us-census.org/inventory/**. One of the few nonprofit census sites. Here volunteers transcribe information from federal census data and digitize it. This is an immense task, and only a small fraction of all census data is available here. The existing material can be searched by location, date, or name. More extensive census information is for sale at the commercial sites listed below.

U.S. Historical Census Browser. University of Virginia. **fisher.lib.virginia.edu/ collections/stats/histcensus**. No individual data but one of the few sites that allows the viewer to plot summary census data spatially. A creative experience in joining map-making with data analysis.

Glossary

abstract: A brief description of the content of a short piece of writing such as a scholarly article. An abstract usually appears at the beginning of the piece. Periodical databases often contain abstracts. See also **periodical database; scholarly article.**

active voice: A sentence in which the subject is the actor and the verb describes what the subject is doing. Contrast **passive voice.**

ahistorical view: A misinterpretation resulting from applying contemporary values, understandings, and so on, to the past. A failure to place the past in its proper historical context. Sometimes referred to as "presentism." Contrast **historical context.**

appendix: Supplementary information placed at the end of a research paper or after the final chapter of a book. This material (for example, tables, visuals, lists of addresses or Web sites) is separated from the body of the text because of its length.

archive: A place in which public records and historical documents are preserved. On the Web: a site where historical documents are available in digital form.

argument: A thesis, especially the principal ideas and evidence that directly support a thesis. See also **evidence; thesis.**

artifact: A physical object made and used by people in the past, such as a tool, clothing, machinery, a building.

atlas: A bound collection of maps, often including illustrations, informative tables, and textual matter. See also **historical atlas.**

bias: A perspective or prejudice that a person has about a particular subject. Hidden, inherent biases of the author or creator of a primary source can be uncovered by close examination of the source. Secondary sources often reflect the bias of the historian studying the primary evidence.

bibliography: An alphabetical list, often annotated with descriptive or critical comments, of works relating to a particular subject, period, or author; in student papers, a list of the works referred to or consulted. See also **working bibliography.**

biographical dictionary: A specialized reference work containing detailed information about important historical figures.

book review: An essay that comments on a particular work or series of works on a single subject.

call number: A combination of letters and numbers assigned to a book to indicate its place on a library shelf.

cheating: See **plagiarism.**

citation: A reference to a source of information used in preparing a written assignment; usually takes the form of a footnote or endnote. See also **documentation.**

conclusion: The final section of a written document in which the writer summarizes findings and interpretations. More generally, a finding or discovery that a researcher makes about a particular piece of historical evidence.

context: In a text, the material that surrounds a particular statement and affects that statement's meaning. Quoting a statement out of its context can misrepresent the original author's meaning. See also **historical context.**

continuity: The coherent flow of arguments as the author moves from one point to the next.

counterevidence: Evidence that contradicts a thesis.

cyclical school: School of historical thought that holds that history repeats itself, that essential forces of nature and human nature are changeless, and that past patterns of events recur.

database: A large collection of digital data organized for rapid search and retrieval. See also **periodical database.**

date range: The period of time covered by a large collection of books, articles, newspapers, and other documents.

dissertation: An extended, usually written, treatment of a subject; specifically a paper submitted for a doctorate.

documentation: The use of historical or other evidence to support a statement or argument; usually takes the form of footnotes or endnotes or material such as pictures, graphs, tables, and copies of documents.

draft: See **rough draft.**

ellipsis mark: Three spaced dots (. . .) indicating the omission of words from a quotation.

encyclopedia: A work that contains information on all branches of knowledge or that comprehensively treats a particular branch of knowledge; usually comprises entries arranged alphabetically by subject. Online encyclopedias can be searched electronically. See also **historical encyclopedia.**

endnote: See **note.**

evidence: A historical source that supports an argument or thesis. Evidence takes the form of, among other things, written sources as well as nonwritten sources that may be visual, aural, or physical. See also **primary source; secondary source.** Contrast **counterevidence.**

footnote: See **note.**

headnote: A brief introduction that usually includes biographical information about a source's author or creator and provides historical context for the time when the source was written or made.

historical atlas: A collection of maps that illustrate important changes over time and that provide visual representations of such changes.

historical context: The complex environment in which a historical topic is embedded. The historical context includes social, political, cultural, economic, and other factors.

historical dictionary: A dictionary that contains brief explanations of historical terms.

historical encyclopedia: An encyclopedia that contains alphabetically organized short essays on historical topics.

historicism: The view that truly objective examination of the past is not possible, that historical data does not represent "laws" of history, and that interpretation by historians is necessary to give data meaning. Contrast **positivism.**

historiography: The study of changes in the methods, interpretations, and conclusions of historians over time.

index: An alphabetical list of persons and subjects and the page numbers where they are discussed in a book. More generally, any list arranged by subject or by letter (alphabetical) of a specific kind of information source such as magazine articles and books.

interlibrary loan: The lending of a book by one library to another.

introduction: The beginning section of a book or a multipage paper; the introduction sets out the writer's thesis.

journal: For students, a written record, created by a student, of some aspect of a course. Contrast **scholarly journal.**

journal database: A large collection of articles from scholarly journals in electronic, searchable form. A journal database may contain article titles only, titles and abstracts, or the full text of articles.

keyword: Specific word or words associated with a particular research topic. In a keyword search, the search engine looks for the researcher's chosen term in all the records of the database or catalog, or on all the sites on the World Wide Web. Contrast **subject search.**

library catalog: A catalog that organizes all the holdings of a library; most library catalogs can be searched by title, author, or keyword. See also **online catalog.**

library stacks: Shelves on which a library's books and journals are stored.

linking paragraph: A paragraph that indicates how and why an essay is moving from one important point to another.

linking sentence: A sentence that ties together the points made in two paragraphs. It almost always comes at the end of one paragraph or at the beginning of the very next one.

microfiche: A sheet of microfilm containing pages of printed matter in reduced form.

microfilm: A film bearing a photographic record on a reduced scale of printed or other graphic matter.

monograph: A book-length study of one specific topic.

note: A note of reference, explanation, or comment. A note placed at the end of an essay or paper is called an "endnote"; a note placed below the text on a printed page is called a "footnote." See also **documentation.**

note cards: Small paper cards (3-by-5 or 4-by-6) that are convenient for note taking and the indexing of notes when researching. Such "cards" can also take the form of computer "files."

online catalog: An electronic catalog that enables the user to search the holdings of a library or database.

paraphrase: A restatement of a passage, idea, or work in different words. Like direct quotations, paraphrases of original work require proper documentation. See also **plagiarism; summary.** Contrast **quotation.**

passive voice: A sentence in which the subject is the receiver of the action and the verb describes what is happening to the subject rather than what the subject is doing. Contrast **active voice.**

peer editing: See **peer reviewing.**

peer reviewing: Examining the work (usually written) of a classmate or colleague. The purpose is to offer constructive comments so that the work can be improved. Articles in scholarly or academic journals are often peer-reviewed or vetted to ensure that the scholarship is of high quality. See also **refereed article.**

periodical: A publication that appears on a regular basis — daily, weekly, monthly, quarterly.

periodical database: A large collection of articles from journals, magazines, or newspapers in electronic, searchable form. Periodical databases may contain article titles only, titles and abstracts, or the full text of articles.

plagiarism: Presenting someone else's ideas or words as if they were one's own; using material without crediting its source; presenting as new and original an idea or product derived from an existing source. Plagiarism is a serious act of academic dishonesty. See also **paraphrase; quotation; summary.**

positivism: The view that historical "truth" can be uncovered by objective examination. Contrast **historicism.**

postmodernism: A philosophy or school of history that questions whether we can truly uncover the past.

primary document: See **primary source.**

primary source: Firsthand evidence — published or unpublished, written or nonwritten — that comes directly from a historical actor such as a person or an organization. Written primary sources include letters and diaries, newspaper articles, official records and statistics, and transcripts of legal proceedings and interviews. Nonwritten primary sources include photographs, audiotapes, video, and artifacts. See also **artifact.** Contrast **secondary source.**

progressive school: School of historical thought that believes that human history illustrates neither endless cycles nor divine intervention but continual progress, and that the situation of humanity is constantly improving.

proofreading: A careful rereading of written work to correct errors of style or grammar.

providential school: School of historical thought that believes that the course of history is determined by God and that the flow of historical events represents struggles between forces of good and evil.

quotation: A statement that repeats a source exactly, word for word. Such a statement must be enclosed in quotation marks and be properly documented. See also **plagiarism.** Contrast **paraphrase; summary.**

refereed article: An academic article that is published only after a group of scholars has agreed that it represents high-quality scholarship. See also **peer reviewing.**

reference source: A work, such as an atlas, a dictionary, or an encyclopedia, containing useful facts or information.

research paper: A formal writing assignment on a specific topic that requires the reading and synthesis of primary and secondary sources, as well as documentation by means of notes and a bibliography.

research question: A carefully framed question that guides research on a specific topic and later serves as the basis for a thesis.

research strategy: A plan for organizing research tasks: what kind of sources to look for, which to read, and in what order.

revise: To look over again in order to correct or improve; to make a new, amended, improved, or up-to-date version of an essay or paper.

revisionism: The replacement of one historical interpretation of a topic by another. Later historians often "revise" the findings of earlier ones.

rough draft: The first version of a written assignment; it is polished and revised in later drafts.

scholarly article: An article, the product of serious scholarly research, on an academic topic. Such articles usually appear in scholarly journals.

scholarly journal: A periodical containing peer-reviewed articles on scholarly topics. See also **peer reviewing.**

secondary source: The work of a researcher who did not have firsthand knowledge of a topic and whose findings came from his or her examination of primary sources. Contrast **primary source.**

source card: The first in a series of note cards or computer files that a writer creates to hold (and later organize) information from a particular source. The source card contains all the information the writer will need to cite that source in a note or list it in a bibliography.

stacks: See **library stacks.**

subject bibliographies: Lists of books, articles, and other material organized by subject.

subject headings: Words or phrases that are assigned to materials in a library catalog or database in order to classify them.

subject hierarchy: A series of subjects that moves from the broadest category to the narrowest. Most online library catalogs and databases base their subject hierarchy on the official set of headings compiled by the Library of Congress.

subject search: A search by subject of a library catalog, database, or Web directory. A subject search finds all of the information in the catalog, database, or directory that is categorized under a given subject heading. Contrast **keyword.**

summary: A brief restatement *in the writer's own words* of facts or ideas taken from a source. See also **paraphrase; plagiarism.** Contrast **quotation.**

thesis: A clear statement, usually appearing at the beginning of an essay or research paper, that informs the reader of the central point or claim the writer intends to make. See also **argument; working thesis.**

topic: A broad subject area chosen or assigned for research.

working bibliography: A list of sources that may be needed to research a topic for a formal paper; it includes publication information and the location of the materials.

working thesis: A tentative thesis that helps the writer organize research tasks. As research proceeds, it may need to be revised.

yearbook: A book that is published yearly and contains a report or summary of statistics or facts.

Index

NOTE: Page numbers followed by an asterisk (*) indicate resources listed in the appendixes.

Abstracts, 30, 34, 104, 197
Accuracy, 115, 140
Active voice, 57–58
African American history, 250–51*
African history, 234–35*
Ahistorical view, 46
Analyzing sources
  artifacts, 48–50, 49 (fig.)
  books, 71–77
  graphs, 39, 40, 41 (fig.)
  illustrations, 41–43, 43 (fig.),
    44 (fig.)
  maps, 36–39, 37 (fig.), 38 (fig.)
  nonwritten materials, 36–50
  photographs, 41–43, 45 (fig.),
    46 (fig.)
  primary sources, 31–32, 63–70
  for research, 117–18
  scholarly articles, 32–35, 76–77
  secondary sources, 70–77
  sound recordings, 45–48
  statistical data, 39–41, 39 (fig.), 40
    (fig.), 42 (fig.)
  video recordings, 45–48, 47 (fig.)
  written sources, 30–36
Ancient history, 221–23*
Annotated databases, 101
Annotations, textbook, 13–15, 14 (fig.)
Anthologies, 35
Appendix, 139
Archives, 30, 90, 95, 106, 245–46*,
  264*
Argument
  anthologies with, 35
  book reviews and, 71
  comparative reviews and critiques
    and, 77
  evidence and, 11

research paper with, 128, 135
scholarly articles with, 30, 34, 101
secondary sources and, 70
short essay with, 78
summarizing, 118
thesis and, 129
visual materials supporting, 139
Article critiques, 76
Articles. *See* Magazine articles; News-
    paper articles; Scholarly journal
    articles
Artifacts
  evaluating, 113
  interpreting, 3, 48–50, 49 (fig.)
  as primary sources, 25, 27 (fig.),
    29, 105, 111, 113, 264
Artwork and paintings
  citation models for, 195–96
  incorporating into a paper, 140
  as primary sources, 106, 113
  See also Illustrations
Asian history, 236–37*
Atlases, 94, 100, 201, 202, 206–07*
Audio recordings. *See* Recordings
Audiotapes, as primary sources, 25, 106
Australian history, 239*
Authenticity, 115
Authors
  bias of, 31–32, 110–11, 115
  citation models for, 174, 176–78,
    192
  evaluating sources and, 5, 109,
    112–13
  library catalog searches using, 98
  plagiarism and, 126
  understanding the points of, 117,
    118
  Web-based sources and, 115

Bias, 5, 31–32, 110–11, 115, 140
Bibliography
  creating, for a research paper, 174

directory to documentation models
for, 175
documentation models for,
176–200
documentation with, 173
evaluating a book for research
using, 109
format of, 146, 170, 174
form of typical, 176
length of paper and, 136
library catalog research and, 98, 99
primary sources listed in, 28
quotation sources in, 139
research paper example of,
170–72
research process and, 94
resource lists in, 218*, 242–43*
secondary sources with, 109
subject, 100–01
textbook reading assignment
and, 13
working, 94, 98
Biographical dictionaries, 90
Biography collections, 207–09*
Blogs, 23
Bookmarks, 109
Book reviews, 63, 71–76
citation models for, 174
comparative, 76–77
example of, 71–74
guidelines for writing, 75
subject bibliography listing of, 100
Books
citation models for, 170, 179–86
as primary sources, 29, 111–13
reading, 30, 31–32
as secondary sources, 28, 109–11
subject bibliography listing of,
100–01
See also Textbooks
Britain
history, 228–32*
public documents, 212–23*
Business history (U.S.), 261–62*

Call numbers, library, 98–99
Canada
history, 241–42*
public documents, 212–23*
Caribbean history, 239–40*
CD-ROMs, 195, 202*
Charts, 39, 139, 196
Chat rooms, 23
Cheating, and plagiarism, 126
Chicago Manual of Style, The, 146, 173

Chinese history, 237–38*
Chronological organization, 132, 133
Citations
plagiarism and, 61–62
for quotations, 139
in a research paper, 140–41,
173–74
in scholarly articles, 35
See also Documentation; Endnotes;
Footnotes
Civil War, U.S., 248–50*
Clarity, 56–57, 61, 136–37
Class lectures, note taking in, 15–21
Classroom participation, 12, 21–23,
78–79
Clear thinking, in essay exams, 84, 86
Clear writing, 51, 84, 86, 136–37
Colonial history, U.S., 246–48*
Communication online, 23–24
Comparative analysis of primary
sources, 67–70
Comparative book reviews, 76–77
Comparative critiques, 76–77
Conciseness, 57
Conclusions
essay draft with, 55, 59–60
example of, 59–60
reading sources and, 30, 35
research paper and, 88, 128, 131,
136, 142
research paper example of, 163–64
revising, 60, 142
secondary sources and, 71
summarizing, 118
thesis and, 30, 135, 142, 164–65
Consistency, 32, 33 (fig.), 140
Context, 112, 120, 138. *See also*
Historical context
Continuity, 59, 135, 136–37, 142, 144
Copying source material, 123
Corroboration, tests of, 32, 33 (fig.)
Counterevidence, 55, 75, 94, 131, 133
County history (U.S.), 265–66*
Critiques
of articles, 76
comparative, 76–77
Cultural history, 10, 254–56*
Cyclical school, 5

Databases
accessing sources on, 29, 30
annotated, 101
citation models for, 187, 189
date range for search in, 104
full-text, 101, 104, 105

Databases (cont.)
  guidelines for using, 104
  journal, 211–12*
  library research using, 95, 101–05
  magazine, 105, 211*
  newspaper, 105, 209–10*
  periodical. *See* Periodical databases
Date of publication
  evaluating secondary sources
    using, 110
  note taking and recording, 121
  subject bibliographies and, 100–01
Date range, in database research, 104
Diagrams. *See* Illustrations
Diaries, as primary sources, 25, 112
Dictionaries
  biographical, 90
  citation models for, 183–86
  historical, 90, 201, 202, 203–04*
  library research using, 100
  reading sources using, 117
  research using, 90, 201*
  resource list of, 203–04*
Digital media
  interpreting, 45, 48
  note taking from, 20–21
Digital note "cards," 121–23, 124
    (fig.), 126 (fig.)
Direct quotations, 118–19,
    120–21, 137
Discussion lists, citation models for, 200
Dissertations, citation models for, 197
Documentation, 173–200
  directory to models for, 175
  plagiarism and, 126
  in a research paper, 141, 142
  of visual materials, 139, 140
  of Web resources, 115–16
  See also Bibliography; Endnotes;
    Footnotes
Documents, bibliographic citations
    of, 171–72, 174
Downloading content, 123, 127
Draft
  of an essay, 55
  of a research paper, 135–36
  revising and rewriting, 60–61,
    142–43
DVDs, citation models for, 193

Early American history, 246–48*
Early modern history (Eur.), 226*
Eastern European history, 233*
Economic history (U.S.), 9, 261–62*
Editing. *See* Rewriting

Editorials, citation models for, 190
Electronic journals, citation model
    for, 187, 189
Electronic reference sources
  accessing, 29, 30
  citation models for, 183–86
  library research using, 99–100
  See also CD-ROMs; Databases;
    Online library catalogs
Ellipsis marks, 120–21, 138, 161
E-mail
  citation models for, 199–200
  communicating using, 23–24
  group work using, 22
  note taking using, 123
Encyclopedias
  citation models for, 183–86
  historical, 90, 100, 201, 202,
    204–06*
  library research using, 100
  reading sources using, 117
  research using, 90, 201
  resource list of, 204–06*
  Wikipedia and, 99–100
Endnotes
  directory to documentation models
    for, 175
  documentation models for,
    176–200
  format of, 173–74
  form of typical, 176
  number to use, 141
  placement of numbers for, 148,
    173–74
  plagiarism and, 62, 119, 126, 141–42
  quotation sources in, 139
  research paper example of, 148,
    166–69
  research paper with, 136, 140–42
  revising and rewriting and, 142
  scholarly articles with, 35
  when to use, 140–42
Environmental history, resources on,
    10, 260–61*
Essay exams
  in-class, 78, 82–83
  take-home, 82, 83–87
Essays
  body of, 56–59
  building, 51–62
  clear writing and, 51
  conclusion to, 59–60
  drafting, 55
  examining sources for, 52
  guidelines for revising, 61

introduction to, 55–56
paragraphs in, 58–59
plagiarism and, 61–62
preparing to write, 51–60
questions before beginning, 51–52
revising, 60–61
rough draft of, 55
sentences in, 56–58
spell- and grammar-checkers for,
  60–61
thesis statement for, 53–54
writing outline for, 54–55
Ethnic history (U.S.), 10, 252–54*
Ethnohistory, 10
European history
historical encyclopedias, 205*
resources in, 223–28*
Evidence, 25–50
artifacts and, 3
bias and, 32
comparative reviews and critiques
  and, 77
counterevidence and, 75, 94,
  131, 133
family history and, 264
forms of. *See also* Primary sources;
  Secondary sources
interpreting and organizing, 11
introduction and, 55
notes and, 128
organizing, 11, 131–35
peer reviewing of, 22
questions by historians about, 4–5
reliability of,
research paper and, 25, 88, 129,
  131, 135
research strategy and, 92–93
revised views of, 8
rough draft using, 55
secondary sources and, 71
short essays with, 78
thesis and, 128, 129
work of historians using, 3, 4, 10
writing assignment and, 52
writing outline and, 54, 130,
  131–35
Exams, 79–87
in-class essay, 82–83
note taking from class lectures
  and, 15, 80, 83
objective and short-answer exams,
  80–81
reading before, 79–80
sample questions to prepare for,
  80, 83

take-home essay, 82, 83–87
taking, 83
Explanatory footnotes, 141

Family history (genealogy), 10,
  264–65*, 266–67*
Film reviews, citation models for, 191
Films
citation models for, 172
interpreting, 45–48, 47 (fig.)
note taking from, 20
Web access to, 106
Folders, in digital note taking, 121,
  124 (fig.), 126
Footnotes
directory to documentation models
  for, 175
documentation models for,
  176–200
format of, 173–74
form of typical, 176
number to use, 141
placement of numbers for, 148,
  173–74
plagiarism and, 62, 119, 126,
  141–42
quotation sources in, 139
research paper with, 136, 140–42
revising and rewriting and, 142
scholarly articles with, 35
when to use, 140–42
Foreign relations (U.S.), resources on,
  259–60*
Format
of bibliographic entries, 146,
  170, 174
of endnotes or footnotes, 173–74
of quotations, 138–39, 176, 177
of a research paper, 146
of sources, 29
of visual materials in a paper,
  139, 140
of a writing outline, 133
Full-text databases, 101, 104, 105

Genealogy. *See* Family history
Glossary, textbook, 13
Government publications. *See* Public
  documents
Grammar, checking for, 61, 142
Graphics. *See* Graphs; Illustrations;
  Maps; Photographs; Tables
Graphs
analyzing data on, 39, 40,
  41 (fig.)

Graphs (cont.)
    citation models for, 196
    incorporating into a paper, 139–40
Group work, 21–22, 23, 127
Guidelines
    avoiding plagiarism, 127
    citing articles in electronic
        databases, 189
    citing articles in print
        journals, 188
    citing books, 180
    citing information from Web
        sites, 194
    citing letters in published collec-
        tions, 184–85
    developing an effective thesis, 130
    evaluating material on Web
        sites, 116
    evaluating nonwritten primary
        sources, 113
    evaluating secondary sources, 111
    evaluating Web sites, 114
    evaluating written primary
        sources, 112
    giving an oral presentation, 78
    identifying scholarly articles, 34
    incorporating visuals, 140
    interpreting nonwritten
        sources, 36
    peer reviewing, 22
    research process, 89
    revising and rewriting, 143
    revising your essay, 60–61
    speaking in class, 21
    taking lecture notes, 16
    using periodical databases, 104
    working with written sources, 31
    writing a book review, 75
    writing in-class essay exams, 82

Headnotes, 106
Highlighting information in a text-
    book, 13–15, 14 (fig.)
Historians
    bias of, 5
    choice of subject by, 4
    evidence and, 25
    fields of historical research and,
        8–10
    linking past to present by, 1–3
    questions asked by, 4–5
    research question and, 25
    work of, 3–4
Historical atlases, 100, 201, 202,
    206–07*

Historical context, 8
    of artifacts, 48
    choosing a topic and, 89
    comparative analysis of primary
        documents and, 67
    evaluating primary sources
        and, 114
    family history and, 264–65*
    historiography and, 8
    of media, 68
    note taking and, 121
    primary sources and, 63
    rough draft and, 135
    thesis and, 130
Historical dictionaries, 90, 100, 201,
    202, 203–04*
Historical encyclopedias, 90, 100,
    201, 202, 204–06*
Historical novels, 35–36
Historicism, 7
Historiography
    career skills and research in, 11
    earlier historical writings exam-
        ined in, 7–8
    philosophies of, 5–7
    ways to use, 11
    what it can tell you, 1–3

Identification exams, 80, 81
Illustrations
    artistic style of, 41
    citation models for, 172, 196
    comparative analysis of primary
        sources with, 67–70, 67 (fig.),
        68 (fig.)
    evaluating, before reading
        sources, 30
    incorporating into a paper, 139
    interpreting, 41–43, 43 (fig.),
        44 (fig.)
    as primary sources, 25, 27 (fig.)
    research paper examples of, 152,
        155, 158
Immigrant history (U.S.), resources
    on, 252–54*
In-class essay exams, 82–83
Index cards. *See* Note cards
Indexes
    journal, 211–12*
    magazine, 105, 211*
    newspaper, 105, 209–10*
    periodical, 101, 104–05, 210–12*
    scholarly journal, 104–05
    textbook, 13
Indian history, 237*

Inherent bias, 32
Interlibrary loans, 93, 104, 105
International history, 259–60*
Interviews
	citation models for, 174, 193–95, 197, 199
	evaluating as a source, 112
	family history research, 264–65*
	as primary sources, 107, 112
Introduction
	book review and, 75
	comparative reviews and critiques and, 77
	conclusion and, 59
	essay draft with, 55–56
	evaluating a book before reading using, 30, 106
	evaluating secondary sources using, 109, 110
	example of, 56
	research paper example of, 148
	research paper with, 128, 142
	revising, 142
	rough draft and, 135
	section in a research paper with, 135
Irish history, 232–33*

Japanese history, 238–39*
Journal articles. *See* Scholarly journal articles

Key, to a map, 38
Keyword searches, 95, 97–98, 101, 107, 108
Korean history, 238–39*

Labor history (U.S.), 261–62*
Latin American history, 239–40*
Lectures
	citation models for, 199
	keeping up with reading assignments and, 12
	note taking from, 15–21, 80, 82
Letters
	citation models for, 182, 184–85, 198–99
	as primary sources, 25, 105, 112
Letters to the editor, citation models for, 190
Library
	archives in, 106
	call numbers for locating materials in, 98–99
	doing research in, 94–95

home page for, 94–95, 96 (fig.), 99, 111
	interlibrary loans and, 93, 104, 105
	periodical databases in, 100
	reference sources in, 94
	resources available in, 94, 96, 201–02
Library catalogs
	author and title searches in, 98
	keyword searches in, 95, 97–98
	research using, 95–99
	searching for journals, magazines, and newspapers in, 105
	subject searches in, 95–96
Library of Congress Subject Headings, 95–96
Library stacks, 94, 104, 105
Linking paragraphs, 59
Linking sentences, 59, 135
Listservs, 23
List-type outline, 133, 134 (fig.)
Local history (U.S.)
	overview of, 265–66*
	resources for, 245–46*, 265–66*
Logic, 88

Magazine articles
	citation models for, 187
	databases and indexes of, 105, 211*
	evaluating, 109
	searching for, 105
	as secondary sources, 109
Maps
	citation models for, 172, 174, 196
	incorporating into a paper, 139
	interpreting, 36–39, 37 (fig.), 38 (fig.)
	key to, 38
	as primary sources, 25, 39, 106
	research paper example of, 152
	scale of, 38
	textbooks with, 13
	Web access to, 106
Medicine (U.S.), history of, 260–61*
Medieval history (Eur.), 224–25*
Message boards, 23–24
Microfiche, 94, 202*
Microfilm, 94, 202*
Middle Eastern history, 235–36*
Modern history (Eur.), 226–28*
Monographs, 35
Movies. *See* Films
Multimedia sources
	citation models for, 192–96

Multimedia sources (cont.)
    note taking in lectures using, 20–21
    as primary sources, 45–48
Multiple-choice objective exams, 80, 81
Museum archives, 106
Musical compositions, citation models
    for, 198
Musical recordings, citation models
    for, 195

Native American history, 248*
Newspaper articles
    citation models for, 187–90
    databases and indexes of, 105,
      209–10*
    as primary sources, 25, 112
    searching for, 105
New Zealand history, 239*
Nonwritten materials
    bibliographic citations for, 172, 174
    evaluating, 113–14
    guidelines for evaluating primary
      sources, 113
    guidelines for interpreting, 36
    note taking in lectures using,
      20–21
    as primary sources, 25, 105, 106,
      111, 113–14
    "reading," 36–50
    See also Artifacts; Illustrations; Maps;
      Photographs; Recordings;
      Tables; Videos
North African history, 235–36*
Note cards
    digital, 121–23, 124 (fig.),
      126 (fig.)
    note taking using, 121, 122 (fig.)
    writing outline using, 132
Notes, in a paper
    bibliography and, 174
    directory to documentation models
      for, 175
    documentation style for, 173
    length of a paper and, 136
    quotation sources in, 13
    use of term, 141
    See also Endnotes; Footnotes
Note taking
    article critiques and, 76
    avoiding plagiarism using, 61–62,
      126–27
    from class lectures, 15–20, 80, 82
    computers used for, 121–23, 124
      (fig.), 125 (fig.), 126–27
    e-mail used in, 123

    examples of, 16, 17 (fig.), 18 (fig.),
      19 (fig.)
    exam preparation and, 80, 82
    guidelines for taking, 16
    library online catalog research
      using, 99
    multimedia content ("wired" class-
      room) and, 20–21
    note cards for, 121, 122 (fig.)
    oral presentations and, 78, 79
    organizing, 121–23
    paraphrasing in, 118, 119–20,
      121, 123
    photocopying, downloading, and
      printing Web-based material
      and, 123
    plagiarism and, 126
    quotations copied in, 118–19, 123
    reading anthologies and, 35
    reading monographs and, 35
    reading scholarly articles and, 35
    rewriting, 16, 17–20, 19 (fig.)
    from slides and films, 20
    from sources, 116, 123
    subject headings used in, 121, 122
      (fig.), 123
    summarizing information in, 118,
      121, 123, 126, 127
    textbook reading assignment and,
      13, 14 (fig.)
    thesis and, 128
    writing outline using, 132, 133
Novels, historical, 35–36

Objective exams, 80–81
Objects. *See* Artifacts
Online communication, 23–24
Online library catalogs
    author and title searches using, 98
    call number searches using, 98–99
    example of a catalog entry page
      for a book, 97 (fig.)
    keyword searches using, 95, 97–98
    research using, 94–99
    searching for journals, magazines,
      and newspapers in, 105
    subject headings in, 96
    subject searches using, 95–96
Opinions, footnotes
    documenting, 141
Oral presentations, 78–79
Outlines
    note taking reflecting, 15
    oral presentations and, 78
    See also Writing outline

Paintings. *See* Artwork and paintings
Pakistani history, 237*
Pamphlets, citation models for, 197
Paper. *See* Research paper
Paragraphs
    clear writing and, 136
    cohesive and connected, in essays,
        58–59
    introduction with, 55–56
    linking, 59
    reading, 30
    in a research paper, 136, 142
    revising, 60, 142
    in a thesis statement, 53–54
Paraphrasing
    examples of, 118–19
    note taking and, 118, 119–20, 121,
        123, 127
    plagiarism and, 118–20, 126, 127
    research paper and, 137
Passive voice, 57–58
Past tense, 58
Peer-reviewed scholarly articles, 34
Peer reviewing, 22, 143
Periodical databases
    annotated, 101
    full-text, 101
    guidelines for using, 104
    library research using, 101–05
    locating articles in, 101–05, 102
        (fig.), 103 (fig.)
    resource listing of, 210–12*
Periodicals, 100
    citation models for, 170–71,
        186–91
    indexes and databases of, 210–12*
    library research using, 101–05
Philosophies of history, 5–7
Photocopying source material, 123
Photographs
    citation models for, 174, 195–96
    evaluating as a source, 113
    incorporating into a paper, 139
    interpreting, 41–43, 45 (fig.), 46
        (fig.), 113
    as primary sources, 25, 105,
        106, 113
    Web access to, 106, 115
Physical objects. *See* Artifacts
Pictures. *See* Illustrations
Plagiarism
    avoiding, 61–62, 116, 126–27
    footnotes and, 126
    group work and, 127
    guidelines for avoiding, 127

note taking and, 126–27
paraphrasing sources and,
    118–20, 126
quoting sources and, 120–21
summarizing sources and, 118
take-home exams and, 87
working online and, 126–27
Political history (U.S.), 9, 256–58*
Positivism, 7
Postmodern school, 6
PowerPoint presentations, 79
Presentations, 78–79
Present tense, 58
Primary sources
    accessing, 29–30
    anthologies and, 35
    bias in, 31–32
    as category of evidence, 25
    comparative analysis of, 67–70
    context of, 112
    description of, 11, 25–28, 63
    evaluating, 31–32, 111–14
    examples of, 26 (fig.), 27 (fig.)
    family history and, 264*
    guidelines for evaluating non-
        written, 113
    guidelines for working with, 31
    interviews as, 107
    magazine and newspaper articles
        as, 105
    maps as, 39, 106
    museum archives and, 106
    nonwritten, 25, 105, 106, 111,
        113–14
    periodicals as, 210*
    published collections of, 106
    reading for an assignment and, 12
    reliability of, 31–32, 109, 112–13
    research strategy and, 93
    scholarly journal articles as, 101
    searching for, 105–07
    secondary sources as, 28–29
    single-source analysis of, 64–66
    tests of consistency and corrobora-
        tion for, 32, 33 (fig.)
    thesis and, 31
    thesis supported by, 129
    types of, 25
    Web access to, 115–16
    Web searches for, 105–06
    writing about, 63–70
    writing assignments and, 51, 63–64
    written, 111–13
Printing, 115–16, 123, 127, 142
Progressive school, 5–6

Proofreading, 60–61, 79, 83, 142
Providential school, 5
Publication date
 evaluating secondary sources
  using, 110
 note taking and recording, 121
 subject bibliographies and, 100–01
Public documents
 citation models for, 191–92
 resource list of, 212–15*
Public speaking, 78–79

Quantitative data, 9. *See also* Statistics
Quantitative history, 9
Questions, in classroom discussions, 21
Questions, in interviews, 107
Questions, on exams
 in-house exams and, 82–83
 objective and short-answer exams
  with, 80–81
 sample, in exam preparation, 80,
  82–83
Quotation marks, 62, 76, 121, 123,
 126, 127, 138–39
Quotations
 article critiques with, 76
 book reviews with, 75, 76
 citation models for, 140, 198
 ellipsis marks in, 120–21, 138, 161
 formatting, 138–39, 146, 161, 162
 note taking and, 118–19, 121, 123
 plagiarism and use of, 62, 118,
  119, 120–21
 research paper examples of, 137,
  138, 156, 161, 162
 understanding author's meaning
  and, 120–21
 when to use, in a research paper,
  137–38

Reading
 anthologies, 35
 artifacts, 48–50, 49 (fig.)
 assignments, importance of, 12
 exam preparation and, 79–80
 graphs, 39, 40, 41 (fig.)
 historical novels, 35–36
 illustrations, 41–43, 43 (fig.),
  44 (fig.)
 maps, 36–39, 37 (fig.), 38 (fig.)
 monographs, 35
 nonwritten materials, 36–50
 photographs, 41–43, 45 (fig.),
  46 (fig.)
 primary sources, 31–32

scholarly articles, 32–35
sound recordings, 45–48
sources in research, 117–18
statistical data, 39–41, 39 (fig.),
 40 (fig.), 42 (fig.)
textbook, 13–15, 14 (fig.)
 underlining information during,
  13, 14 (fig.)
video recordings, 45–48, 47 (fig.)
written sources, 30–36
Recordings
 authorship of, 46, 47–48
 citation models for, 174, 195
 evaluating as a Web source, 115
 interpreting, 45–48
 note taking from, 20
 as primary sources, 105, 113, 114
Refereed scholarly articles, 34
Reference works
 choosing a topic and, 89
 library research using, 99–100
 list of resources, 218*, 242–43*
Regional history (U.S.), 245–46*
Reliability of primary sources, 31–32,
 109, 112–13
Religious history (U.S.), 9, 10, 262*
Research, 88–127
 avoiding plagiarism in, 126–27
 atlases, dictionaries, and encyclopedias in, 100
 beginning, 88–94
 choosing a topic in, 89
 conducting, 94–109
 evaluating sources in, 109–16
 fields of, 8–10
 group work for, 21, 127
 guidelines for process of, 89
 how historians work and, 3–4
 Internet search tools and, 107–09
 interpreting sources in, 116,
  117–18
 library's online catalog used in,
  95–99, 96 (fig.), 97 (fig.)
 narrowing a topic in, 90
 note taking in, 116–23, 132
 organizing, 132–33
 overview of process of, 88
 periodical databases in, 101–05,
  102 (fig.), 103 (fig.)
 philosophies of history and, 5–7
 primary source evaluation in,
  111–14
 primary source searches in,
  105–07
 reference works used in, 99–100

research question in, 90–92
secondary source evaluation in,
109–11
sources for, 201–63*, 264–68*
subject bibliographies in, 100–01
Web-based sources in, 114–16
Wikipedia and, 99–100
writing a short essay using, 77–78
Research paper, 63, 88
documenting sources in, 173–200
downloading from the Web, 127
example of, 143–72
formatting, 146
writing, 88, 128–72
Research plan, 92–93
Research question, 25, 88
debatable aspect of, 91
formulating, 90–92, 128
narrow aspect of, 91
researchable aspect of, 92
significant aspect of, 91
thesis and, 92, 129, 130, 131
Research strategy
description of, 92
keeping an open mind in, 93–94
planning, 92–94
time budgeting in, 92–93
working bibliography in, 94
writing outline and, 131–32
Resources, lists of, 201–62*, 263–67*
Reviews. *See* Book reviews; Film reviews
Revised draft, 60
Revising
an essay, 60
guidelines for, 61, 143
a research paper, 142–43
spell- and grammar-checkers
in, 142
a writing outline, 54, 136
Revisionism, 8
Revolutionary War history (U.S.),
246–48*
Rewriting
guidelines for, 143
of notes, 16, 17–20
a research paper, 142–43
Rough draft
of an essay, 55
peer reviewing of, 22
of a research paper, 135–36
revising and rewriting, 142–43
Russian history, 233–34*

Scale of a map, 38
Schedule, 92–93, 142

Scholarly journal articles
abstracts to, 30, 34, 104
accessing, 29–30
citation models for, 170–71, 174,
186–87, 188
critiques of, 76
databases of, 30, 101–05, 211–12*
date ranges in search for, 104
evaluating before reading, 30, 109
guidelines for identifying, 34
indexes to, 101, 104–05, 211–12*
library research using, 101–04
as primary sources, 210*
reading and interpreting, 32–35
refereed or peer-reviewed, 34
as secondary sources, 29–30,
32–35, 70, 210*
subject bibliography listing of, 100
Science (U.S.), history of, 10, 260–61*
Scottish history, 232–33*
Search engines, 108
Searching library catalogs
by author and title, 98
by keywords, 95, 97–98
by subject, 95–96
Searching periodical databases, 101,
102 (fig.), 103 (fig.)
Searching Web sites, 107–09
advanced searches and, 108
advantages of, 107
efficient use of, 107–08
guidelines for evaluating Web
sources and, 114
keyword searches using, 108
previewing results from, 108–09
subject searches using, 108
Secondary sources, 11, 28
accessing, 29–30
article critiques and, 76
bias of authors and, 110–11, 115
book reviews and, 71–76
as category of evidence, 25
comparative reviews and critiques
and, 76–77
description of, 63
evaluating, 109–11
example of, 28 (fig.)
monographs as, 35
periodicals as, 210*
as primary sources, 28–29
reading for an assignment and, 12
research strategy and, 93
scholarly articles as, 29–30,
32–35, 70
thesis support using, 130

Secondary sources (cont.)
 writing about, 70–77
 writing assignment and, 51, 70–71
Sections of a research paper
 introductions to, 135
 length of, 135, 136
 transitions between, 135, 150
Sentences
 active voice versus passive voice in,
  57–58
 clarity in, 56–57
 conciseness in, 57
 essay body with, 56–58
 in essay exam answers, 56–58
 linking, 59, 135
 paragraph construction with,
  58–59
 past tense versus present tense
  in, 58
 revising, 60–61, 142
Short-answer exams, 80–81
Short essays, 77–78
Single-source analysis, 64–66
Slavery (U.S.), resources on, 248–50*
Slides
 citation models for, 196
 note taking from, 20
Slide shows, 79
Social history (U.S.), 10, 254–56*
Sound recordings
 citations of, 174, 195
 interpreting, 45–48
 reading, 36
Source cards, in note taking, 121
Sources
 accessing, 29–30
 accurate and authenticity of,
  115, 140
 analyzing and organizing, 11
 avoiding plagiarism with, 61–62,
  116, 126–28, 126–27
 bias and, 5, 110–11, 115
 categories of, 25
 comparative reviews and critiques
  of, 77
 evaluating, 109–14
 examining before writing, 52
 interpreting, 11, 116–23
 note taking from, 116, 123
 paraphrasing, 118–20, 127
 photocopying, 123
 primary. *See* Primary sources
 reading, 30–36, 117–18
 research paper and, 88–89
 research strategy for finding, 93

secondary. *See* Secondary sources
 summarizing, 118, 127
 tests of consistency and corroboration for, 32, 33 (fig.)
 understanding the author's thesis
  in, 117
 Web-based, 115–16, 123
 when to document, 140–42
 working bibliography of, 94, 98
 writing assignment and, 51–52
 See also Research
Soviet history, 233–34*
Speaking in class, 21, 78–79
Spelling, checking, 60–61, 142
Sri Lankan history, 237*
State history (U.S.), 245–46*
Statement of thesis, 148. *See also*
 Thesis
Statistics
 analyzing data in, 39–41, 39 (fig.),
  40 (fig.), 41 (fig.), 42 (fig.)
 evaluating as a source, 112
 quantitative history and, 9
 resource list for, 215–18*
Studying for exams. *See* Exams
Subject bibliographies, 100–01
Subject headings, 96, 121,
  122 (fig.), 123
Subject searches, 95–96, 100, 105,
  107, 108
Subject of sentences, 57, 58
Summaries
 note taking using, 118, 121,
  123, 127
 plagiarism and, 118, 126, 127
 research paper examples of, 164
 research paper with, 137
 secondary sources and, 71
 textbook reading assignment
  using, 15
 thesis versus, 129
Superscript note numbers, 148,
  173–74

Table of contents, book, 13, 110
Tables
 analyzing data in, 36, 39–41
 citation models for, 196
 examples of, 39 (fig.), 40 (fig.),
  42 (fig.)
 incorporating into a paper, 139
 reading textbooks with, 13
Take-home exams, 82, 83–87
Technology (U.S.), history of,
  260–61*

Tense, 58
Tests. *See* Exams
Tests of consistency and corroboration, 32, 33 (fig.)
Textbooks
  exam preparation with, 82
  navigating, 12–13
  note taking from class lectures and, 15
  reading, for an assignment, 13–15, 14 (fig.)
  underlining information in, 13, 14 (fig.)
Thesis
  abstract summarizing, 30, 34
  arguments in support of, 128
  article critiques and, 76
  author's, in sources, 117, 118
  bias and, 110
  book review on, 71, 75
  comparative reviews and critiques and, 77
  conclusion and restatement of, 30, 135, 142, 164–65
  effectiveness of, 129–31
  essay with, 53–54
  example of, 131
  family history and, 263*
  guidelines for developing, 130
  introduction using, 56, 57
  monographs with, 35
  need for, 129
  note taking and understanding author's, 117, 118
  paragraphs in an essay and, 58–59
  peer reviewing of, 22
  primary sources and, 31
  quotations in a research paper supporting, 137
  reading sources and, 30, 31, 117
  research question and, 92
  resources for research on, 201
  revising and rewriting and, 60, 136, 142,
  rough draft and, 135, 136
  scholarly articles with, 34, 101
  secondary sources and, 70, 71
  short essay with, 78
  summary versus, 129
  writing a research paper using, 128–31, 135
  writing outline for, 145–46
Thesis statement
  drafting, in an essay, 53–54
  examples of, 53, 54

  introduction and, 55
  research paper with, 131, 135
  revising, 60
  rough draft and, 135
Title of a book
  library catalog searches using, 98
  note taking and, 121, 122 (fig.)
  secondary source evaluation using, 109–10
Title page of a research paper, 146, 147
Topic
  choosing, 89, 201
  examining sources and, 52, 264*
  narrowing, 90, 128
  note taking and, 116
  reading and preliminary research on, 30
  research paper and, 88–90, 135
  research question and, 90
  secondary sources and, 110
  single-source analysis and, 66
Topical organization, 132–33, 145–46
Transition sentences, 150
Transitions between sections, 135,150

Underlining information in a textbook, 13–15, 14 (fig.)
United States history
  biography collections, 208–09*
  general resources in, 242–44*
  historical atlases, 207*
  historical dictionaries, 203–04*
  historical encyclopedias, 206*
  historical statistics, 216–18*
  newspaper indexes and databases, 210*
  public documents, 213–15*
  specialized resources, 245–62*
  Web sites, 243–44*
Urban history (U.S.), 261–62*

Verb tense, 58
Videocassettes, citation models for, 172, 193
Videos
  authorship of, 46, 47–48
  citations of, 174
  evaluating as a Web source, 115
  interpreting, 45–48, 47 (fig.)
  note taking from, 20
  as primary sources, 25, 113, 114
  reading, 36
Visual material
  artistic style of, 41

Visual material (cont.)
documenting sources of, 139, 140
formatting, 139, 146
guidelines for, 130
incorporating into a paper, 139–40
interpreting, 41–43, 43 (fig.),
44 (fig.)
reproducing, 139
research paper examples of, 152,
155, 158
textbooks with, 13
See also Artwork and paintings;
Illustrations; Maps;
Photographs; Tables
Voice, in sentences, 57–58

War (U.S.), history resources on,
259–60*
Web forums
citation models for, 200
communicating in, 23–24
Web sites
accuracy and authenticity of
sources on, 115
bias of authors on, 110–11, 115
citation models for, 172,
192–93, 194
communicating using, 24
documenting sources on, 115–16
downloading and printing material from, 123, 127
evaluating material on Web sites,
115–16
evaluating Web sites, 114–15
guidelines for evaluating material
on Web sites, 116
guidelines for evaluating Web
sites, 114
library home pages on, 94–95, 96
(fig.), 99
maps on, 106
primary sources on, 105–06, 107
print sources for documents on,
115–16
research using, 114–16
resource lists for, 202, 219–21*,
243–44*
search tools on, 107–09
sources accessed on, 29, 30, 100,
114–16

subject bibliographies on, 100, 101
Wikipedia and, 99–100, 115
Wikipedia, 99–100, 115
"Wired" classroom, 20–21
Women's history (U.S.), 252*
Working bibliography, 94, 98
Working thesis, 53
Works of art
citation models for, 195–96
See also Artworks and paintings
World history
biography collections, 207–08*
general resources in, 218–21*
growth of, 10
historical atlases, 206–07*
historical dictionaries, 203*
historical encyclopedias, 204–05*
public documents, 213*
specialized resources, 221–42*
Web sites, 219–21*
World Wide Web. *See* Web sites
Writing assignments. *See* Essays;
Research paper; specific
assignments
Writing outline
chronological organization of,
132, 133
counterevidence and, 55, 131, 133
essay with, 54–55
examples of, 54–55, 133, 145–46
format of, 133
list-type, 133, 134 (fig.)
organizing, 132–33
preparing, 131–35
research notes used in, 132, 133
research paper example of,
145–46
revising, 54, 136
topical organization of, 132–33,
145–46
writing a research paper using,
128, 131–35
Written sources
accessing, 29–30
guidelines for working with, 31
primary, 111–14
reading, 30–36
See also Books; Magazine articles;
Newspaper articles; Scholarly
journal articles